COMMUNICATE!

THIRD EDITION

RUDOLPH F. VERDERBER

University of Cincinnati

Wadsworth Publishing Company
Belmont, California
A Division of Wadsworth, Inc.

Senior Editor: Rebecca Hayden

Production Editor: Kathie Head

Design Management: Cynthia Bassett

Designer: Don Fujimoto

Copy Editor: Catherine Lavin

Cartoonist: Corbin Hillam

Cover: Michael Rogondino

Photo Credits: *Part I*—© Fredrik D. Bodin/Stock, Boston; *Part II*—© 1979 Jim Richardson/Black Star; *Part III*—© Philip Jon Bailey/Jeroboam; *Part IV*—© 1980 Jim Anderson/Woodfin Camp & Associates

Printed in the United States of America
5 6 7 8 9 10—85 84 83

ISBN 0-534-00885-2

Library of Congress Cataloging in Publication Data

Verderber, Rudolph F
  Communicate!

  Includes bibliographies and index.
  1. Communication. I. Title
P90.V43   1981   001.51   80-36768
ISBN 0-534-00885-2

PREFACE

The success of this new edition of *Communicate!* will be measured by how well it contributes to your understanding of communication principles. I have enjoyed the opportunity of improving the material so that you will find this book both informative and interesting.

This third edition maintains the premise that since people spend more time in communicating than in almost everything else, it is important that they learn to communicate as effectively as possible. As in past editions material is included under the headings of Foundations, Personal Communication, Small-Group Communication, and Public Speaking. This arrangement is not meant to imply that the material covered relates only these specific settings. In fact the material is cumulative: The foundations provide a base for communicating in all settings; the personal communication skills provide a base for consideration of both group and public-speaking skills that follow. The book, then, offers a unified whole that is the product of all related communication skills.

The first unit provides a communication base. The opening chapter includes the communication variables that occur in any form or setting. The second chapter focuses on perception, an ability that is needed to make the most of communication. Each of the three major units that correspond with major communication settings is preceded by a short communication self-analysis.

The second unit, Personal Communication, begins with chapters on verbal and nonverbal communication, with emphasis on basic skills that are useful in all communication settings. This unit also includes chapters on communicating ideas and feelings, listening and responding, and understanding communication relationships. The third unit, Small-Group

Communication, includes chapters on the characteristics of work groups, participating in work groups, and leadership in groups. The fourth and final unit, Public Speaking, contains chapters on speech preparation, information exchange principles, practice in information exchange, principles of persuasion, and practice in persuasion. An Appendix includes a sample of an interpersonal conversation, two speeches with analyses, the rationale and forms for writing communication contracts based upon results from self-analyses, directions for an employment interview, and various analysis checklists.

Any study of fundamental skills calls not only for clear explanation but also for well-conceived ideas directed toward helping you put those fundamentals into practice. Throughout the text realistic, workable exercises are included for practice of the skills discussed. These exercises are of two kinds: (1) those you can work with on your own with paper and pencil; and (2) those you can do orally individually or with other persons in small groups. In each exercise some behavioral objective is sought; and there are convenient tearout sheets in Appendix B for use in personal, group, and public speaking analyses.

Through the practice, observation, and analysis model, you can help yourself to learn quickly and efficiently. You will also find, particularly in the public speaking chapters, exercises including performance assignments that give you different kinds of practical application of the various communication skills.

This third edition could not have been completed without the help of many persons. Mostly, I would like to acknowledge the help of my colleagues at various colleges and universities who offered prerevision suggestions or who read the completed manuscript for the third edition and offered many good suggestions: David Branco of Northern Illinois University; Anthony P. J. Cerniglia of Lincoln Land Community College; Norma Flores of Southwestern College; Donna L. Friess of Cypress College; Martha K. Goodman of Central Virginia Community College; Richard Hess of Indiana-Purdue University; Thomas F. Hitchell of St. Louis Community College; Joan Holm of Northern Virginia Community College; H. Rodman Jones of the University of Tulsa; Audrey S. Kirby of Forsyth Technical Institute; Kenneth R. Lane of Arkansas State University; Dale B. Lumsden of Cape Cod Community College; Sylvia S. Malone of Jacksonville State University; Peggy M. Rypsam of Iona College; Patricia Smith-Pierce of Harper College; David E. Switzer of Indiana-Purdue University; James I. Walling, formerly at Central Michigan University; Joy E. Wilkison, formerly of Vincennes University; and I would like to give special thanks to James Mancuso, Mesa Community College, who has offered excellent suggestions on all three editions of *Communicate!*

CONTENTS

COMMUNICATE!

PART 1

ESTABLISHING A COMMUNICATION FOUNDATION

The wise old political philosopher Plato once cautioned against ever launching into a discussion of ideas without defining terms. In this two-chapter unit, we want to gain a perspective on the meaning and importance of communication.

CHAPTER 1

COMMUNICATION PERSPECTIVE

"Hello?"

"Hi—you sound a little groggy—like you just got up."

"No . . ."

"Well, it's just something about your voice. You sound a little groggy to me. But I didn't call to talk about voices. Listen . . ."

"Who is this?"

"Come on! Now I know you're a little groggy. But, come to think of it, it might not be your voice, it might be the connection. Maybe I should hang up and call again?"

"Is this Jack?"

"Jack! Jack hasn't got here by nine o'clock in the morning for a month."

"What's going on here? I feel so silly when I can't recognize a voice. Who is this?"

"I know what you mean. Phyllis was telling me she talked to her sister for about ten min-utes the other morning before she caught on to who she was. The mind plays tricks—especially in the morning. Well, like now—if you had been the one who called I wouldn't know who it was either because your voice sounds so different."

"Who's this? Phyllis?"

"Come on, Brenda—you know darn well Phyllis is my wife."

"Brenda! I'm not Brenda!"

"You're not? Then where's Brenda?"

"Who are you?"

"I'm Claude."

"Well, I don't know any Claude and I'm not Brenda and no Brenda lives here and . . ."

"Oh—uh—then this isn't 532–7649?"

"No, it certainly isn't!"

"Well . . . uh . . . it's been good talking to you."

Click.

Have you ever had an experience like Claude's? He and "Brenda" were talking with each other, but it is obvious that they were not communicating very effectively. What is this phenomenon we call communication? What determines whether communication is effective or not? The key to communication is *meaning*. If we get meaning from a person, an idea, an action, a painting, a building, a room, or whatever we are dealing with, we say that it communicated. Communication depends upon stimulating or bringing about meaning. However, we are not so much concerned with meaning stimulated by things, buildings, or barking dogs. We are concerned with meaning stimulated by people—like Claude, your classmates, and *you*.

Stimulating meaning alone, however, does not result in *effective* communication. One person may communicate with another in such a way that they have different meanings. Effective communication is communication in which the meaning that is stimulated is like, similar to, or the same as that within the communicator. In short, effective communication is shared meaning. So the goal in this book is to learn about communication, stimulating meaning, and to learn effective communication, sharing meanings. In this chapter we want to get an overview of the communication process, looking at its elements, settings, and functions in order to get some understanding of effective communication.

ELEMENTS OF THE PROCESS

Communication is a dynamic, ongoing, transactional process. It is dynamic because it is constantly in motion; it is ongoing because it has no fixed beginning or end; it is transactional because the elements occur simultaneously and the people communicating are interdependent.

In order to get a mental picture of communication, envision yourself at a party. You join three or four people who are conversing. After ten or fifteen minutes you leave the group to fix yourself a sandwich and to get a drink. Communication was going on when you joined the group and it continued after you left. Eventually that particular group disperses, but within the context of the party communication continues.

For purposes of analysis let's freeze this dynamic communication process and isolate the elements that blend together to form the total transactional process. We can isolate the *people* involved, the *context* in which the people are communicating, the *rules* that guide their communication, the *messages* that are being communicated, the *channels* through which the communication occurs, the presence or lack of *noise,* and the verbal and nonverbal responses that communication scholars call *feedback.*

People

The people in a communication transaction play the roles of sender and receiver, sometimes—as in interpersonal communication—simultaneously. As senders we form messages and attempt to communicate them to others through symbols. As receivers we process the messages that are sent to us and react to them both verbally and nonverbally.

Each person is a product of his or her individual experiences, feelings, ideas, moods, sex, occupation, religion, and so forth. As a result the meaning sent and the meaning received may not be exactly the same. For instance, when politician Art speaks of the importance of developing good jobs for the constituency, he may mean jobs that are highly paid; but Glen, a member of his audience, may consider a good job as one that is stimulating, regardless of pay. A successful communicator must take advantage of every skill available to present and interpret meanings as clearly as possible.

Context

Context is the physical and social setting in which communication takes place. The context affects expectations, meaning, and behavior. If you go out for an evening with friends of the same sex as yourself (the social context) and you end up at a disco (the physical context), your communication transactions will be different from what they would have been if you had gone with a church group of men and women (social context) to visit the home of your minister (physical context). Why? Because the context provides a basis for the rules (the norms) operating within a transaction. Likewise, a conversation with a friend in a secluded corner of a dimly lit restaurant provides a far different context than does a group discussion held with your peers in a classroom or a public speech given in an auditorium.

Rules

Rules are the guidelines that we establish or perceive as established for conducting transactions. Rules exist at the beginning of a communication encounter and grow, change, or solidify as people get to know each other better. Rules tell you what kinds of messages and behavior are proper in a given context and with a particular person or group of persons. For instance, students who pepper their conversations with four-letter words

CONTEXT IS THE PHYSICAL
AND SOCIAL SETTING IN
WHICH COMMUNICATION TAKES PLACE.

when talking with friends in a dorm are likely to use a much different vocabulary when giving a speech to their class.

Do we always know the rules? Not always. We have to learn the rules through experience. For instance, people who are used to raising their hands to be recognized at business meetings may find themselves unable to be heard in a group meeting where participants are allowed to break in whenever they feel like it.

The rules for communication may be formal (such as parliamentary procedures for organizational meetings), may be proven social guidelines (such as the cliché "never discuss religion at a party"), or may simply develop within the context of a particular setting.

Messages

The *message* is the content of the transaction. Messages have at least three elements: meaning, symbols used, and form or organization.

Meanings are ideas and feelings. You have ideas about how to study for your next exam, where to go for lunch, and whether marijuana should be legalized. You have feelings such as hunger for a good steak, joy over beating your best competition in racquetball, and guilt over failure to remember a parent's birthday. These meanings cannot be moved in total from one person's mind to another. You need some vehicle to communicate your meaning and to create similar meaning in the mind of someone else.

To express our ideas and feelings to others we use the vehicle of symbols. *Symbols* are words or actions that represent meaning. Symbols can be communicated with both voice and body. As we speak, our mind chooses words to convey the messages. At the same time, however, facial expressions, gestures, and tone of voice (all nonverbal cues) accompany our words and affect the meaning of the message. As we listen, we receive the verbal and nonverbal cues and assign meanings to them. The process of transforming ideas and feelings into symbols is called *encoding;* the process of transforming the symbols we receive into ideas and feelings is called *decoding*.

The communication process has become such an automatic process for you that it is unlikely you think consciously of either encoding or decoding messages. When your eyes grow bleary and you say, "I'm tired," you are not likely to think, "I wonder what symbols will best express the feeling I am now having?" Moreover, when you hear another person say "I'm tired," you are not likely to think "*I* stands for the person doing the talking, *am* means that the I is linked to some idea, and *tired* means growing weary or feeling a need for sleep." Nor are you likely to consider whether you have exactly the same mental picture of "tired" as the person using the word. Note that I said you are not likely to be conscious of these processes. At certain times when you grope for words, especially when you feel the right word is just on the tip of your tongue, you may become aware of the process itself.

The symbols that carry our meanings are not always used intentionally. Most communication is done with purpose. Yet sometimes when persons are carefully selecting symbols to carry thoughts and feelings, they may also be sending complimentary or conflicting messages through unintentional nonverbal cues. Let's look at an example to see how this works: Martha turns to Paul and says, "You can get me that report by noon tomorrow, can't you?" and Paul replies, "Sure, no problem." Even though Paul's response is positive, Martha notes a tone of uneasiness in his voice. Paul intends to convey a note of confidence with the words "Sure, no problem," but at the same time the nonverbal cues he is sending through his tone of voice betray, unintentionally, his verbal message. In this case, the unintentional message contradicted the intentional one. Both the intentional and the unintentional use of symbols are important to the sharing of meaning.

The third element of message is form. When an idea or feeling has many parts, the sender may need to communicate it in sections or in a certain order so that the receiver will not become confused. Message form is especially important in the public speaking setting when one person is talking uninterrupted for a relatively long time. But even in the give and take of interpersonal conversation, form can affect message understanding. For instance, when Julia tells Connie about the apartment she looked at yesterday if her description moves logically from room to room, Connie is far more likely to be able to follow her than if Julia attempts to describe bits and pieces drawn from all over the apartment in a random order.

Channels

The *channel* is both the route traveled by the message and the means of transportation. Words are carried from one person to another by air waves; facial expressions, gestures, and movement by light waves. Usually the more channels that can be used to carry a message, the more likely the communication is to succeed. Although human communication has basically two channels—light and sound—people can and do communicate by any of the five sensory channels. A fragrant scent and a firm handshake may be as important as what is seen or heard.

Noise

A person's ability to interpret, understand, or respond to symbols is often hurt by noise. *Noise* is any stimulus that gets in the way of sharing meaning. Your success as a communicator frequently depends on how you cope with external, semantic, and internal noises.

External noises are the sights, sounds, and other stimuli that draw people's attention away from the message. For instance, during a lecture in American history, your attention is drawn to the sound of a power lawnmower outside the window. The sound of the lawnmower becomes external noise. Trying to concentrate on the lecture might be fruitless unless the noise is eliminated. External noise does not have to be a sound to be a distraction—it may also be a sight. Perhaps during the same lecture an extremely attractive man or woman looks toward you with what you perceive as a particularly engaging look. For that moment at least your attention is likely to be drawn toward that person.

Internal noises are the thoughts and feelings that intrude their way into your mind while you are attempting to pay attention to someone or something else. Perhaps while your economics professor uses an example of food distribution to make a point, the thought of food causes you to daydream about what you are going to have for lunch. If you have tuned out the lecture and tuned in a daydream, a past conversation, or an irrelevant feeling, you have created an internal noise.

The third type of noise, and perhaps the most difficult to cope with, is semantic noise. *Semantic noises* are those message symbols that inhibit or prevent shared meaning. Because your perceptions and experiences differ from those of a person speaking to you, you may hold different meanings for even relatively simple words. Suppose your instructor excitedly tells you that she will be reading a paper at a forthcoming convention. If you think "reading a paper" just means reading a newspaper (rather than giving an oral report on research), you may not understand her enthusiasm. Since meaning depends on your own experience, you may at times decode a word or phrase differently from the way the sender intended. When this happens, you get semantic noise.

Feedback

Whether receivers decode messages properly or not they have some mental or physical response to the messages, and it is the response of the receiver that enables us to determine whether communication—stimulation of meaning—really took place. This response—called *feedback* in most com-

EXTERNAL NOISES ARE THE SIGHTS, SOUNDS, AND OTHER STIMULI THAT DRAW PEOPLE'S ATTENTION AWAY FROM THE MESSAGE.

munication books—tells the person sending a message whether that message was heard, seen, or understood. If the verbal or nonverbal response tells the sender that the communication was not received or was received incorrectly or was misinterpreted, the person can send the message again, perhaps in a different way, so that the meaning the sender intends to share is the same meaning received by the listener.

During this course you will be involved in different kinds of communication situations. The situations or settings themselves are the reason for the differing amounts and differing types of response. A *zero-feedback* situation is said to exist when it is virtually impossible for the sender to be aware of a receiver's response. Suppose that right now I stated in this book: "Stop what you are doing and draw a rectangle resting on one of its sides." I would have no way of knowing whether you understood what I was talking about, whether you actually drew the rectangle, or, if you drew it, whether you drew it correctly. As the source of that message—as well as the other messages in this textbook—I cannot know for sure whether I am really communicating. The lack of direct feedback is one of the weaknesses of any of the forms of mass communication. The source has little or no immediate opportunity to test the impact of his or her message. Suppose, however, that instead of being the author of a book, I am your instructor in a class of fifty students. Now suppose that I asked you to draw a rectangle resting on one of its sides. Even if you said nothing, my presence would enable me to monitor your nonverbal feedback directly. If you drew the rectangle, I could see it; if you refused, I would know; in some cases I could see exactly what you were drawing. A person in a public speaking setting must be sensitive to this type of basically nonverbal feedback. Now suppose that in this classroom, as I asked you to draw the rectangle, you were free to ask me any direct questions and I were free and willing to respond. The free flow of interacting communication that would take place represents the highest level of feedback. This type of feedback is most likely in a personal communication setting.

How important is feedback to effective communication? Leavitt and Mueller conducted an experiment similar to the one just described.[1] They reported that communication improved markedly as the situation moved from zero feedback to complete interaction. In our communication, whether personal, small-group, or public speaking, we want to stimulate as much feedback as the situation will allow.

As we will see later in this textbook, feedback can be used more than just as a test of the understanding of the message; it also can be used to

[1]H. J. Leavitt and Ronald A. H. Mueller, "Some Effects of Feedback on Communication," *Human Relations*, Vol. 4 (1951), p. 403.

help us gain insight into ourselves as persons, to stimulate personal growth, and to verify or validate our perceptions.

In order to summarize and to get a kind of three-dimensional look at the *communication process* in action, trace with me the variables in a simple two-person encounter. Upon leaving the classroom, Joe catches up with Mary. After a few introductory comments about the class, he pauses for a moment and then in a hesitating and almost reticent way says, "Say, Mary, how about—uh—how about going out with me tonight?" Mary, with a neutral expression on her face, replies, noncommittally, "What do you mean 'go out with me,' Joe?" Joe, gaining a little more confidence, says, "Well, I thought we could go to Charley's for dinner and then take in a new flick at the Grand." Mary, breaking into a smile, responds, "That sounds great, Joe, I'd love to."

Let's analyze what happened. In the physical context of a hall outside a classroom, Joe, the sender, conveys his meaning (encodes) in verbal symbols: his statement, "Say, Mary, how about going out with me tonight?" is the verbal representation of his thoughts; his hesitant voice, the breaks in the sentence, and his slightly reticent behavior are probably the non-verbal representations of his feelings of embarrassment. Mary, in decoding the message, finds herself unsure of what Joe is trying to say verbally. She encodes her question in the words, "What do you mean 'go out with me'?" Since she does not wish to convey any positive or negative feelings, her nonverbal response also is noncommittal. Her entire response represents her feedback to his initial message. Joe then decodes Mary's feedback. Realizing that she does not yet share his meaning, he sends another message. This time he encodes his meaning verbally as, "Well, I thought we could go to Charley's for dinner and then take in a new flick at the Grand." Nonverbally he portrays a little more hope in the form of increased enthusiasm—a more positive approach. This time Mary decodes the message into meaning that correlates with the meaning Joe was sending. Since she is pleased with the invitation and wishes to show her approval, she encodes her response verbally with, "That sounds great, Joe, I'd love to" and nonverbally with a smile and a sincere tone of voice. *Meaning is shared; effective communication is now complete.*

In this example we analyzed but one act of communication. In an extended conversation each person acts as sender and receiver many times during the communication event.

COMMUNICATION SETTINGS

Although all our communication includes the seven variables we have just considered, our communication is not the same under all circumstances.

During the course of our study we will be looking at communication in each of the three major settings in which it occurs: personal, small-group, and public speaking.

Personal Communication

Personal communication is the spontaneous, usually informal communication we engage in with self and others. We generally think of communication as involving two or more persons. But just think of the time you spend talking to yourself! Sometimes, the conversation is a silent one, but sometimes you actually speak aloud. Were you ever embarrassed by someone pointing out that you "were mumbling to yourself"? This communication that takes place within you is often called *intra*personal communication.

Of course, much of our personal communication involves the kind of interaction that most of us have referred to as conversation, which is the person-to-person interaction with one other person or with a small informal aggregate of persons. So, talking to a friend on campus, talking on the phone with a classmate about an upcoming test, discussing a movie with the gang over a beer are all personal communication. Intimate relationships and friendships are formed and maintained through personal communication. In this setting, feedback is immediate—total interaction is the rule. This informal communication with others is called *inter*personal communication. For purposes of simplification I have combined the two (*intra-* and *inter-*) under the heading of personal communication.

How we relate to others is strongly influenced by our ability to use the communication skills most associated with conversation: shaping messages, listening and responding, understanding nonverbal cues, and forming relationships. *Personal communication is spontaneous, fast moving, and at times difficult to recall accurately.* Still it is subject to analysis, and how we communicate in personal informal settings can be changed and improved.

Small-Group Communication

Another large portion of our communication occurs in group settings. Each of us belongs to many groups: the family, social organizations, church organizations, work committees, and others. Although our communication in these groups is basically personal in nature, when several persons formalize their relationships by meeting to combine talents to solve a problem or make a decision, they form a *work group*.

The purpose of a work group, achieving a goal that represents and is shaped by the thinking of the entire group, introduces additional variables that are not found in spontaneous, informal communication: elements of group structure, the need for task and maintenance functions by group members, leadership, and formalized methods of group problem solving and decision making.

Still, group communication is not a separate, unrelated activity. Think of group communication as a format building upon personal communication skills.

Public Speaking

At times, on both formal and informal levels, we address others, not as interacting participants, but as an audience. When communication follows a one-to-many model, all the variables of communication are present, but in public speaking they are used much differently than they are in the other settings. For most persons, *public speaking* is more difficult than personal or small-group interaction. The major sources of this difficulty are that public speaking requires careful message preparation, willingness and ability to face a large group, and sensitivity to what are often very subtle feedback responses.

Unfortunately, most persons are least effective in public speaking. Their speeches are often long, tedious, and easily forgotten. However, the true value of public speaking should not be measured by the average or the typical effort. Since public speaking can serve both to disseminate information and to act as a catalyst for change, it is important to master the fundamentals and learn to apply them effectively. In this text we will consider the skills of message preparation, information exchange, and persuasion that you can use to become a more effective speaker.

FUNCTIONS OF COMMUNICATION

We have seen what communication is; we have seen where communication takes place—now let's look at the most important question: Why? We study communication because communication matters. All communication has social and decision-making functions that touch and affect every aspect of our lives.

Social Function

People are basically social animals. Without at least some social interaction, they hallucinate, lose their motor coordination, and become generally maladjusted.[2] Of course, hermits do exist but they are rare. Most of us need to interact, to show feelings, to be wanted, to love.

On one social level people communicate for the sheer pleasure of interaction. At such times the subject of the conversation really is unimportant. Two people may sit talking for hours about apparently inconsequential matters. When they part they may have exchanged little real information, but they may carry away from the interaction a truly good feeling caused solely by the experience of talking with another human being.

On a second social level people communicate to demonstrate their ties with other people. Why do you say, "How you doing?" to a fellow you sat next to in class last quarter but haven't seen since? You may get pleasure out of the interaction—you may also see it as meeting a social need. When you see people you know, you openly recognize them so that they will continue to recognize you. By saying, "Hi, Skip, how's it going?" you conform to our societal norms—you acknowledge a person you recognize with one of the many statements you have learned to use under these circumstances. Failure to communicate is seen as a slight—the person may think you are stuck up. Recognition efforts serve to demonstrate your ties with people.

On a third social level people communicate to build and to maintain relationships. When you do not know a person at all, you may communicate with that person to try out the relationship. If you find that you have things in common, the relationship may grow. Depending upon the results of the interaction, you may be content with an acquaintance relationship or a school-friend relationship, or you may seek a deeper, more intimate relationship. Some conversation is conducted for purposes of moving the relationship to higher level of intimacy; some, for reinforcing the satisfactory nature of the relationship that has been achieved. Few relationships stay the same—especially during college years. You may find yourself moving into and out of a variety of relationships even within a single term. This is part of living—and it is an important purpose of communication.

Decision-Making Function

Just as we are social animals, we are also decision makers. Today, starting with whether you were ready to get up and get going, through what to have for breakfast, whether to go to class, how to study for a test, you

---

[2]John A. R. Wilson, Mildred C. Robick, and William B. Michael, *Psychological Foundations of Learning and Teaching*, 2nd ed. (New York: McGraw-Hill, 1974), p. 26.

have made countless decisions already. Some of these decisions you made alone; others you made in consultation with one or more persons. Even more important, every one of the decisions involved some kind of language usage. Some of your decisions were made as emotional responses to stimuli—some were carefully considered. The more important the decision, the more carefully you may have gone through the various steps of problem awareness, problem analysis, possible solutions, and selecting the best solution. Unless the decision was a spontaneous emotional reaction, it involved processing information, sharing information, and, in many instances, persuasion.

One important aspect of decision making is information exchange. No one can function in our society without data. Some of these data are obtained through observation, some through reading, some through television, and a great deal through interpersonal communication. Jeff runs out to get the morning paper. As he comes through the door hurriedly, Tom asks, "What's it like out there?" Jeff replies, "It's cold—couldn't be more than twenty degrees." Tom says, "I was going to wear my jacket, but I guess I'd better break out the old winter coat." Such conversation is typical of countless exchanges that involve sending and receiving information. Since decisions generally are better when they are based on information, anything that you can do to make your information exchange more accurate will help you make better decisions.

A second important aspect of decision making is to win support for your decisions. This may well involve changing people's attitudes and behaviors. You try to get your friends to go to a particular movie; you try to get an acquaintance to vote for you; you try to persuade your father to let you use the car this weekend; or you try to get an instructor to drop a final written examination. These are but a few examples of attempts to influence people in order to make or carry out decisions. Some theorists argue that the purpose of all communication is to influence behavior of others.

SUMMARY

We have seen that effective communication is a complicated transactional process that results in shared meaning. Although the dynamic nature of the process is very difficult to isolate, it involves sending and receiving messages through various channels within a specific context while competing with noise. Upon receiving a message a person may or may not feed back verbal or nonverbal responses or may do both.

Communication takes place intrapersonally in one's own head, interpersonally with one or more persons in informal settings, in small groups, and in public speaking settings. The communication that takes place serves the social function of communicating for pleasure, demonstrating ties with others, and building and maintaining relationships. It also serves a decision-making function by giving information on the basis of which decisions may be made and by changing attitudes and beliefs.

SUGGESTED READINGS

If you would like more detailed information about the communication process, you may want to consult one or more of the following:

Dean C. Barnlund (Ed.). *Interpersonal Communication: Surveys and Studies.* Boston: Houghton Mifflin, 1968. See particularly pages 3–29 for a good discussion of communication goals and a worthwhile analysis of the evolution of communication models.

David K. Berlo. *The Process of Communication.* New York: Holt, Rinehart & Winston, 1960. Berlo discusses the interaction process in detail.

Gerald R. Miller and Mark Steinberg. *Between People: A New Analysis of Interpersonal Communication.* Chicago: Science Research Associates, 1975. See pp. 3–86 for a comprehensive discussion of communication as transaction.

Paul Watzlawick, Janet H. Beavin, and Don D. Jackson. *Pragmatics of Human Communication.* New York: W. W. Norton, 1967. This book and Barnlund's and Berlo's books are becoming classics of communication theory.

CHAPTER 2

PERCEPTION, SELF-CONCEPT, AND YOUR COMMUNICATION

"Can I use the car Saturday?"

"You've had it pretty often."

"Well, Tim gets the car more than I do."

"That's Tim's family's decision."

"Please? I really need it."

"Where are you planning to go?"

"To dinner and a movie with Jeff and Sue."

"Can't Jeff drive?"

"He drove last time. Listen, I'll pay for a whole tank of gas—and I'll even sweep the inside of the car!"

"That's nice, but . . ."

"You're not planning to use it, are you?"

"I don't have any plans at the moment, but Irene said she might like to go out."

"But this is really important."

"What makes it especially important?"

"Don't you remember? It's Phyllis's birthday—and we always go out to dinner and to a movie on her birthday."

"I'm sorry, I did forget—go ahead, Dad."

"Thanks, son," Claude replies gratefully.

The success of the punchline of this story depends upon your original perception of who is doing the talking. Perception is a key factor in any form of communication. For example, suppose you are asked to give a speech at a sales meeting. What you say in that speech may depend upon your perception of the people listening to you, while the success of your speech may depend upon the audience's perception of you as a speaker. Would you like to get to know the person who shares a microscope with you in biology? Your desire to know that person probably stems from your perception of him or her; likewise, how far you get may depend upon that person's perception of you! Although you may not be aware of it a great deal of your communication behavior and its success or failure is likely to be based upon the nature of perceptions.

Some people have very accurate perceptions of their world and its environs; others, for one reason or another, distort what comes to them through their senses so much that their perceptions of self, others, and their environment have very little to do with reality. In this chapter we want to take a look at the perceptual process itself and its relation to communication.

PERCEPTION

Perception is the process of assigning meaning to sensory information. Your eyes, ears, nose, skin, and taste buds gather information; perception is what your brain does with that information. You assume that what you see, hear, feel, taste, and smell is reality. I'm sure you remember making such statements as "Of course that's the way it was—I saw it happen!" Yet when two or more people see the same event, they are likely to report it differently. Why? Because the reality each person reports is a product of his or her individual perceptions. When someone sees or hears, his brain responds in three stages: it selects, it organizes, and it interprets. The result is perception.

Stages

Although the three stages of perception occur almost simultaneously, we will consider each separately.

Selection   Every second you are bombarded by millions of sensory stimuli. If you were consciously trying to be aware of each sensory stimulus, you could go insane. You have learned to cope with this bombardment by focusing attention on relatively few of these stimuli. Right now you are reading this book so your visual attention should be focused on the words on the page—and you are probably not listening to anything. Stop for a minute and look around—try to become aware of all the sights and sounds you could be focusing on right now. Once you focus on a particular object or sound, the rest of the sights and sounds blend into an indefinite background. At any one time your mind focuses on one thing, and the rest becomes part of the background.

Since the focal point of any given scene may be at any of an infinite number of places—depending upon what each person selects as the focal point—ten persons viewing the same scene may have ten different perceptions. The nature of focus and how it can be shifted is illustrated with the drawing in Figure 2-1. Look steadily at Figure 2-1. What do you see?

Figure 2-1

At first glance you probably noticed either the goblet or the faces in Figure 2-1. As you look at the drawing, notice that the goblet and faces come in and out of focus. The focus from one to the other may give you the impression that you are seeing both the faces and the goblet at one time. Actually you are focusing on one at a time. Likewise, you may be able to switch focus so rapidly that you give yourself the impression of seeing or listening to two different stimuli at once, but you can focus on only one at a time.

What you choose to focus on is a matter of selection. Sometimes the selection is conscious: If you are listening to a song you like very much and your mother is trying to talk with you at the same time, you may well decide to listen to your mother or to the song. Sometimes the selection is unconscious: You may be intending to listen to your mother, but without even seeming to think about it, your attention (focus) may shift to that song you like so much.

Organization   Data are received from the senses by the brain. The brain selects certain stimuli to focus on and then tries to sort the data into some intelligible order. This process of organization is a second major element of perception. When we encounter a group of stimuli, we are likely to arrive at an organization by *patterns*, by *proximity*, and by *good form*.

You are grouping by *patterns* when you see within a set of stimuli something that is similar. Look at the three sets of shapes in Figure 2-2. In Figure 2-2a the dots and circles may seem to separate into two groups because of the similarities of the dots and circles. In Figure 2-2b you may see four columns of figures rather than sixteen individual figures. In Figure 2-2c you may perceive an X surrounded by small circles. Similarly, when you consider a group of people you may perceive them as groups of men and women or adults and children.

You are grouping by *proximity* when you group those things that are physically close together. Look at Figure 2-3. What do you see? Figure 2-3a probably appears as three pairs of parallel lines rather than as six individual parallel lines. Figure 2-3b probably appears as four sets of circles rather than as sixteen individual circles. In a classroom if you see a group of five students sitting apart from the rest of the class, you may decide that they have something in common.

You are grouping by *good form* when your mind supplies missing information that completes a pattern with a gap in it or when your mind thinks in terms of a recognizable form even when the stimuli are not arranged perfectly. Look at Figure 2-4. Because of the tendency to complete

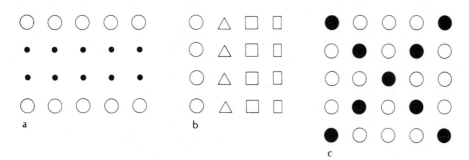

Figure 2-2

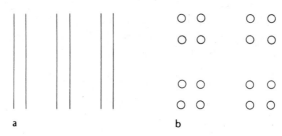

Figure 2-3

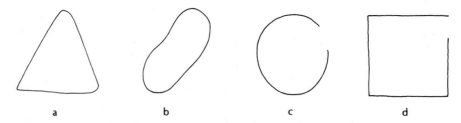

Figure 2-4

a form, you probably perceive Figure 2-4c as a circle and Figure 2-4d as a square; likewise, because of the tendency to see a group conforming to a recognizable form you are likely to perceive Figure 2-4a as a triangle and Figure 2-4b as an oval. This search for good form explains why you may read a neon sign correctly when a portion is burned out and why you may finish a sentence correctly when a speaker leaves out a word.

Interpretation   As the mind selects and organizes, it completes its perception by interpreting the information it receives. The interpretation gives the perception meaning. Thus when we have selected a stimulus and organized it we are likely to identify it or draw some conclusion related to it. Each of the methods of organization mentioned so far led to a kind of identification. We are walking down a street when our attention is drawn to something between two buildings. At once our mind selects stimuli to focus on, organizes those stimuli, identifies the perception as a cat, and perhaps tells us there is no need to be startled.

Let's consider the link between perception and communication by turning attention to Figure 2-5. Look at the drawing. Describe what you see. Talk about what you see in a way that identifies and evaluates what you see.

Through the perception process (selection, organization, and inter-pretation) you probably identified the drawing as that of a woman. If you saw a young woman, your description was much different from what it

Figure 2-5

would have been if you had seen an old woman. Which did you see? Look again. Keep looking at the drawing until you have seen both women. Was your verbal explanation of your first perception appropriate to your second perception? Quite unlikely. "Ah," you say, "but this is just a trick. No real life situation could possibly fool me like this one." Don't believe it. People are fooled every day. We make mistakes with objects, with people, with places. Examples abound of people perceiving a sparkling glass trinket as a diamond, perceiving a stranger as a close friend because of a similar hair style, or perceiving a place as familiar because of a similarity of name, color, or surroundings.

We're often fooled because so many factors affect the accuracy of our perceptions. Let's examine some of the most common.

Factors Involved

Consider each of the following factors carefully. When you make mistakes in perception it is usually because you have been fooled by one or more of the following:

1. *Limitations of the senses.* If your eyes are weak, you will have trouble recording accurately what you see. So it is with all the senses. Any problem in sight, hearing, touch, taste, or smell will affect perception. Even when the senses are working properly they have limitations. For example, human eyes perceive only certain rays; they do not see the infrared or ultraviolet ends of

the color spectrum. Likewise, human ears cannot pick up many of the sounds that come to them; they are limited to a range of between 20 and 20,000 cycles per second. This is why you cannot hear certain kinds of whistles for dogs.

2. *Familiarity.* With each new perception the mind must select, organize, and interpret. If stimuli are not strong enough to catch attention (to be selected) or are difficult to organize into recognizable patterns, then the likelihood of interpretation is not great. For instance, if you do not own a car and you have not made any special effort to study sizes, shapes, or designs, you could walk through a parking lot without having any specific perceptions other than the presence of cars in general. Suppose, however, that you buy a car. In the buying process you become familiar with the styling, shape, and design of your new car. Now when you walk through a parking lot, your eye is drawn to those cars similar to yours. Your attention is focused on the familiar type of car.

Suppose you witnessed a robbery in which you saw a person rush from a store, get into a car, and drive away. Later a police officer asks you for a description of the vehicle. Your ability to describe it would probably depend on your familiarity. For instance, if the "getaway car" happened to be the same type as yours, you would describe it with great accuracy. If, on the other hand, it were a make, model, or year with which you were not familiar, your description could be as vague as, "It was a big, dark colored car."

3. *Expectation.* As you become familiar with objects, places, and people you develop a capacity to recognize them, which works in favor of accuracy of perception. But your familiarity also carries with it the likelihood of expectation which may well lead you to "see" things that aren't there. For instance, if you were told that the person who rushed past you as you entered the store had just robbed the store, your familiarity with the concept of a "robber" might lead you to believe you had seen the person carrying a gun or a knife. In your description you might include some features that you expect from a robber—perhaps a mask the robber was wearing. The fact is that when a number of witnesses to a crime are questioned, there will be much conflicting testimony, and most of the conflict is a result of expectation.

4. *Context or situation.* The nature of your perceptions is likely to be affected greatly by the total context. Take a man with a hat and a top coat. First put that man in the context of midafternoon on a busy street walking toward you; next put that man in the context of midnight on a dark narrow street walking toward you. You are likely to see two entirely different men. As a result of the time of night, the darkness, and the element of fear of attack you will probably see a man much differently at midnight than walking toward you in midafternoon.

5. *Emotions and attitudes.* Ordinarily your perception is affected by what you are thinking and feeling at the moment. For instance, when you are hungry—I mean really hungry—you are likely to see everything in terms of food. If you're driving down a street you will see restaurants, markets, bakeries—perhaps places you never noticed before. If you are walking along a street, you may become especially aware of the aroma of food being cooked somewhere. Whatever your emotion or attitude at the moment, it will affect your perception.

Improvement

When you understand the factors that affect attention, you will probably learn how to improve the accuracy of your own perceptions. Let me offer several suggestions.

1. *Realize that your perceptions may be inaccurate.* Too many people are caught up in the "I was there—I know what I saw" syndrome; that is, people accept their perceptions without question. Start by saying, "I know what I *think* I saw, heard, tasted, smelled, or felt, but I *could* be wrong." By questioning the accuracy of perceptions you may seek further verification. If the accuracy of perception is important, taking a few seconds to double check it may be worth the effort.

2. *Be willing to change a perception when its accuracy is in doubt.* If you see a person you know do something mean, you will develop the perception that the person is "mean." This one perception may lead you to *expect* mean behavior from this person at all times. Willingness to change means taking the time to observe this person's behavior at other times. If the person shows a different kind of behavior under different circumstances, you should be able to change your perception of that person.

3. *Keep from jumping to conclusions; separate fact from inference.* Remember that the third facet of gaining a perception is interpretation. Interpretation often means drawing an inference from a set of observed facts. One part of the problem deals with how you reason things out. Although changing your entire approach to reasoning may be difficult, you can improve. (You will want to study carefully the analysis of reasoning on pp. 321–322.) A second part of the problem deals with how to recognize when the perception is factual and when it is an inference. This differentiation is something you can learn to do *now* with just a little concentration.

A *fact* is a verifiable statement—usually a statement about something that can be or has been directly observed. An *inference* is a conclusion about what has been observed. Separating fact from inference means being able to tell the difference between a verifiable observation and an opinion related to that observation. Let's clarify this with an example. Ellen tells a friend that she saw a Bob's TV Repair truck in her neighbor's driveway for the fifth time in the last two weeks. Ellen is reporting only what she saw; she is relating a perception of the facts. If, however, Ellen adds, "She's having a terrible time getting her TV fixed," she would be making an inference. Ellen would be concluding—without actually knowing—that the truck was at her neighbor's house because someone was trying to repair a television set. This interpretation of the fact—this inference drawn from the fact—may be true, but it may not be. The driver of the truck might be a friend of Ellen's, or maybe they're having an affair, or maybe a special system is being installed, or whatever. The reporting of the presence of the truck is fact; the explanation for the presence of the truck is inference.

There is nothing wrong with drawing inferences—they are necessary if one is to make sense out of the world. However, (1) you should know when you are inferring and when you are reporting observation; (2) you should recognize that although your inferences may be true, they may *not* be—and inferences should not be stated as if they were; and (3) you should not act as though your inferences are facts.

EXERCISE _____

Read the following statement. Assume that all information presented in it is definitely accurate and true.

> The only vehicle parked in front of 725 Main Street is a red truck. The words "Bob Jones TV Repair" are spelled in large letters across the side panels of the truck.

Can you tell the difference between fact and inference? Read the statements about the story, and answer according to the following:

F—fact
I—inference

1. ____   The color of the vehicle in front of 725 Main Street is red.
2. ____   There is lettering on the side panel of the truck.
3. ____   Someone's TV needs repair at 725 Main Street.
4. ____   The red truck parked in front of 725 Main Street belongs to Bob Jones.

> *Answers*
> 1. F.
> 2. F.
> 3. I. There may be, but the story does not tell.
> 4. I. It may, but the story does not say. Both 3 and 4 are inferences that you may have made, but neither is necessarily true.

Try again. This one is a little more difficult.

> A girl had just opened the door to the apartment when a man appeared and demanded money. The tenant opened her purse. The contents of the purse spilled out on the floor. The man took the money and left. The tenant called the apartment manager.

1. _____ A man appeared after the tenant opened the apartment door.
2. _____ The robber was a man.
3. _____ The purse contents were spilled on the floor.
4. _____ The money was in the girl's purse.
5. _____ The apartment manager was called.
6. _____ The man ran from the apartment.
7. _____ The story involves three persons: a female tenant, the robber, and the apartment manager.

Answers
1. I. A girl opened the apartment door. The story does not say whether the girl was the tenant.
2. I. A man demanded money, but whether the man was a robber, or an agent from a collection company, or something else is never stated.
3. F. The purse contents were spilled on the floor.
4. I. The money was somewhere, but the story does not say where.
5. F. The tenant called the manager.
6. I. The man *left*, but whether he ran or not is not stated.
7. I. The story may involve four persons if the girl who first opened the door is *not* the tenant. The story does not say.

PERCEPTION AND COMMUNICATION ABOUT SELF

Now that we have taken a brief look at the perceptual process, we need to understand the role perception plays in communication. In this section we will study perception and communication about self; in the next section we will study perception and communication about others.

Almost all of our communication reveals something about our selves. The simple question, "Isn't it a beautiful day?" not only speaks of what people in general would call a beautiful day but reveals what is for that speaker a beautiful day. Even silence can be revealing. If we remain silent during a discussion, it reveals that we are unable or unwilling to talk about that particular matter. Let's take a look at the interrelationship between perception and self-concept; then we will see how the self reveals itself through communication.

Formation of the Self-Concept

Your self-concept is a collection of perceptions of every aspect of your being: your appearance, physical and mental capabilities, vocational potential, sexual capabilities, size, strength, and so forth. Your self-concept

SELF – CONCEPT IS FORMED
BY YOUR VIEW OF YOURSELF.

is formed by (1) self-appraisal, (2) reactions and responses of others, and (3) roles you play.

Self-Appraisal   You form impressions about yourself partly because of what you see. You look at yourself in the mirror and make judgments about your weight and size, the clothes you wear, and your smile. These judgments affect how you feel about yourself. If you like what you see, you may feel good about yourself. If you don't like what you see, you may try to change. Perhaps you will go on a diet, buy some new clothes, get your hair styled differently, or begin jogging. If you don't like what you see and you cannot or are unwilling to change, you may begin to develop negative feelings about yourself.

Your impressions of yourself may result from your reactions to your experiences. Through experience you learn what you are good at and what you like. If you discover that you can throw a ball or a stone from distances of as much as twenty or thirty feet and hit your target, you are likely to see yourself as having a good arm. If you can read a recipe, modify it, and produce something that tastes good, you will probably consider yourself a good cook. Keep in mind that a single satisfying experience may not give you a positive perception of your throwing or your cooking (just as a single negative experience may not give you a negative perception), but if additional experiences produce similar results, then the initial perception will be strengthened. The greater the number of positive experiences you have—whether as a cook, lover, decision maker, student, or parent—the more positive your self-concept becomes. Likewise, the greater the number of negative experiences you have, the more negative your self-concept may become.

Reactions and Responses of Others   Your self-concept is also a result of how others react and respond to you. Suppose a person looks at you and says, "You have beautiful hair." Or suppose that after you've given your opinion on developing alternate means of power to some friends, one of them tells you, "You're a logical thinker and convincing speaker." Sometimes even one comment like either of these might make you think that you have beautiful hair or that you are a logical and influential speaker. Moreover, if you respect the person making the comment, it will have an even greater effect on your perception of self. Just as positive comments may have a great impact, so also negative comments have similar impacts.

You are likely to use other people's comments to validate, reinforce, or alter your perceptions of who and what you are. The more positive comments you get about yourself, the more positive your total self-concept becomes.

Roles You Play   A third aspect of self-concept is a product of the first two. As a result of how you appraise yourself and how others respond to you, you may choose or be forced to play various roles. Roles are products of the value systems of society, or groups, and of the self. Society's value systems are easy to illustrate. Consider, for example, some of the roles that society expects you to play. In this era of the women's rights movement, we hope that sex-role expectations are changing. Nevertheless, some people still expect little girls to play with dolls and homemaking toys to prepare them for the nurturing roles of wife and mother. Little boys learn to hold back tears, to be aggressive in sports, and to play with mechanical toys—in preparation for their roles as husband, father, and bread winner. If these children are caught playing with "inappropriate toys," a boy is called "sissy," a girl "tomboy." Both are derogatory terms and could injure self-concepts.

In addition to social values, the value system of a specific group may also dominate your role. Your family, your social and service organizations—every group you belong to approves or disapproves of things you do or say and of what you are. They help determine the kind of person you are. For instance, if you are the oldest in a large family, your parents may cast you in the role of disciplinarian, brothers' and sisters' keeper, or housekeeper depending on how they see family relationships. Your peers may look upon you as a "joker"; you may go along by playing your role. You laugh and tell stories when you really feel hurt or imposed upon.

Other roles are products of your own value system. You may portray "easygoing," "fashion model," or "bookworm" to fit your perception of self based upon your own experience, to conform with impressions of others, or to reflect a role you have chosen to play.

We all play a number of roles: Some roles that we play in private may be the same as or directly opposite to those we play in public. For instance, Samantha, who is perceived as a warm, quiet, sensitive person in private or with a close friend, may play the role of a boisterous party girl in a group. In each new encounter, you may test a role you have been playing or you may decide to play a new role.

A key question is "How real or accurate are your self-estimates?" The answer depends on the accuracy of your perceptions. We all experience both successes and failures at things we do; we hear both praise and blame. In determining your self-concept if you think about mostly successful experiences and positive responses, your perception of self will be positive, and your self-concept will probably be high. If, on the other hand, you think about mostly negative experiences and remember only the criticism you receive, your perception of self will be negative, and your self-concept will be low. In neither case does that self-concept necessarily conform to reality. Yet in terms of behavior those perceptions of self are likely to have far greater effect than reality, assuming that one can determine some objective reality.

Functions of the Self-Concept

Now that we have seen what the self-concept is and have given a brief analysis of how it is formed, let's consider what part this self-concept plays in your communication. Your self-concept serves at least four basic communication functions: (1) It expresses predictions of behavior. (2) It filters messages received from others. (3) It influences word selection and tone of voice. (4) It moderates competing internal messages.

Predictor of Behavior   An important communication function of your self-concept is to express predictions of behavior. The higher your self-concept is, the more likely you are to talk in ways that predict positive experiences. The lower your self-concept is the more likely you are to talk in ways that predict negative experiences. Soon your self-concept begins to shape reality—you begin to profit or lose by what are called "self-fulfilling prophecies." A self-fulfilling prophecy is a prediction that comes true *because* you predicted it. For example, Ed sees himself as a good test taker; he says, "I'm going to do well on the economics test." Then, as a result of his positive self-concept, he remains relaxed, studies, takes the test confidently, and just as he predicted, does really well. On the other hand, Jeff believes himself to be a poor test taker; he says, "I just know I'll blow the econ test!" Then, because he fears tests, his study is interrupted by negative thoughts; he goes into the test tired, irritable, and worried; and, just as he predicted, he does poorly. Positive thoughts and positive language do in fact often produce positive results; and, unfortunately, negative thoughts and negative language may produce negative results.

Filter of Statements   Self-concept may also affect our communication by filtering what others say to us. Even though you may receive all messages adequately (that is, your ears receive the messages and your brain records them), you do not *listen* equally to each. Moreover, what you choose to listen to is likely to be those messages that reinforce your self-concept. If someone says something that contradicts your perception, you are likely to act as if it had never been said. For example, you prepare lunch for your study group, and someone comments that you're a pretty good cook. Because this remark contradicts your self-concept, you may ignore it, not really hear it, or perhaps reply, "No, this was more like a lucky accident," or "Thanks for being kind to me, but it really wasn't that good." On the other hand, if you think you are a good cook, you will seek out those messages that reinforce this positive view and screen out those that don't.

Perhaps you have spotted what appears to be a contradiction in this analysis of self-concept. Earlier I said that your self-concept is formed partly by listening to other people's statements. Now I am saying that it is the self-concept that determines whether you listen to those statements or screen them out. The fact is that your self-concept is *both* a result of others' comments and a filter of others' comments. It seems that certain comments help to form a self-concept. Then the self-concept begins to work as a filter, screening out certain messages. At times, however, comments will get past the filter and change the self-concept, and then the newly changed self-concept begins to filter other comments. As a result, change in self-concept does occur.

Influencer of Word Selection and Tone of Voice   There seems to be a definite link between self-concept and a person's word selection and tone of voice.[1] A person's self-concept is likely to be revealed by the kinds of statements he or she makes about himself or herself. Continued use of self-criticism, weakness, and self-doubt is often a sign of low self-concept. Constant statements like "I never was any good at . . . ," "I don't know why I'm even trying, I know it won't work," and "I know you're disappointed with me, I just can't seem to get it right" are examples of such statements. On the other hand, a speech style that is characterized by confidence, honest effort, and probability of success is a sign of a positive self-concept. "I know it will be tough, but I look forward to trying," "You can count on me, I'll be giving it my best," or "I'll get the job done and you'll be pleased" are examples of the positive approach.

Signs of self-concept are especially prevalent in statements about competition. People with a low self-concept are often pessimistic and use statements such as "Why should I try? I won't win." People with a high self-concept look forward to the challenge of good competition; their statements show that they will give a good accounting of themselves whether they do win or lose. Constant blaming and cutting down the accomplishment of others may also be signs of low self-concept. "I might have done better if Tom started better," or "Sally gets A's because she butters up the instructor" are illustrative of these kinds of statements. Moreover, people with low self-concepts frequently adopt a whining voice when they are asked to explain their thoughts, feelings, or behavior.

Moderator of Competing Internal Messages A fourth, particularly interesting function of self-concept is to moderate internal messages. When you are thinking, you are in fact talking to yourself (some people even go so far as to do much of their thinking aloud). When you are faced with a decision, you may be especially conscious of the different and often competing voices in your head. Perhaps this morning when your alarm went off you had a conversation much like Carl's: "There goes that blasted alarm. I'm so tired—maybe if I lie here just a few more minutes. Hold on—if I don't get up now, I'll go back to sleep. Oh, who cares—I need sleep! If I slept just another fifteen minutes. No! It's already later than I wanted to get up—come on Carl, move it." Notice that several of the messages in this internal conversation are competing. What determines which voice Carl listens to? Self-concept is the moderator in the choice. If Carl feels good about himself and the day he has in store, he will probably get up right away. If, on the other hand, things aren't going well for him or there are

---

[1]In his material on "Developing a Healthy Self-Image," Don Hamacheck offers a lengthy analysis of the symptoms of inferiority and self-acceptance. See Don Hamacheck, *Encounters with the Self* (New York: Holt, Rinehart and Winston, Inc., 1971), pp. 232–237.

A PARTICULARLY INTERESTING FUNCTION
OF SELF-CONCEPT IS TO MODERATE
INTERNAL MESSAGES.

important decisions to be made, Carl might seek to escape reality through sleep.

Eric Berne, a psychologist, developed a system of analyzing these internal messages. He called his system Transactional Analysis (TA).[2] Thomas Harris's book *I'm OK—You're OK*,[3] a best seller a few years ago, is a readable treatment of Berne's theories. In brief TA says that the kinds of thoughts that Carl experienced come from three ego states: the *Parent*, the *Child*, and the *Adult*. Statements from the Parent ego state are critical, evaluative statements; they are the voice of conscience. In effect they are the kinds of statements that your parents were likely to have made to you when you were young, such as "Don't touch the stove, you'll get burned," "Cheating on tests is wrong," and "Eat your vegetables, they're good for you." Statements from the Child ego state are emotional reactions. If you are being criticized and you burst into tears and say, "Don't say another thing—I don't want to hear it," or if you are on a roller coaster and you

[2]See Eric Berne, *Games People Play: The Psychology of Human Relationships* (New York: Grove Press, 1964).

[3]Thomas A. Harris, *I'm OK—You're OK: A Practical Guide to Transactional Analysis* (New York: Harper & Row, 1967).

scream as you start down the steepest dip, you're giving voice to pure emotional reaction—you're literally becoming childlike. Statements from the Adult ego state, on the other hand, encourage rational decision making. Statements like "Let me examine this carefully," or "I could go either way on this; I've got to see both sides clearly" are Adult statements.

Everyone listens to statements of all three types on occasion. If we find, however, that we almost always react emotionally or we almost always fall back on parental guidelines, our decisions may not be meeting our personal needs best. Especially when what we're deciding is critical, we need to pay attention to those Adult voices of reason.

Although Transactional Analysis is not the only way to explain these voices in the head, my students have found some of its concepts helpful in understanding or identifying certain communication events. It is useful to know what kind of statements you are inclined to listen to and under what circumstances.

PERCEPTION AND COMMUNICATION ABOUT OTHERS

When people meet, they form quick impressions of one another. As they interact, their impressions may be changed, reinforced, or intensified. The perceptions that develop as a result of these impressions determine such things as how much people like each other and how they will communicate with and about each other.

Think about your own comments about others. Notice how often you verbalize impressions that are based upon limited information. For instance, after a party in which Jack talks to Marty while they are at the buffet table making a sandwich, Jack may later say, "Marty's a nurd," or perhaps, "That Marty's a pretty right guy." Notice that these statements follow a brief one or two sentence interchange! In some instances a person does not even need an in-person encounter to form an impression. For instance, merely looking at a photograph may cause a person to have a strong perception. Show your friend a picture of your uncle or grandmother, and your friend may well form some perception of the person's personality on the basis of that photo alone.

So we know that we will form perceptions about people. Likewise, we know that these perceptions will form the bases of our interaction with these people. The question then becomes, "How accurate are our perceptions of others likely to be?" Research results are inconclusive: Some people make reasonably accurate judgments rather consistently; others make judgments that are neither consistent nor accurate. Given the inconclusive nature of the research, I argue that you are better off not relying solely on your impressions to determine how another person feels or what that person is really like. Perhaps what you need to consider is not whether an impression is or is not accurate at any given time but what it is that affects the relative accuracy of perception of other people. You will understand why you perceive others as you do if you understand each of the following:

1. *How you are feeling at the moment of perception.* Your feelings at the moment affect the nature of your perception. If, for example, you are having a down day, you will probably have a more negative perception of a person you don't know than if you were having a good day. When you come out of a class in which you just received a low grade on a paper you were sure you had done well, your perceptions of people around you will surely be colored by your negative feeling. If on the other hand you receive an A on a paper you were unsure of and that was important to you, you're likely to perceive everything and everyone around you positively. So, regardless of whether your perception of another person is positive or negative, before you act upon that perception ask yourself how your feelings could have affected that perception.

2. *How similar to you others are assumed to be.* The more similar to you you assume another to be, the more likely you are to perceive that person positively. If you like parties and plenty of action and perceive that another person likes the same things, you will be positive, especially if that person is similar to you in age, race, national origin, income level, and other factors. This kind of perception is similar to what psychologists call *projection:* your perception of another person may not be influenced as much by what that person is like as it is by what *you* are like.

3. *A likelihood to rely on stereotyping.* A common tendency of most behavior is to take shortcuts in judging others. Very rarely do we wait until we have all the data about another person before we form a perception. It seems to be human nature to make judgments quickly and then rely on our judgments regardless of what contradictory evidence we may receive. This procedure is called stereotyping. By *stereotyping* we mean forming generalizations about groups of people and then treating individuals as if they are carbon copies of the stereotype we have formed. As we go through life it is common to form stereotypes about groups. In terms of nationalities we have impressions of Arabs, Italians, the English, and Orientals; in terms of religion we have impressions of Protestants, Catholics, Jews, and Moslems; in terms of social groups we have impressions of fraternities and sororities. Then, when we meet a person who is an Arab or a Catholic or member of a fraternity, we don't have to take the time to get to know the person. We fall back on our stereotype. This procedure saves us time and energy.

When we don't have a stereotype, we form one. For example, we meet Hans—who is German. We have no stereotype for Germans so we interact with Hans until we form opinions. Let's say we see Hans as very task oriented and driven to achieve. From now on, we have a stereotype of Germans: They are task oriented and driven to achieve.

The problem with stereotypes is that even though they contain a grain of truth or may apply to one or more members of a group, as generalizations about groups they are *inaccurate!* There is no stereotypic view that is true of all the members of any group. In fact, with some stereotypes there is no connection between the stereotype and even a majority of the members of the group.

Unfortunately, combating the tendency to stereotype is very difficult. Sometimes stereotypes are reinforced when you meet a member of a group who does have many characteristics of the stereotype. However, the greatest problem with stereotypes is that they often underlie prejudices, and in some cases we don't want to see people as individuals. We prefer the comfort of our prejudice and our stereotype.

As communicators, however, whether it be in interpersonal settings, group settings, or public speaking settings, we cannot make the kinds of mistakes that result from stereotyping.

Our perceptions of people are affected by two other tendencies that are similar to stereotyping: relying on central traits and awarding value traits. In our observation of people we see certain traits. For instance, as Carla talks with Nancy she may perceive Nancy as a very warm person. Carla's perception of warmth may come as a result of something that Nancy says or does. Having established the presence of warmth in Nancy, Carla may perceive companion traits without any evidence of those traits. For instance, if Carla sees Nancy as a warm person because she smiles and talks pleasantly, then Carla may also decide that Nancy is friendly, empathic, easygoing, and likeable, even though she has no direct evidence of these companion traits.

Likewise, people tend to award value traits to others on the basis of whether they have evaluated those others as good or bad. Let's say that Carla sees Nancy as a good person as well as a warm person. Carla may award Nancy accompanying characteristics such as honesty. However, Carla perceives Gloria as a bad person. As a result, Carla awards Gloria those traits that accompany badness, such as dishonesty. One day Carla, Nancy, and Gloria are eating lunch together. Each person leaves her books, notebooks, and other belongings on the end of the table. Nancy and Gloria finish eating first and leave the table. When Carla is finished, she gathers up her belongings and notices that her purse is missing. Only two people could have taken it. Whom is Carla likely to accuse?

Whether you are participating in interpersonal communication, group work, or public speaking, you will be making perceptions about people you are working and talking with. Once you understand that initial perceptions can be inaccurate, you should test out your perceptions before acting upon them.

SUMMARY

Perception is the process of assigning meaning to sensory information. Our perceptions are a result of our selection, organization, and interpretation of sensory information. Inaccurate perceptions cause us to see the world not as it is but as we would like to see it or as we want it to be. The accuracy of our perceptions is based on such factors as limitations of the senses, familiarity, expectation, context of the situation, emotions, and attitudes.

A person's self-concept is a collection of perceptions that relate to every aspect of that person's being. The self-concept is formed by views of self and experiences, other people's comments about self and behavior, and roles played. The self-concept serves at least four basic communication functions: it predicts behavior, it filters messages from others, it influences word selection and tone of voice, and it moderates competing internal messages.

Perception also plays an important role in forming impressions of others. Because research shows that the accuracy of people's perceptions and judgments varies considerably, you will have more successful communication if you do not rely entirely on your impressions to determine how another person feels or what that person is really like. You will improve (or at least better understand) your perception of others if you will take into account how you are feeling at the moment of perception, how similar to you others are assumed to be, and your likelihood to rely on stereotyping.

SUGGESTED READINGS

Gerald M. Goldhaber and Marylynn B. Goldhaber. *Transactional Analysis: Principles and Applications.* Boston: Allyn & Bacon, 1976. A good contribution to the theory of Transactional Analysis that combines the Goldhabers' explanations with a representative selection of readings.

E. Bruce Goldstein. *Sensation and Perception.* Belmont, Calif.: Wadsworth, 1980. See especially Chapter 12 on perception of speech.

Don E. Hamachek. *Encounters with the Self,* 2nd ed. New York: Holt, Rinehart & Winston, 1978. A good analysis of self-awareness and self-concept.

R. D. Laing, H. Phillipson, and A. R. Lee. *Interpersonal Perceptions: A Theory and a Method of Research.* New York: Harper & Row, 1966. An analysis of the interaction of perception between two people.

Lawrence S. Wrightsman. *Social Psychology,* 2nd brief ed. Monterey, Calif.: Brooks/ Cole, 1977. One of the many excellent social psychology books available.

Ruth C. Wylie. *The Self-Concept.* (2 volumes.) Lincoln: University of Nebraska Press, 1974. This work provides a comprehensive analysis of research related to formation and development of self-concept.

PART 2

PERSONAL COMMUNICATION

By far the greatest percentage of your communication is personal—it involves the day-to-day conversations that are so fundamental to your very existence. This five-chapter unit focuses on the causes and effects of that personal communication.

PERSONAL COMMUNICATION: SELF-ANALYSIS

Our personal communication is our informal interaction with self and others. For many of us the effectiveness of our personal communication is fundamental both in our understanding of self and others and in the development and maintenance of our relationships with others. How we communicate with others is largely a matter of "doing what comes naturally." Most people think they communicate about the same as everyone else. In fact, people run the gamut from superior to rather poor communicators. What kind of a communicator are you? The following analysis looks at ten specifics that are basic to a communication profile.

For each of the statements listed, encircle the number that best indicates how you perceive your behavior on a continuum from one extreme to another. The numbers 1, 2, and 3 represent the negative end of the continuum—they suggest a need for work on the item; the numbers 5, 6, and 7 represent the positive end of the continuum—they suggest a perceived competence in terms of the behavior. The number 4 represents a midpoint between the extremes that shows either a neutral position on the issue or perhaps a question about where you stand.

When I have something to say I don't worry about how it comes out or how another person might take it	1 2 3 4 5 6 7	When I have something to say I try hard to word my thoughts and feelings carefully, taking into account the feelings of others
I have trouble wording my ideas precisely	1 2 3 4 5 6 7	I speak clearly in specific and concrete language
My speech is cluttered with meaningless expressions like "uh," "well uh," and "you know," or I stumble and search for words	1 2 3 4 5 6 7	I speak fluently without interjecting meaningless expressions or without searching around for the right word

I either withhold my negative feelings about others' behavior toward me or I blow up at what they've said or done	1 2 3 4 5 6 7	I describe objectively to others my negative feelings about their behavior toward me without withholding or blowing up
When I listen to others I do not pay full attention so I miss words and ideas	1 2 3 4 5 6 7	I am attentive and listen carefully
When I don't understand something I act as if I do	1 2 3 4 5 6 7	When I'm not sure whether I understand I seek clarification
The way I respond to others makes them react defensively—they feel as if I'm attacking them	1 2 3 4 5 6 7	The way I respond to others seems to encourage them to talk openly and honestly with me
I have little interest in hearing about what others may think of me or my behavior	1 2 3 4 5 6 7	I am willing to listen to what others think of me and my behavior—in fact I often ask others for their reactions to me
I am completely oblivious to the nonverbal cues that others give	1 2 3 4 5 6 7	I look for and try to understand what other peoples' nonverbal behavior is saying
I am easily intimidated and will seldom give my opinion when I feel the likelihood of conflict	1 2 3 4 5 6 7	I am willing to state what I think and how I feel regardless of the other person's status

Consider your analysis. Is the number you encircled indicative of where you would like to be on that item? If not, in a different colored ink or pencil, encircle the number that represents your goal for this term.

Select one of the areas in which your goals are farthest from your current behavior. Write a communication improvement contract similar to the sample contract on pp. 361–362 in Appendix C. Why a written contract?

Because there is often a great deal of truth to the old adage: "The road to hell is paved with good intentions." It is all too easy to resolve something like, "I'm going to listen better in the future," but it is also all too easy to ignore that resolution. Without a clearly drawn plan and a written commitment, you are less likely to follow through.

Now that you have completed your self-analysis you may be wondering about its accuracy. One way to verify your analysis is through feedback. Feedback is the verbal or nonverbal response you receive to what you are, what you have said, or what you have done. You begin to question the new program and your boss frowns; you state which movie you would like to see and your date smiles; you tell your father that you really like his new car and he says, "Would you like to drive it?" All these responses are feedback. No matter what you say or do, as long as you are interacting with others, you will get some kind of feedback.

In a study of communication we want to use feedback to help ourselves grow. Communication growth is a product of learning about ourselves; and much of what we learn comes to us through feedback from others. How feedback affects your communication growth depends upon whether you are sensitive to the feedback you get, whether you can interpret the feedback, and whether the feedback is useful to you.

Although later in this course you will have an opportunity to get direct feedback from your classmates and from your professor on various aspects of your communication, you may well want some immediate feedback from people you know and have worked with, feedback that will help to reinforce or to correct your self-analysis. Ask two or three persons whom you know and have worked with to take a few minutes to complete the analysis sheets in Appendix B-1, Feedback Analysis. On the basis of the feedback you receive from them, you can validate your self-analysis, making any modifications that seem necessary.

CHAPTER 3

VERBAL COMMUNICATION

As Claude was leaning over the ladder and tapping the wall lightly he called to Phyllis, "Would you bring me that thing on the whatdoyacallit?"

"Sure," Phyllis replied. A moment later she returned and handed a small, plastic object to Claude. "Is that the thing you find the hickies with?" she asked.

"Right—those little fellows are hard to find without one. Blast it! I'm going to need one of those other doodads, too."

"Get it in a minute, Claude," Phyllis said as she went back to the closet where they kept tools. "Here you go," she said as she returned.

"We're going to put that one whatchamacallit here, right?" he asked.

"Looks good to me," Phyllis answered.

"You know," Claude said, "I was just wondering about something Morrison said at work today. I was really puzzled."

"What was it, Claude?"

"Well, we were working on the Whathisface account when Morrison says, 'Claude, I just can't understand what you're trying to say sometimes.' You could have knocked me over with a feather."

"What in the world was he talking about? I never have any trouble understanding you."

"Beats me. Well, I don't think it's worth losing any sleep over. Say," Claude continued, "we need a couple more of these gizmos for over by the whatsis."

"Good idea," Phyllis replied, "I think that will do it!"

Does Claude have a problem? Phyllis doesn't think so. Can you figure out what they're talking about? Claude is hanging pictures on the living room wall. He needs a stud finder to locate the metal nails that will indicate where the two-by-fours are. He also needs a simple plumb line to help him make sure that he's hanging the pictures straight.

Claude has problems that are probably a little more dramatic than most of ours but not all that different. We could all improve our verbal communication if we took time to work on it. And that's exactly what we will be doing in this chapter.

As you complete your work this term, you will discover that accomplishing the various interpersonal, group, and public-speaking assignments will require proficiency with the English language. Since you have studied some aspect of the English language during every year that you have spent in school, the basics should be part of your general knowledge. Thus instead of focusing on basic grammar or vocabulary, we will suggest some ideas you can use to develop effective oral communication skills.

LANGUAGE AND MEANING

Because of the way that words and meaning are related, a skilled communicator must be careful when making assumptions about either word selection or word understanding. Although such expressions as "picking exactly the right word" seem to leave the impression that the master of language need only learn enough words, the role of language in communication is far more complicated. You can help yourself get the proper perspective on language if you are consciously aware of how words get whatever meaning they may have. Let's take a look at the arbitrary, conventional, and learned nature of language.

Meaning Is Arbitrary

When we say that something is *arbitrary*, we are saying that it is a matter of choice. Whether the word is *chair, sister,* or *predilectory* we know that someone at some time had to use those letters (sounds) in that order for the first time. So someone chose to try a certain word to convey some meaning. What happened then?

Meaning Is Conventional

When we say a word is *conventional* we mean that it is a choice of a large number of people. At some point in history it may have been a single person's idea to call a female sibling a *sister*. But the use of *sister* as a symbol with some specific meaning wasn't possible until others started using that word when they wanted to express the idea of female sibling.

Every day people begin using certain sound patterns to stand for meaning as a matter of preference; the word does not become a part of the language until other people have used the word often enough to make it conventional.

Meaning Is Learned

Because of the preferential, conventional nature of words, each new generation must learn the language anew. Children's brains enable them to think, and they have a vocal mechanism that allows them to form any number of sounds. But how to determine which sounds go together to form which words must be taught from generation to generation.

By the time children are between three and five years old, they have learned enough vocabulary to communicate almost all their basic ideas and feelings and have mastered enough grammar to be understood. From then on, they enlarge their vocabulary and sharpen their understanding of grammar.

The implication of the fact that meanings are learned is that all people do not learn exactly the same meanings for words, nor do they learn exactly the same words. You must never assume, therefore, that another person will know what you are talking about just because that person uses words that you have learned.

COMPLICATIONS IN USING WORDS

The ideal form of communication would be some form of telepathy. Science fiction writers have for years worked on the premise that advanced societies will develop some form of telepathy so that a person will be able to share meanings directly with another. But until such a time (and I doubt any of us are going to see it), we must share our ideas and feelings indirectly through a system of symbols, that is, through words. This symbol system is often an imperfect means of sharing. If you are going to be effective as a communicator, you must be able to distinguish between the denotative and the connotative meanings of a word.

Denotation

Denotation means the direct, explicit meaning or reference of a word; denotation is the meaning given in a dictionary. Although knowing dictionary

DICTIONARY DIFFERENCES

definitions is useful in communication, even with a firm grasp of word denotations you can still encounter problems. Let us examine a few:

Dictionary Differences   There are very few words that are defined exactly the same way in each of the most popular American dictionaries. And although the differences are minimal in most cases, they illustrate the problems we face when we try to communicate precisely with others. Let's take the word *dog. Webster's New World Dictionary* says a dog is "any of a large and varied group of domesticated animals related to the fox, wolf, and jackal."[1] *Webster's New Intercollegiate Dictionary* (published by another company even though the word *Webster's* is in both titles) says a dog is "a carnivorous domesticated mammal, type of the family Canidae."[2]

Why do these differences occur? Most dictionaries are compiled in the same way: Companies survey printed materials to see how people use words. Then, based upon these surveys, someone writes a definition. Depending upon what written work is surveyed and who writes the definition, there are going to be some differences. Both of the above definitions attempt to classify and differentiate. Nevertheless, if the only knowledge

---

[1]*Webster's New World Dictionary*, 2nd College Ed. (Cleveland, Ohio: William Collins & World Publishing Co., 1978), p. 414.

[2]*Webster's New Collegiate Dictionary* (Springfield, Mass.: G. C. Merriam Co., 1979), p. 334.

you had about a dog was from these two dictionary definitions, you can see that you might have rather different views of the animal.

Multiple Meanings   But an even more confusing fact is that a great many of the words we use daily have more than one distinct meaning. If we looked up the 500 most commonly used American words in any dictionary, we'd be likely to find more than 14,000 definitions. Some of these definitions would be similar, but some would be much different. Take the word *low* for instance. *Webster's New World Dictionary* offers twenty-six meanings for *low*. Number 1 is "of little height or elevation"; number 8 is "near the equator"; and number 16 is "mean; despicable; contemptible."[3] No matter how we look at these three definitions we have to admit that they are quite different.

As words get more difficult we begin to find fewer and fewer definitions. Thus it is usually with our most common words that we get into the most trouble. These common words have so many different meanings that unless we carefully examine context, we may get (or give) the wrong idea. On the other hand, if we use the more precise word, there may be some in our audience who are not familiar with it.

Changes in Meanings   As time goes on, words both acquire and lose meanings. According to W. Nelson Francis in the 700 years *nice* has been in the English language it "has been used at one time or another to mean the following: foolish, wanton, strange, lazy, coy, modest, fastidious, refined, precise, subtle, slender, critical, attentive, minutely, accurate, dainty, appetizing, agreeable."[4]

If we think about it, we all know some words that have changed their meaning over a relatively short period of time. Our communication is most affected when these changes are quick and/or dramatic. Take the word *gay*, for instance. In the fifties and sixties, people spoke of having a "gay old time," of Jack being a "gay blade," and the state of "being gay" as being happy. In each case *gay* meant joyous, merry, happy, or bright. Today having a "gay time," being a "gay blade," and the state of "being gay" are most likely to refer to a person's sexual preference. Although *gay* as joyous is still heard sometimes, it is becoming obsolete. If you describe another person as "gay" and you mean happy or joyous, you will probably be totally misunderstood.

Influence of Context   The position of a word in a sentence and the other words around it may change the denotation. When a young girl says,

[3]*Webster's New World Dictionary*, p. 839.
[4]W. Nelson Francis, *The English Language* (New York: W. W. Norton, 1965), p. 122.

"Dad, you owe me a dime," the meaning is somewhat different from when she says, "Dad, I need a dime for the machine." In the first case, she is looking for two nickels, ten pennies, five pennies and a nickel, or a single ten-cent piece. In the second case, she is looking specifically for that small coin that we call a dime.

Examples of influence of context abound. Think of the difference between "George plays a really *mean* drum" and "The way George talked to Sally was downright *mean*."

Connotation

Whereas denotation refers to the most basic, explicit definition of a word, *connotation* refers to the feelings that a particular word arouses.

When a word is spoken (especially a specific, concrete word for which there is a clearly defined referent), if a person has had any experience with the referent of that word, it is likely that the person is also going to have some feelings about it.

Earlier we defined the word *dog* as a domesticated animal. But because at some time in your life you have had experience with dogs, you have feelings that define dog for you much differently than they might for me. Suppose that as a child you had a dog that was a constant companion, that slept with you at night, licked you when you came home from school, lay at your feet as you watched television, and wagged its tail at the sight of you. You will have a far different meaning for *dog* than a person who never had a dog for a pet, had been bitten six times by dogs for "no reason," and who is allergic to dog hair.

We can illustrate further with the word *home*. If home to you is a place filled with fun, love, understanding, warmth, and good feelings, it means something far different to you than it would if home were a place filled with fighting, bickering, punishment, confinement, and harsh rules.

Each of these words (*home* and *dog*) carries a potential for feelings and values for the person using them. As a communicator, then, you must take into account both the standard denotative meaning and the potential connotative meaning of the word to the specific person or persons with whom you are communicating.

So, when Carl says to Paul, "I'm buying a dog this week," Carl must understand that his sentence denotes the purchase of a domesticated mammal—a denotation that Paul is likely to share. But it also carries a connotation that will be shared only if Carl and Paul have had similar experiences with dogs and as a result feel much the same way about them.

A person's or a group of people's feelings about words do vary considerably. As a result scientists have been trying to find ways of measuring intensity of feelings. Let me briefly describe one method that has gained wide use among psychologists and communication scholars. Charles Osgood and his associates developed an approach to word connotation that focuses on dimensions of meaning.[5] Each dimension of meaning is part of the total feeling a person has about a word. The method used by Osgood involves describing feelings about words through *bipolar adjectives* (adjectives that are the opposite of each other).

Why did Osgood and his associates focus their study on adjectives? If you list the responses that come to your mind when someone says words like *dog* or *home*, you will see that many, if not all of the words you use, are adjectives. You may think of *dog* and *home* in terms of pleasant or unpleasant, big or small, happy or sad, attractive or unattractive.

As they studied the various responses, Osgood and his associates grouped them in identifiable categories called *dimensions*. There are many of these dimensions, but the three most common are adjectives of evaluation, adjectives of potency or intensity, and adjectives of activity or movement. They found that good-bad, awful-nice, ugly-beautiful, and valuable-worthless are pairs that can be used to measure the *evaluation dimension*. Strong-weak, light-heavy, and large-small are used to measure the *potency dimension*. Hot-cold, active-passive, and fast-slow are used to reveal the *activity dimension*. The end result of their work was a Semantic Differential Test that can be administered to groups and individuals alike.[6] A test using only the ten pairs just cited can be used to compare how one person or one group feels in comparison to another person or another group on a specific word like *dog* or *home*.

The value of such a test is that it gives us the ability to compare results. First, the test enables us to compare one person's feeling with another's. For example, is one person's feeling about the word *home* more or less positive? Stronger or weaker? More or less active? Second, it enables us to compare a person's reaction to several different words. Does the person see *home* differently from *resort, farm, camp,* or *trailer*? Third, the test enables us to compare a person's feeling about a word at different times. Does a person feel differently about *camp* after she has spent six weeks at one?

What is the value of this kind of knowledge to you in your communication? If you know how others feel about the words they use, you can understand them and communicate better with them. Consider a schoolteacher who wants to develop a teaching unit on the theme "A community is a group of people who help one another." It would be useful

[5]Charles E. Osgood, George J. Suci, and Percy H. Tannenbaum, *The Measurement of Meaning* (Urbana, Ill.: University of Illinois Press, 1957).
[6]Ibid., pp. 36–38.

for that teacher to discover how the class feels about such words as *community, home, police,* and *businessperson* before beginning the unit. Or consider the value of the semantic differential to the congresswoman who would like to know how the people in her district feel about words like *busing, schools,* and *taxes* before she begins preparing speeches for her campaign.

EXERCISES

1. Make a list of current slang or "in" words. How do the meanings you assign to these words differ from the meanings your parents or grandparents assign?
2. Working in groups of three, select several common words like *home* and *dog.* Each person will list at least five adjectives that he or she associates with the word. When you have finished, compare the results. In what ways are your meanings different?

LANGUAGE HABITS

In a sense the remainder of this textbook is about the development of good language habits. Nearly every chapter considers skills that you can learn, sharpen, and use to help you use language effectively. Nevertheless, there are some ideas and skills that we can look at now to help lay a foundation for later skill development.

What kinds of language habits have you developed over the years? Many people find they have at least three habits that distort or hinder good communication.

Forcing a Response

Communication is supposed to be open and honest, but we have learned that some things people tell us can be unpleasant. To avoid hearing those things we don't want to hear or are afraid to learn about ourselves, many of us "stack the deck" by phrasing thoughts and feelings in such a way that the nature of the response is shaped. Consider the following set up. Tom says to Gordon, "I'm really interested in your opinion, Gordon (so far so good). I've really got a good backhand, haven't I?" As noted, Tom opens with a statement that sounds as if he wants honest feedback, but the phrasing says "Tell me what I want to hear, Gordon." Or Phyllis says to Nancy, "That was really a good movie—you'd go along with me on that, wouldn't you?" Both Tom and Phyllis are manipulating by attempting to force a response they want to hear. In each case Gordon or Nancy has the freedom to say something different, but the wording of the statements makes it difficult. It is likely that both Gordon and Nancy will give the expected response regardless of what they really think or feel.

Do you make statements or ask questions in ways that leave the other person little room for free response? If so, perhaps you can change your behavior patterns. For assistance look at the discussion of feedback skills in Chapter 6.

Misrepresenting

We can make something sound good or bad, better or worse by the phrasing we select. Advertisers are good at finding ways of saying things that sound better than what is actually true. For years the advertisers of Anacin have said, "Two of three doctors recommend the ingredients in Anacin." These advertisers are aware that some people will think this statement says "Two of three doctors recommend Anacin," or at least "Two of three doctors recommend ingredients that can only be found in Anacin." These advertisers may say, "We can't be responsible for how people interpret our message." What the sentence says is that two of three doctors recommend aspirin for headaches and other minor problems. And aspirin is one of the ingredients in Anacin. They do not tell you that other brands like Bayer, Excedrin, and St. Joseph also have aspirin as a major ingredient.

At one time or other, we all give a different impression to our words by the way we say something. "Hector," his mother asks, "why were you out until 3 A.M. this morning?" Hector replies indignantly, "I wasn't out anywhere near 3 A.M." (he got in at 2:20!). Marjorie says to Allison, "I want you to know that I was not the one who told your mother that you were smoking. I'd never do that!" What Marjorie fails to say is that she did tell Brenda and suggested to Brenda that perhaps she could tell Allison's mother! Many times we say to ourselves, "I did not tell a lie," and then we feel rather good about our character. Yet we may well know that we did leave an impression that was *not* really correct.

Shifting Perspective

Our study of perception shows us that much depends on how we look at something. People are often quick to use language that is kind to them personally but often derogatory of others. For instance, how many times have you heard such statements as "I like to have a late afternoon drink, but Tom can't get through the day without a drink"; or "I'm confident of my ability, but George is always praising himself, and Bill is a braggart";

or "I don't like to make a decision unless I have all the facts, whereas Tim is overly cautious, and Pete is afraid to make a decision"; or "I've smoked a little weed in my day, but Glen smokes dope, and Bill is a pothead." In none of these examples is there any evidence that the behavior for the various individuals is materially different from that of the speaker. What we can see is different phrasings depending upon the perspective. Like most people, the speaker always chose a label that was generous in respect to himself, but the same restraint was not exercised with others. The truth is that the more removed a person is from us in time, space, or interest, the more likely we are to use a more negative word.

This list is not meant to be exhaustive. It is meant to develop an awareness that some language habits are bad because they are inaccurate, they misrepresent, or they totally distort reality. Problems like these can often be avoided by adopting descriptive language rather than evaluative language.

Descriptive language means reporting the nature of the action, statement, or behavior. Consider these three statements: "I like a late afternoon drink; George can't get through the day without a drink; and Pat is becoming a lush." They represent a move from nearly descriptive to totally evaluative. In answer to the question "What are the drinking habits of the people in question?" the answer might be "I, George, and Pat all have at least one drink before dinner each day."

The more descriptive your communication, the more objective it will be. The more objective your communication, the more effective you will become. Many of the skills in the chapters on forming messages and listening and responding will help you develop a descriptive perspective.

GUIDELINES

As you begin to work with interpersonal communication, group communication, and public speaking you must become conscious of your verbal communication. The main language goals you should strive for in your communication are clarity and appropriateness. The following guidelines are offered to help you lay a foundation for language use that will improve your interpersonal, group, and public speaking skills:

1. *Choosing vocabulary.* The vocabulary you use and the vocabulary of those with whom you communicate will affect the degree of communication. The issue of vocabulary is vital to your choices in message formation and to your ability to listen.

In general the smaller your vocabulary, the greater the potential difficulty in communicating effectively. As a speaker you will have fewer choices from which to select the word that you want; as a listener you will be limited in your ability to understand the words used. So, the first guideline is to choose your words with care.

2. *Developing accuracy.* For any idea or feeling you wish to communicate you have many words from which to choose. Some of the choices will enable you to communicate an accurate picture; others will destroy your ability to get your idea across. Suppose that this morning Tom told you he was concerned that he would be late for class. As Tom leaves the dorm you observe him going to class. You see that Tom is moving very quickly. Later when you are talking with Mary you mention that this morning Tom was afraid he would be late for class so he "skipped" to class. Now there are many words that would denote moving quickly, but "skipping" is not one of them. So we would say that your description of Tom's behavior was not accurate. On the other hand, if you told Mary that Tom ran to class, she would get a picture of Tom in motion that would roughly approximate what Tom did. In this case we would say that your word choice was accurate.

The better your vocabulary, the more accurate your communication is likely to be. Yet just because you use the most accurate word does not necessarily mean you will communicate well.

3. *Being specific and concrete.* We have noted that accuracy of word selection is very important. But using language effectively is as much a product of specificity as it is of accuracy. When you spoke of Tom "running" to school, you selected an accurate word. But as a word *run* still leaves room for interpretation. Was Tom's run a gallop or a sprint? A *gallop* is a run that is fast but is designed to take a person a rather long distance at a reasonably fast pace. Contrast this with *sprint*, an all-out, go as fast as you can run. "Run" is accurate—but saying either "galloping" or "sprinting" would be even more specific. The more specific a picture your wording creates in the mind of the listener the better your communication will be.

4. *Being aware of audience and appropriateness.* Let's continue our extended illustration by assuming that you said to Mary that Tom ambled to school. In this case you would have two problems. Problem one is that "amble" is an inaccurate word choice. Those who know the word *amble* use it to mean a smooth, easygoing, unhurried gait. Yet Tom was very much in a hurry. But the second problem is that Mary may not know what amble means—it may be outside her vocabulary. Thus amble is not only inaccurate, it is also inappropriate.

We say words are appropriate when they adapt well to the people with whom we are talking. You should be reasonably certain that the person or the group will know the meaning of words you use. Moreover, you must be sure that a word does not have a potential for strong connotation that will color the meaning. For instance, if you say the pigs picked you up last night for speeding, the people you are talking with will probably know that "pigs" denote police. The problem is that *pigs* has many connotations nearly all of which will so color the thinking of the listener that unless you were trying both to use the most abusive word possible and create a strong feeling, "pig" would surely be an unfortunate word choice.

5. *Responding to pressure.* Under pressure a person is likely to make mistakes in word choice. If a person is relaxed and confident, communication usually flows smoothly and words that communicate are selected. If the same

THE PIGS PICKED HER UP LAST
NIGHT FOR SPEEDING.

person is put under pressure, the effectiveness of communication begins to deteriorate. For instance, if you come from a large family, you may have heard your mother or father go through the names of all the children before getting the right name when your mother or father felt pressure.

Your brain is like a computer: It is a marvelous instrument, but it does fail to work sometimes. More often than not, the failures happen when you are under pressure or when you speak before you think. People sometimes think one thing and say something entirely different. Consider a familiar scene: The math professor says, "We all remember that the numerator is on the bottom and the denominator is on the top of the fraction, so when we divide fractions . . ." "Mrs. Jones," a voice from the third row interrupts, "you said the numerator is on the bottom and . . ." "Is that what I said?" Mrs. Jones asks. "Well, you know what I meant!" Did everyone in the class know? Probably not.

The point then is that the greater the degree of pressure you feel, the greater your effort will have to be for your language to meet the goals of clarity and appropriateness.

SUMMARY

Language is a system of symbols used for communicating. Language communicates when words are arranged in certain learned ways. Even though you have worked years to develop a good vocabulary and to understand the grammar of the English language, you are still likely to have some communication problems.

You will be a more effective communicator if you recognize that the meaning of words is arbitrary, the meaning of words is conventional, and the meaning of words is learned.

A word's denotation is its dictionary meaning. Despite the ease with which we can check a dictionary meaning, word denotation can still present problems. Why? Because most words have more than one dictionary meaning, changes in meanings occur faster than dictionaries are revised, words take on different meanings as they are used in different contexts, and meanings can become obscured as words become more abstract.

A word's connotation is the emotion and value significance the word arouses. Regardless of what a dictionary says a word means, we carry with us meanings that are a result of our experience with the object, thought, or action the word represents. Connotations can be quantified and tested by comparing scores achieved on a Semantic Differential Test.

Through the years we may develop negative language habits that distort or hinder our communication. Forcing a response, purposeful or unconscious misrepresentation, and shifting perspective are but three of the kinds of habits that we must avoid. Many negative language habits can be corrected by learning to speak descriptively.

Students of language must understand how the issues of vocabulary, of clarity, of appropriateness, of general versus specific, and of pressure relate to communication.

SUGGESTED READINGS

Samuel C. Brownstein and Mitchel Weiner. *Basic Word List*. Woodbury, N.Y.: Barron's Educational Series, 1977 (paperback). An excellent vocabulary building book.

Stuart Chase. *The Power of Words*. New York: Harcourt Brace Jovanovich, 1953. A pioneer work in general semantics. A good place to begin the study of problems with meaning.

Joseph DeVito. *The Psychology of Speech and Language*. New York: Random House, 1970. A short, informative work.

W. Nelson Francis. *The English Language: An Introduction*. New York: W. W. Norton, 1965. An excellent introduction to linguistics.

Edwin Newman. *Strictly Speaking: Will America Be the Death of English?* Indianapolis: Bobbs-Merrill, 1974. A popular book that is well worth reading.

Charles E. Osgood, George J. Suci, and Percy H. Tannenbaum. *The Measurement of Meaning*. Urbana: University of Illinois Press, 1957. Good for a complete discussion of the Semantic Differential Test.

CHAPTER 4

NONVERBAL COMMUNICATION

"I'm going to buy that denim jacket we looked at this morning. You don't want me to, do you?" Claude asked.

"What do you mean 'I don't want you to'?" Phyllis replied.

"You've got that look on your face."

"What look, Claude?"

"You know the look—the one you always get on your face when you don't want me to do something I want to do. But no matter, I'm going to get that jacket."

"I still don't know what look you're talking about, Claude."

"Sure you do—you know how I can tell you do? Because now you're embarrassed that I know and so you're raising your voice."

"I'm not raising my voice, Claude."

"Hear that little quiver in your voice, Phyllis? It's a dead giveaway."

"Claude, you're making me angry."

"You're just saying that because I'm on to you."

" 'On to me'? Claude, I don't care whether you get that jacket or not."

"Of course you do—you don't have to tell me in so many words."

"Claude, it's your decision. If you want to get the jacket, get it."

"Well, I don't think I want to—but don't think you talked me out of it."

We have all heard—and said—that "actions speak louder than words." Actions are so important to our communication that researchers have estimated that in face-to-face communication as much as 90 percent of the social meaning may be carried in the nonverbal message.[1] Still, as Claude found out, interpreting these actions is not always the easiest thing to do. Through the years most of what we know about nonverbal usage and understanding has been instinctive—a result of what you might call "doing what comes naturally."

In this chapter we will consider nonverbal communication very carefully. There are several important reasons: (1) because you communicate nonverbally whether you know it or not (hence, the saying "you cannot *not* communicate"); (2) because your nonverbal communication—whether it is intentional or unintentional—has tremendous influence on all forms of your communication; and (3) because at least some of your nonverbal communication *can* be controlled. We will begin by studying both the differences between verbal and nonverbal messages and the way verbal and nonverbal communication interrelate. We will then look at the elements of nonverbal communication and will discuss the skill of perception checking, a means of improving understanding of nonverbal cues.

VERBAL AND NONVERBAL COMMUNICATION

Verbal and nonverbal communication differ in at least three major ways. First, whereas verbal communication is discrete, nonverbal communication is continuous. Speech communication begins when sound starts to come from the mouth and ends when vocalization stops. Nonverbal communication, however, continues for as long as a person is in your presence.

Second, whereas verbal communication is a single-channeled phenomenon, nonverbal communication is multichanneled. Have you ever tried to participate in a conversation when you were wearing ear plugs? If the plugs worked properly, you could not hear at all and there was little if any communication. Verbal symbols—words—come to us one at a time, in sequence; we hear the spoken words, see the printed or written words. We send and receive various kinds of nonverbal messages simultaneously—in, for example, tone of voice to be heard or lift of an eyebrow or a hand gesture to be seen. By nonverbal messages we communicate more than most of us realize.

[1]Albert Mehrabian, *Silent Messages*, 2nd ed. (Belmont, Calif.: Wadsworth, 1981), p. 77.

Third, whereas verbal communication is almost always under your voluntary control, you may not realize—let alone control—your nonverbal communication. You are likely to think about or plan what you are going to say—verbal communication is usually well under control. On occasion words will "slip out," but in most instances you determine what you wish to say. In your nonverbal communication you may consciously control some of your "body language," but more often than not, you are unaware of all the nonverbal signals you are sending.

These contrasts are not meant to give the impression that you have two communication systems, verbal and nonverbal, operating totally apart from each other. Actually, verbal and nonverbal communication usually are both operating as you send and receive messages.

In the ideal relationship nonverbal communication *supplements* verbal communication. Gesturing to show the size of a ball or the direction the car went reinforces the words. The dejected look accompanying the words "I lost" or the smile that goes with the exclamation "Congratulations!" are complementary. When the coach grips your arm and says, "I want you to try harder," the grip emphasizes the meaning explicit in the words.

Under some circumstances, nonverbal communication is sufficient by itself—no verbal communication is needed. When the team comes into the dressing room after a game, the looks, posture, and tones of voice tell the story of who won the game—no one needs to ask. Likewise, when the umpire jerks his thumb into the air you know the runner is out.

The most important point to understand about the potential of non-verbal communication, however, is that it can contradict verbal communication. When you slam the door behind you but say you don't care, when you perspire profusely but claim you are not nervous, when you shout and say you are not angry, your verbal and nonverbal messages are contradictory. So, which is to be believed? According to most communication scholars, nonverbal communication defines the meaning in most social situations. This means that observers are more inclined to believe what is expressed nonverbally, because it is less subject to conscious control. You will not fool anyone if you should say, "Oh, I'm so sorry!" and your eyes are dancing and a smile is twitching at the corners of your mouth. You are not fooled by someone who says, "Let me help," then disappears when there is work to be done. The contradiction of verbal statements is carried to an art when the tone of voice is sarcastic. Such statements as "Great play, George!" said in a sarcastic tone are always perceived as negative, regardless of the positive nature of the words themselves.

In this next section we will examine several elements of nonverbal behavior. Although Larry Barker and Nancy Collins[2] have identified some eighteen categories, we will group the most important aspects under the four headings of environment, personal style, body motions, and paralanguage.

MANAGING THE ENVIRONMENT

Control of nonverbal communication begins with means of managing your environment. The principal elements of your environment over which you can exercise control are space, color, temperature, and lighting.

Space

One useful way of categorizing space is as fixed-featured, semi-fixed featured, and personal.[3]

Fixed-featured space includes the elements of your environment that are relatively permanent. The buildings that you live and work in and the parts of those buildings that cannot be moved are all fixed-featured. Although you may not have much conscious control over the creation of such elements, you do exercise control in your selection. For instance, when you rent an apartment, or buy a condominium or home you raise questions about whether or not the structures are in tune with the kind of statement you wish to make as a person. If you select a fourth-floor loft instead of a one-room efficiency, you might be saying something about how you wish to be perceived as a person. Business persons, doctors, or lawyers usually search with care to find surroundings that fit the image they want to communicate.

Whatever your choice, elements of that choice affect your communication within that environment. The amount of time neighbors spend talking with each other is likely to differ between people whose homes are less than twenty feet apart and those whose homes are a quarter of a mile apart. Moreover, people who live in apartment buildings tend to become acquainted with neighbors who live across the hall and next door but are

---

[2]Larry L. Barker and Nancy B. Collins, "Nonverbal and Kinesic Research," in Philip Emmert and William D. Brooks (Eds.), *Methods of Research in Communication* (Boston: Houghton Mifflin, 1970), pp. 343–372.

[3]Edward T. Hall, *The Hidden Dimension* (Garden City, N.Y.: Doubleday, 1966).

less likely to know those who live on other floors. Also, your chances of knowing people who live in your building are greatly enhanced if you live near an elevator, a staircase, or a door.

Semi-fixed-featured space consists of objects that remain in a fixed position unless they are moved. You manage your semi-fixed-feature space by arranging and rearranging objects until they create the kind of atmosphere you wish. In general, the more formal the arrangement, the more formal the communication setting.

Consider a situation in which you make an appointment with your professor to discuss some aspect of the course. You can tell a lot about your professor and about the kind of climate your professor is trying to establish just by the arrangement of the office and where you are expected to sit. So, at 3 P.M., you go in to see George Hamilton, your history professor. If he shows you to a chair across the desk from him, he may be implying "Let's talk business—I'm the professor and you're the student." This formal arrangement (the desk between you and the professor) is likely to contribute to a formal conversation. On the other hand, if he shows you to a chair at the side of his desk, he may be indicating "Don't be nervous—let's just chat." In this case the lack of any formal barrier between you and the relatively small space should lead to much more informal conversation. Although you must be somewhat tentative about the conclusions you draw about any setting, the use of space is nevertheless a pretty good index of how people are going to treat you and how they expect you to treat them.

Whether it be your dormitory room, your living room, or the family room, you can arrange the furnishings to create the kind of effect you want. In a living room you can arrange furniture in a way that will contribute to conversation or will encourage attention to, say, a television set. A room with Victorian furniture and hard-backed chairs arranged formally will produce an entirely different kind of conversation from a room with a thick carpet, pillow, beanbag chairs, and a low, comfortable sectional sofa.

The relationship between semi-fixed-featured space and communication can be illustrated by thinking about your various classrooms. The atmosphere of a classroom in which several rows of chairs face the lectern differs from that of a room in which chairs are grouped into one large circle or one in which there are four or five smaller circles. In the first environment most students anticipate a lecture format. In the second they might expect a give-and-take discussion, with the instructor and members of the class participating. In the third setting they might expect the class to work on group projects.

Regardless of the nature of arrangements, you can change them if you want to change the communication atmosphere.

Informal space refers to the space around us or the space we are occupying at the moment. The study of informal space is called *proxemics.* Managing your informal space requires some understanding of attitudes toward space around us and attitudes toward our territory.

You are probably aware that communication is influenced by the distance between us and those with whom we communicate. Edward T. Hall, a leading researcher in nonverbal communication, has discussed the four different distances that most people perceive.[4] By far the most important to us is the intimate distances, up to about eighteen inches from us, which we regard as appropriate for intimate conversation with close friends, parents, and younger children. People usually become uncomfortable when "outsiders" violate this intimate distance. Consider your last ride in a crowded elevator, for example. Most people get rather rigid, look at the floor or the indicator above the door, and pretend that they are not touching. Being forced into an intimate situation is only acceptable when all involved follow the "rules." When there is no apparent good reason for your intimate space to be intruded upon, you may be alarmed. Notice people coming into a movie theater that is less than one-quarter full: Couples tend to leave a seat or more between them and another couple. If you are sitting in a nearly empty theater and a stranger sits right next to you, you are likely to be upset; if a person you do not know violates this intimate distance in conversation, you may move away instinctively.

The other three distances are personal—eighteen inches to four feet—appropriate for casual conversation; social—four to twelve feet—for impersonal business (a job interview, for instance); and public distance—more than twelve feet. Determining these four distances was not some arbitrary decision; these are but descriptions of what most people consider appropriate in various situations. Individuals do, of course, vary. Oftentimes problems occur when one person has for one reason or another developed a slightly different standard. For instance, Paul may come from a family that conducts informal conversations with others at a range closer than the eighteen-inch limit that most Americans place on intimate space. So, when Paul talks to Dan or Mary, people he has met in class for the first time, he may move in closer than eighteen inches for his conversation. He then may be very much surprised when both Dan and Mary seem to be backing away from him during the conversation.

Normally our intimate or personal space moves when we move, for we are likely to define these spaces as distances from us. Yet in many situations we seek to put claim to a given space around us whether we are

[4]Edward T. Hall, *The Silent Language* (Garden City, N.Y.: Doubleday, 1959), pp. 163–164.

occupying it currently or not—that is, we are likely to look at certain space as our *territory*. Territory is space over which a person claims ownership. If Marcia decides to eat lunch at the school cafeteria, the space at the table she selects becomes her territory. Let's say that Marcia goes back to the food area to get butter for her roll. The chair she left, the food on the table, and the space around that food are "hers" and she will expect others to stay away. If while she is eating her lunch someone across the table moves a glass or a dish into the area that Marcia sees as her territory, she may be at least a little upset.

Many people stake out their territory with markers. George is planning to eat in the cafeteria. Before he gets his food he finds an empty table and puts his books on the table and his coat on a chair. These objects are indicators of occupied territory. If someone came along while George was gone and put the books and coat on the floor and then occupied that space, that person would be in big trouble when George returned.

Our needs for territory and the way we treat territory are culturally determined. As a result what an American would consider the boundaries of territory may be different from what an Arab or an Oriental would consider to be territorial boundaries. Misunderstandings between people of different cultures often occur as a result of their different ways of perceiving territory.

Thus in our management of personal space we must understand that others may not look at either the space around us or our territory in quite the same way as we do. Because the majority of Americans have learned the same basic rules does not mean that everyone has or will treat either the respect for the rules or the consequences of breaking the rules in the same way.

Temperature, Lighting, and Color

When it comes down to it, almost every facet of the environment has a communication potential. To manage your environment effectively you must consider any or all facets that you have control over. Three facets that people seem sensitive to and over which you are likely to have considerable control are temperature, lighting, and color.

Temperature acts as a stimulant or deterrent to communication. The ideal temperature for communication is one that is perceived as neither too high nor too low. Americans seem most comfortable when the temperatures are between 68 and 75 degrees. If you doubt the importance of temperature, recall your grade-school days when the June or September heat made listening to the teacher especially difficult. Many Americans are finding it difficult to adjust to the warmer temperatures of offices in summers and cooler temperatures in winters as we try to conserve energy.

Lighting can also act as a stimulant or deterrent to communication. In lecture halls and reading rooms, bright light is expected—it encourages good listening and comfortable reading. In a chic restaurant, a music listening room, or a television lounge you expect the lighting to be soft and rather dim. Soft, dim lighting makes for a cozy atmosphere and leads to intimate conversation.

Color seems particularly important to how we behave. For instance, many people react predictably to various colors: red as exciting and stimulating; blue as comfortable, soothing, calming, peaceful; yellow as cheerful, jovial. As a result interior designers who are trying to create a peaceful, serene atmosphere will decorate in blues rather than in reds and yellows. If, on the other hand, they want to create a stimulating atmosphere, as for a playroom, they will use reds and yellows.

Of course, much of our reaction to color comes from expectation: mashed potatoes are supposed to be white; butter, yellow; and broccoli, green. When a color does not meet expectation, reactions are unpredictable. Mashed potatoes tinted green in honor of Saint Patrick's Day may nauseate diners who are not color-blind, even before they attempt to eat.

You can create a communication climate by adjusting the variables of temperature, lighting, and color.

EXERCISE

1. Define your territories. What do you do when those territories are invaded? Discuss this matter with groups of three to six. Are your attitudes the same? Under what circumstances do they differ?

2. What are your expectations about space when (a) you are talking with a professor? (b) you are talking with a good friend? (c) you are talking with a person for the very first time?

3. Consider the color, temperature, and lighting of the room in which you are reading. To what extent does the nature of each help or hinder your study mood? What if you were using the same setting for a party? A discussion with an intimate friend?

YOU AND YOUR STYLE

You control a great deal of your nonverbal communication. This is especially true in the way you present yourself. Several major aspects of your personal style are body shape, clothing, and the way you treat time.

Body Shape

The way people perceive us is based in part upon the way they perceive our bodies. The three basic body types are endomorph, mesomorph, and ectomorph. The *endomorph* is soft, round, and fat; the *mesomorph* is muscular, hard, and athletic; the *ectomorph* is thin, fragile, and brittle.

A study by Wells and Siegel indicates how physical proportion affects others' perceptions of you.[5] In their study, 120 adult subjects were shown silhouette drawings of the three body types and asked to rate them on such paired adjectives as lazy-energetic; intelligent-unintelligent; dependent-self-reliant. The results showed that endomorphs are seen as older, lazier, weaker but more warmhearted, good-natured, agreeable, and trusting; mesomorphs are seen as stronger, more masculine, better looking, younger, taller, and more mature; ectomorphs are seen as younger, more ambitious, more suspicious, more tense and nervous, more stubborn, and quieter.

We saw in Chapter 2 that perceptions of others are not necessarily accurate. Nevertheless, you must understand that people will draw conclusions about you based on body type alone.

Clothing

On a day-to-day basis we exercise more control over the clothing we wear than over the body the clothes adorn. You have the power to greatly affect others' perception of you solely by the way you dress. Times change and values change; the perceptions people drew from a style of dress may not be the same today as they were years ago. Although reactions may be different at different times, it does not affect the point that people will and do react. It is for you to determine what you are trying to say and then to dress appropriately.

John Molloy has achieved a tremendous amount of discussion the last several years with his books *Dress for Success* and the *Woman's Dress for Success Book*. Molloy is not setting up arbitrary standards for dress. He is simply reporting what people—particularly employers—perceive as a result of dress. Molloy's methods may not meet the tests of research that scientists demand; still, he has demonstrated that what people wear and how they wear it makes a difference.

[5]William D. Wells and Bertram Siegel, "Stereotyped Somatypes," *Psychological Reports,* Vol. 8 (1961), pp. 77–78.

YOU HAVE THE POWER TO AFFECT OTHERS'
PERCEPTION OF YOU BY THE WAY YOU DRESS.

We all have a right to dress any way that we want; and when there are no consequences to our dress we have complete freedom of selection. Nevertheless, there are times when it is in our best interests to meet the expectations of others. The manager of a business may have a clear idea of the image she wants her business to portray. If you want to prosper with that business, you will want to dress in a way that is in line with that image.

It is up to you to determine what is appropriate or expected; then you can deviate from expectation at your own risk. The man who goes into an interview with a major oil company in a rumpled sweatshirt, levis, and tennis shoes had better have a lot going for him if he expects even to be heard, let alone hired. A defendant charged with assault and battery runs a risk of alienating the jury if he shows up in the courtroom wearing a black leather jacket, jeans, and boots. A rape victim who has the courage to testify risks savage cross-examination and alienation of the jury if she wears a low-cut blouse and a tight skirt when she takes the stand. Lawyers are very careful to tell their clients exactly how to dress in order to favorably impress judge and jury.

People have the right to their individual differences, and I believe modern society is moving in the right direction in allowing persons to express themselves as individuals. Nevertheless, your clothes are still perceived by others as clues to your attitudes and behaviors. Clothes do communicate, however accurate or inaccurate you may believe that communication to be.

Time

Although we have no control over time, how we manage our time and how we react to others' use and management of time are important aspects of personal style.

For each of us there is a length of time that we regard as appropriate for certain events. For instance, Sunday sermons are 20 to 30 minutes, classes are 50 minutes (Tuesday and Thursday classes of 75 minutes never seem right to many of us), a movie is roughly two hours. Television programs are 30 minutes or 60 minutes *unless* they are a movie or a sporting event. When the length of an event does not meet our expectation, that time itself becomes an obstacle to communication. We get angry with the professor who holds us beyond normal class time; we become hostile if someone asks us to cut short our lunch hour or coffee break.

In addition to an appropriate length of time there is also an appropriate time of day for certain things to happen. We work during the day, sleep at night, eat at noon, have a cocktail at 5 P.M., and so on. We make judgments about people who accept "time" for events that differ from ours. Joe is strange if he gets up at 4:30 A.M. The Martins eat dinner at 4:30 P.M. and the Smiths don't dine till 8 P.M.—we may consider both families peculiar. Adam works on his books from midnight until 4 A.M. and then sleeps till noon—we are aware that he is "different." So, *when* people do things communicates something to us.

But perhaps most basic to our perception of people is how they treat time designations. For instance, suppose you are holding a party. When you invited people you told them to come at about 8 P.M. What do you think of Rob if (a) he arrives at 7:30? (b) if he arrives at 8 P.M. exactly? (c) if he arrives at 8:30? (d) if he arrives at 10 P.M.? Now, for sake of argument, let's change the setting. Suppose you have a test scheduled for tomorrow. After today's class, suppose that a group of five of you decide to study together. Since your place is as good as any you say, "Stop by about 8 P.M." Now what do you think of Rob if he arrives at (a) 7:30? (b) 8 P.M. exactly? (c) 8:30? and (d) 10 P.M.? Depending upon how you see time, you will make a value judgment upon the basis of when he comes; moreover, you may view his arrival time differently depending upon the occasion.

Time does communicate. We must be sensitive to our own perceptions of time, as well as those of others, so that the variable of time facilitates or at least does not inhibit communication.

EXERCISE _____

1. Do you dress to achieve any special goal? If so, what? If not, does how you dress still affect your relations with others?

2. Next time you go to class, dress completely differently from your normal dress. Notice what effect, if any, this has on your communication with those around you.

3. How do you treat time? Consider Rob's arrival at the party and at the study session. Compare your views with other members of the class.

4. Bring to class a picture of a person taken from a magazine article or advertisement. Divide into groups. Each person in the group should write three to five adjectives about each of the pictures. Then the persons in the group should compare their assessments and discuss them on the basis of perception of clothes, hair style, and other aspects of personal habits.

BODY MOTIONS

Of all nonverbal means we are probably most familiar with *kinesics*, the technical name for such body motions as facial expression, eye behavior, gestures, movements of the limbs and body, and posture. To the unobservant all body motion may appear as random movement growing from peculiarities of culture, personality, or nationality (Italians talk with their hands; British have a stiff upper lip) but Ekman and Friesen[6] see these movements as emblems, illustrators, affect displays, regulators, and adaptors.

Emblems

These body motions or gestures take the place of a word or two or a phrase. Their meanings are every bit as clearly defined and universally accepted as verbal dictionary definitions. Thumbs up for "everything is Go"; extension of fist and second finger in V shape for "peace"; the waved hand for "hi" or "how are you doing?"; shaking the head for "no" and nodding for

[6]Paul Ekman and W. V. Friesen, "The Repertoire of Nonverbal Behavior: Categories, Origins, Usage, and Coding," *Semiotica*, Vol. 1 (1969), pp. 49–98.

"yes"; shrugging the shoulders for "maybe" or "I don't care" are but a few of the nonverbal emblems that we use consistently to replace speech.

Our verbal vocabulary consists of words that we know and use regularly in our daily speech, words that we can recognize if others use them but that are not in our working vocabulary, and words that we have to look up. Our nonverbal vocabulary has these same three classifications. For instance, nearly everyone in our culture nods his head for "yes"; this is an example of a nonverbal emblem that each of us knows and uses to regulate daily communication. Examples of emblems that you recognize but don't use are those that do not fit your personality, or do not have enough meaning for you. Many obscene emblems may be in your understanding vocabulary even if you rarely or never use them. Likewise, there are many emblems that just are not familiar to you. New emblems come into vogue just as new words are constantly being coined (the "generation gap" is reinforced by both verbal and nonverbal language usage). Moreover, some ethnic groups have sign languages whose meaning is known only to members of the group.

When do we rely on emblems to carry our messages? Emblems are probably used most when we are too far apart for speech to be heard and when there is so much noise present that we cannot hear, or when we just do not feel like verbalizing. Emblems also are used nearly exclusively when our auditory receptors do not work properly (the deaf have developed an extremely elaborate sign language) or when we are trying to exclude someone who is not a member of the "in" group.

Illustrators

These sets of nonverbal body movements or gestures are used to accent or emphasize what is being said verbally. Often when we say, "He talks with his hands" or "He couldn't talk if we tied his hands," we mean that the person's speech and body movement are totally complementary.

What is the nature of these movements that illustrate or complement speech? A sharp downward thrust of the hands as a person says, "Don't bug me" helps *emphasize* the act. The movement of the hand on an imaginary continuum as the person says, "The papers went from very good to pretty bad" illustrates a *path* or *direction* of thought. Pointing as the person says, "Take that table for instance" illustrates *position*. Using the hands to show the size as the person says, "The ball is about three inches in diameter" *describes*. Nodding your head as you say, "Did you see the way he nodded?" *mimics* a behavior. Thus any body motion that emphasizes, shows a pattern of thought, points, describes, or mimics is an illustrator.

Like emblems, illustrators are used intentionally and receivers process their use in determining meaning. Also, illustrators are socially learned and can be taught. The body action we will refer to under public speaking is largely comprised of illustrators. In the old days, training of public speakers involved detailed study of illustrators. You have probably heard older people talk about "elocution," which was in part a study of how to gesture "properly." Today, when we teach public speaking, we talk of letting the body action follow naturally from the thought. We are not, therefore, advocating that you learn and put into practice a set of illustrators. Our goal is to raise your awareness of their use. If you use them inappropriately or if your use calls attention to them rather than facilitating meaning, you should try to correct the use.

Affect Displays

When you feel some strong emotion, you are likely to *affect display* the nature of that feeling through a facial configuration or some concurrent body response. For instance, you get out of bed in the morning and as you walk sleepy-eyed to the bathroom you stub your toe. You are likely to show the pain with some verbal comment (do you have a pet word for these occasions?) and with an accompanying grimace. More often than not, these reactions—spur-of-the-moment emotional displays—are not intended as conscious communication. One of the apparent reasons for labeling the body motion a "display" is that your reaction will take place automatically whether you are alone or whether someone else is present, and it will probably be quite noticeable.

Of all the body motions we have considered thus far, it is through affect display that we reveal most about ourselves. For although the response we make is automatic, it is conditioned by a set of cultural, familial, and personal norms that alter the nature of the display. So if we are aware, we can learn a lot about a person by how he displays his emotions. The behavior we witness will probably be of four different kinds. Consider these carefully—they are very important to increasing your awareness of nonverbal communication. (1) *A person may deintensify the appearance of clues.* For instance when a person is extremely afraid, happy, or hurt, he feels he must attempt to look only slightly afraid, happy, or hurt. Perhaps a person bangs his head on the door frame getting in the car so hard that a bump appears, but the person acts as if it were a minor injury. (2) *A person may overintensify or amplify.* In this instance, when a person is only slightly afraid or happy, he may show extreme fear or happiness. Perhaps a child who suffers a little pain screams as if he has been grievously injured.

(3) *A person may take a neutral position.* If a person is happy, afraid, sad, or angry, he shows no difference. We call this the "poker face." (4) *A person may mask the clues.* This means that the person purposely looks different from what we would expect. If a person is happy, he may sneer or look angry. If he is angry, he may smile.

These display rules are usually learned—perhaps at home, perhaps in a social group, or perhaps in keeping with a self-image a person is trying to project. Especially in relation to family or social group, a person tries to conform to the established norms. For instance, if in your family it is considered bad form to show fear, then you learned from early childhood when you were afraid to de-emphasize your display or to adopt a neutral posture or perhaps to mask the display. Of course, the stronger the stimulus the harder it is to follow your personal rule. When you step sleepily out of bed and stub your toe, the display is likely to be directly proportional to the degree of pain. Ordinarily, however, your rules are your guide. Of course, you may portray yourself differently under different circumstances depending on how well you know people, what you think of them, and what you want them to think of you.

In this area of affect display we as students of communication need to be very careful about the conclusions we draw. For if we do take the nonverbal behavior as the true meaning of the communication, we can be fooled. Later in this chapter we will discuss the principal means for clarifying our perceptions of nonverbal behavior.

Regulators

Less dramatic but equally important as a form of body motion are the *regulators*, the nonverbal acts that regulate the flow of conversation by telling the speaker to continue, to repeat, to elaborate, to hurry up, and the like. Think for a minute. How do you know when someone has finished speaking? Or when someone will continue speaking for a while longer? How do you know when you should talk more slowly? Or faster? We pick up such communication clues from movements such as shifting eye contact, slight head movements, shifts in posture, raising eyebrows, and nodding of the head. Incidentally, you may have noticed that nodding the head has been used to exemplify an emblem meaning "yes" and a regulator meaning "good, go on." Like words, nonverbal responses have different meanings in different contexts.

Regulating occurs on the periphery of our awareness. We usually do not know when we are doing these things, and we are not necessarily conscious of others' doing them. But, if we were restrained from doing them we would become quite frustrated—we expect and need these regulators.

Regulators penetrate our awareness when their usage reaches a state that we describe as rudeness. If while we are talking a person gives signs of impatience, we think, "How rude of him to do these things when I'm talking!" For instance, if in the midst of what you think is a good conversation the other person gathers up his things, puts his coat on, and starts to leave while you are in the middle of a statement, you would usually be upset. Yet, we do regulate communication on a subtler level constantly.

Adaptors

In the fifth and the most difficult to define classification are the *adaptors*. Researchers have called them adaptors because they are thought to be adaptive efforts to satisfy needs, perform actions, manage emotions, develop social contacts, or to perform many other functions. Of all the nonverbal movements we have discussed, these are the least capable of being coded—yet, in some ways they are the most fascinating. You may be familiar with one or more of the books that trade on the mystery of adaptors. Some years ago Fast's *Body Language*[7] had everyone who read it trying to "psych out" the hidden messages that people were unaware of or were trying to repress. A close reading of these books shows that such things as a person crossing her legs may (or may not) have something to do with her attitude toward the person she is with or the crossing of her arms may (or may not) have something to do with her rejection of the other's ideas. Usually, we just are not aware of our adaptive behavior.

Yet, if someone believes he senses something in our nonverbal behavior it may greatly affect the communication. When we talk with a person we often get an instinctive feeling of what he is like, what he is thinking, or what he is feeling. For instance, when the boss takes off his coat, rolls up his sleeves, and pitches in, he is telling something about himself that is somewhat different from the boss who dresses rather formally, stands apart from his workmen, and looks disgusted at the thought of getting his hands dirty. Many times we say we are attracted to a person because he or she just exudes sexuality or has a kind of grace or just seems comfortable. Sometimes we are repelled by a person because he or she seems stern,

---

[7]Julius Fast, *Body Language* (New York: M. Evans & Co., 1970).

strict, formal, uptight. Many of these impressions are projected by adaptive behaviors on the part of the persons in question.

In the following exercise, the goal is for you to determine your own reactions to nonverbal behavior you perceive. Of course, in normal conversation you should check out the accuracy of your perception. As mentioned before, a means of checking out perceptions will be discussed later in this chapter.

EXERCISE

1. Divide into groups of three to six persons. Have an individual describe a game he saw, a place he had just been, where he had lunch, or the like. Give the person a minute or so to talk. Note the nature of his illustrators. Did he use body action to describe, to emphasize, to mimic, or in some other way? Compare the use of body movement by the various people in the group. Who used more? Under what circumstances?

2. Two members of the group discuss a textbook, a course, the school cafeteria. As they talk, monitor facial expression, hand movements, and posture. Discuss what if any of the movements acted as regulators.

3. Write out on a piece of paper what you believe are your normal nonverbal means of displaying anger, pain, boredom, surprise, happiness, and disgust. In your groups, discuss the various nonverbal means you have listed. Is there any common denominator in your group?

4. Do you ever emphasize? De-emphasize? Neutralize? Or mask? Why? When? How?

5. With your group discuss the kinds of facial expressions, postures, or movements suggestive of being sexy, fun-loving, a bore, pushy, and the like. What kinds of behavior seem to be conscious—in control of the person? What kinds seem to be unconscious or subconscious?

PARALANGUAGE

Kinesic behavior relates to the bodily movements we see; *paralanguage* relates to the sounds we hear. In simple terms, the study of paralanguage deals with how something is said and not what is said. We have all developed some sensitivity to the clues people give through their voices. Let's consider two major categories of paralanguage.

Vocal Characteristics

The four major characteristics of voice are *pitch* (highness or lowness of tone), *volume* (loudness), *rate* (speed), and *quality* (the sound of the voice).

Each of these by itself or in concert with one or more others either complements, supplements, or contradicts the words used. People talk loudly when they wish to be heard greater distances, but some people also talk louder when they are angry and softer when they are being loving. People tend to raise and lower their pitch to accompany changes in volume. They may also raise pitch when they are nervous or lower pitch when they are trying to be forceful. People may talk more rapidly when they are happy, frightened, or nervous; they will talk more slowly when they are unsure or trying to emphasize a point.

In addition to combined changes in volume, pitch, and rate, each of us uses a slightly different quality of voice to communicate a particular state of mind. We may associate complaints with a whiny, nasal quality; seductive invitation with a soft, breathy quality; and anger with a strident, harsh quality. To each of these different qualities, we assign some kind of a value judgment about how persons are feeling or what they are thinking.

None of these particular differences in voice quality necessarily has the meaning we assign. Some people have high-pitched or breathy or nasal or strident voices all the time. Perhaps some people use these different qualities for reasons other than what we assign. Nevertheless, *how* the person says what he says does convey meaning, whether intended or not. Although paralanguage is learned, it is quite difficult to change. If you have some vocal characteristic that works to contradict the meanings you intend to send, you may need professional help in changing those patterns. My purpose here is more to make you aware of the meanings received through paralanguage than to suggest the need for change of your own paralanguage. If you have concerns, talk them over with your professor. If she believes you do in fact have some problem, she can refer you to a speech therapist for help.

Vocal Interferences

By *vocal interferences* we mean those sounds that interrupt or intrude into fluent speech, causing distraction and occasionally total communication breakdown. Vocal interferences are the bad speech habits that we develop over a period of time. The most common interferences are the "uh's," "er's," "well's," and "OK's" that creep into our speech, and that nearly universal interrupter of thought, "you know."

Vocal interferences are hard to eliminate from our speech. They are often caused by a fear of momentary silence. In some instances, this fear of silence is real. Americans have been taught that it is impolite to interrupt another person until the flow of sound stops. A problem occurs for the speaker when he pauses for the right word or idea. The split second it takes for him to come up with the word may be perceived by others as "dead air time." For fear that another person may perceive the pause as a full stop, the sender often fills that dead air time with sound. More often than not, the sound has no meaning. For some, the customary filler sounds are "uh" or "er"; for others, they may be "well uh" or "um." Although the fear of being interrupted may be real (some people will seek to interrupt at any pause), the intrusion of fillers is a terrible price to pay for occasional interruption.

Equally prevalent, and perhaps even more irritating than the "uh's" and "um's," is the incessant use of "you know." The "you know" habit may begin with a person seeking to find out whether what he is sending is already known by a receiver. For some, "you know" may be a source of identification; the sender seeks to show that sender and receiver have common knowledge as a binding element. For most people, however, the flooding of sentences with "you know" is just a bad habit.

Curiously, no matter how irritating the use of "you know" may be, receivers are unlikely to acknowledge their irritation. Seldom if ever does anyone say openly to another person anything like "Your use of 'you know' at every break in thought is really very irritating to me." Yet passages like the following are quite common: "You know, Maxwell is, you know, a good, uh, a good, you know, lecturer." In addition to one "uh" and one repetition,

VOCAL INTERFERENCES DISTRACT AND CAN CAUSE TOTAL COMMUNICATION BREAKDOWN.

the short sentence contains three "you knows"! I wish such uses were exaggerations. Unfortunately, they are not. Perhaps you should start pointing out this irritant in others' speech; most important, you should request feedback from others and monitor your own speech for such use and do what you can to eliminate it.

In the normal give and take of conversation, even the most fluent speakers may use an occasional "uh" or "you know"; few people can completely avoid their use at all times. However, with some practice, you can *limit* their occurrence in your speech. Remember, although people may not be willing to tell you about it, they are likely to be distracted or irritated by your nonfluencies. So, what do you do? Try these suggestions:

1. *Become aware of usage.* One problem is that people are seldom aware of their use of vocal interferences. You may believe that you never use them, when in fact they may be a major part of your sending style. There are two easy ways of learning to be aware. One way is to tape-record yourself talking for several minutes and then listen to the recording. Turn the recorder on and talk about the game you saw yesterday, the course you plan to take next term, or anything else that comes to mind. When you play it back, you can notice your uses. A second way is a little more traumatic but may bring even quicker results. Have a close friend listen to you and raise her hand or drop a penny in a tin can every time you say "uh" or "you know." You may find the experience traumatic or nerve-racking, but your ear will soon start to pick them up as fast as the listener.

2. *In practice sessions see how long you can go without using a vocal interference.* Start out by trying to talk for fifteen seconds. Continue to increase the time until you can get to two minutes. In these practices, meaning may suffer. You may spend a disproportionate amount of time avoiding nonfluencies. Still, it is good practice.

3. *In regular conversation mentally note your usages.* You will be making real headway when in the heat of conversation you can recognize your own *interferences.* When you reach this stage, you will find yourself beginning to avoid their use.

Ridding yourself of these habits is hard work. You will have to train your ear to catch your use. But the work is worth it. Conversation would be a lot more pleasant if everyone would work to reduce vocal interferences by just 50 percent.

PERCEPTION CHECKING

In Chapter 3 we talked about how difficult it is to understand what a person really means even when the words used are understandable. As you read this chapter you are probably thinking that understanding the meaning of nonverbal communication is even more difficult. The only way you can be reasonably sure that you have interpreted a person's nonverbal response accurately is to verbalize your interpretation. The perception check is the skill used to accomplish your goal. A *perception check* is a verbal statement that reflects *your* understanding of the meaning of another person's nonverbal cues.

If we always said what we were thinking or feeling and if our statements were always accurate representations of those thoughts and feelings, then perception checking would not be needed. Because some people do not verbalize what they are thinking or feeling and because what they do say sometimes seems at odds with other clues they are sending, we, as receivers, must interpret the words and actions. There is no way of judging the accuracy of our perceptions without putting them to the test. Examine the following situations and the efforts at checking out perceptions.

> George, through various visual and auditory clues that connote displeasure (speaking in short, precise sentences with a sharp tone of voice, and the like), gives Bill his day's assignment. Bill says: "I get the impression that you're upset with me, George. Are you?"

> Ted delivers a note to Mary from her friend Gary. As she reads the note her eyes brighten and she breaks into a smile. Ted says: "You seem particularly pleased with Gary's note, Mary. Is that so?"

> Al offers Suzy directions for revising the advertisement she has written for a new product—an advertisement that took her many hours to prepare. As Al talks, Suzy's face reddens, and she sets her lips. Al says: "Am I right that you're angry with the suggestions I'm making?"

> Martin listens to what Greg says with virtually no expression other than a slight smile. As Greg speaks Martin occasionally nods and he looks Greg straight in the eye. Greg says: "I'm not sure whether your expression means that you're satisfied or unsatisfied with my proposal."

In each of the above examples, the final sentence is a perception check that is intended to test the receiver's perceptions of the nonverbal communication of the sender. Notice that the statements do not express approval or disapproval of what is being received—they are purely descriptive statements of the perceptions.

How do you phrase a perception check? As you perceive the nonverbal behavior of another ask yourself, "What does that behavior mean to me?" Then put your interpretation of the behavior into words. After you verbalize your understanding, the other person has a chance to report the accuracy of your interpretation. When should you use a perception check? Whenever the accuracy of your understanding is important to your current communication or to the relationship you have with that other person. Most people use this skill far too little, if at all. They *assume* that they have a perfectly accurate understanding of another's nonverbal cues; too often, they are wrong.

Let's see what happens when we respond without checking the accuracy of our perceptions. We'll examine a rather typical conversation based upon the situation described in the first example just given.

If, in place of the descriptive perception check ("I get the impression that you're upset with me. Are you?"), Bill were to say: "Why are you so upset with me?" Bill would not be describing his perception—he would be making a judgmental statement related to that perception. Replying as if your perception is "obviously" accurate involves reliance on mind reading, and few of us can read minds. When mind reading is substituted for perception checking, the result is all too often trouble. Perhaps you are thinking, "Well, I know when another person is upset with me." Perhaps you are correct in your certainty that you can properly identify such feelings accurately most of the time. If you do not respond at all, you are guessing that you know how the other person is feeling. If you choose the judgmental reply, any person so spoken to would be inclined to be rather defensive about his feelings that you appear to be challenging. In response he might say, "Who said I'm upset?" or more harshly, "What the hell are you talking about?" Such responses might soon lead to further emotional outbursts, and very little communication takes place when communicators lose their tempers.

Because a perception check is descriptive rather than judgmental, the original sender will be less likely to become defensive. The purpose of checking out any perception of behavior is to give a person the opportunity to deal with that perception—to verify it or to correct it. Let's carry through with George and Bill's conversation. When Bill says, "I get the impression that you're upset with me, George. Are you?" George may say either (1) "No, whatever gave you that impression?" in which instance Bill can further describe the clues that he received; or George may say (2) "Yes, I am," in which instance Bill can get George to specify what has been the cause of the upset. If George is not upset, then Bill can deal with what caused him to misinterpret George's feelings; if George is upset, then he is given the opportunity to explain why in more detail, and Bill has the opportunity of changing the behavior that caused George to be upset.

A perception check will not eliminate defensive behavior. There are times when the emotional stress is so great that calm, logical communication is nearly impossible. Through the use of perception checking, however, you can reduce the probability of defensiveness.

Of all the possible barriers to communication, defensiveness is the easiest to elicit and perhaps one of the most difficult to deal with. We are all sensitive human beings; without giving it conscious thought, we become attached to our own ideas and feelings because they are ours. Then, when we believe that one of our ideas or one of our feelings is being questioned, challenged, or in some way attacked, our immediate reaction is to strike out at the one doing the attacking. If, however, we feel that a person is not attacking us, we may develop an empathic bond, and we are less likely to get defensive. Although we will have occasion to talk about defensiveness later, for now let's try checking perceptions in a way that is least likely to elicit a defensive reaction.

EXERCISE

1. Respond to the following situations with well-phrased perception checks:

   Vera comes rushing into the room, throws her books on the floor, and sits at her desk with her head in her hands. You say:

   Bob comes out of the professor's office with pale face and slumped shoulders. Glancing at you with a forlorn look, he shrugs his shoulders. You say:

   As you return Jim's tennis racket you borrowed, you smile and say, "Here's your racket." Jim stiffens, grabs the racket, and starts to walk away. You say:

   In the past your advisor has told you that almost anytime would be all right for working out your next term's schedule. When you tell him you'll be in Wednesday afternoon at 4 P.M. he pauses, frowns, sighs, and says "Uh," and nods. You say:

2. Work in groups of three. A talks with B and C observes. A role plays a situation in which he gives off various clues to his feelings through words and actions. B uses perception checking to test his perception of A's feelings. C discusses the conversation. The exercise continues until everyone in the group has a chance at being sender, receiver, and observer. After the exercise, each person discusses how it feels to check out perceptions. Did the perception checking help or hinder the communication? How?

SUMMARY

Although verbal and nonverbal communication work together best when they are complementary, nonverbal communication may take the place of or even contradict verbal communication.

The environment is one aspect of nonverbal communication that is often overlooked. Yet the way a person arranges and reacts to space and the way he controls or reacts to color, temperature, and lighting contribute to the nature of the communication that will occur. Likewise, a person's own style as manifested by such things as clothing, hair style, and use of time further affects communication.

Perhaps the most obvious of the nonverbal means is what and how a person communicates through body motions and paralanguage. Movements of hands, arms, and other parts of the body act as emblems, illustrators, affect displays, regulators, and adaptors. Likewise, a person's vocal characteristics and vocal interferences affect the meaning communicated.

Perhaps the most important skill a person can develop to test her understanding of nonverbal meanings is the perception check, a statement that tests the receiver's understanding of how a person feels and what that person means by his or her nonverbal responses.

Nonverbal communication is not easily controlled, but it can be understood and taken into consideration more consciously by those who understand its various aspects.

SUGGESTED READINGS

Judee K. Burgoon and Thomas Saine. *Unspoken Dialogue.* Boston: Houghton Mifflin, 1978. This book provides a comprehensive analysis of nonverbal communication.

Edward T. Hall. *The Silent Language.* Garden City, N.Y.: Doubleday, 1959 (paperback). This classic work by Hall is fundamental to any comprehensive study of time and space.

Mark L. Knapp. *Essentials of Nonverbal Communication.* New York: Holt, Rinehart & Winston, 1980 (paperback). Excellent analysis and summary of research studies.

Marianne LaFrance and Clara Mayo. *Moving Bodies.* Monterey, Calif.: Brooks/Cole, 1978. This book is especially good for analyzing nonverbal communication in the context of relationships.

Dale G. Leathers. *Nonverbal Communication Systems.* Boston: Allyn & Bacon, 1976 (paperback). Another detailed account with an excellent bibliography.

Albert Mehrabian. *Silent Messages,* 2nd ed. Belmont, Calif.: Wadsworth, 1981 (paperback). A short, highly readable book focusing on the role of nonverbal communication in social interaction.

John T. Molloy. *Dress For Success.* New York: Warner Books, 1976.

John T. Molloy. *The Woman's Dress for Success Book.* New York: Warner Books, 1977.

CHAPTER 5

COMMUNICATING IDEAS AND FEELINGS

"Claude, when that man asked you whether you'd rather have stuffing than potatoes, you said 'yes'!"

"Yes," Claude responded nodding his head.

"But you never told me you prefer stuffing."

"Well . . . No, I guess I never did."

"Claude, we've been married more than twenty years and I'm just now learning that you like stuffing more than potatoes."

"Well, I'm sorry Phyllis," Claude said sheepishly.

"Claude," Phyllis asks, "are there other things that you like or don't like that you haven't told me about during these more than twenty years?"

"Well, probably, Phyllis."

"Claude—why aren't you telling me about these things?"

"Well, I don't know, Phyllis. I guess I didn't think they were all that important."

"Not important? Claude, every night I make potatoes. I make mashed potatoes, baked potatoes, scalloped potatoes, potatoes au gratin, french-fried potatoes, home-fried potatoes. Claude, I hate potatoes. I wouldn't care if I never saw a potato again. Now I find out you like stuffing better!"

"Phyllis, why didn't you ever tell me that you don't like potatoes?"

"Well I, uh-uh . . ."

Poor Claude—poor Phyllis—in fact, poor marriage. But is their experience all that unusual? Do we take the time to tell others what we're really thinking and feeling? Do we do it clearly and concisely? For a lot of people the answer is a resounding *no*. In fact one study showed that many married people talk to each other only 27½ minutes per week![1] And little of that time involved sharing ideas and feelings.

In this chapter we want to look at message formation. Specifically we will consider some of the skills that will help you communicate your ideas and feelings.

MESSAGE FORMATION

Communication may be a dynamic, transactional process; nevertheless, someone must initiate a topic of conversation. Moreover, even in the midst of a give-and-take interaction, a person may be focusing on presentation of his or her own idea and feelings rather than on responding to ideas presented. The material presented in this chapter has three goals: (1) to suggest ways that will help you be better understood, (2) to present ideas in ways that sustain a neutral if not a positive communication climate, and (3) to be more revealing of the person doing the communicating.

For any communication to be mutually satisfying there must be a climate that will allow all parties to share ideas and feelings freely. In the chapter on nonverbal communication we talked about how difficult it is to keep our mind on communicating if, for instance, the temperature is so low that our attention is drawn toward feelings of discomfort. Yet, a psychological climate formed through verbal and nonverbal communication is every bit as important as a physical climate. We have it within our power to say things in such a way that the other person will be encouraged to continue communicating and will achieve a feeling of satisfaction with the transaction.

Let's begin by looking at several of the skills that you can use to communicate your ideas clearly with less chance of provoking defensiveness. The skills we will consider are dating, indexing, and provisional phrasing.

Dating

Dating is a simple skill that means including in your statements a specific time referent that indicates when a given fact was true. Conclusions we

[1] Beth Dunlop, "A Good, Deep Talk Isn't Cheap Anymore," *The Cincinnati Enquirer* (Jan. 21, 1980), p. B6.

draw are based on information we have or get. When the information is accurate, it is more likely that the conclusions drawn from that information will be accurate. Many times when we share information we leave the impression that the information is fresh when in fact it may be outdated. For instance, Park says, "I'm going to be transferred to Henderson City." Bill replies, "Good luck—they've had some real trouble with their schools." On the basis of Bill's statement Park is going to be concerned with what this move might mean to his family. What he doesn't know is that Bill was talking about a problem that Henderson City had *five years ago*! Henderson City still may have problems, but it may not. Had Bill originally replied, "Five years ago they had some real trouble with their schools, but I don't know what the situation is now," Park would look at the information differently.

The fact is that nearly everything changes with time: Things age, grow, learn, wear out. Some changes may be nearly imperceptible, but some changes are so great as to make the person, idea, or thing nearly unrecognizable. As a result whatever you are talking about, you should actually or mentally indicate the date when your view of that phenomenon was true. Consider each of the following examples:

> When we were in Palm Springs *two years ago,* it was really popular with the college crowd.

> Powell brings great enthusiasm to her teaching—at least she did *last quarter* in communication theory.

> *Four years ago* the Death Ride was considered the most exciting roller coaster in the country.

> You think Mary's depressed? I'm surprised. She seemed her regular high-spirited self when I talked with her *the day before yesterday.*

Because you have no power to prevent change, you should recognize the reality of change by dating the statements you make.

Indexing

Indexing is a companion skill to dating. Dating accounts for differences caused by the passing of time. *Indexing* accounts for the innate differences among groups of people, objects, or places. Indexing is the mental or verbal practice of accounting for individual differences.

Indexing counters the tendency to make sweeping generalizations. To some extent generalization is an important part of our reasoning. It allows us to use what we have learned from one experience and apply it to another. When George tells Glenda that he caught five beautiful bass near a fallen tree on the eastern shore of Eagle Lake, a spot that seems to attract bass, Glenda is likely to look for a similar place to fish. When Sam notices that his girl friend seems to enjoy the fragrance of the new cologne he is wearing, he is likely to wear it again when they are together. When Marie learns that three of her fellow teachers have been promoted for excellence in teaching, she may try to improve her teaching. Glenda, Sam, and Marie have used what they learned from one experience and applied it to another. They have generalized.

Yet, misuse (or overuse) of this power can cause at least two serious communication problems. One is the tendency to take the characteristics of a class of people or objects and assign them to all the individual members within that class. For instance, just because men (a class) have greater strength in general than women (a class) does not mean that Max (a member of a class) is stronger than Barbara (a member of a class). Just because a university is ranked among the top twenty in the nation does not mean that every department in that university is so ranked.

A second problem is the tendency to transfer a characteristic of one person (or object) to another person (or object) just because that other person (or object) is within the same class. For instance, just because Klaus, a German, is industrious does not mean either that all Germans are industrious or that Fritz, who is also German, is industrious. Likewise, just because one Chevrolet goes 50,000 miles without a brake job does not mean that all Chevrolets can or that my Chevrolet can.

Now that we've considered the need for accounting for individual differences, let's see how the skill of indexing is used. Indexing calls for us to assign numbers to each member of a class. So in the class of men, we have man^1, man^2, man^3, and so forth; in the class of Chevrolets we have $Chevrolet^1$, $Chevrolet^2$, $Chevrolet^3$, and so forth. Let us consider how this works in a conversation. We will use each of the four examples just cited in explanation of problems of generalization. In each case we'll make a statement that involves generalization; then we'll make a similar statement that is properly indexed.

Men are stronger than women; Max is stronger than Barbara.

Men are in general stronger than women; Max is probably stronger than Barbara but not necessarily.

It's got to have a good department; the university is ranked among the top twenty in the nation.

Since the university is among the top twenty in the nation you can figure the department should be a good one although it doesn't necessarily have to be.

Fritz is likely to be industrious; Klaus is, and they're both German.

Fritz is likely to have the same industrious nature as Klaus (they're both German), but Fritz could be different.

Your Chevrolet should go 50,000 miles before you need a brake job; Jerry's did.

Jerry got 50,000 miles before he needed a brake job on his Chevrolet. You might be able to do as well, but you may not.

Thus if Bill tells Art, "I'm really ticked—I've got a graduate assistant as my teacher in speech class. The last time I had a graduate assistant in class it was a real waste." Art would be indexing if he had said, "I know graduate assistants as a group are not the most experienced teachers, but your teacher is not the same one you had before. I would at least give him a chance."

In short, before you make a statement about an object, person, or place, consider whether your statement is about that specific object, person, or place or whether it is a generalization about a class to which the object, person, or place belongs. If you discover that your statement is not based on specific knowledge, inform your listener of that fact.

Here are some additional examples of the use of indexing in normal conversation:

I think this house is probably well built—Conway, the builder, has a reputation for solid construction. *This house may be an exception,* though, so I'm going to have it inspected before I buy it.

Listen, I know Professor Barker was a poor teacher in business fundamentals, but organizational behavior is his specialty. We'd better see what he is like *in that course* before we decide to take a different class.

In general white clothes can be bleached without hurting them, but *this fabric may be an exception* so you'd better double check before you try to bleach it.

As a human being you cannot avoid generalizing, but indexing your statements can help you avoid the problems that hasty generalization sometimes creates.

Provisionalism

Another skill you can use to improve communication is to state your ideas provisionally. As a communicator you should try to phrase ideas so they will not create or add to a defensive communication climate. Whereas provisional statements will facilitate good climate, dogmatic statements—the opposite—will create defensiveness. By *provisional statements* we mean phrasings that suggest a lack of certainty or dogmatism.

Consider the following statements: Willie Stargell was the most valuable player in the 1979 World Series; paying cash is always better than installment buying; this is no time to buy a house. All three statements are asserting the "truth." Although the first statement is a matter of record (it can be validated by looking at a baseball record book), as stated it is *not* necessarily true. The other two statements are matters of opinion—they are inferences drawn from facts, but again, not necessarily true. If the three statements are made dogmatically, that is, in such a way that "they cannot be refuted" they could arouse defensiveness.

Let's reconsider the same three ideas. This time they will be stated provisionally: If I remember rightly, Willie Stargell was the most valuable player in the 1979 World Series; I've been brought up to believe that paying cash is always better than installment buying; it's my opinion that this is no time to buy a house. What are the differences? Why are these phrasings more likely to result in better interpersonal communication? First, the tone is different. Although we can't see a difference in vocal tone, the tentativeness of the phrasings is likely to result in a less certain tone of voice; but also, the tone of the phrasing is better. The words themselves convey a tentativeness that is going to be less antagonizing. Second, in all three cases there is the recognition that the words come from the speaker—and that speaker may have it wrong. "Willie Stargell was the most valuable player . . ." says "I'm telling you what's right." By saying, "If I remember rightly . . ." the speaker is saying that he thinks he's right, but there is some chance for a mistake. Recognizing the possibility of error makes it all right for the other person to offer his opinion without feeling that he is going to be in for a fight.

Speaking provisionally allows for different opinions. On certain topics it acknowledges that something that seems to be true under these circumstances may not be entirely true or may not be true at all under different circumstances.

Speaking provisionally may seem unassertive and wishy-washy, and if carried to some extreme it may be. But there is a world of difference in coming forward to say what's on your mind and saying it in a way that is likely to arouse hostility.

EXERCISE _____

1. Write a two- to five-sentence conversation about each subject below. Include two persons in the conversation. Use indexing and dating skills for shaping key statements.

   Datsuns as economical metropolitan vehicles
   Minority groups in colleges
   Dogs as pets
   Nuclear power plants as a means of generating electricity

2. Working in groups of three to six, have two persons discuss topics like the ones above. The rest of the group should observe when indexing and dating are used, how well they are used, and when they should have been used. Each person in the group should have an opportunity to practice.

SELF-DISCLOSURE

Perhaps two of the most important skills we can discuss in a chapter on communicating ideas and feelings come under the heading of self-disclosure: describing feelings and assertiveness.

Self-disclosure means sharing biographical data, personal ideas, and feelings that are unknown to another person. The first of these reveals facts about you as an individual. A statement such as "I was too small to make the team in high school" discloses biographical information; "I don't think the idea of rehabilitation of criminals is working" discloses a personal idea; "I get scared whenever I have to make a speech" discloses feelings. Through such self-disclosures others get to know you and understand you. The problems illustrated in the chapter opening are basically problems of failure to self-disclose. Biographical disclosures are the easiest to make, for they are, in a manner of speaking, a matter of public record. Disclosures of personal ideas and feelings are at the same time more threatening and more important. They are more threatening because they are not a matter of record. They are truly revealing of you as a person; they are more important because they represent the kinds of statements that enable someone to really know you.

Although there is considerable agreement that some self-disclosure leads to more effective communication, there is little evidence about the amount of self-disclosure that is most desirable.

Students of communication learn that the more we know about a person the more likely we are to feel closer to that person since we gain an understanding of the person. (You have probably spoken of a given professor becoming a "real person" to you as a result of what he or she said in class.) If self-disclosure is so valuable to interpersonal relationships,

SELF-DISCLOSURE CAN BE RISKY.

why are some people so cautious about revealing anything about themselves? This is true because self-disclosing carries with it a degree of risk. For just as knowing a person better is likely to result in closer interpersonal relations, learning about a person *may* result in alienation. You've heard the statement "Familiarity breeds contempt." It means that some people can learn too much about another person; eventually they learn something that detracts from the relationship. For instance, a professor you've always liked as a teacher may disclose information that causes you to change your mind about him or her. The risk that consequences of disclosure may be negative is more of a risk than some people wish to take—they prefer neutral reactions to themselves.

People find that disclosing may also make them vulnerable. For instance, let's say you don't like to be teased. If you keep this a secret, the person may not know it and, therefore, cannot hurt you. If on the other hand you tell a person you don't like to be teased, if and when that person wants to hurt you, the person knows how: to tease you.

But without disclosure the person is not going to get to know you, and a close, satisfying relationship is nearly impossible. A risk-free life (probably impossible to attain) may be safe, but it would not be very satisfying. Some risk is vital to achieving a gain. Too much risk can be more costly than we wish. So, what do we do? The following are guidelines for determining an appropriate amount of self-disclosure. They will give you a chance to get close to a person and develop a good relationship without making yourself too vulnerable.

Guidelines for Self-Disclosure

If you are not used to disclosing information about yourself, doing it is not easy, especially if you're not sure how much about yourself you wish to reveal. As you read the following guidelines, keep in mind that the goal of self-disclosure is to help you to be known to others as you know yourself.

1. *Self-disclosure should come when you believe the disclosure represents an acceptable risk.* There is always some risk involved in disclosing, but if you trust another person, you may perceive the disclosure as "safe." Incidentally, this guideline explains why some people engage in self-disclosure to bartenders or people they meet in travel. The disclosures they make are perceived as safe (representing reasonable risk) because the person either does not know them or is in no position to use the information against them. It seems sad to me that these people do not trust their husbands, wives, or other members of the family enough to make the disclosures to them.

2. *Self-disclosure should move gradually to deeper levels.* Since receiving self-disclosure can be as threatening as giving it, most people become uncomfortable when the level of disclosure exceeds their expectations. As a friendship develops, the depth of disclosure increases as well.

3. *Intimate or personal self-disclosure is most appropriate in ongoing relationships.* Disclosures about deep feelings, fears, loves, and so forth are most appropriate in an established relationship. When people disclose deep secrets to acquaintances, they are engaging in potentially threatening behavior. If disclosure is made before a bond of trust is established, the person making the disclosure may be risking a great deal. Moreover, people are often embarrassed by and hostile toward others who try to saddle them with personal information in an effort to establish a relationship where none exists.

EXERCISE ──────────────────────────────

Working alone, label each of the statements below L (low risk), meaning you believe it is appropriate to disclose this information to almost any person; M (moderate risk), meaning you believe it is appropriate to disclose this information to persons you know pretty well and have already established a friendship with; H (high risk), meaning you would disclose such information only to the few friends you have great trust in or to your most intimate friends; or X, meaning you would disclose it to no one.

____ **1.** Your hobbies, how you like best to spend your spare time.

____ **2.** Your preferences and dislikes in music.

_____ 3. Your educational background and your feelings about it.

_____ 4. Your personal views on politics, the presidency, and foreign and domestic policy.

_____ 5. Your personal religious views and the nature of your religious participation.

_____ 6. Habits and reactions of yours that bother you at the moment.

_____ 7. Characteristics of yours that give you pride and satisfaction.

_____ 8. The unhappiest moments in your life in detail.

_____ 9. The occasions in your life when you were happiest—in detail.

_____ 10. The actions you have most regretted taking in your life and why.

_____ 11. The main unfulfilled wishes and dreams in your life.

_____ 12. Your guiltiest secrets.

_____ 13. Your views on the way a husband and wife should live their marriage.

_____ 14. What to do, if anything, to stay fit.

_____ 15. The aspects of your body you are most pleased with.

_____ 16. The features of your appearance you are most displeased with and wish to change.

_____ 17. The person in your life whom you most resent and the reasons why.

_____ 18. Your favorite forms of erotic play and sexual lovemaking.

_____ 19. The people with whom you have been sexually intimate and the circumstances of your relationship with each.

Discussion (optional)

Working in groups of five to seven, discuss your labeling of the statements. You are not required to make any of the disclosures, only to discuss circumstances, if any, under which you are likely to make them. The purpose of discussion is to see how people differ in what they view as acceptable disclosures.

Description of Feelings

Having feelings is not an issue. Everyone has feelings! The issue is how to _deal_ with the feelings we have. Basically people will (1) hold feelings inside of them, (2) nonverbally and/or verbally express their feelings, and/or (3) describe their feelings. Holding feelings inside is psychologically bad for a person; expressing feelings is good psychologically but could be bad interpersonally; describing feelings is the most desirable way of dealing with feelings, especially when those feelings are negative.

Holding feelings inside means keeping others from knowing how we feel about anything. Good poker players often develop a "poker face," a neutral look that is impossible to decipher. The look is the same whether the players are dealt cards that are amazingly good or cards that are amazingly bad. Whether poker players are telling the truth or bluffing with their bet cannot be revealed through their expression.

Unfortunately, many people use poker faces for all their interpersonal relationships. Whether they hurt inside or are extremely excited, no one knows. Psychologists say this is very bad. If negative feelings are withheld, people develop ulcers, neuroses, and psychoses. If positive feelings are withheld, people simply aren't much fun to be around. Who wants to do something nice for people who never reveal how they feel about it? If this is your style, I can do nothing but suggest to you that there are better ways of dealing with your feelings.

More common than holding feelings is to react nonverbally and/or verbally by expressing feelings openly and spontaneously. With positive feelings, open expression is usually a good thing both psychologically and interpersonally. If someone does something nice for you, a positive emotional outburst will probably be well received. Have you seen the bumper sticker "Have you hugged your kid today?" There's nothing wrong with being a bit demonstrative. And at times a hug is the ideal way of showing a positive feeling. Squeals of delight, saying "wow," "great," and the like are verbal expressions of positive feelings. Again, they are likely to be well received and particularly appropriate.

Expression of feelings starts to be bad interpersonally when the feelings are negative. If someone steps on your toe and hurts you, you may have an urge to lash out at that person either nonverbally with a sudden slap, punch, or hit, or verbally with "Watch what you're doing, stupid."

The more appropriate procedure would be to describe your feelings verbally. Describing is best not only because it gets them out in the open but mostly because it teaches people how to treat you. Let me emphasize this point. Describing feelings is a starting point in educating others about your feelings. Consider the following statements: "Cliff, when you borrow my jacket without asking, it makes me angry with you"; "Rick, I know you think I don't mind it when you tease me about how I talk, but it makes me feel self-conscious about what I say"; "Maria, I get the feeling that you think it's a compliment to my ability to get things done when you leave me with the dirty work, but in fact I resent being left with those jobs"; "Paul, it really makes me feel good when you take the time to tell me I've done a good job."

We all like to feel that we are in control of our lives and our environment. We like to feel that we have the power to determine what will happen to us. When we are confronted by situations that show us to be defenseless and/or powerless, it is not only bad for us psychologically, but it also interferes with our communication. If you are able to let people know what hurts you, what makes you feel good, and when you are hurt or feeling good they will probably behave toward you in ways that you find more comforting. If you tell Paul that it really makes you feel good when he compliments you, such a statement should encourage Paul to keep on complimenting you when you have done a good job; likewise, when you tell Cliff that you get angry when he borrows your jacket without asking, he is more likely to ask the next time he borrows a jacket. Thus in each case you exercise a measure of control over others' behavior toward you.

However, before you think describing feelings is a perfect method for controlling behavior, understand that describing your feelings will not always get people to change their behavior toward you. After all, people behave as they choose. Paul might not feel like complimenting you all the time, and Cliff might not care whether you get angry or not. Still, a great deal of what we're talking about in our discussion of skill development is increasing the probability of desirable outcomes. If, therefore, you can raise the chances of desirable behavior significantly by describing feelings, isn't it worth it to try? And even if people do not behave as you would like, at least they will know the consequences of their behavior—they will have a rational base for what they do.

If describing feelings is so great, why don't more people do it regularly? Well first, as we have discussed, many people confuse describing feelings with expressing feelings. I begin discussion of this point with my students by asking them, "How many of you describe your feelings to others?" Often 50 percent or more will raise their hands (I had one class where nearly everyone said they did). Instead of challenging them, I get them to talk about what should be counted as "describing feelings." Then I say to my students, "For the next two days, I want you to be very conscious of each of the times you describe feelings. During our next class I will want to discuss some of the examples you provide me." At the next class meeting I find that very few have really described feelings much if at all. At first many students had confused describing and expressing feelings. Only when they examined their behavior carefully did they see that they were not really describing feelings.

But beyond just not understanding the difference between describing and expressing there seem to be at least three reasons why many people are reluctant to describe feelings even when they understand what describing is all about.

1. *If you describe your true feelings, they will reveal too much about you and you will become vulnerable.* As we mentioned earlier in this section, there is an element of risk attached to any self-disclosure. If you tell people what hurts you, they have the option of behaving in that way when they want to hurt you *on purpose.* This is true. It is a risk you run when you describe. But again, I ask you to look at the benefits. If Pete has a nickname for you that you don't like, and you tell Pete you don't like it because it hurts your feelings, Pete has the option of calling you by that name when he wants to hurt you. *But,* if you don't describe your feelings to Pete, he's probably going to call you by that name all the time because he doesn't know any better. When you say nothing, you are in fact reinforcing the current behavior. So even though you are running some risk by disclosing, you're likely to be far better off. Now the level of risk varies with each situation. However, you will be better off far more often than you will be hurt by describing feelings.

2. *If you describe your feelings, you will have to feel guilty about them.* At a very tender age we all learned about "tactful" behavior. Based on the premise that "the truth sometimes hurts" we learned to avoid the truth by not saying anything or by telling "little" lies. Perhaps when you were little your mother said, "Don't forget to give grandma a great big kiss." You replied, "Ugh—it makes me feel yucky to kiss grandma. She's got a mustache." If your mother then responded, "That's terrible—your grandma loves you. Now you give her a kiss and never let me hear you talk like that again!" you probably felt guilty for having the feeling "that you shouldn't have." But the point is that the thought of kissing your grandma made you feel "yucky" whether it should have or not. There may be times when describing feelings will not result in desirable outcomes, and perhaps under those circumstances you shouldn't describe them. But they still must be dealt with. For instance, had your mother said, "Oh, I see why you don't like to kiss grandma. Well grandma is old and there is nothing she can do about her 'mustache.' And since we love grandma and she won't understand why we don't kiss her, perhaps you could kiss her anyway to show her that you do love her even though it doesn't make you feel good."

3. *If you describe your feelings, you will cause harm to another person or to a relationship.* Let's say that it really bothers Max when people bite their fingernails. And let's say further that Max's girlfriend Dora bites her fingernails. If Max describes his feelings to Dora, Dora may be hurt and the knowledge may drive a wedge into their relationship. So, it's better if Max says nothing, right? Wrong! If Max says nothing, he's still going to be bothered by Dora's behavior. As time goes on it is likely that being bothered by this will cause Max to lash out at Dora for other things because he can't bring himself to talk about the behavior that really bothers him. What's the net result? Dora will be hurt—and Max's behavior will drive a wedge in their relationship. Only this time Dora won't understand why. So there's a very good chance that not describing feelings will result in negative outcomes. Let's go back to describing Max's feelings. If he tells Dora how he feels, she might quit or at least try to quit biting her nails. Or they might get into a discussion in which he finds out she doesn't want to but that she just can't seem to stop, and he can help her in her efforts to stop. Or they might discuss the problem and Max may see that it is a small thing really and not let it bother him as much. The point is that describing feelings has more chances of positive outcome than not describing them has.

In summary, a description of feelings statement puts your emotional state into words: (1) it clearly labels the feeling, (2) it indicates what has triggered the feeling, and (3) it credits you, the person having the feeling. For instance, "Your compliment (trigger) makes me (the person) feel very warm inside" (the feeling); or "The way you criticize my cooking (trigger) makes me (the person) very angry" (the feeling).

You may find it easiest to get started describing positive feelings: "You know, your taking me to that movie really cheered me up." As you gain success with positive descriptions, you can try negative feelings attributable to environmental factors: "It's so cloudy; it really makes me feel gloomy." Finally, you can move to negative descriptions resulting from what people have said or done: "Your stepping in front of me like that hurt my feelings." Or, "The tone of your voice makes me feel very defensive."

EXERCISE

1. In each of the following sets of statements, place a *D* next to the statements that describe feelings; place an *X* next to the statements that convey feelings by expressing them or by showing the effect of a feeling without actually describing it. Such statements can be called *evaluative*.

   1. ____ a. That was a great movie!

      ____ b. I was really cheered up by the story.

      ____ c. I feel this is worth an Oscar.

   2. ____ a. I feel you're a good writer.

      ____ b. Your writing brings me to tears.

      ____ c. Everyone likes your work.

   3. ____ a. If things don't get better, I'm going to move.

      ____ b. Did you ever see such a hole?

      ____ c. I feel depressed by the dark halls.

   4. ____ a. I'm not adequate as a leader of this group.

      ____ b. I feel inadequate in my efforts to lead the group.

      ____ c. I'm depressed by the effects of my leadership.

   5. ____ a. I'm a winner.

      ____ b. I feel I won because I'm most highly qualified.

      ____ c. I'm on cloud nine after winning that award.

Answers

1. a, expressive/evaluative; b, descriptive; c is an evaluation dressed in descriptive clothing. Just because the word *feel* is in a statement does not mean the person is truly describing feelings. "This is worth an Oscar" is an evaluation, not a feeling.

2. a, expressive/evaluative (there's that word *feel* again); b, descriptive; c. expressive/evaluative.

3. a, the result of feelings, but not descriptive of the feelings; b, evaluation in question form; c, descriptive.
4. a, expressive/evaluative; b, descriptive (similar to a except that here the feeling is described, not stated as an evaluation); c, descriptive.
5. a, evaluative; b, evaluative; c, descriptive.

2. Select five subjects (like a movie you saw, a place you visited, something that happened to you) and write a good personal description of feelings statement for each.

Assertiveness

Another skill associated with self-disclosure has been the subject of more recent discussion than nearly any other subject in this book: assertiveness. The women's movement and affirmative action programs that help minorities and people in subordinate positions try to get ahead have revealed that large numbers of people are unable to take advantage of opportunities to advance themselves because they lack assertiveness. For this reason, more and more people are enrolling in courses, programs, and workshops on assertiveness training.

Assertiveness means stating important ideas and feelings openly in interpersonally effective ways. The ability to be assertive is a direct outgrowth of your feelings about your self-worth and importance. Assertiveness is not a single individual skill, but the mastery of—and willingness to use—several skills, with special emphasis on describing feelings.

Why are some people less likely to assert themselves? For the most part it seems due to a feeling of a lack of power growing from or related to a lack of self-importance. Jack and Marsha both have something important to say. They begin talking at the same time. Marsha lets Jack go first. Is this a matter of politeness? Maybe. It is also possible that Marsha defers to Jack because he's a man and men "have the right to speak first." Mark gets a C on a test. As he reads his paper over he's sure that what he said was worth more than a C. He thinks about going in to talk to his professor but says to himself, "He's not going to listen to me—I'm just another student." Angie buys a new hair dryer. She takes it home and finds that a piece is broken off the end of the handle. What's missing does not affect how the hair dryer works. Angie is angry at getting an appliance that is not all that it should be, but Angie says to herself, "Well I got rooked, but at least it works all right."

Each of these three situations illustrates a person who makes a choice not to be assertive. Each choice may be the result of that person feeling a lack of personal power. What is social power? *Social power is the potential for changing attitudes, beliefs, and behaviors of others.* The presence of power

I DEFINITELY FEEL THAT WE SHOULD MAYBE GO AHEAD AND DO WHAT THE MAJORITY WANTS TO DO, I THINK.

ASSERTIVENESS MEANS STATING IMPORTANT IDEAS AND FEELINGS IN EFFECTIVE WAYS.

does not insure change, but the absence of power makes it nearly impossible for people to be willing to assert themselves.

Several social psychologists have offered analyses of social power. The one that seems to make the most sense in understanding interpersonal action is French and Raven's analysis that discusses the bases of social power: coercive, reward, legitimate, expert, and referent.[2]

Coercive power involves actual or threatened force. The use of coercion can be physical or psychological. The elements of physical coercion are size, strength, and possession of weapons. It doesn't matter whether a person exercises any of these elements. If we perceive the person as being able to exercise them, then we grant that person power.

Many people are not inclined to be assertive because they are intimidated by a person's coercive power. I'm sure you are familiar with the old vaudeville routine that opens with "Where does a gorilla sit when he comes into a room?" and ends with "Anywhere he wants to!" But the fact is that many people feel so intimidated by aggressive people that they grant coer-

[2]John R. P. French, Jr., and Bertram Raven, "The Bases of Social Power," reprinted in Dorwin Cartwright and Alvin Zander (Eds.), *Group Dynamics*, 3rd ed. (New York: Harper & Row, 1968), pp. 259–270.

cive power to people who in no way deserve it. Some people see others as intimidating when they're not even trying to be.

Reward power involves the giving of monetary, physical, or psychological benefits. Reward power works when a person being rewarded sees the reward as large enough or important enough to compensate for the pain of the action called for. In this situation, the person believes that the one who promises has the power to give that reward. For instance, you may know you'll be rewarded with an A grade if you write a good paper. If the course is not important to you, you may not think getting an A in that course is worth working for. Or, if your boss promises you consideration for promotion if you do a particular job well, you may not do it well because you doubt your boss really has the power to grant you a promotion at this time.

Some people are not inclined to be assertive because they fear that what they say may get in the way of their receiving a reward. For instance, if Jack's boss is giving him more to do than what Jack thinks is fair, Jack may be reluctant to assert his position because his boss may decide not to reward him in the future. Many people let others run over them because they think that giving in will help them get a reward they seek.

Legitimate power involves having influence as a result of being elected, selected, or holding a position. The rationale for bestowing legitimate power is the belief that people in certain positions have the responsibility of attempting to exert influence. Thus people give power to presidents, senators, and members of Congress because they were elected; to teachers, cabinet members, and committee chairpersons because they were appointed; and to older members of a family, parents, or oldest children because of tradition or cultural norms.

Legitimate power is highly valued in our society. Yet some people are excessively intimidated by position. Just because a person is a senator or a teacher or a parent does not mean that the person is infallible. Some people bestow such power to these individuals that it goes beyond what the person deserves or wants. We have all heard of persons giving in to officials or currying favor from those who have legitimate power. Both of these powers are thought to be negative because they ask people to reduce their own self-worth. Yes, legitimate power *is* legitimate—but only in the areas related to the position.

Expert power involves having knowledge in a specific field. Expert power is influential when you admit that another person holds information in a particular field that you need. Your instructors have the potential for expert power in your classes because they have knowledge and expertise you need; coaches have potential for expert power because they have knowledge that players seek.

Some people are not inclined to be assertive because they downplay their own expertise whatever the subject being considered. It's unlikely that a student should challenge the professor on a matter in which the professor is far more knowledgeable than the student. On the other hand, to grant the professor expert power over you on any subject being considered just because the person is your professor is foolhardy. We are far too often blinded by the perception of expert power. For instance, when buying clothing people are often intimidated by a salesperson just because that person is selling a particular line of clothes. Salespeople are not usually assigned because they are masters of information; they are assigned because they are persuasive. As salespeople work with a certain line of goods they may develop true expert power. But no one should be intimidated by the fear of being shown up by another person's knowledge. Whether it be buying a coat, having a repair made on the car, or having the furnace fixed, a customer must have the right to ask questions about what is happening and why.

Referent power involves having a potential to influence others through the image, charisma, or personality of the person. Many of us will listen to a person for no reason other than that we like that person or have a certain respect for the person's judgment. Many times it is in our best interests to grant this kind of power. We seldom have the time and energy to solve every issue that comes before us. If your best friend recommends a movie he saw or a restaurant she went to, you may well decide to attend that movie or eat at that restaurant because the person is a friend.

But on many important issues our reliance on the power of person is misplaced. Too often we vote for someone only because "there's something about him" that we like; too often we do things that may not be in our best interest because someone said we should. We are often not inclined to assert ourselves because we don't think highly enough of our own judgment to trust it—we rely too much on the word of others.

Whether it is because of coercive power, reward power, legitimate power, expert power, referent power, or some combination of them we sometimes give up our right to be heard, and that's a mistake.

People who are not assertive are inclined to be either passive or aggressive. Let's first look at passive behavior. Many American women are passive because they play the role that society has taught them. Women must be soft, warm, and loving; women have no power; any signs of assertiveness that suggest a kind of power are unwomanly. Fortunately, passive behavior is no longer seen as an ideal way for women to act. Women are flocking to courses on assertiveness training because they have spent the better portion of their lives being passive and now they need to learn to assert themselves.

What are some signs of passive behavior? People who are passive are often shy. People who are passive are reluctant to state their opinions, share their feelings, or assume responsibility for their actions. They often give in to the demands of others, even when doing so is inconvenient or against their best interests. They often pay dearly for their passivity. The failure to describe or to express negative emotions often results in resentment, depression, or sickness.

Another kind of nonassertive behavior is aggressiveness. Unfortunately, too many people equate assertiveness with aggressiveness, although the difference between the two is distinct. Assertiveness involves stating what you believe to be true for you, taking responsibility for your actions and feelings, but not attacking another individual personally. Aggressiveness, on the other hand, is judgmental, dogmatic, and often fault-finding.

We will illustrate how passive, aggressive, and assertive behaviors differ by examining two different situations.

Bill has just purchased a new color television set at a local department store. When he uncrates the set at home, he notices a large, deep scratch on the left side of the cabinet.

If Bill's behavior were passive, he would be angry about the scratch, but he would keep the set and say nothing to the store clerk from whom he purchased it. He might complain to his family about how the customer constantly gets ripped off, but he would say nothing to anyone associated with the store. He would probably be resentful and might even refuse to shop there again, but he would say or do nothing about the specific situation.

If Bill's behavior were aggressive, he would be angry about bringing home a damaged set. He might storm back to the store, loudly demand his money back, and accuse the clerk of intentionally selling him damaged merchandise. He would threaten the store with a lawsuit, and he would not stop until he received satisfaction.

If Bill's behavior were assertive, he would be angry about bringing home a damaged set—the feeling of anger is common to each type of behavior. Assertive behavior involves the special way of dealing with the anger. Bill might call the store and ask to speak to the clerk from whom he had purchased the set. When the clerk answered, Bill would describe his anger that resulted from discovering a large scratch on the cabinet when he uncrated the set. He would then go on to say that he was calling to find out what he had to do to return the damaged set and get a new one.

Both the aggressive and the assertive behavior would probably get Bill a new set. But the assertive behavior would achieve the result at lower emotional costs to both Bill and those with whom he talked.

Now let's change the situation from one involving an object to one involving direct interpersonal relations. Betty arrives late to a large lecture class. Because all the seats in the front section are occupied, she is forced to sit in the back of the room. Two men in front of her are talking noisily, but Betty assumes they will quiet down when Professor Green begins his lecture. Several minutes into the lecture, however, they are still talking.

If Betty's behavior were passive, she might just sit there boiling inside and feeling powerless to do anything.

If Betty's behavior were aggressive, she might lean forward and in a loud voice say, "Hey, would you knock off the talk—I'm trying to listen." She might then turn to a neighbor and say, "If I were Green, I'd have come down on these two creeps long ago."

If Betty's behavior were assertive, she might tap one of the men on the shoulder and say, "Excuse me, I'm having a hard time hearing Professor Green. Would you please keep your voices down?" If she achieves nothing with her statement, she might then get up and move to another section of the room where she could hear better.

Remember, you are important enough to be in control of your environment. You have every right to make necessary changes so long as you proceed in interpersonally sound ways.

EXERCISE

Identify five situations from your life where you were nonassertive or aggressive. Write a dialogue for each situation and insert an assertive response as a substitution for the nonassertive or aggressive reaction in each case.

PITFALLS TO AVOID

We've looked at several of the skills that will facilitate your communication of ideas and feelings. Let's conclude this chapter with a brief look at some of the problems of message formation that are very typical.

Transfer Stations

Communication is likely to be most effective when it is sender to receiver. If for any reason you find yourself using a relay system, you are likely to be setting up a problem by the method itself.

You've probably played the game called "telephone" (or "gossip") in which one person whispers a statement to another who in turn whispers what he thinks he heard to another who whispers what she thinks she heard to the next person and so on until it has gone through five, six, or more transfer stations. By the time it reaches the last person, the message may be so garbled that it is unintelligible.

Why is the transfer station doomed to failure? First because of the very nature of the system. The original sender may have all the information needed to communicate a relatively complex idea. When Dora encodes the message into language, she has already simplified, limited, and perhaps interpreted the original idea. Glen, who represents the first transfer station, does not have the benefit of the entire background for the idea. All he has is the words Dora used. Glen may not be able to remember all the words; he may not understand all the words; he may let semantic noise interfere with his understanding of the words. Nevertheless, he communicates what he now perceives as the message to Pauline, who communicates what she perceives. As the message moves on down the line, each transfer station affords another opportunity for selection and interpretation. If there are enough transfer stations (and it does not take many), the message may be totally lost.

Unscrupulous persons have used the technique to spread rumors for as long as human beings have used speech. Rumors are statements that are passed from person to person and usually embellished along the way, becoming bigger, bolder, bloodier all the time. (It is interesting that messages with many facts are not only distorted in transmission but also shortened. Messages that are storylike usually get embellished—certainly they are distorted—but instead of becoming shorter, they often become longer.)

You can avoid the problems of transfer stations by giving information directly to those who need it. If you are caught in the middle of chain-link communication, you will need to work very hard checking the accuracy of your ideas. Do not pass a message until you have taken the opportunity to make sure you have it right.

Information Overload

Since we are human beings, there is a limit to the amount of information we can process at any given time. If we are hit with more than we can handle, much of it will just be lost.

Sometimes in the interests of accuracy or objectivity we pack so much into such a short period of time that we lose nearly everything.

Giving directions is a good example to use to show how much or how little most of us are able to process. Very few people can listen to a recipe, how to get to a certain place, how to play a game *once* and really understand. In general, the more new information you attempt to communicate, the more careful you must be.

At this point, let me refer you to Part 4, Public Speaking, which is offered to help communicators deal with information effectively.

Hidden Agenda

A *hidden agenda* is a reason or motive for behavior that is undisclosed to other participants. For instance, if the account exec called Sanders in to talk about the Morris account but really wanted to find out why Sanders had seemed so depressed lately, the discovery of the reason for the depression would be the exec's hidden agenda that controls his behavior. In this example the problem with such behavior is not obvious. Let me cite another example that may pinpoint the problem more directly. If Carla called Susan to ask her over to study for the econ test when all Carla was really interested in was Susan's notes for the days Carla had missed class, that would be Carla's hidden agenda.

At best hidden agenda seems like an easier way of dealing with a difficult issue; at worst, hidden agenda is gross manipulation.

Interpersonal communication is supposed to be open and honest. When people start trying to achieve their goals in indirect ways that are designed to keep the other person from knowing what is happening or why, a potential for barriers between the people exists.

Some people go so far as to use the hidden agenda as a strategy to play psychological games with other people. A game is nothing more than one person's attempting to manipulate another person's behavior until the manipulator gets some payoff, usually a predictable behavior. Glen knows that Judy gets angry when he smokes in the bedroom, so he lights up in the bedroom and acts amazed when Judy loses her temper. Rachel knows that Steve is likely to become very uncomfortable with a discussion of his former girl friend, Doris. So in his presence, Rachel "innocently" asks, "Say, has anyone seen Doris lately?" In both cases, the person's hidden agenda was to create a painful experience. If the behavior gets the desired response, the person "wins." And it is this win-lose element that makes such statements games.

Are hidden agendas always detrimental to communication? Usually, if not always. Although as a matter of tact or propriety (or lack of nerve) you may sometimes stipulate one agenda when in reality you support another one, the behavior is still manipulative. If Collins suspects June of taking home company material (paper, paper clips, pencils) for her personal use, she may call June into the office to talk about a report and try to get at the subject of misappropriating indirectly. In this instance, the hidden agenda may appear to be beneficial to Collins, but when the real subject is revealed the attempt to keep it below the surface may become a bigger issue than the theft. When hidden agendas are discovered, the fragile bond of trust is often frayed or perhaps even broken; and, once trust is gone, the chance for good working relations is gone.

Despite the often painful thought of approaching a difficult problem directly, it is usually superior. If Collins suspects June of taking office supplies—or if she has seen her do it directly—she is better off saying, "June, I called you in here today because I believe you may be taking office supplies home for your personal use and I'd like to talk to you about this issue." Dealing with the issue may prove difficult, but at least the difficulty will be the issue itself and not something else.

SUMMARY

In this chapter we looked at message formation skills. The language skills of dating, indexing, and phrasing provisionally are directed at sharpening the clarity of the message in a way that will not arouse unnecessary defensiveness.

Self-disclosure—revealing information about yourself that is unknown to others—is considered the major skill for helping others to know you better. Describing feelings and assertiveness are two of the major skills under the self-disclosure heading. Describing feelings helps teach people how to treat us. Although expressing feelings is good psychologically for the person doing the expressing, describing feelings is a more interpersonally sound way of handling feelings. Assertiveness is the skill of stating your ideas and feelings openly in interpersonally effective ways. Assertiveness results from people believing that they have power over their fate. Passive people are often unhappy as a result of not stating what they think and feel; aggressive people get their ideas and feelings heard but may create more problems for themselves because of their aggressiveness.

Any speaker must be aware of the potential problem of transmitting information from person to person in chain-link fashion, information overload, and hidden agenda.

SUGGESTED READINGS

John C. Condon, Jr. *Semantics and Communication*, 2nd ed. New York: Macmillan, 1975. This short paperback provides an excellent explanation of semantics.

Jack R. Gibb. "Defensive Communication." *Journal of Communication,* Vol. 2 (September 1961), pp. 141–148. This landmark article provides an excellent analysis of communication climates.

W. Barnett Pearce and Stewart M. Sharp. "Self-disclosing Communication." *Journal of Communication,* Vol. 23 (December 1973), pp. 409–425. Not only does this article present an excellent overview of the subject, but it also contains a good review of the research.

John L. Wallen. "Developing Effective Interpersonal Communication." In R. Wayne Pace, Brent D. Peterson, and Terrence R. Radcliffe (Eds.), *Communicating Interpersonally—A Reader.* Columbus, Ohio: Charles E. Merrill, 1973. This article has a particularly good section on describing feelings.

CHAPTER 6

LISTENING AND RESPONDING

"Ah, Meg—it's so good to have someone to talk with, someone who really understands my problems."

"I know what you mean, Phyllis."

"I'm not sure just what I should do, Meg. Claude came home last night and just looked so tired."

"Tired—I know exactly what you mean. I've been just exhausted lately myself. . . ."

"You see, Claude's been doing Terry's work while Terry's been out sick the last couple of weeks. Now, a couple of days were all right, but a couple of weeks are just too much for Claude to handle. Why, his own job takes as much energy as one man has to spend. . . ."

"But then it's no wonder why I've been exhausted what with walking Sally to kindergarten every morning and getting her at noon, taking Jill to the doctor on the bus after school Monday, Jill and Tom both to crafts class at the Community Center on Tuesday. . . ."

"I think Claude's just going to have to put his foot down. I said to him this morning, 'Claude, talk to Mr. Grooms—tell him you can't take it,' but he just says, 'I can handle it—and Terry would do the same for me.' "

"Now, to top it off, Grandma Schmidt's staying with us for a few weeks while she recovers from her operation. Geez, my whole life is spent waiting on others. . . ."

"I know he wants to help Terry out, but he can only do so much before he's going to go under. . . ."

"Exhausted or not, I have to keep going. Well, have to run, Phyl, the merry-go-round is about to start."

Phyllis thought, "Thank God I have a friend like Meg—someone who really listens to me."

Do you listen carefully to others? Do you respond in ways that will add to the effectiveness of the communication? Do you ever try to check out whether you really understand what another person is saying? Or are your conversations more like the one between Meg and Phyllis?

In conversation people respond to each other in many ways. The kind of response influences the interpersonal relationship of which the conversation is a part. Response choices can heighten or sever the fragile bond of communication.

Responses can be divided into two basic categories: those that are helpful or appropriate and those that are less helpful or inappropriate. Helpful responses are the empathic responses that make communication easier. They confirm people's rights to their thoughts and feelings, and they help to sharpen understanding. Less helpful or inappropriate responses hinder communication. They plant seeds of discontent within people about both themselves and what they are thinking or feeling, and they ignore or scuttle efforts at understanding.

In this chapter we will look at both appropriate and inappropriate responses. But because all response skills begin with and depend on listening, let's begin with that important skill.

IMPROVING YOUR LISTENING

You may already be aware that in our daily communication we spend far more time listening than we do speaking, reading, or writing. Yet, of all our skills, we are most complacent about our listening. We think that if our ears are normal we can hear everything that goes on around us. This line of thinking is good as far as it goes, but listening and hearing are not the same. *Hearing* means registering the sound vibrations; *listening* means making sense out of what we hear. Research studies have shown that most of us listen with only 25 to 50 percent efficiency—that means that 50 to 75 percent of what we hear is never processed.

In this analysis of listening, let us first consider those listening factors that are a function of your heredity and of your environment, hearing acuity, vocabulary, and ear for language.

Some people have real hearing problems. Although accurate data are difficult to come by, authoritative estimates indicate that as many as 10 percent of any adult audience have some hearing difficulty. If you know you have a hearing problem, you may now wear a hearing aid or you may have learned to adapt to the problem; but if you are not aware of the problem, poor hearing alone may limit your listening effectiveness. If you suspect that you may have a hearing problem, your school probably has facilities for testing your hearing. The test is painless and is usually provided at minimal if any cost.

Listener vocabulary is a second element of effective listening. If you know the meanings of all or at least most of the words you receive, you will understand what is said and will have a good chance to retain much of what you hear. If many of the words you hear are meaningless to you, your listening is bound to be affected. Many poor students have average or better intelligence but are handicapped by poor vocabulary. If you have a below-average vocabulary, you must work that much harder to develop listening skills—or work to improve your vocabulary. One way to help yourself is to ask what a word means when you don't know the meaning. So many people pretend they know the meaning of a word because they feel foolish asking. I know, sometimes it is very difficult to call attention to your ignorance, but isn't it far more detrimental to you in the long run to try to act on information or respond to a person when you didn't understand? Listening and vocabulary are definitely related; don't let your listening suffer because you are afraid to ask what a word means.

A third element of effective listening is an ear for language—specifically, good usage, effective word selection, and good sentence structure. If you come from a family in which conversation about ideas is a part of family life, there is a good chance that you have a natural "ear for language." The people around you have provided models that you have learned from. If you have not developed an ear for language at home, then your ear may not be attuned to the difficult kinds of listening you may encounter at school.

You may have some listening problems, but you can improve your listening ability. The following suggestions can be put into practice if you are willing to concentrate and practice.

1. *Get ready to listen.* Listening efficiency increases when the listener follows the apparently elementary practice of really being ready to listen. "Getting ready" involves both mental and physical attitudes. Mentally you need to stop thinking about any of the thousands of miscellaneous thoughts that constantly pass through your mind; all your attention should be directed to the speaker and to what he is saying. Daydreaming, or wool gathering as it is sometimes called, is one of the leading causes of poor listening. Physically, you need to assume a posture that keeps you alert. Since physical alertness encourages mental alertness, you may find it helpful to look the speaker in the eye as he talks or to sit upright in your chair.

2. *Make the shift from speaker to listener a complete one.* In a classroom in which you are planning to be a listener, it is relatively easy to get ready to listen. In conversation, however, you may switch roles from speaker to listener and back to speaker again quite frequently. If as a listener, you spend your

time preparing your next speech (that is, how you are going to say something clever or try to recall something you can use to make your point), your listening efficiency will nose dive. We have all been in or at least witnessed situations in which two persons—like Phyllis and Meg in our opening story—talked right past each other under the guise of "holding a conversation." In real life, the results of such "communication" are often pathetic; in comedy routines, such situations are often hilarious. The next time you are conversing, double check what you are doing: Are you "preparing speeches" instead of listening? Although making the shift from speaker to listener may be the most difficult suggestion to put into practice consistently, it is especially important.

3. *Listen actively.* Because you are likely to think faster than you can talk, you can use your thinking capacities to make you a better listener. As noted in points 1 and 2, if you let your mind wander or if you prepare speeches while you are supposed to be listening, your efficiency will go down. On the other hand, if you use your time to raise questions about the nature of the material—both the content and the intent; if you try to couple what the speaker is saying with your own experience; if you mentally repeat key ideas or associate key points with related ideas, you may be able to raise your listening efficiency. Too often we think of the listening experience as a passive activity in which we act as a sponge soaking up what is coming to us. In reality, good listening is hard work that requires concentration and a willingness to mull over what is said. If you have really listened for a class period, you may actually feel tired—that's good; it shows you have been working.

4. *Withhold evaluation.* Are there any words or ideas that serve as red flags while you are listening? Do you ever find yourself turning off because of your emotional response to what is being said? Often poor listeners are given an emotional jolt by a speaker invading an area of personal sensitivity. When a person trips the switch to your emotional reaction, let a warning light go on before you go off. Instead of quitting or getting ready to fight, work that much harder at being objective. Good listening depends upon comprehension of what is being said. Withhold your evaluation of the message until you have mastered the content and the intent.

EXERCISE

1. Now let's put our listening skills to the test. Ask someone to read the following news item to you once, at a normal rate of speech. Then give yourself the test that follows. Although the temptation is great to *read this news item to yourself*—try not to—you will miss both the fun and the value of the exercise if you do.

   A 23-year-old Stafford woman remained in serious condition at the St. Eli Hospital after she was shot in the chest at the Black Watch Motorcycle Clubhouse, 2726 Main St., Stafford, early Saturday.
      Police said Miss Olga White, 23, 621 Crescent Ave., Stafford, was shot once in the chest.

Inside the clubhouse at the time of the shooting, officers said, were: Gill Bower, 20, Bishopville; Ron Lister, 23, Stafford; L. W. McShane, 25, Bishopville; and Timothy Berton, 23, 414 Ottawa St., Elmira.

The four witnesses told police they were all seated at a table. Miss White was sitting on a bar stool playing a pinball machine, the four said, when they heard what sounded like a "cap gun."

The door of the clubhouse "splintered," witnesses said, and Miss White fell to the floor saying she was shot.

Berton, who police said was Miss White's boyfriend, said he checked the outside of the building but saw only "a car with lights on top going north" on Main.

Miss White was rushed to St. Eli Hospital by the Stafford lifesquad. She was placed in the hospital intensive care unit.

Five holes made by bullets fired from the outside were found in the clubhouse door, investigating officers said. A 38-caliber slug was also found inside the building, officers said.

Answer the following questions either T for True, F for False, or ? for not stated in the story.

1. _____ Miss White was shot five times in the chest.

2. _____ The Black Watch Motorcycle Club is in Stafford.

3. _____ There were five men in the clubhouse with her at the time of the shooting.

4. _____ Two men and a woman were standing outside at the time of the shooting.

5. _____ Miss White was sitting on a bar stool playing table shuffle-board at the time of the shooting.

6. _____ Miss White was killed instantly.

7. _____ Two of the men were from Bishopville.

8. _____ The witnesses said they heard what sounded like a "cap gun."

9. _____ Miss White said she was shot as she fell to the floor.

10. _____ Miss White's boyfriend could not be found.

11. _____ One of the men said he saw a car with lights on top of it going north on Main.

12. _____ The investigating officer was named Shane.

13. _____ The clubhouse door had five holes in it.

14. _____ A .45 caliber slug was also found inside the building.

15. _____ Miss White was dead on arrival.

Answers
(1—F) (2—T) (3—F) (4—?) (5—F) (6—F) (7—T) (8—T) (9—T) (10—F) (11—T) (12—?) (13—T) (14—F) (15—F)

2.   How did you do on the test? If you need to work on this skill, why not write a "listening contract" to focus your work. See Appendix C for directions.

RESPONDING APPROPRIATELY

Conversations involve a give and take on the part of the people involved; effective communication requires that this give and take contain empathy. If the participants in a conversation truly empathize with each other, their responses are likely to be appropriate.

Empathizing is being able to detect and identify the emotional state of the other person. Thus when you empathize with another person you understand another person's feelings as a result of your own experience in a similar situation or your fantasized reaction to that situation. For example, when Agnes talks with Glenna, Agnes is conscious of the cues that her gestures, movements, and posture may be giving; Agnes also hears the words Glenna speaks, hears the changes in vocal quality and pitch, and detects the presence or absence of interferences in her speech. From all of these cues, Agnes not only perceives what Glenna is saying but feels and understands Glenna's total meaning. If Glenna says, "And out of the blue he slapped me—for no reason!" from both the words and the nonverbal cues Glenna gives, Agnes is able to feel what the unexpected slap would be like—Agnes would be empathizing. Agnes might respond to Glenna in any number of ways. Her empathy with Glenna would provide the framework for an appropriate response that reflected her empathy.

EMPATHIZING IS BEING ABLE TO
DETECT AND IDENTIFY THE EMOTIONAL
STATE OF THE OTHER PERSON.

Let's now look at several appropriate responses. We will focus on questioning, paraphrasing, supporting, interpreting, and giving helpful feedback.

Questioning

Many times how appropriately you can respond depends upon your getting enough information from the other person. For any number of reasons a person may not have given you enough information in a conversation to work with. Under these circumstances the most appropriate response would be a question asking for additional information.

Although you have been asking questions ever since you learned to talk, you may occasionally find that a question irritates or flusters the other person. Such reactions are usually a result of poorly phrased questions. Let's first look at the most important goals of questioning; then we will discuss appropriate phrasing.

Questions are often used to get more details:

Ann: I'm going to need some more paper.

Nell: Will a pad be enough, or will you need a whole ream?

Fred: Morgan hit us with another paper.

Sam: Will it have to be as long as the last one?

Questions are used to clarify the use of a term:

Martha: He's just so sanctimonious.

Adelle: What do you mean by 'sanctimonious'?

Phil: Parker's actions have been irresponsible!

Bob: What has he done that would be called 'irresponsible'?

Questions are frequently used to elicit a person's feelings about an issue:

Cal: What a day—to top it off it snowed three more inches.

Pete: Does the new accumulation of snow bother you?

Norm: Billy called, but he's not coming over.

Kay: Are you disappointed that he is not coming?

For questioning to succeed as an appropriate response, it must be perceived as an honest effort to discover information that will aid the questioner in helping with the particular problem. If the person perceives the questions as actual or veiled attacks, the questioning will be construed in a negative way. For instance, if in reply to Fred's statement, "Morgan hit us with another paper," Sam had replied, "Well, you've got to expect some work—it is a college course, you know!" Fred might very well perceive the statement as an attack on Fred's attitude toward college, resulting in conflict rather than discussion.

When you believe you really need additional information to be helpful in reply, then ask a question. Determine specifically what kind of information you need and then phrase a question that will get that information without making the sender defensive. Ask your question in a sincere tone of voice—not one that could be interpreted as sarcastic, cutting, or evaluative. Questioning should come out of a spirit of inquiry and support and not from a real or an apparent need to make the person look bad.

Paraphrasing

Paraphrasing means restating the message you heard *in your own words*. Paraphrasing is the response that is most appropriate when you think you understand what a person means, but (1) you are not absolutely sure or (2) you recognize that clear understanding is very important in that context. Some of our most serious communication problems arise when we are "sure" we understand. Because the likelihood for misunderstanding is so great, the paraphrase should be a working part of your communication repertoire.

When we say that paraphrasing is restating the message you hear in your own words, we do not just mean repeating words:

Charley: I'm really going to study this time.

George: You're really going to study this time.

Repetition shows that George heard the words. It does not show that George really understands what Charley is saying. To paraphrase a message effectively you should (1) listen carefully to the message, trying to absorb every clue to its meaning and (2) restate the message but this time in your own words. Let's try again on this same one-sentence statement:

Charley: I'm really going to study this time.

George: From the way you're talking I take it that this time you're going to outline each chapter and do all the exercises.

Charley: Well, at least most of the exercises.

George's paraphrase was an attempt to show what the words "really study" mean to him.

Perhaps you're thinking, "If I were in this situation I'd ask Charley the question, 'What do you mean by study?' " And to be sure, a sincere, well-worded question is appropriate when you are looking for additional information. But in this case, most people think they know what "really study" means. At least in our example George thought he did. So George isn't really looking for new information; he's checking to make sure that what he (George) thinks of when he says "really study" is the same as what Charley meant.

When you paraphrase, you may concentrate either on the content, the substance of the message, or on the speaker's feelings about the message. Either or both are appropriate, depending on the situation. Let's go back to Charley's statement, "I'm really going to study this time," to illustrate. George's statement, "I take it that this time you're going to outline each chapter and do all the exercises," is a paraphrase focusing on content. It shows George's understanding of the substance, the meaning of "really study." Now had George replied "From the way you say that I get the idea you were pretty upset with your grade on the last test," the paraphrase would have focused on Charley's feelings, in this case the perception that Charley was "pretty upset."

This initial example was based upon a one-sentence statement. Although you may well find yourself paraphrasing single sentences, you will probably listen to someone speak several sentences for several minutes before a paraphrase is appropriate. Let's illustrate paraphrasing one more time—this time with a series of sentences that are somewhat more similar to the length of statements you will be working with.

Donna: Five weeks ago I sent the revised manuscript of my novel to the publisher. I was elated with my work because I felt the changes I had made were excellent. You can imagine how I felt when I got it back yesterday with a note from the editor saying he couldn't see that this draft was much different from the first.

Marcia: *(Before continuing the conversation with any of her own thoughts, Marcia wants to make sure that she really understands the substance of Donna's remarks.)* If I have this right, you're saying that the editor who read your revision could see no real differences, yet you think your draft was not only much different but better.

Marcia: *(Or, before continuing the conversation, Marcia could paraphrase with the focus on how she perceives Donna's feelings about what she has just said.)* From the way you talk about the situation I get the idea that you're really disappointed and hurt by the editor's failure to recognize the changes you made.

Usually we don't consciously differentiate between content and feelings paraphrases. The next example represents a combination of content and feelings paraphrase.

> *Marcia:* If I have this right, you're saying that the editor who read your revision could see no real differences, yet you think your draft was not only much different but better. Moreover, I get the feeling that the editor's comments really irk you.

From the examples presented you probably realize that for any statement there are several paraphrases that would be acceptable or appropriate. Now let's see how well you can do. Suppose you were talking with your professor about his summer.

> *Professor Johnson:* I don't know how things went for you, but for me the summer really flew by. And I'm afraid I didn't get nearly as much done as I'd planned, but I guess I'm not surprised. I hardly ever accomplish as much as I plan. Anyway, I'm really looking forward to the new term. I look at it as getting a fresh start.
>
> *You:* (Write a paraphrase here.)

As with most statements people make, Professor Johnson's includes several ideas. Moreover, what he said is only a small part of what he is thinking. In sum, Professor Johnson seems to be both lamenting the fact that the summer went by so quickly and glorying in the fact that a new, potentially exciting term is about to begin. Which is more important to him? There are many acceptable paraphrases. Yours may well have been similar to one of the following:

> I get the feeling that not getting everything done that you intended isn't nearly as important to you as the excitement of starting a new term.

> It sounds like you enjoyed the summer, but that you're really excited about getting back to school.

> If I understand, you're saying that you always expect to get more done during the summer than what you accomplish, but that it doesn't bother you because you're always so excited about starting a new term.

You may be thinking that if people stated their ideas and feelings accurately in the first place, you would not have to paraphrase. Well, accurate phrasing might help you paraphrase better, but I hope that our previous study of perception and language showed you that one person can seldom be sure that he or she has a perfectly accurate understanding of what another person says. So, as a student of communication you must perfect the art of paraphrasing. Perhaps of equal importance to how well you can accomplish this art is the understanding of when you should put the art into practice. Before you state your own ideas or feelings you should paraphrase the ideas or feelings of the other person when

1. You think you understand what a person has said or how a person feels about what was said, but you're not absolutely sure, or

2. Better understanding of a message is necessary before you can continue intelligently, or

3. You perceive that what the person has said is controversial or was said under some emotional strain, or

4. You are inclined to have some strong reaction to what the person has said or how the person has said it—and your strong reaction might interfere with your interpretation of the message.

What paraphrasing is and when paraphrasing is appropriate are easily stated. The test is whether you can paraphrase well on the spur of the moment.

Supporting

How you respond will have great effect on the outcome of a conversation. Your responsibility to make an appropriate response may be most difficult in situations of high emotion or stress. An especially valuable type of response is the supportive statement. Being supportive is saying something that soothes, reduces tension, or acknowledges the right of the person to describe or express a feeling. A supportive statement is a major empathic response; it shows that you can empathize with a person's feelings.

In a conversation a person may show positive emotions (joy, elation, pride, satisfaction) or negative emotions (sadness, anger, sorrow, disappointment). Moreover, the feeling may be so intense that it almost short-circuits the thinking process, or it may be mild. Whatever the direction or intensity of the feeling, the supportive statement shows (1) that you care about the person and what happens to him or her; (2) that you can empathize with that feeling, and (3) that you acknowledge the person's right to that feeling—whether a person "should" be having the feeling is not of concern.

If the feeling is positive, a supportive statement is your attempt to share in the feeling and help sustain it. People like to treasure their good feelings; they don't want them dashed by inappropriate or insensitive words. If the feeling is negative, the supportive statement is your attempt to help the person work through the feeling without intensifying it or in some other way becoming more uncomfortable or unhappy. When a person's feeling is highly negative, it may take that person a few seconds, a few minutes, or even a few hours to calm down and think rationally. When a person expresses a highly negative emotion, you want to say something that will help defuse the emotion so the person can begin to return to normal.

Let's look at some examples and see why the responses would be perceived as supportive.

Julia: *(hangs up the telephone and turns to Gloria)* That was Paul. He asked me to go to the Homecoming Dance. I thought he never even noticed me.

Gloria: Julia, I'm so happy for you. You really seem excited.

Gloria perceives that Julia is very happy with the news. The statement, "You really seem excited," shows that Gloria recognizes Julia's feeling; her statement, "I'm so happy for you," goes on to show that Gloria *cares* about what happens to Julia. Let's turn this example around and make it deal with negative, rather than positive feelings.

Julia: *(hangs up the phone in tears)* That was Paul—he called to break our date, but he wouldn't even tell me why!

Gloria: Oh Julia—that hurts. Anything I can do for you?

Gloria, empathizing with Julia, perceives the blow to Julia's pride. The statement, "Oh Julia—that hurts," verbalizes her recognition of the feeling; the statement, "Anything I can do for you?" indicates that Gloria cares about what happens to Julia and is ready to do something to help her through this moment of disbelief.

Since negative feelings and negative situations are the most difficult to handle, let's look at a few more examples that deal with negative situations.

Jan: *(comes out the door of her history class clutching the paper she had been so sure she would receive a B or an A on)* He gave me a D on the paper. I worked my tail off, did everything he asked, and he gave me a D.

Lois: A D! As hard as you worked I can see why you're so upset. That's a real blow. Is there anything I can do for you?

Lois's response is primarily an empathizing statement. It shows an understanding of why Jan is so upset. Lois's saying "That's a real blow" further shows that she is in tune with Jan's feelings. Perhaps at this point you might be inclined to say, "Jan, I can see why you feel so bad. You deserved an A!" Although such a statement would have supportive qualities, Lois is in no position to judge whether the paper did in fact *deserve* an A. The support comes with Lois showing an understanding of how hard Jan worked and therefore why Jan feels especially bad. You need to be very careful about making statements that either aren't true or that only tell people what they want to hear.

Here's another example:

Alex: (*hits his forehead with his hand*) I forgot all about the two o'clock meeting! Tony's going to kill me.

Hank: Oh boy—I can see why you feel bad. It can really be upsetting when something important slips your mind. Anything I can do to help you work it out with Tony?

Notice that Hank is not blaming Alex; he is being supportive of the bad feeling that results from forgetting something important. The "Anything I can do to help?" statement can be especially useful if you really mean it. In this case, Alex might feel better explaining he forgot if Hank accompanies him.

Sometimes there's virtually nothing you can say. At these times perhaps the very best way of showing your support is just being there and listening. Consider this one:

Nancy: (*With a few seconds left in the basketball game and her team trailing by one point, Nancy steals the ball from her opponent, dribbles down the court for an uncontested layup, and misses. The gun sounds ending the game. Nancy runs to her coach with tears in her eyes.*) I blew it! I lost us the game!

A first reaction might be to say "Don't feel bad, Nancy." But Nancy obviously does feel bad, and she has a right to those feelings. Another response might be "It's OK, Nancy, you didn't lose us the game." But at that moment Nancy's miss did affect the outcome of the game. Perhaps the best thing the coach can do at that moment is to put her arm around Nancy to show that she understands. Perhaps she could say, "Nancy, I know you feel bad—but without your steal we wouldn't even have had a chance to win." Still, for the moment Nancy is going to be difficult to console.

Making supportive statements is not always easy. Instead, you may be tempted to give advice. But if you remember that your goal is to soothe, reduce tension, and acknowledge the feeling, you'll probably do a reasonably good job.

Interpreting

Many times a person will say something that shows a very limited view of a given event. An important but infrequently used response skill is the *interpretation*, the attempt to point out an alternative or hidden view of an event. Many times an interpretation will be applied to what are excessively negative views. Consider the following situation:

George: (*After returning from his first date with Natalie, a woman George thinks he might become very fond of, George is very concerned. He had an excellent time, yet the end of the evening was very disappointing.*) I take her to dinner and a great show, and when I get to her door she gives me a quick little kiss, says "Thanks a lot," and rushes into the house.

George is interpreting Natalie's behavior negatively. He sees her action as a rejection of him as a person. Martin does not know what Natalie thinks, but he sees George as taking a very limited view of the events.

Martin: I wonder whether she might not have been afraid that if she said any more you'd get the wrong idea about what kind of girl she is?

Whose interpretation is correct? We don't know. But neither does George! What we do know is that behavior can frequently be interpreted in more than one way. Too often, especially when we feel slighted, angry, or hurt, we interpret events negatively. Listen carefully to what a person is saying. If there are other ways to look at the event present those potential interpretations. And, when appropriate, preface the interpretive statement with a supportive one. During this procedure, recognize that you are not a mind reader—you cannot know for sure why something was done or said. Your goal is to help a person look at an event from different views.

The following are two additional examples to show how interpreting can work:

Polly: I just don't understand Bill. I say we've got to start saving money, and he just gets angry with me.

Angie: I can understand why his behavior would concern you (*a supportive statement prefacing an interpretation*). Perhaps he feels guilty about not saving money or feels that you are putting him down.

Glen: I just don't seem to understand Professor Aldrich. She says my writing is really creative, but she never gives me an A.

Sid: I can see why you'd be frustrated with her behavior, but perhaps she is trying to motivate you to do even better.

EXERCISE _____

1. Read the following situation and proceed as instructed:

> Martin is leaving Professor Hartley's office where he had just learned that he did not get the position as student assistant in Hartley's large lecture class. Although Martin knew several others had applied, he is very disappointed. Judy, a close friend, is waiting for him as he comes out of the office. Upon seeing her, a look of dejection comes into his eyes and in a trembling voice, Martin says, "I didn't get the job—I've got the highest point average of the bunch, but I didn't get the job."

Judy might make any of several appropriate responses. Label the following four as A, paraphrase; B, supportive; C, questioning; or D, interpretive.

1. __C__ Did he tell you why he was giving the job to someone else? Did he give you any explanation?

2. __D__ Not getting the job is disappointing, but maybe you'll have more time to work on that grant proposal.

3. __B__ I perceive you're really hurt by Hartley's decision.

4. __D__ I can understand your disappointment—you were really sure you would get it.

2. Read each of the following situations. Supply responses that are P, paraphrase (either content or feelings or combined); Q, questioning; S, supportive; and I, interpretive (where indicated).

> I just got a letter from Ann. I never thought she'd write! I've sent her I don't know how many letters.
> P:
> Q:
> S:

> Darn it. My favorite sweater has a hole in it! George bought it for me when we first started dating. I'll bet I wore that thing three times a week for a while.
> P:
> Q:
> S:

> The pie is all gone! I know there were at least two pieces left just a while ago. Kids! They can be so inconsiderate.
> P:
> Q:
> S:
> I:

> I just got a call from my folks. My sister was in a car accident. They say she's OK, but the car was totalled. Apparently she had her seat belt fastened when it happened. But I don't know whether she's really all right or whether they just don't want me to worry.

P:
Q:
S:
I:

My boss was really on me today. I worked hard all day, but things just didn't jell for me. I don't know—maybe I've been spending too much time on some of the accounts.

P:
Q:
S:
I:

Giving Feedback

So far the skills that we have considered are direct responses to statements. Personal feedback may relate to or be based upon what a person has said, but mostly it refers to providing a person with new information or new impressions about him or herself. Personal feedback takes three forms: (1) describing behavior, (2) praise, and (3) criticism.

Describing behavior means accurately recounting specific observable behavior without labeling the behavior good or bad, right or wrong. The most difficult part of describing behavior is avoiding the tendency to put the descriptive in evaluative terms. Beth and Ann are talking. Beth is telling Ann about her experience of buying a new coat. In the middle of her story, Ann interrupts to tell Beth about a similar experience when Ann bought a suit. Beth, annoyed, says: "Why are you so rude, Ann?" Such a statement does not describe the behavior, it evaluates it. Beth would be describing Ann's behavior if she said, "Ann, were you aware that you started telling your experience before I had a chance to finish my story?"

As a method of personal feedback, evaluation has two weaknesses: First, evaluation does not inform. When Beth says, "Why are you so rude!" she is not providing the basis for the evaluation. Anne does not know what she has done that brings about the reaction. Second, evaluation is likely to trigger a counter evaluation that will change the subject and probably destroy the positive communication climate. When Beth says, "Why are you so rude!" Ann is likely to feel attacked. To protect herself Ann may lash out at Beth with: "Who do you think you are calling me rude? I'm not the one who borrows things without asking." Suddenly Ann and Beth are off arguing about a new subject.

On the other hand, if Beth were to say: "Ann, were you aware that you started telling your experience before I had a chance to finish my story?" Ann might reply, "Well I wouldn't have to interrupt if you weren't so long-winded." But since Beth's statement was a description, Ann is not likely to take it as an evaluation.

The following are three more examples of describing behavior as personal feedback:

Jack: Bill, you smile when your other behavior seems to be saying that you are angry.

Wendy: Jed, when you criticize, your voice has a very sharp tone.

Andy: Mark, whenever Alice joins the group you are all smiles.

Nonevaluative description is probably the best form for personal feedback.

Praise is a positive reaction to what a person has said or done. Everyone needs to feel successful at something. When you observe that a person has done something quite well or when you hear a person say something in a particularly good way, you should feel free to tell that person about it.

Sally: Gwenn, that ball was right into the corner. You've got a very good backhand.

Jim: Gail, I really like the way you sing that song. You make the words meaningful to me.

Drew: Guy, that was nice of you to share your lunch with Pete. You're a very warmhearted person.

Criticism is evaluation of behavior, and more often than not it's negative evaluation. When it comes to personal feedback, or any kind of response for that matter, criticism should be avoided if possible. If a person asks for criticism, then you should proceed by first describing behavior and then evaluating it. For instance:

Agnes: How do you like my new hairdo?

Joyce: They fixed your hair a lot curlier than the way you usually wear it; I prefer it the way you had it before.

Dean: What did you think of my paper?

Rick: There were a great number of typographical errors and several mistakes with grammar. I thought your paper was hurried because it looks rather sloppy.

Whenever you are in a situation where you need to give feedback, the following guidelines should prove helpful.[1]

---

[1]Several of these suggestions were first articulated in the *1968 Summer Reading Book* of the National Training Laboratories Institute for Applied Behavioral Sciences.

1. *Make sure that giving feedback is appropriate in the given interpersonal context.* It is safest to withhold any feedback until it is asked for. Feedback becomes dysfunctional if a person is not interested in hearing it. Even the people who seem willing to listen to any kind of comments may not always be receptive to what you might want to say.

If a person has not asked for feedback, but you feel that some feedback would benefit him, you should be careful about your timing. Look for signs of receptiveness; watch verbal or nonverbal cues indicating that some feedback would be welcomed. If you are not sure, ask. You might say, for example, "Would you like to hear my comments about the way you handled the meeting?" Remember, however, that even if the person says "yes," you must proceed carefully.

2. *Preface a negative statement with a positive one whenever possible.* Feedback need not be negative, although for some reason most people think that it is (as if the only things that they hear about are things that are wrong). When you are planning to criticize, it is a good idea to start with some praise. But use a little common sense. Do not start with some superficial praise and then follow it with crushing criticism, such as: "Betty, that's a pretty blouse you have on, but you did a perfectly miserable job of running the meeting." A better approach would be, "Betty, you did a good job of drawing Sam into the discussion. He usually sits through an entire meeting without saying a word. But you seem hesitant to use the same power to keep the meeting on track. You seem content to let anybody talk about anything, even if it is unrelated to the agenda." The praise here is significant; if you cannot give significant praise, then don't try. Empty comments made just to be "nice" are worthless.

3. *Be as specific as possible.* In the situation just discussed, it would not have been helpful to say, "You had some leadership problems." If the person wasn't in control, say so; if the person failed to get agreement on one item before moving on to another, say so. The more specific the feedback, the more effectively the person will be able to deal with the information.

4. *Feedback should concern recent behavior.* No one is helped much by hearing about something the person did last week or last month. Feedback is best when it is fresh. If you have to spend time recreating a situation and refreshing someone's memory, the feedback probably will be ineffective.

5. *Direct criticism at behavior the person can do something about.* It is pointless to remind someone of a shortcoming over which the person has no control. It may be true that Jack would be a better leader if he had a deeper voice, but telling him so will not improve his leadership skill. Telling him he needs to work on stating summaries or getting agreement on issues is helpful because he can change these behaviors.

6. *Show the person you are criticizing what can be done to improve.* Don't limit your comments to what a person has done wrong. Tell the person how what was done could have been done better. If Gail, the chairperson of a committee, cannot get her members to agree on anything, you might suggest that she try phrasing her remarks to the committee differently; for example, "Gail, when you think discussion is ended, say something like 'It sounds as if we agree that our donation should be made to a single agency. Is that correct?' "

FEEDBACK IS BEST WHEN IT IS FRESH.

EXERCISE _____

1. Think of the times you have given someone feedback. What mistakes, if any, did you make in giving the feedback? If you were to do it again, how would you proceed differently?

2. You have a close friend who has an irritating habit that bothers you and other people as well (biting fingernails, saying "you know" several times a minute, talking very loudly). Work out an appropriate phrasing of feedback.

RESPONDING INAPPROPRIATELY

During these last several pages we have looked at appropriate responses that facilitate good interpersonal communication. Inappropriate responses are just the opposite: they increase chances for defensive reaction; they disconfirm a person; and they fail to further the flow of interaction.

A response that increases the chances for defensive reaction is one that threatens a person. It causes that person to feel a need to protect himself or herself from an apparent attack.

A disconfirming response is one that causes a person to question her or his self-worth; it undermines a person's self-concept.

Responses that fail to further the flow of interaction are dysfunctional.

Let's look quickly at some common responses that are inappropriate because they are likely to arouse defensiveness, because they disconfirm, or because they are dysfunctional.

Irrelevant Response

An *irrelevant response* is one that bears no relationship to what has been said—in effect it ignores the sender entirely.

> *Bob:* Carson seems to know his economics, but I just can't seem to understand his explanations.
>
> *Tom:* Did you see the new wheels Barry got?

When the sender is totally ignored it not only causes him to question whether he was heard, but it may well cause him to wonder about the worth of what he was thinking or saying—for anything important will not be ignored.

Interrupting Response

When the receiver breaks in before the sender has finished, the response is interrupting.

> *Bob:* Carson seems to know his economics, but . . .
>
> *Tom:* I know, Carson is quite a character. I remember once . . .

People are inclined to interrupt when they believe they know what the sender is going to say, when they believe their own thoughts are more important, or when they are just not paying careful attention. Any of these reasons shows a lack of sensitivity to the sender. As human beings we need to be able to verbalize our ideas and feelings regardless of whether they are already known or not. Constant interruptions are bound either to damage the sender's self-concept or to make him or her hostile—or possibly both. Whatever you have to say is seldom so important that it requires you to interrupt the sender. When you do interrupt, you should realize that you are building a barrier. The more frequent the interruptions, the greater the barrier will become.

Tangential Response

A *tangential response* is really an irrelevant response in tactful language. At least the receiver acknowledges hearing the sender's statement; but the net result, changing the subject, is essentially the same.

> *Bob:*   Carson seems to know his economics, but I just can't seem to understand his explanations.
>
> *Tom:*   Well, you know Carson. Did you see the new wheels Barry got?

Even though Bob's statement has been acknowledged, Tom appears to be saying that the issue is not important enough to deal with. Again, such responses chip away at the sender's feelings of self-worth. Bob was raising an issue that was important to him, but Tom ignores it.

Incongruous Response

In the chapter on nonverbal communication we indicated that communication problems occur when nonverbal messages appear to conflict with the verbal messages. An incongruous response is a manifestation of this kind of conflict.

> *Bob:*   We really covered a lot of ground in class today!
>
> *Tom:*   (*in sarcastic tones*) Yeah, it was a great class.

On the surface Tom seems to be acknowledging and verifying Bob's statement, but his sarcastic tone causes Bob to wonder whether he is confirming Bob's ideas or whether he's making fun of them. Since nonverbal messages generally override verbal meaning, Bob probably will take Tom's words as sarcasm. If they are in fact sarcastic, a barrier begins to be built as a result of Tom's insensitivity to Bob's honest statement of feelings. If Tom's words are sincere, a barrier begins to be built as a result of Bob's confusion about Tom's meaning.

Evaluative Response

Often a person is inclined to reply with a statement that evaluates the sender or the value of his response. When a person evaluates, it changes the original issue. Such a change usually results in a barrier:

> *Bob:*   Carson seems to know his economics, but I just can't seem to understand his explanations.

> *Tom:* Questioning Carson's methods is idiotic. He's regarded as the best economist in the department.

Tom's response is inappropriate because it changes the subject from Bob's understanding to whether Bob makes idiotic statements. The barrier results initially because the statement has an air of irrelevancy to it; but, more important, it is an attack on Bob—an attack that probably will result in defensive behavior.

How can these and other inappropriate responses be avoided? First, you should really listen to the other person. If you spend your time thinking of what you have to say, your response is likely to be inappropriate and you may come up with an irrelevant or an interruptive response. If, on the other hand, you really listen to what is being said, you are more likely to acknowledge and to come to grips with the idea or feeling the sender is describing or expressing. Second, you should be sensitive to the needs of the other person. Start with the assumption that what a person says is important to that person—even if it is not or does not seem to be important to you. Then deal with the idea or feeling at face value. If what the person has said is not, in your opinion, very important (or worth talking about) then the honest response is one that verbalizes your ideas or describes your feelings.

> *Bob:* Carson seems to know his economics, but I just can't seem to understand his explanations.
>
> *Tom:* *(believing the point may be important to Bob but is not important to Tom at this time)* I can see where you would be concerned about not understanding, Bob, but I'm so wrapped up in this report that I really can't take the time to discuss it with you now.

Notice that Tom's response is honest. Bob will at least know why Tom is not continuing discussion on the subject. Bob has the option of letting the topic drop for now or trying to persuade Tom of its importance. At least, however, he has been acknowledged. If a barrer is going to be built, it becomes Bob's responsibility as much as Tom's.

SUMMARY

As a listener you have as much responsibility for the effectiveness of communication as the person who forms the original message. The tools of effective listening are helpful responses.

Any effective response begins with good listening. Your heredity and environment influence how well you listen. Your hearing acuity, vocabulary, and ear for language will determine some of your effectiveness. Nevertheless, there are many behaviors you can put into practice to become a better listener. Some of the more important are (1) get ready to listen, (2) make the shift from speaker to listener a complete one, (3) listen actively, and (4) withhold evaluation.

Appropriate responses are those that make communication easier: They confirm the person's right to his thoughts or feelings, and they help sharpen understanding of meaning. Supporting, questioning, paraphrasing, interpreting, and giving helpful personal feedback are basic listening and responding skills.

Inappropriate responses hinder communication. They plant the seeds of discontent within people about themselves or about what they are thinking or feeling, and they ignore or scuttle efforts at understanding meaning. Interrupting, irrelevant comments, tangential statements, incongruous replies, and unsolicited evaluation are some of the most common types of responses that should be avoided.

SUGGESTED READINGS

George Gazda, et al. *Human Relations Development: A Manual for Educators*, 2nd ed. Boston: Allyn & Bacon, 1977 (paperback). This entire book focuses on developing "helpful response" skills. It provides a good supplement to material in this chapter.

Robert O. Hirsch. *Listening: A Way to Process Information Aurally*. Dubuque, Iowa: Gorsuch Scarisbrick, 1979. This 45-page booklet contains some excellent suggestions and a good bibliography.

R. Wayne Pace, Brent D. Peterson, and Terrence R. Radcliffe (Eds.) *Communicating Interpersonally—A Reader*. Columbus, Ohio: Charles E. Merrill, 1973. See particularly John L. Wallen's article, "Developing Effective Interpersonal Communication," pp. 218–233 for an excellent discussion of response skills.

CHAPTER 7

UNDERSTANDING COMMUNICATION RELATIONSHIPS

As they walked to the door, she turned and said, "Thanks for the ride home."

"Hey, no problem," Paul replied.

"That Disco Haven is something else, isn't it? I could go there every night. And it's great to dance with someone who really knows how—I was impressed!"

"Well, I go for the music—and having a few lessons doesn't hurt. Maybe we could get together again, huh?"

"Sure. I'm at the Haven a couple of times a week."

"OK, I'll look for you. . . . Listen, I've got tickets to the Led Zeppelin concert next Monday. You want to go?"

"You got tickets for Led Zeppelin? I tried to get tickets, but they sold out the first day they went on sale! I guess I'll go with you."

"Great! I'll pick you up Monday about 7:30?"

"I'll be ready."

"Then it's on," Paul said as he gave her a quick kiss. As she turned and went into the house, Paul danced down the stairs, jumped into the car, and roared up the street. "Look out," he shouted, "I'm in love! . . . Oh, nuts!" he said as he slapped his hands on the steering wheel, "I forgot to ask her name!"

Although we may not fall madly in love with everyone we meet, most of us are excited about discovering people we have a lot in common with. One of the major goals of personal communication is to develop satisfactory ongoing relationships with others.

In a relationship, the members are interdependent with one another. The thoughts and actions of one person affect the thoughts and actions of the other. How do you know when you have a good communication relationship with another? How can you predict the likelihood or endurance of a relationship? What causes you to relate so well to some people and so poorly to others? Although there are no pat answers to these questions, a number of theories provide explanations for these questions. Each theory may shed enough light on some aspect of communication to give you insight into your own communication and your relationships with others.

In this chapter we will look at the nature of a good relationship; then we will consider three theories that help to explain why people form and dissolve relationships. We will consider a means of comparing perceptions of the depth of a relationship through a self-disclosure–feedback ratio, and finally, we will look at means of managing conflict within a relationship.

THE NATURE OF RELATIONSHIPS

A good relationship is any mutually satisfying interaction—on any level—with another person. Perhaps the first thing you need to understand is that interpersonally appropriate behavior depends on the kind of relationship.

Acquaintance Relationships

Acquaintance relationships are those we have with people we know by name and talk with when the opportunity arises but with whom our ties are rather loose. We become acquainted with those who live in our apartment house or dorm or in the house next door, who sit next to us in a class, who go to our church or belong to our club. Acquaintance relationships are likely to be a product of a given context. While Ruth and Ann are in biology class they are friendly, but they make no effort to see each other outside of class, and if they meet it is by chance. Each of us has a nearly infinite number of acquaintances.

Role Relationships

Role relationships are those that are a product of a specific context. You have a role relationship with your parents, your siblings, your children, your coworkers, your doctor, and so forth. Within these role relationships the participants have a great deal of leeway in determining the depth and character of the relationship, but the relationship itself will last so long as they are cast in their roles. With relatives, for example, the role relationships last a lifetime. With coworkers the role relationships last as long as you and the others are employed in the same positions. Criteria for a good relationship vary from role to role: A good working relationship with your boss is much different from a good family relationship with your brother or sister.

Friend Relationships

Friend relationships are those we have with people we want for company. Friends are people we like and who like us; friends seek each other out because they enjoy one another's company. Friendships may be initiated with acquaintances or out of a specific context. People then *become* friends as a result of a shared interest in a specific activity, a mutual attraction, or for some other reason. However they begin, friend relationships are those in which people find satisfaction with each other on many levels. Friends act reciprocally to meet each other's needs. The level of trust between friends is quite high. Friends spend time together because they want to.

Intimate Relationships

Deep friendships or intimate relationships are those we have with that small number of people with whom we choose to share our deepest feelings. A person may have countless acquaintances and many friends but is likely to have only one or a very few truly intimate relationships. In male-female relationships intimacy is likely to include sex. However, a person can be intimate with a member of the same sex or with a relative without having sex. Intimacy implies a deep feeling for another person. Intimates are those we seek out when both something especially good or especially terrible has happened to us. Intimates are often those with whom people choose to spend the most important moments of their lives.

LEVELS OF COMMUNICATION

Just as our relationships can be categorized, so can the communication within the relationships. Let's look at the levels of communication and the circumstances under which they are appropriate. Communication relationships fall into the categories of phatic level, gossip level, idea-exchange level, and sharing-feelings level.

Phatic Level

Phatic level communication represents the lowest level of involvement with another person. On the phatic level you acknowledge or recognize another person, and you are willing to verbalize this recognition. Basically, it says to another person: I know you; I leave the door open for more meaningful communication at some other time. It is identified by such comments as "How are you doing?" "What do you say?" and "Great day, huh?" With none of these comments is more than a perfunctory reply expected. If in response to "How you doing?" the person greeted answered the question with a detailed account of his or her current state of health, you would probably think the person was really weird. Phatic communication is not intended for sharing information; it is used to acknowledge recognition. These phatic-level comments serve the important function of meeting certain social expectations.

Gossip Level

Gossip level communication is communication between two people about a third person. It represents a somewhat greater intensity of interaction but still does not require much, if any, information about self. Such statements as "Have you seen Bill lately? I hear he has a really great job"; or "Would you believe that Mary and Tom are getting married?"; or "Irene is really working hard at her new job. She says it takes her at least ten hours a day to get everything done that she wants to" are typical of conversations on the gossip level.

The gossip level is considered a "safe" level of communication, since you can gossip for a long time with another person without really saying anything about yourself and without really learning anything about the other person. Gossip is a pleasant way to pass the time of day with acquaintances and even with some friends. Sometimes gossip is malicious; more often than not, however, gossip is a pastime—a way of interacting amicably with others without getting involved personally. A cocktail party provides numerous examples of gossip-level communication.

Idea-Exchange Level

Idea-exchange level communication involves sharing facts, opinions, beliefs, and values. Although this level may be experienced with acquaintances, it is more likely to take place among people in role relationships and with friends. At the office Martha may talk with Hal about sports; Zeb may talk with Ann about gardening; or Pete may talk with Nell about new cars. In more serious circumstances, Bart may talk with Joan about energy, and Agnes may talk with Bill about women's roles. Although the discussions of energy and women's roles may be "deeper" than chatter about sports or cars, both sets of conversations are on the idea-exchange level. On this level you learn what the other person is thinking; through such conversations you can determine what you have in common, if anything, and you can decide whether or not you would like to have the relationship grow.

Most idea-exchange statements are disclosures of the low-to-moderate risk level. You can tell what you think about an idea or an action without revealing very much of the "real you." Many relationships, even some seemingly intimate ones, stay on this level. You may know people who intellectualize about situations without ever revealing how they feel.

Sharing-Feelings Level

Sharing-feelings level communication represents the greatest personal involvement with another person. On the sharing-feelings level, people not only reveal what they are thinking but also how they feel about the ideas, actions, and behaviors of themselves and others. As a result, the sharing-feelings level is most likely to be found among close friends and intimates. The describing-feelings skill we discussed earlier represents one end of the sharing-feelings level; what we refer to as having a "heavy discussion" or "really letting loose" represents the other end. Although describing feelings is appropriate even with acquaintances and "distant" friends, sharing our deepest feelings is usually reserved for those with whom we are intimate in ongoing relationships. At the sharing-feelings level, both parties are perfectly free and open in their discussion of feelings with each other.

Some people achieve this level of communication with only one other person at any one time; many are on this level with members of the immediate family as well as with one or a few others; unfortunately, some people seldom if ever achieve this level with anyone. Oh, they may on occasion let another see how they are feeling, but as consistent policy, they try not to. I say "unfortunately" because it is on this level that you come to know and to really understand another person. Although it is unrealistic and may be undesirable to have such a relationship with many others, the presence of a sharing-feelings level of communication with at least some persons is regarded as a highly beneficial interpersonal communication goal.

EXERCISE

1. Of all the persons you know, with what percentage do you relate on the phatic level, gossip level, idea-sharing level, feelings-sharing level?

2. On what basis do you determine on what level you will communicate with another person?

THEORETICAL EXPLANATIONS

Many theories attempt to explain the motivation for moving in and out of relationships. I believe the following three theories are especially useful for giving insights into behavior.

Interpersonal Needs

Whether or not a relationship can be started, built, or maintained may well depend upon how well each person meets the interpersonal needs of the other. William Schutz provides an analysis of needs that is very useful in helping people to determine whether their interpersonal communication is geared to meeting the interpersonal needs of others. Schutz discusses needs for affection, for inclusion, and for control.[1] As you read this analysis you may be able to discover why people form the relationships that they do.

Affection involves the need to express and to receive love. The "personal" individual is one who can express and receive affection naturally. He gets a joy out of his relationships with others. People you know prob-

---

[1]William Schutz, *The Interpersonal Underworld* (Palo Alto, Calif.: Science & Behavior Books, 1966), pp. 18–20.

ably run the gamut of showing and expressing affection. At one end of the spectrum are the "underpersonal" individuals. You have met them: They avoid close ties; they seldom show strong feelings toward others; and they shy away from those who show or who want to show affection. At the other end of the spectrum are the "overpersonal" individuals. You have probably run across them, too: They thrive on establishing "close" relationships with everyone; they think of all others as their close friends; they confide in persons they have met for the first time; and they want all others to think of them as friends.

Inclusion involves the need to be in the company of others. Everyone has some need to be social. Yet again, because we are individuals our inclusion behavior varies widely. At one extreme are the "undersocial" persons who want to be left alone. Although they may occasionally seek company or may enjoy being included with some others if they are specifically invited, being around people is not their normal behavior. Whether they find the company of others threatening, whether they treasure their solitude, or whether they have some other reason, they spend much of their time alone. At the other extreme are the "oversocial" persons who need constant companionship and dislike or even fear being alone. If there is a party, they are there; if there is no party, then they start one. Their doors are always open—everyone is welcome, and they expect others to welcome them. The ideal, of course, is to be comfortable alone or with others. Social persons do not need constant company to feel fulfilled. In effect, their behavior is a cross between the loner and the social butterfly.

Control involves the need to feel that one is a responsible person successfully coming to grips with his environment. Again, how we respond to this need varies somewhere between extremes. At one end are persons who shun responsibility—they do not want to be in charge of anything. The "abdicrats," as they are called by Schutz, are extremely submissive and are afraid to make decisions or accept responsibility. At the other end are persons who like to be—indeed who need to be—in charge. "Autocrats" must dominate others at all times. They usurp responsibility and make every decision. The ideal could be called the "democrats." They are comfortable either leading or following. They can take charge when need be but can follow equally as well. They stand behind their ideas, but they are not reluctant to submit when someone else has a better idea.

On all three of these needs most of us fall somewhere along a continuum rather than at either of the extremes. Through our communication we display where we stand relative to each of these needs. As we interact with others we see whether their affection, inclusion, and control needs seem compatible with ours. As you see your relationships with others forming and breaking apart, you may well see your communication display of these needs determining or at least playing a part in the defining of the relationship.

Cost-Reward Theory

A somewhat different theory for explaining whether you are likely to begin, maintain, or terminate a relationship is offered by John Thibaut and Harold Kelley. They explain social relationships and interaction in terms of rewards received and costs incurred by each member of a relationship or interaction.[2] Rewards are, of course, the benefits received. Some common rewards are good feelings, prestige, economic gain, and fulfillment of emotional needs. Costs are considered in terms of the time, energy, and money spent to accrue the rewards. Whereas a person may be willing to spend a minute of time if she expects to have some good feelings as a result, she may not be willing to spend an hour of time to receive that same amount of good feelings.

According to Thibaut and Kelley, each of us seeks interaction situations in which behaviors will yield us a high reward and low-cost outcome. For example, if Jill runs into Sarah on campus, there are several communication options available to Jill: She can ignore Sarah; she can smile; she can say, "Hi!" in passing; or she can attempt to start up a conversation. What Jill does will depend in part upon her appraisal of the reward-cost outcome of the interaction. For instance, if Jill had been thinking about giving Sarah a call to arrange a game of tennis, she will probably take the time now to attempt to seek that outcome—she will be willing to pay the cost of taking time and using energy in hopes of receiving a suitable reward, a tennis date. If Jill and Sarah do talk, the duration of the interchange will continue until one or both realize that the interaction is falling below the satisfactory level. For Jill this might mean until a tennis game is set. For Sarah this might mean something else. Thibaut and Kelley suggest that the most desirable ratio between cost and reward varies from person to person and within one person from time to time.

If a person's net reward (reward minus cost) is below a comparison level, he will experience an unsatisfactory or unpleasant relationship or interaction; but, if his net reward is higher than the comparison level he sets as satisfactory, he will experience a pleasant and satisfying relationship or interaction. Moreover, if a person has a number of relationships he sees

[2]John W. Thibaut and Harold H. Kelley, *The Social Psychology of Groups* (New York: Wiley, 1959), pp. 100–125.

as giving him a good reward-cost ratio, the comparison level he sets will be high, and he is not likely to be satisfied with low-outcome relationships. Thus if Joan has four or five men she gets along well with, she is not likely to put up with Charley, who irritates her. On the other hand, the person who does not have many positive interactions will be satisfied with relationships and interactions that the person with wider choice would find unattractive. If Joan felt that Charley was the only man who could provide the benefits she sought, she would be inclined to put up with his irritating habits.

While the ratio of outcomes to the comparison level determines how attractive or unattractive a relationship or an interaction might be to a person, it does not determine how long a given relationship or interaction will last. Although it seems logical to leave a relationship or an interaction in which costs exceed rewards, circumstances are sometimes such that a person will stay in a relationship that is plainly unsatisfactory.

The variable that may intervene is what Thibaut and Kelley call the *comparison-level alternative*. They explain that whether a person stays with a particular relationship may depend on what alternatives or other choices he perceives himself to have. Thus durability of a relationship is also dependent upon possible alternatives. If his outcome level drops below the level he can attain elsewhere, the person will leave the relationship or interaction in order to engage in his next-best alternative. If, however, a person is not satisfied with the outcome level, he may continue in the relationship or interaction because no viable alternative exists. The experience, as unsatisfactory as it may seem, is the best he believes he can get *at this time*.

Theories of Balance

A third explanation for change in or maintenance of a relationship is found in balance theories. Perhaps the most widely discussed of these is the one offered by Heider.[3] He says that human beings seek a balance in attitudes and behavior. Psychological consistency, or balance, occurs (1) when there are positive relationships among two people and a topic or (2) when one positive and two negative relationships exist among these three components. Let's cite some examples to show how this balance occurs:

> *Three positive:* Spike likes Susan *(positive)*; Spike likes going to baseball games *(positive)*; and Susan likes going to baseball games *(positive)*.

[3]Fritz Heider, *The Psychology of Interpersonal Relations* (New York: Wiley, 1958), pp. 202 ff.

One positive and two negatives: Spike likes Susan *(positive);* Spike hates cocktail parties *(negative);* Susan hates cocktail parties *(negative).*

or: Spike doesn't like Nick *(negative);* Spike likes subcompact cars *(positive);* Nick doesn't like subcompacts *(negative).*

or: Spike doesn't like Nick *(negative);* Spike dislikes Alice Cooper *(negative);* Nick likes Alice Cooper *(positive).*

Imbalance occurs (1) when three negative relationships are present or (2) when one negative and two positive relationships are present:

Three negative: Spike doesn't like Nick *(negative);* they both dislike living in the dorm *(two negatives).*

Two positive and one negative: Spike likes Susan *(positive);* Spike likes watching football on television *(positive);* Susan dislikes watching football on television *(negative).*

or: Spike likes Susan *(positive);* Spike dislikes live theatre *(negative);* Susan loves the theatre *(positive).*

or: Spike dislikes Nick *(negative);* Spike likes the guys in his chemistry class *(positive);* Nick likes the guys in the same class *(positive).*

The theory is that when a balanced state occurs everything is in order, but when a state of imbalance occurs, a person needs to bring the relationship into balance. At any given time, people in the state of imbalance have three options available to them: They can change their attitude toward the other person, they can change their attitude toward the topic, or they can try to influence others to change their attitude toward the topic. Notice that the third is entirely in the realm of interpersonal communication behavior; the first two, requiring change of attitude, may involve a degree of intrapersonal communication.

The importance of this theory is that it shows the options available even when some elements of a relationship go awry. Rather than experiencing a sense of frustration, you can determine what actions you can take to bring a situation into balance. If for some reason you cannot achieve balance or if you do not wish to make the effort to achieve balance, a relationship may deteriorate. In any case you have some control over the destiny of a relationship.

EXERCISE

1. Consider a person with whom you have a close interpersonal relationship. Analyze it on the basis of (1) meeting interpersonal needs, (2) its costs versus its rewards, and (3) the degree of balance within the relationship.

2. On a 1 to 5 scale (1 low, 5 high) how would you rate yourself on the following?

    A. Need to show affection

    B. Need to receive affection from others

    C. Need to be included with others in bull sessions, informal gatherings, and parties

    D. Willingness to include others in leisure-time activities

    E. Need to be in charge of situations

    F. Willingness to allow others to be in charge of situations

Ask a close friend to rate you on these same six criteria.

THE JOHARI WINDOW

As you examine your relationship with another you may believe that both parties perceive it as being on the sharing-feelings level. If so, that relationship is likely to maintain a mutually satisfying blend of self-disclosure and feedback between the two persons. How can you tell whether you and another are sharing enough to keep the relationship growing? The best method is to discuss it. As the basis for a worthwhile discussion, I suggest the drawing and analysis of Johari windows.

THE JOHARI WINDOW

The Johari window (named after its two originators, Joe Luft and Harry Ingham) is a tool that you can use to examine the relationship between disclosure and feedback. The window is divided into four sections or panes as shown in Figure 7-1.

The first quadrant is called the "open" self pane of the window. The open pane is used to represent everything about a person that is known and freely shared with others. It also shows others' observations of him or his behavior that he is aware of. For instance, most people are willing to discuss where they live, the kinds of cars they drive, the activities they enjoy and countless other items of information. Moreover, most people are aware of certain of their mannerisms that others observe. A person may be well aware that he gets red when he is embarrassed or that he wrinkles his nose when he is not sure of something. If you were preparing a Johari window that represented your relationship with another person, you would include in the open pane all the items of information that you would be free to share with that other person.

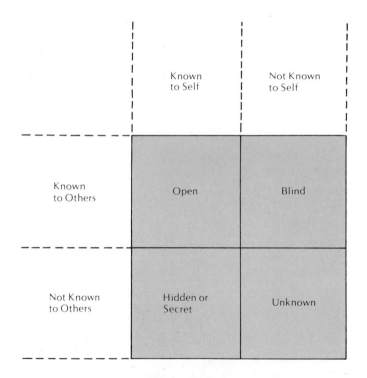

Figure 7-1

The second quadrant of the window is the hidden self or "secret" pane. This pane is used to represent all those things a person knows about himself that he does not normally share with others, for whatever reason. This information may run the gamut from where Tim keeps his pencils or why he does not care for green vegetables to deep secrets that seem very threatening to him. If you were preparing a Johari window that represented your relationship with another person, you would include in the secret pane all the items of information that you are unwilling to share with that other person. Secret information moves into the open part of the window only when you change your attitude about revealing that specific information. If, for example, Angela was engaged at one time but the information is something that she usually does not let people know, it would be in the secret part of her window. If for some reason she decided to disclose this information to you, it would move into the open part of the Johari window that she might draw to represent her relationship with you.

The third quadrant of the window is called the "blind" area. The blind pane is used to represent information others know about a person that he is unaware of. Most people have blind spots—behaviors that are observed by others but for some reason are unknown to the person who does them. If Charley snores when he sleeps, if he always wrinkles up his nose when he does not like something, or if he gets a gleam in his eye when he sees a girl he would like to get to know, these may well be nonverbal behaviors that he is blind to. Information in the blind area of the window moves to the open area through feedback from others. If you were preparing a Johari window that represented your relationship with another person, the size of the blind pane would include your guess as to the amount of information the other person holds about you that either he is reluctant to feed back or that you are unwilling to hear. For instance, if Ken is Charley's roommate at the dorm, he may not tell Charley that he has bad breath. If he does tell Charley directly or indirectly through some nonverbal response, Charley may not choose to "hear" what Ken tells him. In both cases, the blind spot continues. On the other hand, if Charley is receptive to such feedback, the blind pane gets smaller and the open pane enlarges.

The fourth and last quadrant of the window is called the "unknown." It represents aspects of a given person that are not known to anyone—not to the person himself or to others. If, for instance, you have never tried hang-gliding, neither you nor anyone else knows how you might react and behave at point of takeoff—you might chicken out or you might follow through, do it well, and love every minute of flight. Once you had tried, your feelings and abilities would be known by you and probably at least a few others.

Thus as you can see, with each bit of self-disclosure or feedback, the sizes and shapes of the various panes of the window change. For any relationship you have with another person you can construct a window that represents the ratio of openness to closedness. Let us look at four different representations and consider what they mean.

Figure 7-2 shows a relationship in which the open area is very small. The person is not sharing much information about himself and is blind to what the other person knows or thinks about him. This window might represent your relationship with another person during the first stages of getting to know that person; it is also typical of a person who keeps to himself and does not want, desire, or need to interact on more than a superficial level with others.

Figure 7-3 shows a relationship in which a person is willing to share his thoughts and feelings but gets or is receptive to very little feedback from the other person. Such a person may perceive himself to be very open in his communication. Yet his communication is limited by his unwillingness to learn or lack of interest in learning about what others observe.

Figure 7-4 shows a relationship in which a person seeks out and is very receptive to feedback but is quite reluctant to share much of himself. He wants to hear what others have observed, but he is not willing or is afraid to disclose his observations or feelings.

Figure 7-5 shows a relationship in which a person both seeks out and is very receptive to feedback and is willing to share information and feelings he has. This is the kind of window we would expect to see depicting a close relationship of friends or intimates. Even though Figure 7-5 is the best model of communication for friends and intimates, the windows of Figures 7-2, 7-3, and 7-4 depict many of our communication relationships. Although no one need share every idea or feeling with others and no one need be receptive to every person's reaction to him, having a relatively large open pane is conducive to good personal communication.

Figure 7-2

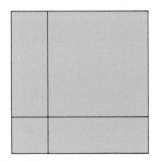

Figure 7-3

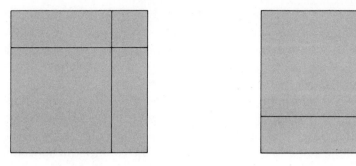

Figure 7-4   Figure 7-5

EXERCISE

Working with an intimate or a close friend, each of you draw a window that represents your perception of your relationship with the other. Then each of you draw a window that represents what you perceive to be the other's relationship with you. Share the windows. How do they compare? If there are differences in the representations, talk with your friend about them.

TENSION IN RELATIONSHIPS—CONFLICT

A certain amount of conflict will occur in any relationship. When there is a clash of attitudes, ideas, behaviors, goals, and needs, tension is created and conflict often results. The key question is not whether conflicts will occur in relationships. The key question is how those conflicts are managed.

Conflicts will range from clashes over ideas ("Charley was the first one to talk." "No it was Mark." or "Your mother is a battle-ax." "What do you mean a 'battle-ax'?"); over values ("Bringing home pencils and pens from work is not stealing." "Of course it is." or "The idea that you have to be married to have sex is completely outdated." "No it isn't."); and perhaps the most difficult to deal with, over ego involvement ("Listen, I've been a football fan for 30 years, I ought to know what good defense is." "Well you may be a fan, but that doesn't make you any expert.").

Dealing with Conflict

Depending on the situation people will deal somewhat differently with each conflict they perceive. Nevertheless, each person usually develops a style that is used with conflict. The following are some of the most common styles:

Withdrawal is a physical or psychological removal from the situation. Although this is a common way of dealing with conflict it is basically negative. Why? Because it does not eliminate the conflict. If Dorie says, "Let's stay home tonight," and Tom replies, "Baloney, you said you'd go to a movie with me," Dorie may withdraw physically by running to the bedroom and slamming the door. Or Dorie may withdraw psychologically by changing the subject and going on as if she never heard what Tom said. In neither case does it resolve the conflict. In the first case Tom may follow Dorie to the bedroom where the conflict will be resumed; if not, the conflict will undoubtedly surface later—probably in an intensified manner—when Dorie and Tom try to cope with another issue. In the second case, Tom may force Dorie to cope with his comment, or he may go along with Dorie's ignoring him but harbor a resentment that will surface later.

There appears to be two cases where withdrawal may work. (1) When a conflict seems likely between people who communicate infrequently withdrawal may be a good solution. Jack and Mark live on different floors of an apartment building. They know each other's first names but don't socialize. For the last two Saturdays Jack and Mark have tried to use the washing machines in the basement at the same time. A potential for conflict exists. The following Saturday when Jack takes his clothes down and finds Mark already there, rather than confronting Mark about dealing with the issue of both wanting or needing to use the washer at the same time, Mark withdraws physically and looks for a different time. (2) When withdrawal can be defined as "disengagement" it may work. Perhaps we could label this "momentary withdrawal," that is, giving a few minutes for temperatures to cool. Bill and Margaret begin to argue over whose responsibility it is to get the car washed. Margaret says, "Hold it a minute. Let me calm down before we discuss this." Margaret goes into the kitchen and makes coffee for the two of them. A few minutes later she returns, temper intact and ready to approach the conflict more objectively. Margaret's action is not true withdrawal; it is not meant as a strategy to avoid confronting the issue. It is a cooling-off period that will probably benefit both of them. Withdrawal is a negative response only when it is a person's major way of managing conflict.

Surrender means giving in immediately to avoid conflict. Some people are so concerned over the potential for conflict that they will do anything to avoid it. For instance, Jeff and Marian are discussing their wedding plans. Jeff says he would like a simple ceremony with just the minister, immediate families, and close friends. When Marian replies, "But Mother and I are already planning a big wedding and reception," Jeff interrupts with "OK, that will be fine." In this example Jeff really wanted a small wedding, but rather than describe his feelings or give reasons for his position, he gives in to avoid conflict.

Surrender is a negative way of dealing with conflict for at least two reasons: (1) Decisions should be made on merits and not to avoid conflict. If one person gives in, there is no testing of the decision—no one knows what would really be best. (2) Surrender can be infuriating to the other person. When Marian tells Jeff of her plans, she would probably like Jeff to see her way as the best. But if Jeff just surrenders, Marian will perceive Jeff not as liking her plan but as martyring himself. His unwillingness to present his reasons could cause even more conflict.

Aggression is the use of physical or psychological coercion to get your way. Through aggression people attempt to force others to accept their ideas. Through aggression a person may "win," but it seldom does anything positive for a relationship.

Aggression is an emotional reaction to conflict. Thought is short-circuited, and the person lashes out physically or verbally. Aggression never deals with the merits of the issue—only who is bigger, can talk louder, or is nastier.

In each of the above reactions, conflict is escalated or obscured. In none is it resolved.

Discussion is a verbal weighing and considering of the pros and cons of the issues in conflict. Discussion is the most desirable means of dealing with conflict in a relationship—it is often difficult to accomplish. It takes cooperation on the part of those involved. It requires an objectivity in the presentation of issues, an openness in stating feelings and beliefs, and an openness to acceptance of the solution that proves to be most logical and in the best interests of those involved.

Discussion follows the problem-solving method: It requires defining the problem, analyzing the problem, suggesting possible solutions, selecting the solution that best fits the analysis, and working to implement that decision. In everyday give-and-take use of the method, all five steps are not always considered completely nor are they necessarily considered in the order given. Its use requires that when two people perceive a conflict emerging, they step back from that conflict and proceed systematically in its resolution. Does it sound ideal? Or impracticable? Well, it is difficult, but when two people have agreed to commit themselves to trying, beneficial results can be achieved. Perhaps most of all, two people who are planning to interact for some extended period need a stated or implied plan for dealing with conflict. We'll see such a plan after we have looked at one more method of dealing with conflict.

Persuasion is the attempt to change either the attitude or the behavior of the other person. Thus at a key point in a conflict, one person can attempt to persuade the other that his or her position is the best.

Persuasion takes a variety of forms. We will study the process of persuasion in detail in the final unit of this textbook, Public Speaking. As far as conflict resolution is concerned, one particular method of persuasion can prove quite valuable; namely, developing good reasons for your position. See particularly pp. 291–293 for guidelines for presenting reasons in support of your position.

Coping with Conflict

Two people who are interested in maintaining a good relationship should be concerned with a plan for dealing with conflict.

1. *Both parties should be consciously aware of when they are in conflict.* Too often people slip into conflicts without even knowing it. When that happens, all too often one or both start engaging in one of the negative means of coping with conflict without even thinking about it. On the other hand, if both parties are aware of a conflict, or if one will say something like "I think we have a conflict here" then they can take steps to put a plan into action.

TWO PEOPLE WHO ARE INTERESTED IN MAINTAINING A GOOD RELATIONSHIP SHOULD BE CONCERNED WITH A PLAN FOR DEALING WITH CONFLICT.

2. *Consciously attempt to discuss the issues involved.* What is at the heart of the conflict? Are you arguing about a fact you could look up? A definition that could be worked on? A value? What? Having once identified the conflict you can go about discussing it rationally.

3. *Look for ways to negotiate.* Negotiation means both parties give up something to gain something in return. Let's say the conflict is over whether to go to a movie or to a concert tonight. If Cal says that he will go to the concert tonight if Susie will go to the movie he wants to see Friday, then the conflict may be resolved. Cal gives up a little tonight, but then Susie has to give up a little Friday.

4. *If negotiation won't work, can someone arbitrate?* Arbitration means finding someone who will make the decision for you. It is important that the arbitrator be a person whose judgment you both trust. The arbitrator also should in some way be competent to make a decision on the issue. Your lawyer may act as arbitrator for you over whether to sue or not to sue over a car accident. Your financial counselor may arbitrate a conflict over whether to invest in a high-risk stock or a high-dividend stock.

Be careful not to ask a close friend or a relative to arbitrate. Not only does this person not have the expertise needed for the particular issue, but more important, a friend or relative is not an independent, impartial agent. Calling on such a person puts him or her in a no-win situation (somebody may well be upset by the decision) or at best makes the person feel very uncomfortable in the role.

5. *If conflict gets out of control, return to basic communication skills.* In recognition of the fact that the best laid plans of mice and men sometimes go astray, we should say something about what happens when conflict gets out of control, when the result is a blow-up from one or both parties, a deep withdrawal, or a loss of all rational capability. Under such circumstances it becomes even more important for participants to use one or more of the three skills essential to good communication.

In the heat of battle, at least one of the people should begin describing feelings. Conflict out of control is most likely to result in a blow-up (perhaps aggression) or withdrawal. As we have pointed out repeatedly, neither is suitable for conflict management. If Sally starts to withdraw, Mike might say, "Sally, I can see that this confrontation is painful for you, but can you understand that when you withdraw it makes me even more angry because I feel frustration; I feel deprived of being able to let you know what is happening to me." Or if Mike starts to shout or in one way or another begins to get aggressive, Sally might say, "Mike, I love you, but when you shout it frightens me, and when I'm frightened I'm most likely to want to withdraw."

Second, at least one of the people involved should paraphrase frequently to help isolate the issues that are being contended. Again, Mike might say, "Sally, I'm getting the idea that the issue is not so much how we spend our money as your feeling that you deserve the right to be in on the decision before it is made. Is that correct?" Or Sally might say, "Mike, I get the feeling that you think it is all right to make decisions unilaterally because you see yourself as the one who makes the money in the first place. Is that correct?"

Third, at least one person should begin to check on perceptions rather than mind-read. Mike might say, "When we get on the subject of budget you start fidgeting in your chair and your voice goes up in pitch. I get the feeling that the subject of the budget makes you very tense. Am I right?" Or Sally might say, "With the subject of money you get a tone in your voice that makes you sound very patronizing. Do you see me as incapable of understanding money matters?"

All three of these skills have the potential of bringing the conflict back to key issues. When well done they also can be used as defusing devices.

ANALYZING YOUR PERSONAL COMMUNICATION

Of all the forms of communication, face-to-face interaction between two or more individuals is the most difficult to analyze and evaluate. Why? Because the greatest amount of our personal communication is in very informal settings with no "audience." Moreover, the flow is quick, speaker and receiver switch roles rapidly, a response may be as short as one or two words, and some or much of the meaning is sent and verified by nonverbal means.

Nevertheless, to say that personal communication is beyond analysis begs the question. Since we become more effective communicators when we see what we are doing and how we are doing it, we need to work out some objective system. In order to make such an analysis then, we need a device that will allow us to view the skills that go together to produce effective communication. To provide a working base for an evaluation instrument, let's take another look at criteria for effectiveness and see how these fit together into a personal analysis profile.

The key to our analysis is determining effectiveness. When is communication effective? Since communication means sharing meaning in the minds of one or more individuals, effectiveness depends upon communicating meaning. If each partner in a conversation really "understands" or "hears" what the other is saying, then communication has taken place. Of course, the analysis of effectiveness, or outcome, is complicated by the importance of the communication, the length of time involved, and the complexity. A one-hour encounter with your boyfriend or girlfriend over an important issue over which you are really at odds requires a considerably higher level of communication skill than a three-minute encounter with an old friend about getting together for lunch. Likewise, the analysis of each encounter would require differing degrees of skill.

All right, let's set forth two sets of questions on which the evaluation instrument will be based:

1. What was the apparent purpose of the encounter? Was it for enjoyment? Fulfilling social expectations? Negotiating with others? Exchanging information? Problem solving? Airing diverse views?

2. How were the elements of communication handled? Did the sender himself or the receiver himself contribute to or detract from the effectiveness? Did the verbal or nonverbal message contribute to or detract from the communication? Were any communication barriers present? Were the barriers reduced or eliminated as the encounter continued? Did barriers interfere with effectiveness?

Before presenting the evaluation instruments themselves, we need to consider who should analyze your personal communication. Because there is seldom a third-party observer present during your conversations, you may have to make the analysis yourself after the fact. Such an analysis is difficult, but it can be done. After an encounter, you have feelings about whether it was satisfactory or not; and it is useful to take the time to "replay" it. You can determine whether your communication is effective and why. Of course, you should be an even more effective critic of encounters you are able to observe.

The first instrument we will consider is a descriptive-analytical, after-the-fact procedure. With this instrument you are focusing on the reasons why communication was or was not successful (Appendix B-2, Personal Communication Analysis—Form A). With this instrument you name the participants, identify the apparent purpose of the encounter, and determine the outcome. Then, after you describe the entire encounter, you conclude by listing and explaining the reasons for the success or failure of the communication.

The second instrument we will consider (Appendix B-3, Personal Communication Analysis—Form B) enables you to evaluate the means. With this instrument you proceed similarly by naming participants, identifying the apparent purpose of the encounter, and determining the outcome. The difference is that this instrument calls for you to replay the confrontation noting the presence or absence of various skills, considering the transactional level, and analyzing barriers.

EXERCISE

Use either Appendix B-2 or Appendix B-3. Analyze a communication encounter of yours. Select one that occurred during the past day or two so that the dialogue is fresh in your mind.

SUMMARY

An effect of, if not the primary reason for, communication is developing relationships. Although at times we seem to fall into and drift out of relationships without rhyme or reason, there are identifiable elements underlying the success or failure of a relationship. A good relationship is any mutually satisfying level of interaction with another person.

People tend to view relationships in the social categories of acquaintances, roles, friends, and deep friends or intimates. Communication in those relationships will occur on the phatic level, the gossip level, the information-exchange level, and the sharing-feelings level.

Many different theories have been set forth to explain how relationships work. Schutz sees relationships in terms of ability to meet the interpersonal needs of affection, inclusion, and control. Thibaut and Kelley see relationships as functions of a cost-reward analysis—the energy, time, and money invested weighed against the satisfaction gained. Heider and others explain the relationship as a function of balance. When imbalance occurs, we either change our attitude or we alter a relationship.

We can test the viability of an intimate relationship through a self-disclosure feedback ratio like the Johari window, enabling us to see whether our perceptions and objective reality coincide.

How a relationship lasts may well be a function of how the participants manage conflict. Interpersonal conflict management depends on the ability of those involved to deal with conflict in a cooperative rather than a competitive way. People have developed their own styles of dealing with conflict. Styles that use withdrawal, surrender, and aggression are basically negative; styles that use discussion and persuasion are basically positive. Conflict management between intimates is best accomplished by following a prearranged plan based on discussion that may well involve negotiation. If negotiation fails, people should have a plan for using arbitration.

SUGGESTED READINGS

George R. Bach and Peter Wyden. *The Intimate Enemy*. New York: Avon, 1970. A readable and useful discussion of conflicts in marriage.

Sidney M. Jourard. *Healthy Personality*. New York: Macmillan, 1974. Although the entire book is worth reading, Chapter 10, "Personal Relations and Healthy Personality," is especially valuable.

Paul Watzlawick, Janet H. Beavin, and Don D. Jackson. *Pragmatics of Human Communication*. New York: W. W. Norton, 1967.

Lawrence S. Wrightsman. *Social Psychology*, 2nd brief ed. Monterey, Calif.: Brooks/Cole, 1977.

PART 3

SMALL-GROUP COMMUNICATION

Ours is a government by committee—small groups of people working together to reach decisions. Indeed, reliance upon the group process as an instrument of decision making extends into nearly every facet of our lives. But as informal conversation moves to the structure of small-group communication, the group itself presents a new set of variables we need to consider.

SITE PLAN

GROUP COMMUNICATION: SELF-ANALYSIS

This second self-analysis considers your behavior in work groups. Work groups are small units whose members interact face to face while working toward a common goal. Group-member roles are characterized by a combination of leadership and participation with each person accomplishing various task and maintenance functions. Task functions are those things that contribute to getting the job done; maintenance functions are those things that help people feel good about what they are doing. The roles that you fulfill may be positive or negative. Positive roles facilitate task or maintenance; negative roles hinder members' work or the group in general.

Most of the personal skills included in the first part of this book are fundamental to effective group work. In this analysis (and in this part of the book) we will focus on those skills that are particularly relevant to group work.

A well functioning group achieves much more and on a much higher level than any individual member of the group could do working on his or her own; on the other hand, a poorly functioning group can result in disaster. Not only is the end product inferior to what a given individual member might have accomplished, but also group members may have bad feelings toward themselves, other members of the group, group leadership, or the group itself.

For each of the statements listed below, encircle the number that best indicates how you see your behavior. The numbers 1, 2, and 3 represent the negative end of the continuum—they suggest a need for work on the item; the numbers 5, 6, and 7 represent the positive end—they suggest a perceived competence with the behavior. The number 4 is the midpoint that represents a position between the extremes. It may also say you are not sure of your behavior.

I believe that participating in groups like committees is a waste of time	1 2 3 4 5 6 7	I enjoy participating in group discussions like committees

I seldom do any research or think very deeply about the problem to be discussed beforehand	1 2 3 4 5 6 7	I prepare well beforehand for group discussions
I tend to contribute in a group discussion only if I am called upon	1 2 3 4 5 6 7	I contribute freely and openly in groups
I am not usually the one who provides key information for the group	1 2 3 4 5 6 7	My contributions are very helpful in the group's effort to accomplish its task
I am not very good at helping develop or maintain a good discussion climate	1 2 3 4 5 6 7	I am good at saying things that help the group work well together
I avoid being in a position to make decisions	1 2 3 4 5 6 7	I enjoy being in a position to make decisions
I prefer to let others lead a group	1 2 3 4 5 6 7	I try to provide leadership for the group
When I am a leader I do not usually prepare a suggested outline for group procedure	1 2 3 4 5 6 7	When I am a leader I provide the members of the group with a carefully thought out suggested procedure
No matter what the group decides to do, I do what I think is right	1 2 3 4 5 6 7	I abide by the group decision even when it is not one I would make on my own

(1) Consider your analysis. Is the number you encircle indicative of where you would like to be in that category? If not, in different colored ink or pencil, encircle the number that represents your goal for this term. (2) If you would like verification of your self-analysis, have a close friend, one parent, and a working acquaintance complete a personal analysis as outlined on pp. 343–346 of Appendix B. (3) Select one of the areas in which your goals are farthest from your current behavior. Write a communication improvement contract similar to the sample contract on pp. 361–363 of Appendix C.

CHAPTER 8

CHARACTERISTICS OF WORK GROUPS

Claude convened the entire family for a Council Meeting. Phyllis, Dottie, Chet, and Paul gathered with him round the dining room table. "Gang," Claude began, "we've always acted democratically when decisions that face all of us have to be made. Now, I know that decision making can be frustrating, but I also know that none of you would willingly give up your democratic right to have a decision made by the entire group; moreover, . . ."

"Dad, I'm doing my homework. I've got a big test tomorrow. Can I be excused?"

"Just a minute, Paul—this is important. Through the years we have developed this family unit with a camaraderie that rivals the cohesiveness of the finest working teams. Why, time after time, we have tried to explore even the smallest of problems to its root to uncover the causes mo-

tivating an action of a specific member of the unit . . ."

"Really, Claude," Phyllis added, "you've picked the darndest time . . ."

"Darndest time! Phyllis—this group has never known the meaning of inconvenience—we've sacrificed ourselves for the good of the group on countless occasions. All I'm asking for is the same kind of careful analysis and consideration of human value that we have exercised since time immemorial . . ."

"OK, Dad—we believe in the family group—now what's the problem?"

"Yeah, Dad," Dottie echoed, "what's the problem?"

Claude looked from Dottie to Chet to Paul to Phyllis. Slowly he asked, "Who gave permission to Mr. Anderson to ride my lawnmower?"

Poor Claude. But really we should be saying poor Phyllis, Dottie, Chet, and Paul. For Claude's display is an example of the worst kind of abuse of the group concept. Because of experiences of this kind, no communication institution has been satirized more than the group. The saying "A camel is a horse designed by a committee" expresses a widely held opinion of group experience. Yet, when we consider our family life, our business or work life, and our social life, we become aware of the tremendous investment of our time in group communication. In each of these settings groups function as decision-making bodies. Since we are not going to change the reliance upon groups as decision makers, we should focus on what we can do to make our group work more profitable.

The greatest criticism of the group process comes from two sources: those who argue that too much group time is wasted on tasks best accomplished by individuals and those who argue that group decisions compromise individual values. Now, let's face it, some kinds of problems *are* best solved by individuals. Usually, if the necessary data are available to an individual who has expertise in an area, the individual will often do a better job of problem solving than a group. If you want to determine the stress that a bridge must bear in order to meet safety requirements, you should ask a structural engineer, not a group. Moreover, an individual can often solve a problem more quickly than a group. If, on the other hand, the question involves judgment as well as the determination of facts, a work group can be more effective than the individual because each person brings to the group a different perspective to help shape and affect the final decision.

As far as compromising basic values is concerned, a group experience should yield the best possible decisions.

"Two heads are better than one" and "The whole is greater than the sum of its parts" summarize the major reasons why work groups are formed. Many problems are too much for one person. Gathering the data alone may require hours of work put in by every member of the group. Moreover, good decision making requires not only objectivity but also vigorous testing at every stage of the decision-making process. A group provides perspective. Because of the stimulation of group effort, the right questions are more likely to be asked. Every solution is given a thorough analysis, and a solution is not selected until it meets the criteria for each person involved. Of course, we are talking about work groups at their best. Since the group is effective only when it exhibits certain characteristics and when its members exhibit certain skills, we need to explore those characteristics and skills. Let's begin by defining the work group.

In our analysis, we are defining a *work group* as a small, cohesive unit, whose members interact face to face, working toward a common goal. To fully understand the implications of this definition and to realize all the characteristics of an effective group, we must examine several interrelated variables: size, cohesiveness, commitment to task, norms, roles, and methods of decision making.

Our goal is not to dictate what should take place in a work group but, rather, to outline what we might term reasonable expectations about group effectiveness. What will or will not happen within a group depends upon the individual members of that group. Our thrust, then, involves analysis of elements of groups for purposes of helping you to make sure that you and the group are doing all within your power to give the group the greatest opportunities for success.

SIZE

An often underestimated characteristic of an effective work group is *size*. Five to eight people may be ideal. Why at least five? Groups with fewer than five members almost universally complain that they are too small. One reason is that in a small group there are not enough people for specialization. To be effective, a group needs certain skills. When the group contains only three or four members, the chances are less that these skills will be present. Moreover, it is hard to generate discussion with only three or four members. If one member does not feel like contributing in a group of three, then you no longer have much of a group.

On the other hand, it has been found that when a group numbers more than eight, reticent members are even less likely to contribute. As the group grows still larger, two, three, or four become the central spokesmen with others playing a more passive part. Once a group gets to twelve, thirteen, or more, it breaks down into subgroups or cliques, destroying both cohesiveness and interaction. Interestingly, sometimes in the spirit of good representation, the organizers of groups may inadvertently make the group so large that it just cannot function—occasionally when the organizers are not really interested in receiving any workable plans this may even be done on purpose.

Even in the ideal group of five to eight, five or seven is better than six or eight. Why? Although taking a vote is not the best way of determining group opinion, when a group finds that it is necessary to resolve an issue upon which it cannot achieve consensus, an even-numbered group often splits evenly and then tends to bog down trying to achieve a majority. So, examine your work group. If it is not functioning well, the reason may be size alone.

EXERCISE

As a basis for completion of all the exercises in this chapter, select for analysis one of the last groups you worked with. Each exercise will call for you to examine that group from a different standpoint. The goal of each exercise will be to increase your awareness of the importance of that variable to group effectiveness.

1. How large was the group? What was the relationship between size and productivity?

2. Alternate exercise: Working with three to six other members of the class, discuss what appears to be an optimum number under differing sets of circumstances. Why are these numbers optimum?

COHESIVENESS

An extremely important characteristic of the effective work group is *cohesiveness*. Remember "The Three Musketeers" who were all for one and one for all? They represent the prototype of a cohesive group. Cohesiveness means sticking together, pulling for each other, being caught up in the "team spirit."

Although the elements of cohesiveness vary, at least three seem particularly important. One of these elements of cohesiveness seems to be *attractiveness of the group;* when the group's goals are particularly appealing to members of the group, they identify with each other. For instance, fraternal groups build cohesiveness out of devotion to brotherhood or service. Another element is *similarity of needs and interests.* A homogeneous group, one in which all members are from the same age group, background, religion, and the like, is likely to achieve cohesiveness more quickly than a heterogeneous group because the members are more likely to identify with each other's needs and interests from the start. Still, a good work group can build cohesiveness by emphasizing similarities in needs and interests. A third element is the *reinforcement of interpersonal needs.* Earlier we identified the three major interpersonal needs as affection, inclusion, and control. Group cohesion seems directly related to belief of individual members that each is included, liked, and respected.

What are some of the things we can look for as hallmarks of cohesiveness? One is the development of *group tradition*. In a cohesive group, common experiences become the subject of group discussion ("Remember the first time we . . . ," "After the meeting we always go together to . . . ," and the like). Another hallmark is the development of *group teamwork*. In a cohesive group all members pull together; any idea is everyone's idea to work with, accept, or reject; no particular or apparent interest is

A HOMOGENEOUS GROUP IS
LIKELY TO ACHIEVE COHESIVENESS
MORE QUICKLY.

shown in who is getting credit—the important thing is getting the job done; and there is an apparent joy of working together.

Of course, cohesiveness is not usually found in the one-meeting group. It is a characteristic of the ongoing group—a characteristic that is generated after initial meetings but is established during or before the group reaches its most productive stages. As an example, I am reminded of a group that was formed as part of a class assignment. For several class periods the individuals acted as would be expected of a "group" that was formed by professorial edict; their attitude was "It's a class assignment so let's go along with it, but let's not take it too seriously." By the third or fourth class meeting, however, this group was acting more vigorously than any of the others. I remember thinking that they were getting into the spirit. About the sixth meeting I happened to go to the local steak house for lunch after class. Much to my surprise, I found the entire group having lunch together. Long after the quarter was over, I ran into one of the members and asked her whether she ever saw any of the others. "Yes," she replied, "we've been getting together for lunch every week or so." This was a case of group cohesiveness surviving long after the original "task" was accomplished. They found they functioned well as a unit, and they had grown to like and respect one another. Now this is not to say they never had disagreements. They did. I remember that some of them occasionally had vociferous arguments in class. One of the positive characteristics of cohesiveness is that it allows the group to handle conflict—in fact, sometimes it even encourages conflict—yet, when the conflict is resolved, the group becomes even stronger.

EXERCISE

Was the last group you worked with a cohesive unit? How can you tell? How did cohesiveness or lack of it affect productivity? Interpersonal relations?

COMMITMENT TO TASK

Another characteristic of an effective group is its *commitment to the task*— its desire to accomplish the goal. A work group is convened as a result of the need to achieve a particular task. Completion of that task is the primary goal that the work group shares, and how effectively the group functions often depends upon the commitment the membership has to that particular task. Sometimes the task is submitted to the group by a person in a superior position or by the parent group that originated the work group. Sometimes the specific task is determined by the work group itself. Whatever the source, in an effective group each member sees the same group goal.

AN EFFECTIVE GROUP IS
COMMITTED TO A COMMON TASK.

One of the first issues that each of us faces upon entering a group is whether we want to belong to that group and work on the task or tasks related to it. Although we are occasionally assigned to a functioning work group without our approval, with most groups we have the option of accepting or rejecting participation, and we should be honest with ourselves and with our superiors when we are asked to participate. Membership in a work group implies commitment, and you should be treated as if you are committed. Sometimes a sense of commitment develops as the group proceeds with its work. But unless at least some sense of commitment is demonstrated by the members, the group will probably have difficulty functioning.

EXERCISE

In the last group you worked with, what sense of commitment did you have to the task? What about the other members? What relationship did commitment have to the productivity of the group?

NORMS

Another characteristic of a work group is establishment of a system of norms. *Norms* are rules of behavior, the do's and don'ts. Norms refer to the "proper" way of acting in a group. They are a set of guidelines that have been accepted formally or informally by the entire group. For some work groups, guides like *Robert's Rules of Order* state group procedures for presenting ideas, modifying ideas, and speaking on those ideas; the rules are formally accepted by the group, and each person has access to the rules and knows what norms are in operation.

Even under a formal set of rules other norms are established informally—that is, they are understood or implied by operating group behavior and group approval of that behavior. A major norm concerns *group demeanor*. Without the subject ever being discussed, one group may proceed informally, use vulgar language, tell obscene stories, and make base references to members' private behavior. Yet, many of the same individuals might belong to another group in which only "proper" language is used and where all business is conducted with utmost propriety. Another area in which norms are clearly seen is in *interaction*. In one group it may be all right to interrupt any speaker at any time; in another, no one may speak until he is recognized. In one group it may be all right for someone to openly express her anger or hostility toward a person or toward an idea; in another group anger and hostility never surface. And finally, in one group member status may determine who speaks first, longest, or most often, while in another group member status may have no effect on interaction. A third area of norm development is *procedure*. In one group it may be accepted that people will come and go as they please; in another group business does not start until everyone is present and the group stops its work when someone has to leave. In one group it may be that members socialize for a few minutes, exchanging greetings or inquiring about family or activities; in another group members may move directly to the task at hand. In one group members may sit in a definite predetermined spatial arrangement; in another group members may sit where they feel most comfortable.

When a new member joins a particular ongoing group (a group that is formed for more than a single meeting), he or she usually adopts the established norms. As the person becomes accepted, the new member may be able to effect some change in the norms of that particular group, but not without group approval. The violator of group norms will usually be punished in some way. Although he is rarely banished, he may be ignored, his ideas may be passed over, or he may be recipient of disapproving expression or speech.

EXERCISE

Try to determine the norms that were operative in your last work group. Had the norms always been the same? Or had they evolved over a period of time? What happened to a person who violated the group norms?

ROLES

A *role* is a pattern of behavior that characterizes an individual's place in a group. In an effective work group, roles are understood by the members. In any group role specialization is inevitable—one or more members will function as task leaders and maintenance leaders. Likewise, the members of the group accept people for the roles they play and agree on the status or importance of each of the roles in helping achieve the goal.

When we enter a work group we start looking for clues to direct our behavior. Whether we recognize it or not, we make systematic decisions to behave in a given way within a group. What determines how we behave? What roles will we assume? We have already discussed group norms as determinants of some of our behavior. And if you will recall our discussion of self-concept in Chapter 2, we considered how our behavior and the roles we play are determined by our own personality and the behavior of others.

How does your personality affect group behavior? A reticent person will not behave in the same way as an aggressive person; a jovial person will perform a somewhat different role from that of a suspicious person. Of course, your reputation from outside the group will often affect the role you play within a group. But, as we said, our behavior may also be a product of how we are treated by others or what others expect our behavior to be. If others look for us to be the clown, we may well live up to that role; if others look to us for leadership, we may provide it even though it was not our initial intention to be the leader of that group.

In addition roles arise out of the functions a group serves. All work groups meet two clearly definable functions. One is task. The *task function* includes all the work a group must do to accomplish the group goal. Thus if the group goal is to determine college entrance requirements, some of the tasks it must do are to find information about requirements and to process that information. The other function is related to keeping the group working smoothly together. This, the *maintenance function*, includes all things that facilitate cohesion and good interpersonal and working relationships.

The major roles in a group then may be classified as task-oriented roles or maintenance-oriented roles. Thus, the task roles accomplish the task function of the group. Such roles as information giver, questioner, and analyzer are three of the task roles we will explore in detail in the next chapter. The maintenance roles meet the maintenance function. Such roles as harmonizer, gatekeeper, and compromiser are three of the maintenance roles we will be considering in the next chapter.

The most important in the group is the role of *leader*. The leader is the person who is designated by outside authority, who is appointed or elected by the group, or who emerges or takes over leadership responsibilities in the group for a given period of time. His or her role is to exert influence toward the attainment of group goals and toward the maintenance of group interpersonal needs. Because leadership is so important to any group, we will reserve an entire chapter for discussion of this vital role.

EXERCISE

In your recent work group, how did members try to meet the task and maintenance functions of the group? Describe their efforts. What kind of role did you see yourself playing?

DECISION MAKING

When we consider decision making, we are talking about both decisions that are imposed and decisions that are arrived at democratically. Especially in an authoritarian group, a common way of making a decision is by decree. After the group has discussed for a while, the leader tells the group what its decision will be. If the leader has enough power, is very persuasive, or very manipulative, he can get the group to approve a decision. This method, called rubber stamping, often destroys group decision making and group morale.

Group members often feel more pleased about the process and more committed to the group decisions when they are arrived at democratically. This democratic decision is usually arrived at by one of three methods. The first, and the best, is to achieve consensus. *Consensus* means total group agreement. For instance, suppose we were discussing the possible criteria for evaluating acting and someone suggested "character portrayal" as a major criterion. If after some discussion the leader posed the question, "Are we in agreement that character portrayal is a major criterion for evaluating acting?" and everyone agreed, the decision would be by consensus.

If it is not possible to reach consensus, then the group tries to make a statement that incorporates divergent viewpoints without compromising the principles behind the viewpoints. Suppose that during the discussion of criteria your group was determining whether "attitude" is a major criterion for evaluating acting ability. When the leader asked "Are we in agreement that attitude is a major criterion for evaluating acting?" suppose several people said, "No, I don't think so." Since some people say "no," you cannot have consensus on the point. Before taking a vote, the group might decide to try to word the idea differently, such as "Willing to give 100 percent at all times, in rehearsal or in the show, big part or small." If everyone is satisfied, then the group has successfully modified the point and gotten consensus.

If consensus still cannot be reached, the group usually takes a vote. Let's say that after fifteen minutes of discussion on the criterion of "attitude" there is still considerable dissent, regardless of the wording. At that point the group should take a vote. If the vote is six to one or five to two in a seven-person group, the decision has been given solid support. If it is a four-to-three decision, there may be some question about later group support of that decision; nevertheless, on some issues, at some times, the principle of majority rule is the only choice open.

EXERCISE _____

In the last group in which you worked, how were your decisions arrived at? Authoritatively? Democratically? By consensus? By vote?

WHEN THE GROUP GOES PUBLIC

Work groups basically operate by private discussion in which the participants attempt to accomplish some task without the presence of an onlooking or participating audience. Occasionally, however, a group is called upon to go public—that is, to do its deliberating in front of a larger audience. Although by far the greatest number of your work groups will function in private, it is useful to look at two major public models for discussion. Except in settings that basically feature information exchange, the public discussion serves more a public relations function than a problem-solving function.

A popular, public discussion model is the symposium—a discussion in which a limited number of participants (usually three to five) present individual speeches of approximately the same length on various aspects of the subject to an audience. After the planned speeches, the participants in the symposium may discuss their reactions with each other or may respond to questions from the listening audience or both. Although the symposium is a popular model for public discussion, it exhibits few of the characteristics we have been discussing. The symposium properly should be discussed as a public speaking assignment.

The other popular public discussion model is the panel, in which four to eight persons discuss a topic spontaneously under the direction of a leader and following a planned agenda. After the formal discussion, the audience is often encouraged to question the participants. So that the discussion can be seen and heard by the audience, the group usually is seated in a semicircle, with the chairperson in the middle, where she can get a good view of the audience and the panelists. Since the discussion is conducted for an audience, the panelists need to be sure that they meet the requirements of public speaking that we will discuss in the next unit. Because a panel discussion encourages spontaneity and interaction, it can be very stimulating for both a listening audience and the participants themselves. A good panel exhibits many of the traits we have considered in this section.

SUMMARY

Whether you are in charge of forming a group or working as a member of a group, your understanding of group characteristics will help you put together a better group or help you get maximum value from the group experience.

Be realistic about your expectations. Groups often get off to a rather rough start. It takes a while for a group to learn to work well together. Work groups are likely to function best with five to eight members. The group probably will achieve cohesiveness if goals are appealing to members, if members have similar needs and at least some common reference points. The group will function best if the members are committed to the task, if members understand and respect group norms, and if task and maintenance roles are assumed and negative roles are kept to a minimum. The group decision will receive the greatest support if members believe those decisions are a product of group thinking.

SUGGESTED READINGS

Ernest G. Bormann. *Discussion and Group Methods: Theory and Practice,* 2nd ed. New York: Harper & Row, 1975. This is an excellent comprehensive look at work groups.

John K. Brilhart. *Effective Group Discussion,* 3rd ed. Dubuque, Iowa: Wm. C. Brown, 1978 (paperback). Good overall view of decision-making discussion.

David Potter and Martin P. Andersen. *Discussion in Small Groups: A Guide to Effective Practice,* 3rd ed. Belmont, Calif.: Wadsworth, 1976 (paperback). Shorter, but still excellent coverage.

CHAPTER 9

PARTICIPATING IN DECISION-MAKING GROUPS

Several of the sales division's leading members were gathered to determine how to proceed with the new advertising program. Claude, head of the sales division, was hoping the group would come through for him. At the beginning of the first committee meeting, Claude began, "You know why I called you together—to determine how to proceed with the new sales program idea. Well, what do you say?"

After a few seconds of silence, Claude said, "Grover, what have you been thinking?"

"Well, I don't know, chief," Grover Davis replied, "haven't really given it much thought. What are we supposed to be doing?"

"I wanted to get your ideas on how we should proceed with this new program."

"Whatever you think is OK with me,

Claude," said Barry Barton.

"Yeah, Claude, what do you want to do?" Grover asked.

"I thought maybe you folks would like to give some input," Claude suggested.

"I'd sure like to talk about it," Sue Maxley said. "If you'd give us the scoop, why I'm sure we could comment."

"But I sent around preliminary data earlier this week," Claude explained.

"Oh, is that what that was?" Mark Jones asked. "I read the part about the meeting, but I guess I didn't pay much attention to the material."

"I'd really like to start using some of the new sales ideas," Claude remarked.

"Sure, go ahead—we'll back you," Ann

Denny replied.

"Well, I'll think it through and make some suggestions next time," Claude announced. "Meeting's adjourned."

As people filed out, Claude overheard Ann commenting to Barry: "These meetings sure are a waste of time, aren't they?"

Is this the way your group works? Maybe this group will come up with a good plan sometime—if Claude works one out. Maybe the problem was Claude's. As leader he could have shown more direction. But for the most part, the problem with the group falls directly on the membership— the participants. Whether your groups work well depends on each and every member of the group—including *you*.

As we said in the last chapter, you have a commitment to a group. If you don't want to be a member or if you don't want to discuss the issue before the group, don't agree to be on the committee or in the group. Once you have agreed to take part, you have an obligation, a responsibility to work. Many people like to meet with a group and "bat around ideas." But your responsibility involves both getting ready to discuss as well as the actual discussion itself. So, instead of the "Well, here I am, what do we do now" attitude, you need to take an active part. Let's look at the responsibilities of effective group participation.

BEING PREPARED

Whether your group is meeting for a one-shot effort or whether your group is ongoing, you need to be prepared for the day's session. You should never go into a group decision-making session unless you have done your homework. In an ongoing group you may need to spend your first meeting or two deciding procedures and so forth, but from then on you should do special preparation for each session. Basically you have several options:

1. *Read circulated information carefully before the meeting.* With many groups you will not be required to gather information. It will be done for you, but the whole idea is short circuited if you don't do the reading beforehand. In a group it's so easy to leave the work to the other guy. Try to adopt the attitude that *you* are the other guy!

2. *Survey your own experience.* There's a chance that the topic being discussed is one that you have thought about or worked with before. For instance, if your group is considering how to arrange available parking space so that it is equally distributed to administrators, faculty, and students, your parking experience may be useful to the group. But whenever possible your experience should be validated. Personal experience can be part of your preparation, but it is seldom enough for your total preparation.

3. *Survey library sources.* For many of the questions you will be considering, you will need solid, documented materials. Suppose you are considering changing college requirements. What are the requirements at similar colleges and universities? Your library should have catalogues of other schools that you can check. Or suppose you are considering instituting a class on television literacy. Your library has various magazines and journals that will have articles related to the issue. The point I'm making is that for any number of topics being considered you may need to do library research to be prepared. The two most basic research tools are the library's card catalogue which indexes all the books and materials held by the library and *Readers' Guide to Periodical Literature,* an index of some 125 popular magazines and journals. You should also talk with your reference librarian who will be happy to suggest various books, articles, government publications, newspapers, or other sources that contain useful data.

4. *Survey public opinion.* For some topics a survey of public opinion is most appropriate. Let's return to the question of distribution of available parking space. Since people at school are currently using the available space, you may be able to take advantage of their experience and opinions. What do they think of the present system? What would they like to see done? Prepare a few well-worded questions, go to the parking lots, and ask your questions. If a personal survey is not practicable, put your survey questionnaire under the windshield wiper of every car. Ask each driver to answer the questions and leave the results at the entry gate or drop them in the campus mail. You need data to work with, and a survey is one good way of getting information. Of course, you need to make sure that you have polled a large enough group and that you have sampled different segments of the larger group before you attempt to draw any significant conclusions from your poll.

5. *Interview for information.* An effective but often overlooked means of preparation is the personal interview. For your subject one interview with the right person may be all that is needed, or you may have to interview several people.

Because interviewing is a method of preparation you may not be familiar with, let's take a more detailed look at this important process.

INTERVIEWING

You are likely to use interviewing as a means to acquire information for an article, paper, report, speech, or, as we are featuring it in this chapter, for a group project.[1] A good interviewing plan involves selecting the best

---

[1]Since interviewing is also an important aspect of getting a good job, some suggestions for the interviewer and the interviewee are included in Appendix C.

person to interview, determining a procedure, and conducting the interview.

Selecting the Best Person

Somewhere on campus or in the larger community, there are people who have or who can get the information you want. How do you find out whom you should interview? Suppose you are going to be discussing a question related to food service in your dormitory. One of the employees can tell you who is in charge of the dining hall. Or you could phone your student center and inquire about who is in charge of food service. When you've decided whom you should interview, make an appointment. You cannot walk into an office and expect the prospective interviewee to drop everything on the spur of the moment.

Before going into the interview, get information on the topic. If, for instance, you are going to interview the dietitian who makes out menus and orders the food, you should already know something about the job of dietitian and something about the problems involved in ordering and preparing institutional food. Interviewees are more likely to talk with you if you appear informed; moreover, familiarity with the subject will enable you to ask better questions. If for some reason you go into an interview

SELECT THE BEST PERSON TO INTERVIEW.

uninformed, then at least approach the interviewee with enthusiasm and apparent interest in the job.

You should also be forthright in your reasons for scheduling the interview. Whether your interview is a part of a class project, for a newspaper article on campus food, or some other reason, say so.

Planning Carefully

Good interviewing results from careful planning. A good plan begins with good questions. Write down all the questions you can think of, revise them until you have worded them clearly and concisely, and put them in the order that seems most appropriate. Your questions should be a mix of open and closed questions and should be neutral rather than leading. Moreover you'll need to be alert to the need for follow-up questions.

Open questions are broad based. They range from those with virtually no restrictions like "Tell me about yourself" to those that give some direction like "Tell me about your preparation for this job." *Closed questions* are those that can be answered "yes" or "no" or with only a few words, such as "Have you had a course in marketing?" to "How many restaurants have you worked in?" Open questions encourage the person to talk; closed questions enable the interviewer to get much information in a short time. You'll probably want to have questions of both types.

Neutral questions are those in which the person is free to give an answer without direction from the interviewer; *leading questions* are those in which the interviewer suggests the answer expected or desired. A neutral question would be "How do you like your new job?" A leading question would be "You don't like the new job, do you?" In the majority of the interviewing you will do, leading questions are inappropriate. They try to force the person in one direction and make the person defensive.

Primary questions are those you plan ahead of time; *secondary questions* follow up on the answers. Some secondary questions encourage the person to continue ("And then?" "Is there more?"); some probe into what the person has said ("What does 'frequently' mean?" "What were you thinking at the time?"); and some plumb the feelings of the person ("How did it feel to get the prize?" "Were you worried when you didn't find her?").

When you list your questions leave enough space between them to fill in answers as completely as possible. It is just as important to leave enough space for answers to the secondary questions you decide to ask. Some interviewers try to play the entire interview by ear. However, even the most skilled interviewer needs some preplanned questions to insure covering important areas. The order and type of questions depend somewhat upon what you are hoping to achieve in the interview.

In the opening stages you should of course start by thanking the person for taking time to talk with you. During the opening try to develop good rapport between you and your respondent. Start by asking some questions that can be answered easily and that will show your respect for the person you are interviewing. For instance, in an interview with the head dietitian you might start with such questions as "How did you get interested in nutrition?" or "I imagine working out menus can be a very challenging job in these times of high food costs—is that so?" When the person nods or says "yes," you can then ask for some of the biggest challenges he or she faces. The goal is to get the interviewee to feel at ease and to talk freely. Since the most important consideration of this initial stage is to create a positive communication climate, keep the questions easy to answer, nonthreatening, and encouraging.

The body of the interview includes the major questions you have prepared. A good plan is to group questions so that the easy-to-answer questions come first and the hard-hitting questions that require careful thinking come later. For instance, the question "What do you do to try to resolve student complaints?" should be near the end of the interview. You may not ask all the questions you planned to, but you don't want to end the interview until you have the important information you intended to get.

As you draw to the end of your planned questions, again thank the person for taking time to talk with you. If you are going to publish the substance of the interview, it is courtesy to offer to let the person see a draft of your reporting of the interview before it goes into print. If a person does wish to see what you are planning to write, get a draft to that person well before deadline to give the person opportunity to read it and to give you opportunity to deal with any suggestions. Although this practice is not followed by many interviewers, it helps to build and maintain your own credibility.

The following example gives you an idea of the method of setting up a question schedule. If you were planning to interview the dietitian, you might prepare the following question schedule:

Background
What kinds of background and training do you need for the job?
How did you get interested in nutrition?
Have you worked as a dietitian for long?
Have you held any other food related positions?

Responsibilities

What are the responsibilities of your job besides meal planning?

How far in advance are meals planned?

What factors are taken into account when you are planning the meals for a given period?

Do you have a free hand or are there constraints placed upon you?

Procedures

Is there any set ratio for the number of times you put a given item on the menu?

Do you take individual differences into account?

How do you determine whether or not you will give choices for the entree?

What do you do to try to answer student complaints?

Could a student get a comparable meal at a good cafeteria for the same money? Explain.

Conducting the Interview

The best plan in the world will not result in a good interview unless you practice good interpersonal communication skills in conducting the interview. Among other things, you should be courteous during the interview. Listen carefully. If the person has given a rather long answer to a question, you should paraphrase what he or she has said to make sure your interpretation is correct. Try to keep the interview moving. You do not want to rush the person but when the allotted time is ending, you should call attention to that fact and be prepared to conclude. Try to be very aware of the impression you are making nonverbally. How you look and act may well determine whether or not the person will warm up to you and give you the kind of information you want.

EXERCISE

Divide the class into groups of five. For each of the following topics, each group should consider procedures for gathering information from written sources, surveys, and interviews:

Reducing crime in the community

Meeting the needs of the commuter student

Revision of college requirements

Extent of drug abuse on campus

DETERMINING A PROCEDURE

Some members of small groups think they have prepared if they have made an effort to gather good information. Unfortunately, they are only *half* right. For in addition to getting information, you should also consider a procedure both to guide the selection of information and to determine how the information will be incorporated into the discussion. You will often hear people grumble as they leave a meeting, "That was a waste of time. We never seem to accomplish anything." Some of this frustration is the direct result of the group format: Good group decision making is often slow. It takes time to pool data, discuss, and draw conclusions about any given issue. By far the greater part of the frustration arises because groups have not considered procedures that allow them to maximize their efforts. Too often group members assume that somehow a procedure will emerge within the framework of discussing a topic, and sometimes it does. Nevertheless, you have a responsibility to see to it that the topic has been carefully considered so that the best possible procedure is followed by the group. This responsibility is on everybody's shoulders—leader and participants alike.

Groups are formed either to consider all issues that relate to a specific topic (a social committee, a personnel committee, a public relations committee) or to consider a specific issue (determine the year's social calendar, determine criteria for granting promotions, develop a long-range plan for university growth). Whether your group is an ongoing group meeting periodically to consider each problem or task in turn or whether the group has but one decision to make, you need to think about (1) a statement of the problem and (2) an analysis of the problem. My suggestion is for you to think about this on your own. Then when the group meets to discuss, it is your responsibility to enter the product of your thinking into the discussion.

Stating the Problem

With many groups much wheel spinning takes place during the early stages of the group discussion. Much of this results from members' questions about the function, purpose, or goal of the group. As soon as possible, the group should decide exactly what it is going to be doing. It is the responsibility of the person, agency, or parent group that forms a particular decision-making group to give it a specific charge. For instance, a group may be formed for the purpose of "determining the nature of the spring social" or "preparing a guideline for implementation of new courses that can be ready for use next autumn." If the charge is not clear, it is up to the leader or a group representative to find out exactly why the group was formed and what its goals are.

Regardless of the clarity of the charge, the group may still want to reword or in some way modify it. Until everyone is in agreement about what the problem is, there can never be agreement about how to solve it. But don't wait for the first group meeting. Figure out how to state the problem beforehand; then you will be in a better position to help the group get the problem stated in its most usable form. There are several criteria that should be used in preparing a statement and that the group should consider *before* accepting wording. Let's look at some of them:

1. *Is the problem phrased as a question?* In this chapter we are focusing on groups that meet primarily to make decisions. The logical starting point for such a group is to phrase its goal in a form that will facilitate the decision-making process. The best form is the question.

Why is an issue to be discussed best phrased as a question? The group discussion format is one of inquiry. A group begins from the assumption that answers are not known. Although some decision-making groups serve merely as rubber stamping agencies, the ideal is for the group to have the freedom of choice. This spirit of inquiry is furthered through questions.

2. *Is the wording of the question clear enough so that all group members understand what they will be discussing?* Sometimes an apparently important question contains a word that is so ambiguous that the group may waste time quibbling over its meaning. Look at the following questions:

Should the small basketball games be returned to the university fieldhouse?

What should the department do about courses that aren't getting the job done?

Should the practices of social clubs be looked into?

All three questions are well intentioned, and participants may have at least some idea about what they're discussing. But vague wording like "small basketball games," "getting the job done," and "looked into" can lead to trouble in the discussion. So, instead of waiting until later, reword questions so they are specific *before* the group begins to get into the issues. With just a little bit of work groups could revise the preceding questions so that the wording is clearer:

Should basketball games whose advanced ticket sale is less than 5000 be played at the university fieldhouse?

What should the department do about courses that receive low scores on student evaluations?

Should the university reexamine criteria for selecting membership in campus social clubs?

3. *Does the question encourage a spirit of free inquiry?* It is possible to phrase a question in such a way that a group is forced in a direction whether it should be or not. Consider the following: "Should our ridiculous set of college requirements be revised?" Right from the start the group has agreed on a phrasing that preordains the outcome of the discussion. What kind of free inquiry is possible if the group agrees that the requirements are "ridiculous"? Or, consider the question "Should our country opt for clean solar energy or for highly dangerous nuclear power?" Again, the scales are tilted before the group even gets into the issues involved. The phrasing of the question should not indicate which way the question will be decided.

4. *Does the question contain only one central idea?* "Should we ban the internal combustion engine and encourage the development of better batteries?" is poorly phrased because it contains two similar but distinct questions. Either one would make a good discussion. And perhaps one would have to be resolved before beginning another; but they cannot both be discussed at once.

5. *Can the question be identified easily as one of fact, value, or policy?* How you proceed in your deliberations will depend on the kind of question. Later we will discuss how the type of question affects organization. For now, let's consider the three types of questions.

Questions of fact consider the truth or the falsity of an assertion. Implied in the question is the theoretical possibility of verifying the answer. For instance, "What is the temperature today?" is a question of fact because the temperature can be recorded and read. "Is Jones guilty of shoplifting?" is also a question of fact. Jones either committed the crime or he did not. Resolving questions of fact is seldom the ultimate goal of a work group.

Questions of value consider relative goodness or relative badness. They are characterized by the inclusion of some evaluative word like "good," "cool," "reliable," "effective," "worthy," or their opposites. The purpose of the question of value is to compare a subject with one or more members of the same class. "Who is the most valuable player in the National (or American) League?" is a question of value. Although we can set up criteria for "most valuable" and measure our choice against those criteria, there is no way of verifying our findings. The answer is still a matter of judgment, not a matter of fact. "Is socialism superior to capitalism?" "Is a liberal education better than a specialized education?" are both questions of value. Although questions of value are widely discussed in social groups these are not so likely to be the ultimate goal of the work group.

Questions of policy judge whether a future action should be taken or not. The question is phrased to arrive at a solution or to test a tentative solution to a problem or a felt need. "What should we do to lower the crime rate?"

seeks a solution that would best solve the problem of the increase in crime. "Should the gasoline engine be banned?" reaches for a tentative solution to the problems of how we could conserve oil and how we can reduce air pollution in the United States. The inclusion of the word "should" in all questions of policy makes them the easiest to recognize and the easiest to phrase of all discussion questions. Most issues facing work groups are questions of policy.

Analyzing the Problem

The second step in determining a procedure is to analyze the problem. Analysis means breaking the question into its component parts to determine the areas (often called "issues") that must be considered to reach a satisfactory decision. Since each of the three major types of questions (fact, value, and policy) are analyzed somewhat differently, we'll consider each separately.

Questions of Fact   Questions of fact, you'll recall, consider discovering the facts and/or determining the truth or falsity of the question. Most questions of fact are resolved by defining and classifying. Sometimes the task is to discover the characteristics of the classification; sometimes the task is to select a choice from among various classifications. The analysis of a question of fact includes at least (1) defining the key terms and (2) finding information that satisfies the definition and/or determines classifications.

For purposes of illustration, let's consider two examples of analyses:

What are the goals of the Republican Party?

1. What do we mean by *goals*? (Defining key terms)
2. What qualifies as a goal? What else qualifies? Anything further to add? (Information that determines each classification)

Is Jones guilty of murdering Smith?

1. What is meant by *guilty of* and *murdering*? (Defining key terms)
2. Did Jones cause the death of Smith? (Information leading to classification)
3. Can Jones's actions be defined as "murder"? (Determining whether information fits classification)

Questions of Value   Questions of value, you'll recall, judge relative goodness or relative badness. They are often identified by the presence of some comparative or evaluative word such as *effective, better, detrimental,* or *worse.*

The judgment of comparative value requires standards from which to work. Since a standard of judgment of value depends upon criteria, analysis calls for establishment of some criteria. The analysis of a question of value then includes at least the following: (1) determining the criteria on which the judgment will be made, (2) determining the facts surrounding the object(s) or person(s) being evaluated, and (3) matching the facts with the criteria.

For purposes of illustration, let's consider analysis of the following question of value:

Is Professor X an effective teacher?

1. What are the criteria for establishing teaching effectiveness? (Criteria)

2. What are the facts about Professor X's teaching? (Determining facts)

3. Do the facts show that Professor X's teaching meets enough of the criteria to be called effective? (Matching facts with criteria)

Questions of Policy Questions of policy, we said, determine whether a future action should be taken. Because questions of policy deal with courses of action, they involve determining the nature of the problem and finding an acceptable solution. The majority of the questions you will work with in decision-making discussions are likely to be questions of policy. The analysis of a question of policy includes at least the following:

1. What is the nature of the problem?

    A. What is the size of the problem?

    B. What are the symptoms of the problem?

    C. What are the causes of the problem?

2. What criteria should be used to test the solutions? (Specifically, what checklist of items must the solution meet in order to solve this problem beneficially and practicably? For instance: **A.** Does the plan eliminate the symptoms? **B.** Is the plan capable of being implemented soon with present resources?

3. What are the possible solutions?

4. What is the best solution?

    A. How does each solution meet the criteria?

    B. Which solution best meets the criteria?

For purposes of illustration, let's consider analysis of one question of policy. Only a few of the possibilities are shown under each heading.

What should be done to equalize athletic opportunities for women on campus?

1. What has happened on campus that signifies the presence of a problem for women? (Nature of the problem)

    A. Have significant numbers of women been affected?

    B. Do women have less opportunity to compete in athletics than men?

    C. Has the university behaved in ways that have adversely affected women's opportunities?

2. By what means should we test whether a proposed solution solves the problem? (Criteria)

    A. Does the proposed solution cope with each of the problems uncovered?

    B. Can the proposed solution be implemented without creating new and perhaps worse problems?

3. What can be done to equalize opportunities? (Possible solutions)

    A. Can more scholarships be allocated to women?

    B. Can time allocated to women's use of university facilities be increased to a level comparable with men's use?

4. Which proposal (or combination) would work the best? (Best solution)

    A. Will increasing women's scholarships solve the problems without creating worse problems?

    B. Can women's time for use be increased without creating worse problems?

TAKING PART IN GROUP DISCUSSIONS

How will a discussion group actually proceed? The answer depends upon such variables as method of leadership, willingness to work, and so forth. As a participant it is your obligation to prepare a tentative wording and a tentative outline of procedure. A good leader, and one or more other members of the group, may also have worked out tentative wordings and procedures.

Early in the discussion the group should decide which wording and which plan or combination of plans they will use. How well a group holds to the plan again depends on both leadership and discipline of the group. In practice very few groups ever work linearly through all the suggested steps. More than likely the group will go on and off the subject, move forward and backward, and sometimes in circles. But if the group has decided on a plan, then at least they will know what has to be accomplished before they are finished. They can as a group work to see to it that all the subquestions outlined are in fact answered.

Since most questions you will work with will probably be questions of policy, let's consider a few guidelines for procedure:

Try to determine the nature of the problem before even mentioning possible solutions. With some questions determining the nature of the problem can be accomplished quickly—perhaps even in a few minutes; with others, determining the nature of the problem may take hours, days, or even weeks. This is the stage of decision making that is most easily sloughed off; but if it is, the penalty is often failure of the solution that is decided upon. Why do I say this? Because it is the natural tendency of groups to want to go directly to possible solutions. For instance, if your charge is to plan a spring party, someone will probably say something like "Let's have a casino party" very early in the discussion. Or, if the charge is to determine priorities for parking, someone is likely to say, "I've got a plan I think will work." Because these statements sound as if they deal directly with the charges given the groups, the tendency is to pursue these prematurely offered solutions. Although it is possible to discuss the nature of the problem concurrently with presenting solutions, groups would work more effectively if they would curb the tendency to try. Consider that a solution or a plan can work only if it solves the problem at hand. Before you can shape a plan you must decide what obstacles the plan must meet, what symptoms the plan must eliminate, and with what other criteria the plan must deal.

Try to suggest as many solutions as possible. Although it is not necessary that the group deal with every one of the possible solutions, participants should not be satisfied until and unless they have considered a wide variety of solutions that could meet the problem stated. For instance, if you are on a committee appointed to raise money, you should take time to find as many ways of making money as possible so you'll have enough options to choose from.

How do you come up with solutions? Some groups like to use the brainstorming method. In *brainstorming*, every member of the group is asked to state ideas, at random, until a long list has been compiled. In a good ten-to-fifteen minute brainstorming session perhaps thirty different solutions can be suggested. Usually the solutions are grouped so that they represent three, five, or ten different categories of solutions.

The key to coming up with many solutions is to avoid evaluating them as they are mentioned. If a person feels free to make a suggestion even if it later proves to be unworkable, he will feel much freer than if the person fears that each idea will be evaluated on the spot.

When it is time to determine the best solution, make sure that each is measured against the criteria. Too often groups get to this stage of discussion and then forget to use much of what they decided on earlier. In general the solution that meets the most criteria or the one which meets several criteria best should be selected.

If a group has been organized to solve one problem, once it has been resolved, the group should disband. If the group is ongoing, once a decision is made, the group should move on to the next item on the agenda or the next problem.

EXERCISE

For one of the subject areas on p. 174, (1) state the topic as a question that meets the tests discussed and (2) outline an analysis of the question.

Talking Productively

Taking part in a group means talking. How you talk, when you talk, and what you say all are important in determining the effectiveness of a group. Let's consider some of the criteria that your "talk" must meet:

Interacting   The concept of interaction is at the heart of effective group work. Earlier, in mentioning the value of discussions, we recalled the adage "Two heads are better than one." This adage is true, however, only when the "two heads" are willing to talk with each other, to share what they are thinking and feeling, and to listen carefully to what others are saying. Thinking, talking, listening are the foundation of interaction, the give-and-take of group encounter. Effective interaction uses every skill that we worked on in the personal communication unit. When you see a group in which the ideas of participants are probed, supported, built upon, questioned, debated, added to, and subtracted from, and finally brought to consensus, then you are seeing the ideal of group interaction.

The ideal of group interaction calls for everyone to have the right to speak, to talk approximately the same amount of time, and to direct contributions to all members of the group. The ideal is hardly ever achieved, but as we will see, good leadership can facilitate coming at least close to the ideal.

Maintaining Objectivity   As you think about, research, and begin discussion of the major issues of a question, you may find yourself becoming an advocate of a particular idea, plan, or procedure. Yet, once you become ego-involved in your material, you lose your objectivity—a quality that is fundamental to good group work. Debate is the format for advocates of opposite sides of a question to present their convictions in an effort to convince a judge or an audience of the merits of a particular point of view. Group communication, on the other hand, is a format in which each participant attempts to present material on any and all sides without bias. Although few people can remain truly objective at all times (in fact, some would argue that objectivity is itself an illusion), there are at least two things that you can do to increase the value of your participation.

First, report data but do not associate yourself with them. If you report that preschool children watch upward of 25 hours of television each week, do not feel that because you presented the information you must defend it. An excellent way of presenting data with a degree of disassociation is illustrated by the following comment: "According to *Newsweek*, children under the age of five watch an average of upward of 25 hours of television per week. If that's true, it is even above the average for adult viewing. *I wonder whether anyone else has any data to support* Newsweek's *statistic?*" The value of the italicized portion of the comment is that it tells the group that you are seeking discussion of the information and that whether it is supported or not, you have no personal ties with it.

Second, try to find material supporting differing views on each of the key issues of the question. Although nothing is wrong with forming tentative opinions based upon the material you've researched, in the discussion you should present material you've found regardless of whether it supports or opposes your tentative position. After all material has been presented you may tell why you think one position is stronger than another. But conclusions should not be drawn until all the available material is pooled. If the group arrives at a conclusion opposite from your original tentative position, you will not be put on the defensive. In fact, by being objective, you may find that during the discussion your views will change many times. Remember, if the best answer to the topic question could be found without discussion, no discussion would be necessary.

Managing Group Conflicts If the group is doing a good job, some conflicts will occur. Keep in mind that conflict need not mean arguing and fighting. Any clash of opinion may result in conflict. Just as with interpersonal conflict the issue is not whether conflict will occur but what should be done about it. When group members resort to negative means of dealing with conflicts (withdrawal, surrender, or aggression) someone will have to try to change the direction of the response. Sharply opposing views will need to be resolved, but during the resolution the conflict sometimes serves as a test of the validity of the ideas presented, and its function can be beneficial to the group discussion. A total lack of conflict may be a sign of group indifference. When members are not committed or when the task seems neither very important nor very interesting, a group may work quickly to reach a decision, but it is doubtful that such a decision has been given much thought.

Conflicts often arise because people care very much about what is happening. Because they care, they are willing to show their feelings and some of these feelings may be negative and may result in conflict.

Conflicts can also arise from within an individual. Each participant may have a personal strategy that determines the nature of his or her participation in the group. These various strategies may be classified as distributive or integrative.[1] A *distributive situation* is one in which a win-lose strategy is developed—that is, if one person wins, it must be at the other person's expense. Conflicts that develop from this situation will be largely negative and difficult to deal with. An *integrative situation* is one in which the members of the group integrate their resources toward a common task. The game of poker may be contrasted with a group working a jigsaw puzzle. In poker an individual is working at the expense of others; in working a jigsaw puzzle each person cooperates with the others.

The National Training Laboratories have described two opposite modes of behavior, one that results in negative conflict and one that either avoids conflict or results in positive or useful conflict. Let's look at what appear to be the five most important of these contrasts:

Behavior That Will Result in Negative Conflict	Behavior That Will Reduce Conflict or Result in Positive or Useful Conflict
1. Purposefully pursuing your own goals	1. Purposefully pursuing goals held in common
2. Being secretive	2. Being open
3. Disguising or misrepresenting your own needs, plans, and goals	3. Accurately representing your own needs, plans, and goals
4. Being unpredictable—using the element of surprise	4. Being predictable—using behavior consistent with past experience
5. Using threats and bluffs	5. Avoiding threats and bluffs

One of the common negative strategies we considered earlier, the hidden agenda, is the source of many conflicts in problem-solving groups. In fact, probably no one in any group is free from some hidden agenda. Recall that a hidden agenda is a reason or motive for behavior that is undisclosed to the other participant or participants. Thus, as the group gathers, Tom may be wanting to make sure the group has finished by 3 P.M. so he can get to another meeting. Bill might be willing to go along with anything unless it is advocated or presented by Joan. Angelo might be a member of another group that has a vested interest in a particular

[1]Based upon analysis made in the *1968 Summer Reading Book* of the National Training Laboratories Institute of Applied Behavioral Sciences, pp. 57–58.

outcome of this group. Joan might feel that she was forced to take part in this group and wants to get the job done quickly so she can get out of it. If a hidden agenda is deep-seated enough to cause actual conflict, then it is probably best to take time to decide what hidden agenda is affecting group productivity and deal with it before going on. (Some suggestions for dealing with hidden agendas were discussed on pp. 103–104.)

So, regardless of the motivation for the conflict, you will be a more productive group member if you can pattern your behavior after that described in the second column of the list on page 184.

Being Responsible for Leadership Once a leader has been designated, participants often think "OK, it's your show." However, just because someone else is called upon to be the leader does not excuse you from leadership responsibility. Everyone shares the responsibility for showing leadership when it is appropriate. For instance, if you believe that one or two people seem to be dominating the discussion, you could say to yourself, "I think it's hurting our group. I wish the leader would do something about it, but what the heck, it's not my responsibility" or "I'm lost. I think we're still talking about the Howard plan, but I'm not sure—oh well, it's not my concern." Refusing to respond to such concerns means you are not fulfilling your responsibility. To be sure, designated leaders should exercise leadership. But what if they don't? What if a leader misses something you notice? If there is something wrong and you know what it is, you have the responsibility to do something about it. Readiness to exercise leadership on a single point is each participant's responsibility.

Fulfilling Roles

One way to analyze group participation is through the roles that group members play. As you recall, a role is a behavior that you determine for yourself or that is determined for you by expectations of a group. Sometimes a person plays one role and one role alone throughout the duration of a group. At other times, a person may play several roles simultaneously or alternately, and, of course, more than one person can play a given role in a group.

Sometimes the role played is a conscious or deliberate effort on the part of the participant. Some people choose roles because they feel comfortable playing them; some people deliberately try to play a new or different role in a group. More often than not, however, the group is responsible for determining role-playing behavior. By rewarding people for roles that please the group and by punishing people for playing roles that the group sees as unbecoming, nonessential, or "someone else's" a group will mold the behavior of its members.

Group pressure is not always "correct" and certainly not always in the best interests of the individual or of the group. Often, however, it explains why people behave as they do in a group. So, as a person who is trying to learn to become a more productive group member, you might on occasion need to overcome the efforts at applying pressure that members of a group or the whole group will exert on you.

As we noted earlier, group roles consist of both task and maintenance functions. The task function involves doing the job in the best manner; the maintenance function involves how group members talk about their task, the nature of their interactions, and how they deal with the feelings of the group members. For a group to reach its potential, both functions must be satisfied. In the remainder of this chapter we will look at several task and maintenance functions that need to be met in a group. We will also look at some of the negative roles that can detract from group effectiveness and/or group satisfaction.

Task Roles   In most groups there are at least five major task roles that can be identified.

1. *Information or Opinion Giver.* In this task role a person provides content for the discussion. Actual information provides about 50 percent of what is done in a group. Without information and well-considered opinions the group will not have the material from which to draw its decisions. Probably everyone in the group plays this role during the discussion. Nevertheless, there are usually one or more persons who have really done their homework. Either as a result of past experience with this or a related problem, long conversations with people who have worked with similar problems, or a great deal of study, these persons are relied upon or called upon to provide the facts. In some groups there is a designated resource person or consultant called in solely to fulfill the information-giving role. In most groups one or more persons take it upon themselves to be especially well prepared. The information giver identifies himself by such statements as "Well, when the Jones Corporation considered this problem, they found . . ." or "That's a good point you made—just the other day I ran across these figures that substantiate your point . . ." or "According to Professor Smith it doesn't necessarily work that way. He says . . ."

2. *Information Seeker.* A second task role, similar to but opposite from the information giver, is the information seeker. This role is played by the member of the group who sees that at a given point the group will need data in order to function. Again, in most groups more than one person will take this role during the discussion, yet one or more are especially perceptive in seeing where more information is needed. The information seeker may be identified by such questions as "What did we say the base numbers were?" or "Have

we decided how many people this really affects?" or "Well, what functions does this person serve?" or "Have we got anything to give us some background on this subject?"

3. *Expediter.* The expediter is the individual who perceives when the group is going astray. Whether the group is meeting once or is an ongoing group, almost invariably some remarks will tend to sidetrack the group from the central point or issue in front of them. Sometimes apparent digressions are necessary to get background, to enlarge the scope, or even to give a person an opportunity to get something off his chest. Often in a group these momentary digressions lead to tangents that take the group far afield from its assignment. But because tangents are sometimes more fun than the task itself, a tangent often is not realized for what it is and the group discusses it as if it were important to the group decision. The expediter is the person who helps the group stick to its agenda—she helps the group stay with the problem at hand. And when the group has strayed, she helps lead it back to the mainstream. This role is revealed by such statements as "Say, I'm enjoying this but I can't quite see what it has to do with whether permissiveness is really a cause" or "Let's see, aren't we still trying to find out whether these are the only criteria that we should be considering?" or "I've got the feeling that this is important to the point we're on now, but I can't quite get hold of the relationship—am I off base?" or "Say, time is getting away from us and we've only considered two possible solutions, aren't there some more?"

4. *Idea Person.* The idea person is the individual with imagination who thinks originally, rattles off alternative ideas, and often comes up with an idea that serves as the base for the ultimate decision. Although everyone in the group may bring information, usually only one or two members seem truly inventive. When many members of the group seem unable to see past tried-and-true solutions, the idea person invents a new one; when the group thinks it has exhausted possibilities, he comes up with another one; when the group seems up against a stone wall, he finds an outlet. As we might expect, all of his ideas are not "world beaters." The creative mind is constantly mining ideas, but from among all those that come, only a few are golden. But when he is being serious and is working, the idea person is indispensable. This role may be seen in such statements as "Hey, I've got just the thing! . . ." or "Wait a minute, listen to this . . ." or "We've been looking at this all backward. If we turn it around, we'll see that . . ."

5. *Analyzer.* This is the person who is the master of technique. She knows the problem-solving method inside out. The analyzer knows when the group has skipped a point, has passed over a point too lightly, or has not taken a look at matters it needs to. More than just *expediting*, the analyzer helps the group penetrate to the core of the problem it is working on. In addition, the analyzer examines the reasoning of various participants. The tests she applies may be seen by looking at the explanation of common forms of reasoning discussed on pages 321–322. The analyzer may be recognized from such statements as "Tom, you're generalizing from only one instance—can you give us some others?" or "Wait a minute, after symptoms, we have to take a look at causes" or "I think we're passing over Jones too lightly—there are still two criteria we haven't used to measure him by."

Maintenance Roles   Now that we have looked at the roles that facilitate accomplishing the task, let's look at the major roles participants play in facilitating good interpersonal relations. The following roles are called *maintenance roles*.

1. *Active Listener*. People participating in groups are likely to feel better about their participation when their thoughts and feelings are recognized. It is the role of the active listener to feedback specific reaction to group members. In any group we expect nearly everyone will exhibit active listening traits at some time, but people tend to get so wrapped up in their own ideas that they may neglect to reward the positive comments that are made. The true active listener responds verbally and/or nonverbally whenever a good point is made.

The active listener is recognized through such nonverbal cues as a smile, a nod, or a vigorous head shake. Verbally he or she is recognized by such statements as "Good point, Mel," "I really like that idea, Susan," "It's obvious you've really done your homework, Peg," and "That's one of the best ideas we've had today, Al."

2. *Game Leader*. Folklore has it that "all work and no play makes Jack a dull boy." When group members really get working on their tasks, they sometimes get so involved and try to work so hard that they begin to wear themselves down. Nerves get frayed, vision becomes cloudy, and the machine of progress grinds to a halt. The game leader is the person who recognizes when the process is boring, when the group is getting tired. He has an uncanny sixth sense for when to tell a joke, when to take off on a digression, when to get the group to play a little before returning to the task. In some situations, a single well-placed sentence will get a laugh, break the monotony, and jolt the group out of their lethargy. At other times, the group can be saved only with a real break—sometimes a minute or so and sometimes even five, ten, or fifteen minutes. The game leader always has an idea for getting the group interacting on some point not related to the task at hand. He adds nothing to the content of the discussion, but improves the spirits of the participants immeasurably. Of all the roles we will be discussing, this is the least capable of being played consciously. If someone has to try to be a game leader he usually will fail. Although not every group has a member who fills the bill completely, most groups include at least one person who can meet it well enough to break tension and fatigue. Even if a group can accomplish its task without a game leader, it certainly is not as much fun. Attempts at characterizing this role with examples seldom read well—suffice it to say that you will know, recognize, and be thankful for the person playing this role when you encounter him or her.

3. *Harmonizer*. It is a rare group that can expect to accomplish its task without some minor—if not major—conflicts. Even when people get along well they are likely to get angry over some inconsequential points in heated discussion. Most groups experience some classic interpersonal conflicts caused by different personality types. The harmonizer is responsible for reducing and reconciling misunderstanding, disagreements, and conflicts. She is good at "pouring oil on troubled waters." She encourages objectivity and

is especially good as a mediator for hostile, aggressively competing sides. A group cannot avoid some conflict—if there is no one present to harmonize, participation can become an uncomfortable experience. The harmonizer may be recognized by such statements as, "Bill, I don't think you're giving Mary a chance to make her point" or "Tom, Jack, hold it a second. I know you're on opposite sides of this, but let's see where you might have some agreement" or "Sue, I get the feeling that something Todd said really bugged you, is that right?" or "Hold it, gang, we're really coming up with some good stuff, let's not lose our momentum by getting into a name-calling thing."

4. *Gatekeeper.* The gatekeeper is the person who helps to keep communication channels open. If a group has seven people in it, the assumption is that all seven have something to contribute. But if all are to feel comfortable in contributing, those who tend to dominate need to be held in check and those who tend to be reticent need to be encouraged. The gatekeeper is the one who sees that Jane is on the edge of her chair, ready to talk, but just cannot seem to get in, or that Don is rambling a bit and needs to be directed, or that Tom's need to talk so frequently is making Cesar withdraw from the conversation, or that Betty has just lost the thread of discussion. As we said earlier, a characteristic of good group work is interaction. The gatekeeper assumes the responsibility for facilitating interaction. The gatekeeper may be recognized by such statements as "Joan, I see you've got something to say here . . ." or "You've made a really good point, Todd, I wonder whether we could get some reaction to it . . ." or "Bill and Marge, it sounds like you're getting into a dialogue here, let's see what other ideas we have."

5. *Compromiser.* Whenever two persons get together, there is the likelihood of two different points of view. If it is hard to mesh two points of view, you can realize how hard it is to get five, seven, or ten persons to agree. Now, a group need not necessarily come to complete agreement on every point that is made, but it cannot afford to favor several positions on all issues. The compromiser is the person who senses that two apparently different positions can be brought together with some minor modification on the part of the disputing sides. If the compromiser is involved, she will often seek a mediating position herself. If she is not involved, she will help the disputing sides find a middle ground that will win wider approval. Compromising is not always the best way, but during the course of a lengthy discussion there will inevitably be several times when some give-and-take is necessary or the group will bog down and die. The compromiser can be recognized from such statements as "I don't want us to end at an impasse—Jack, if I remove my point about having to get agreement from every agency, will you back the plan?" or "Dick, you and Jerry both have good ideas—I wonder whether you're as far apart as you seem. Maybe if we . . ." or "Look, we can't go back to the group with two different ideas. Now what can we do to reconcile the differences without making anyone feel that he's being betrayed?"

6. *Public Relations—The Front Person.* The front person is the member of the group who possesses skills at dealing with external bodies and individuals outside the group. This is a very important role, because the decisions that a group makes are usually relevant to other groups, persons, and sometimes institutions. If a group decides that the quarter system would better serve a school that is currently on the semester system, this decision must get to the group that has the power to implement it. It will be for the front person to develop channels of communication to other persons. He may have to sell the larger group, the establishment, or some other agency on the value of that decision. In addition to being likable and competent, this person must have both interpersonal and public-speaking skills to fulfill his role.

The roles that we have considered so far are those we call positive. In any good group we look for all or most of these roles to be served by members of the group. Several other roles that are seen in group work are negative. Rather than facilitate the task or maintenance functions of the group, they inhibit them. We want to point out the negative roles so they can be prevented; if they are permitted to develop, they may destroy the group. In some situations people play these negative roles inadvertently— that is, they are not trying to be negative but are acting impulsively or responding to what they believe to be the tenor of the group.

Negative Roles   Now that we have examined positive task and maintenance roles, let's look briefly at seven *negative roles* that you are likely to encounter in group discussion.

1. *Aggressor.* The aggressor is the person who works for his own status by criticizing almost everything or blaming others when things get rough. His main purpose seems to be to deflate the ego or status of others. One way of dealing with the aggressor is to confront him. Ask him whether he is aware of what he is doing and what effect it is having on the group.

2. *Blocker.* The blocker, related to the aggressor, is the person who goes off on tangents or argues without giving up, or rejects ideas on a personal basis in order to block ideas from gaining group acceptance. The blocker usually has some vested interest in the status quo or some personal reason for not favoring the suggested plan. Blocking is a strategy a leader must be concerned with. The leader should seek group backing for a point before the blocker can establish his position. If everyone or nearly everyone favors a point, then the leader can present a united front.

3. *Competer.* The competer, similar to the aggressor, is the person who always feels a need to compete with another person or idea, mostly for purposes of getting attention. Her ideas are not as important as her getting an audience. For instance, if Dick seems to be presenting ideas that the group favors, the competer, Jane, will bring up another point of view whenever Dick talks so that the group will see him as a thinking person. She takes on a person solely for the joy of the competition. The leader should not let the competition continue. Once the competer has made her point the leader should solicit comments from others and not let the competer dominate.

4. *Special Pleader.* The special pleader has one or two pet ideas. Regardless of what kind of a group, what its real purpose, the special pleader works in "his thing." He is especially difficult in a new group that is not onto him. An ongoing group soon learns what "his thing" is and finds ways around it without hurting his feelings too badly.

5. *Joker.* Whereas the game leader plays a positive role, the joker is negative. Her behavior is characterized by clowning, mimicking, or generally disrupting by making a joke of everything. She too is usually trying to call attention to herself. She must be the center of attention. A little bit of a joker goes a long way. The group needs to get the joker to consider the problem seriously, or she will constantly be an irritant to other members. One way to proceed is to encourage the joker when tensions need to be released but to ignore her when there is serious work to be done.

6. *Withdrawer.* The withdrawer refuses to be a part of the group. He is a mental dropout. Sometimes he is withdrawing from something that was said; sometimes he is just showing his indifference. Try to draw him out with questions. Find out what he is especially good at and rely on him when his skill is required. Sometimes complimenting him will bring him out.

7. *Monopolizer.* The monopolizer needs to talk all the time. Usually she is trying to impress the group that she is well read, knowledgeable, and of value to the group. The monopolizer should be encouraged when her comments are helpful. But when she is talking too much or when her comments are not helpful, the leader needs to interrupt her and draw others into the discussion.

Now that we have examined the roles that are played in a group, you may be wondering about how all of these fit together in a "normal" group. One of the leading researchers in group interaction processes, Robert Bales, has noted (1) that 40 to 60 percent of discussion time is spent on giving and asking for information and opinion, (2) 8 to 15 percent of discussion time is spent on disagreement, tension, or unfriendliness—behavior that we have discussed as *negative maintenance functions*, but that (3) 16 to 26 percent of discussion time falls under headings of agreement, friendliness, or dramatization—behavior that we have discussed as *positive maintenance functions*.[2] So the two norms we can use as guidelines are that approximately half of all discussion time be concerned with information sharing and that group agreement far outweighs group disagreement.

EVALUATING GROUP COMMUNICATION

Now that we have considered the criteria for group effectiveness, we can consider instruments for analyzing the group decision, individual participation, and the group process.

[2]Robert F. Bales, *Personality and Interpersonal Behavior* (New York: Holt, Rinehart and Winston, 1971), p. 96.

The Decision

The first instrument (Appendix B-4, Group Communication Analysis—Form A, Decision) to be considered gives us an opportunity to look at the group *decision*. The theory behind this instrument is that since the group's goal is to arrive at a decision, a decision-based critical instrument will consider the end product of group communication. As you will see, this instrument calls for you to discuss three major questions:

1. *Did the group arrive at a decision?* Just because a group meets to discuss does not necessarily mean that it will arrive at a decision. As foolish as it may seem, there are some groups that thrash away for hours only to adjourn without having arrived at a decision. Of course, some groups discuss such serious problems that a decision cannot be reached without several meetings, but I am not talking about a group that plans to meet later to consider the issue further. I mean the group that "finishes" without arriving at some decision. Not arriving at a decision results in total frustration and disillusionment.

2. *What action is taken as a result of the discussion?* Problem-solving discussion implies implementation. After the group has "finished" if no means for putting the decision into action has been considered, then there is reason to question the practicability of the decision.

3. *Was the group decision a good one?* This may be the most difficult question to answer. Whether a decision is good or not is of course a value judgment made by the evaluator. I would suggest applying six criteria for such an evaluation: (1) Was quality information presented to serve as a base or foundation for the decision? (2) Were the data discussed fully? (3) Did interim conclusions relate to information presented or were they stated as opinions that had no relationship to content? (4) Did a given conclusion seem to be the product of group consideration, or was it determined by the persuasive or authoritarian power of the leader? (5) Was the final decision measured against some set of criteria or objectives? (6) Did the group agree to support the decision?

Individual Members

Although a group will have difficulty without good leadership, it may not be able to function at all without members who are willing and able to meet the task and maintenance functions of the group. The next critical instrument of group analysis (Appendix B-5, Group Communication Analysis—Form B, Individual) incorporates each of the elements considered earlier in the chapter and provides a relatively easy-to-use checklist that can be kept for each individual.

The Group Process

Perhaps the most revealing method of analyzing group behavior is to do some kind of process analysis. Although Robert F. Bales has developed a very sophisticated method called the Interaction Process Analysis, discussed in his book *Personality and Interpersonal Behavior*,[3] in this section we want to outline a type of process analysis that is based upon the language defined and discussed in this chapter. This relatively simple analysis (Appendix B-6, Group Process Analysis) should prove beneficial for you in seeing how much each person is participating, determining the nature of the participation, and comparing the group's participation with Bales's norms given on page 191. From your comparison, you can see whether your group seems to be acting in a "normal" way. If not, your group can take time to find out what is causing the variations. If your group does not seem to be functioning very well, the process analysis may lead you to the causes of the difficulty.

EXERCISE

1. Each group has ten to fifteen minutes to arrive at a solution to the following dilemma: Five people are boating. The father, a 55-year-old heart specialist reputed to be the best in the state; his 36-year-old wife, a dermatologist; their 8-year-old child; their neighbor, a 43-year-old industrial salesman for a major corporation; and his wife, a 35-year-old former model who appears in frequent local television commercials. If some tragedy ensued and only one of the five could be saved, who should it be?

    After the exercise, the group should determine (1) what roles were operating in the group during the discussion, (2) who were performing those roles, and (3) what factors helped or hurt the discussion process.

2. Try to use one of the three instruments (Appendix B-4, Appendix B-5, or Appendix B-6) to analyze a group discussion.

SUMMARY

As an effective group participant, you have many responsibilities. The first is to be prepared. Preparation begins with a good working knowledge of the material related to the subject. If information is gathered for you, you should take the time to read it carefully before the group's first meeting. If you are responsible for research, you will want to survey your own experience with the subject, survey appropriate library sources, survey

[3]Bales, pp. 99–134.

public opinion, and interview. Since so many of the subjects you will be discussing are likely to be current and about issues close at hand, you will find some of your best material coming from carefully planned and executed interviews.

But preparation goes beyond just finding material. You will also want to determine a procedure for analyzing the topic. Such a procedure involves testing the phrasing of the question for discussion and identifying the question as one of fact, value, or policy. If you can identify the type of question, you will then be able to identify the questions you will need to ask in order to resolve the topic question.

Once you are adequately prepared, you can begin to think about taking part in the discussion. Effective participation involves talking productively and fulfilling positive roles. By interacting with other participants, maintaining objectivity, managing conflict, and being responsive to the requirements of leadership, you can insure productive participation. By fulfilling task and maintenance functions, you can insure a positive rather than a negative contribution. You may perform one or more of the task roles of giving and seeking information, expediting, analyzing, and coming up with creative ideas; you may perform one or more of the maintenance roles of active listening, harmonizing, gatekeeping, compromising, or reducing tension through humor. You will want to try to avoid the negative roles of aggressor, blocker, competer, special pleader, joker, withdrawer, or monopolizer.

SUGGESTED READINGS

David W. Johnson and Frank P. Johnson. *Joining Together.* Englewood Cliffs, N.J.: Prentice-Hall, 1975 (paperback).

Bobby R. Patton and Kim Giffin. *Decision-Making Group Interaction.* New York: Harper & Row, 1978 (paperback).

Stewart L. Tubbs. *A Systems Approach to Small Group Interaction.* Reading, Mass.: Addison-Wesley Publishing Company, 1978.

CHAPTER 10

LEADERSHIP IN GROUPS

Claude paused as he walked through the huge set of doors. "The Summit," he said to himself. "I never dreamed I'd ever go through these doors." All he had ever heard or read came rushing through his mind. The Leader's Summit. Here was where the decisions were made. Here was where the policy of the nation was decided. The all-knowing Leader sat daily on his throne at the Summit—and today Claude would have an audience. He had grappled with his problem for months. Starting the project could affect the lives of nearly everyone in the community. He had taken the question to both the local and regional Councils, but both said the decision needed the special attention—the special wisdom—of the Leader. And so here he was.

He made his way into the foyer. At each checkpoint leading to the Throne Room—the heart of the Summit—he showed his credentials.

At last he was led by the Chief Appointment Maker to the Throne itself. The Leader sat in regal splendor with Gold Scepter in his hand.

"You have come a long way for guidance," the Leader said quietly. "State your problem, my son."

Claude, momentarily overwhelmed by the presence of the great Leader, slowly began to pour forth the complexities underlying the decision that had to be made.

"Well stated," the Leader said. And now came the moment Claude had been waiting for. The Leader gazed at him intently. Slowly he reached into his gold lamé tunic and drew out what appeared to be a tiny metal disc with the seal of the Leader stamped on the surface. And with a sweep of his hand, he propelled the disc into the air..The Leader whispered, "Heads you start the project—tails you don't."

Leadership means many things to many people. To some it is an inherent, almost divine complex of traits that sets one person apart from his or her peers. To others it is the lucky providence of being in the right place at the right time. Yet, within most of us is some deep feeling that whatever leadership is—we have what it takes. Although it is fashionable to talk publicly about how "we wouldn't take the job of leader for all the tea in China," in private we may see ourselves as the only logical candidates for the job.

The premise of this chapter is that there is absolutely nothing wrong with thinking you are the best person for the job. However, leadership is not something that can be thought of lightly. Our goal in this chapter is to show what it means to be the leader of a work group, how to proceed if you want to try for leadership, and what you are responsible for doing in the group after you get the job. Although much of this discussion is applicable to all leadership situations, we will focus on the question of leadership in the work group context.

WHAT IS LEADERSHIP?

What is leadership? The definition differs from person to person. Yet, common to most definitions are the ideas of influence and accomplishment. Leadership means being in charge—exerting influence; and leadership means getting things done. Let's explore these two ideas. (1) *Leadership means exerting influence.* The exercise of influence is different from the exercise of raw power. When you exercise raw power you force a person or a group to submit, perhaps against their will; when you influence others you show them why an idea, a decision, or a means of achieving a goal is superior in such a way that members of the group will seek to follow those ideas of their own free will. Members will continue to be influenced as long as they are convinced that what they have agreed to is right, or is in their individual best interest, or in the best interest of the group. (2) *Leadership results in getting things done.* In the context of task or problem-solving discussion this means accomplishing the task or arriving at a solution that tests out to be the best solution available at that time.

So, you say that you think you are good at exerting influence and you think that you are good at getting the job done, and now you want to be a leader. Well, let's see how you might get there. Perhaps you have heard that leaders are born and not made, so you might raise the question: "Is there a way of making sure that I have the leadership traits that are necessary?"

LEADERSHIP TRAITS

What kind of a person is most likely to be the leader of a group? Are there such things as "leadership traits" that if discovered within a person will predict his success as a leader? For many years researchers operated under the assumption that special leadership traits could be isolated. The goal was to isolate them and then work out some kind of a test that any person could take to determine whether he was or should be a leader. But after some years of work, researchers concluded that a trait approach to the question of leadership was not going to yield means to uncover or predict leaders.

Does this mean that there are no specific traits that a leader shows? No, it means only that there is not a high correlation between traits and instances of leadership. Or to put it another way, leaders and nonleaders alike exhibit many of the same traits. However, Shaw, a leading authority in group research, states: "Although the correlations between individual traits and leadership measures are not large, there is nevertheless enough consistency to permit some generalizations."[1] What generalizations does he then go on to draw? He concludes that leaders exemplify traits related to ability, sociability, and motivation to a greater degree than do nonleaders. As far as ability is concerned, leaders exceed average group members in intelligence, scholarship, insight, and verbal facility. In sociability, leaders exceed group members in regard to such things as dependability, activity, cooperativeness, and popularity. In motivation, leaders exceed group members in initiative, persistence, and enthusiasm. Remember, this does not mean that a person in the group with superior intelligence, or the one who is most liked, or the one with greatest enthusiasm will necessarily be the leader. I believe it does mean that a person is unlikely to be the leader if he or she does not exhibit at least some of these traits to a greater degree than do other group members.

Do you perceive yourself as having any or many of these traits? If you see these traits in yourself, then you are a potential leader. Since several individuals in most groups have this potential for leadership, who ends up being the leader depends upon many things other than possession of traits. Modern research indicates that the path to leadership (or maintaining leadership after you get there) grows out of the context of the group, the needs of the members, and their goals.

---

[1]Marvin E. Shaw, *Group Dynamics: The Psychology of Small Group Behavior,* 2d ed. (New York: McGraw-Hill, 1976), p. 275.

EXERCISE

1. What do you believe are your strongest leadership traits?
2. In your discussion groups, discuss your opinion about the relative importance of various leadership traits.

WHO WILL LEAD?

Most of us consider as normal a model in which a person is appointed or elected to act as leader. We sometimes are not aware that, regardless of whether there is a designated leader, a group ends up being led by a "real leader"—a person who emerges from the group. The appointed leader may prove to be the real leader. Sometimes the appointed leader and one or more others share leadership, and sometimes early in the group's existence or after a long series of tests of leadership one person emerges as the real leader of the group. So, just because there is a designated leader does not mean that you are kept from either sharing leadership or becoming the real leader. The following are suggestions of what you can think about, do, and say that will show you to be worthy of leadership. If you are looking for some tried and true formula, forget it. Although people who do not consider these things very seldom achieve or maintain leadership, considering them does not guarantee attainment of leadership.

   1. *Think carefully about group expectations.* People are not likely to support leaders who call for a group to achieve far-reaching programs that entail great risk and require great personal change. Although a new direction or a new method of procedure might be best for the group, the risk is often too great for individual members of the group to undertake. The promise of revolutionary change is very threatening to member positions. For a person to gain leadership or to maintain leadership he must show the ability to set forth achievable goals and procedures.

   2. *As a potential leader, you must have knowledge related to the particular group tasks.* Remember that context determines emergence and success of the leader far more than possession of any leadership traits. You must have enough grasp of the context of the task to recognize which members are contributing effectively and which are not.

   3. *Closely related to point 2, be prepared to work harder than anyone else in the group.* Leadership is often a question of setting an example. When a group sees a person who is willing to do more than her fair share for the good of the group, group members are likely to support that person. Of course, such effort often takes a lot of personal sacrifice, but the person seeking to lead must be willing to pay the price.

   4. *A leader must be willing to be decisive at key moments in the discussion.* When a leader is unsure of himself, the group may ramble aimlessly; when the leader is unskilled at making decisions the group can become frustrated and short-tempered. When decisions are not made by the designated leader, then one or more other persons must assume leadership. Sometimes a leader must make decisions that will be resented; sometimes he must decide between two competing ideas about a course of action, and any decision he makes may cause conflict. Nevertheless, a person who is not willing and able to be decisive is not going to maintain leadership very long.

5. *The leader must be personally committed to the group goals and needs.* It is quite possible that in any given group for any given situation there may be several who can perform as leaders. To gain and maintain leadership, you need greater enthusiasm for the particular job. When you lose commitment, your leadership may wane and may be transferred to others whose enthusiasm is more tuned to a new set of conditions.

6. *A person who wishes to be leader must interact freely.* No one will opt for a leader who remains silent most of the time. Now this does not mean that the leader always dominates the discussion—but no one can know how you think, how you feel, what insights you have unless you are willing to share your ideas in discussion. Too often people sit back silently, thinking: "If only they would call on me for leadership, I would do a real job." Groups do not want unknown quantities. Perhaps by talking you run the risk of showing your lack of qualifications for leadership, but it is better to find out now whether you can talk sensibly and influence others.

7. *The person who wishes to be leader must develop skill at maintenance functions as well as at task functions.* The leader must make others in the group feel good; he or she must be able to contribute a group cohesiveness; she must be able to give credit where it is due. Although a group often has both a task leader and a maintenance leader, the overall leader is equally if not more likely to be the one who shows maintenance skills.

So, if you want to be a leader, these are some of the behaviors you must exhibit. However, becoming a leader and then carrying out leadership are two different things. Many people reach the top of the leadership pole only to slide slowly to oblivion. Perhaps the first question you must ask yourself when it becomes obvious that you are the leader is "How am I going to handle myself?"

LEADERSHIP STYLE

The way a person handles himself is called *style.* A casual examination of groups in operation will reveal a variety of kinds of style on the part of leaders. Some leaders give orders directly; others look to the group to decide what to do. Some leaders appear to play no part in what happens in the group; others seem to be in control of every move. Some leaders constantly seek the opinions of group members; other leaders do not seem to care what individuals think. Each person will tend to lead a group with a style that reflects his or her own personality, needs, and inclination. Although people have a right to be themselves, an analysis of operating groups shows that groups themselves work better and/or feel better about the work they have done depending upon the style of leadership.

What are the major leadership styles? Which is best? In their pioneer study, White and Lippitt describe three types of leadership behavior.[2] Their discussion forms a foundation for a discussion of styles of leadership. In effect, their analysis describes a kind of continuum of leadership. At one extreme is the authoritarian leader who maintains total control; at the other extreme is the laissez-faire style that for all practical purposes is nonleadership; somewhere in between is democratic style. Few people fall into any of the three categories Lippitt and White describe; moreover, few people behave consistently in all situations.

If we go back to the definition of leadership as exerting influence to get things done, we can see that by definition an effective style is one in which the leader takes some active role in the discussion in order to influence its outcome. If that's the case, then why isn't the authoritarian style the ultimate form for leadership? Although there are situations when authoritarian leadership may in fact be most desirable, as a consistent style it fails to meet the definition of leadership because it denies the value of members of the group. Let's explore characteristics of leadership style a little more deeply.

The authoritarian leader exercises complete control over the group. Authoritarian leaders will determine the statement of the question. They will make the analysis of procedure and dictate how the group will proceed to arrive at the decision. They are likely to outline specific tasks for each group member and suggest the roles they desire members to play. They also make personal praise or criticism of individual contributions. In the end they determine the decision with or without the help of the group.

The laissez-faire leader, on the other hand, does almost nothing except to get the group together and to supply information and material when asked. Laissez-faire leaders do not take part in or even suggest directions for decisions of the group. The group itself has complete freedom in determining every aspect of the decision-making process. Laissez-faire "leaders" are nonleaders.

Somewhere between these two extremes lies the ideal of democratic leadership. Democratic leaders *suggest* phrasings of the question, *suggest* procedures, *suggest* tasks and roles for individual members. Yet in every

---

[2]Ralph White and Ronald Lippitt, "Leader Behavior and Member Reaction in Three 'Social Climates,' " in Dorwin Cartwright and Alvin Zander (Eds.), *Group Dynamics: Research and Theory*, 3rd ed. (New York: Harper & Row, 1968), p. 319.

facet of the discussion, democratic leaders encourage group participation to determine what actually will be done. Everyone feels free to offer suggestions to modify the leader's suggestions. What the group eventually does is determined by the group itself. Democratic leaders may well exert influence at various places; that is, they may give reasons for the procedures they suggest. And groups may well decide that the leader's suggestions are in the best interests of the group. But in the final analysis, it is the *group* that decides. So, democratic leadership is not wishy-washy, it is not laissez-faire—nor is it authoritarian.

The contrasts indicate the characteristics of leadership style. But the more important question for you is: What are the results of these styles? The following analysis considers White and Lippitt's conclusions but also includes other research to verify, supplement, and occasionally modify their conclusions.[3]

1. *More work is done under either a democratic leader or an authoritarian leader than in a laissez-faire setting.* For all practical purposes, laissez-faire means no leadership at all. When a group is truly directionless, it tends to flounder. So, the laissez-faire style is least effective under all circumstances. This is very important to note for at least one additional reason: often when leaders who tend toward authoritarianism try to be more democratic they become laissez-faire. Many people just can't seem to lead without controlling. Thus, when they give up control, chaos reigns. Be very careful not to confuse laissez-faire with democratic leadership.

2. *More work is done under an authoritarian leader than under a democratic leader.* Whether this is true most of the time or only some of the time is open to question. According to Shaw,[4] either the authoritarian group is more productive or there is no significant difference. This means that if the sole criterion is getting a job done quickly, the authoritarian style of leadership is usually more effective and seldom if ever less effective than the democratic style.

3. *Work motivation and originality are better under a democratic leader.* Evidence for this conclusion is consistent. In a democratic group the members "have a piece of the action"; they feel as if they have been active in the decision-making process. As a result, under democratic leadership individual members are more likely to blossom. Not only is individual growth potential the greatest, but also individuals feel better about the group process. In most group settings this factor is a very important consideration.

4. *Authoritarian leadership seems to create aggression and discontent, even though the discontent may not appear on the surface.* Again, research substantiates this point. Take notice that under an authoritarian leader members may not be vocal about their discontent during the group process. In fact, an authoritarian group often gives the impression of complete harmony. But dis-

---

[3]White and Lippitt, "Leader Behavior," p. 334.
[4]Shaw, *Group Dynamics*, p. 279.

content, although below the surface, manifests itself in many ways: It may be complaining about what took place during discussions in informal comments after the meeting; it may be footdragging in putting the group's plan into action; it may be abandoning the group decision if the going gets rough during implementation; it may be indifference or hostility about taking time to work with the group.

5. *There is more dependence and less individuality in authoritarian groups.* Whereas democratic leadership may help the individual to blossom, authoritarian leadership seems to stifle the individual. Because the authoritarian leader is quick to exercise coercive power, everyone looks to him or her to see what to do and how to do it so there will be no "mistakes." As a result there is little likelihood that individuals will be willing to take the initiative. Moreover, if the leader is absent for any reason, the authoritarian led group tends to flounder. People aren't used to contributing.

6. *People enjoy the group process more when they work under a democratic leader.* They often look forward to meetings, get caught up in the group action and become oblivious to time, and look back on the group activity as a positive experience.

This analysis of the literature indicates that most researchers favor democratic leadership. True. Yet, there are times when the democratic way is not the best choice. Participatory democracy has its limits. For instance, during a closely contested basketball game the coach who calls a time-out has one minute to help the players handle a particular defensive alignment

THERE ARE TIMES WHEN
THE DEMOCRATIC WAY IS NOT
THE BEST CHOICE.

the other team is using. The coach will not use the minute in democratic processes—asking players if they have any ideas, or suggesting a plan and giving the players the opportunity to evaluate it. Instead, the coach will tell the players how to proceed, make a substitution if needed, and give the players encouragement to do what they have been told. When the accomplishment of the task is or appears to be more important than the feelings of members, then authoritarianism may be appropriate. (This is not to say that a basketball coach or any other leader who adopts the authoritarian style for the moment can disregard group feeling.) As studies have shown, a job gets done as fast or faster and often with fewer errors under an authoritarian leader. Authoritarian leadership also seems to work well when the authority really is much superior in knowledge and skill to the participants. Again, the basketball example bears this out. The coach is the coach because of what he knows—as long as the players respect his superior knowledge, they will work under the authoritarian style.

There is at least one other favorable aspect of the authoritarian form of leadership—it is easier. Learning to be a good democratic leader sometimes ends in the frustrations of laissez-faire nonleadership. In other words, some people confuse being a democratic leader with not leading at all. Since there is little ambiguity in authoritarian leadership—the leader gives directions and the group follows them—it is far easier to understand and administer.

If authoritarian leadership is your thing—and many authoritarian leaders do exist, are effective, and even win the approval of their groups— perhaps it would be well to consider one other point. The best authoritarian model seems to be "benevolent dictatorship." If the authority arises out of the need to control—and perhaps even to crush dissent—authority leads to tyranny. Even an authoritarian can be likable. Let's go back to our coach one last time. Even though authoritarianism is an approved model in coaching, the tyrant is seldom successful. Any group process is partly inspiration. Inspiration is seldom nurtured in a climate of hate.

Is there no place for laissez-faire procedure? There appears to be only one set of circumstances that calls for the laissez-faire approach. A group of experts who are largely self-motivated, such as a research staff of a "think tank" or scientific laboratory, may do best if left pretty much to their own creative devices. Usually, however, laissez-faire is *least* satisfactory.

My advice is that you examine your own style very closely. What is your natural inclination? How has it worked in the past? Would it be useful to blend some of the characteristics of another style with what comes naturally to you? Remember, these categories are not necessarily hard and fast. Still, the style you adopt is *yours*. If you have determined your approach, now you must consider your leadership behavior.

EXERCISE

1. What is your leadership style? What are the strengths and weaknesses of that style?
2. What kind of leadership style do you work best under? Why?
3. Compare your answers with those of other members of your group.

LEADERSHIP RESPONSIBILITIES

We have looked at how you can become a leader and what kinds of style you can use in leadership. In our discussion of style, we tried to show the advantages of democratic leadership under most circumstances. Assuming then that you want to try to become a better democratic leader, how do you go about it? You know that you will want to try to bring members closer together in a cohesive unit, maintain a high morale among the members, encourage a sociability that allows for freedom of expression, and help get the job done. Now let's look at some of the specific behaviors of democratic leadership.

Establish a Climate

Your first job is to set up a comfortable physical setting that will encourage interaction. The leader is in charge of such physical matters as heat, light, and seating. Make sure the room is at a good comfortable temperature; make sure that there is enough lighting; and most important make sure the seating arrangements are conducive to spirited interaction.

Too often, seating is too formal or too informal for the best discussion. By "too formal," I mean board-of-directors style. Imagine the long polished oak table with the chairman at the head, leading lieutenants at right and left, and the rest of the people down the line, as illustrated in Figure 10-1a. Seating is an indication of status. Thus how the seating is arranged can facilitate or kill real and total interaction. In the board-of-directors style a boss-and-subordinate pattern emerges. People are less likely to speak until they are asked to do so. Moreover, no one has a really good view of all the people present.

However, an excessively informal setting may also inhibit interaction. In an informal arrangement people just sit where they can be most comfortable. In Figure 10-1b three people sitting on the couch form their own little group; the two seated next to each other form another group. A couple of members have placed themselves out of the main flow. The group interaction will be casual, but may not be the most effective.

The ideal is the circle, represented by Figure 10-1c. Here everyone can see everyone else. At least physically, everyone has equal status. If the meeting place does not have a round table, you may be better off with either no table at all or a setting of tables that make a square (Figure 10-1d), at which the members can come close to the circle arrangement.

Plan the Agenda

The second leader responsibility is to plan the agenda. You may do this alone or in consultation with the group. When possible the agenda should be in the hands of the group several days before the meeting. A group needs the opportunity to think about the task before it. How much preparation any individual member will make is based upon many factors, but unless the group has an agenda beforehand members will not have an opportunity for any preparation. Second, we have already talked about the importance of commitment on the part of the participant. When a group has little idea of why it is meeting or what will happen during the meeting, morale suffers and commitment wanes. Too often, when no agenda is planned, the group meeting is a haphazard affair, often frustrating and usually unsatisfying.

What goes in the agenda? Usually a sketch of some of the things that need to be accomplished. If a meeting is for the purpose of accomplishing a single task, the agenda should include a suggested procedure for handling the task logically. For instance, suppose that at the meeting someone moved to raise the dues three dollars per session. The group then voted to refer the issue to a committee that you chair. Although some of your committee members will have ideas on the issue, think of how much better the discussion could be if each committee member were given the following agenda a few days before the committee meeting:

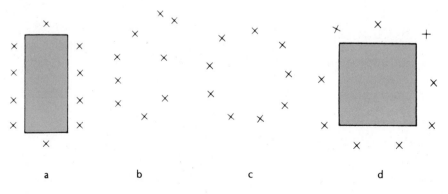

a   b   c   d

Figure 10-1

Question: Should the dues be raised $3 per session?

Is the group in need of additional funds? In what areas?

Are there areas in which money can be saved?

If dues were raised $3, would it enable the group to achieve its goals?

What would be the effects of a $3 raise in dues on the membership? Can members afford it? Would it result in a drop in membership?

Notice that the agenda does not indicate what will be done; it does suggest the kinds of questions that need to be considered if the group is to come up with the best solution.

For an ongoing group, the agenda indicates the business that will be handled at that particular meeting. Suppose that this week is the fifth meeting of the long-range planning committee.

Goal: What should be the requirements for the College of Liberal Arts?

Today's business: Discussion of the Miller Report of student questionnaire.

How good was the sample?

How accurate are the results?

What effect if any should student views have on the issue?

What should be the next step?

If the group is an ongoing group that meets more or less regularly to conduct the business of the organization, then the agenda is more formal in following established procedure:

Calling meeting to order
Reading of the minutes
Officers' reports
Committee reports
    Social
    Curriculum
    Library
Old business
    None
New business
    Jones proposal to limit expenditures on travel
    Hanley proposal to conduct quarterly personnel evaluation
    Other
Adjournment

Introduce the Topic

A third responsibility, and one that is especially important for a group's first meeting, is for the leader to introduce the topic. Again, at the beginning of a group's existence, commitment may be low for some members, expectations may be minimal, general attitude may be questioning. The stance of the individuals may likely be "we know that many group sessions are a waste of time and we take a wait-and-see attitude." A good leader will start the group by drawing a verbal contract and motivating members to live up to it. The leader will answer such questions as Why are you here? Who got you together? What is your mission? How much has been done already? When are you supposed to finish? To whom are we responsible? What kinds of responsibilities will each group member have? How much will each member be expected to do? Some of these questions will already have been discussed with individuals, but the first meeting gives the leader a chance to put everything together.

Direct the Flow of Discussion

The leader is responsible for directing the flow of discussion. It is in this area that leadership skill is most tested. Let's examine carefully several of the most important elements of this responsibility.

Keep the Interaction Balanced   In Chapter 9, we discussed the role of the gatekeeper—he is the one who keeps channels of communication open. The leader should certainly be one of the people who takes this role of determining who talks and of facilitating the flow of the interaction. The nature of the interaction directly affects the quality of the end product. Consider the three patterns of group discussion (Figure 10-2, where lines represent the flow of discussion among the eight participants). Figure 10-2a represents a leader-dominated group. The lack of interaction often leads to a rigid, formal, and usually poor discussion. Figure 10-2b represents a more spontaneous group. However, since three people dominate and a few are not heard, conclusions will not represent group thinking. Still, this pattern is by far the most common in work groups. Left to their own devices, some will elect to speak out more frequently and some will elect

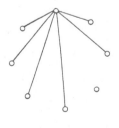   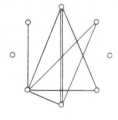   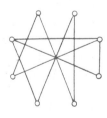

a   b   c

Figure 10-2

not to speak at all. Figure 10-2c represents something closer to the ideal pattern. It illustrates a great deal of spontaneity, a total group representation, and theoretically at least the greatest possibility for reliable conclusions.

Although the ideal is difficult to achieve, it is up to the leader to try for as much balance as possible. The two most important questions involve to whom a person may talk and when he may talk. If a member thinks that he may talk only to the leader, then the pattern of Figure 10-2a is likely to emerge, as it will also if a person thinks that he may talk only when recognized. Although more than one person should not be talking at once and members should not interrupt others rudely or constantly, there must be a freedom of expression that allows anyone to talk when and to whomever he needs to talk. The ideal (Figure 10-2c) gets a bit messy at times—pandemonium may rage momentarily—but everyone feels part of the group.

Perhaps the best attitude for the leader is a slightly permissive one. Although he needs to protect the rights of all, informality would be the key note.

See That the Points Are Carefully Weighed and Considered   Not only must the leader see to it that the key ideas are discussed but also that maximum value is achieved from each point that is made. The skill that helps a leader most is appropriate questioning.

Although the members of any group bring a variety of skills, information, and degrees of motivation to the group, they do not always operate at peak efficiency without help from the leader. Perhaps one of the most effective tools of good leadership is the ability to question appropriately. This skill involves knowing when to ask questions and knowing what kinds of questions to ask.

By and large, the leaders should refrain from questions that can be answered "yes" or "no." To ask a group member whether she is satisfied with a point that was just made will not lead very far. After she answers "yes" or "no," either you must ask another question to bring her out or you must change the subject. The two most effective types of questions are those that call for supporting information or the completely open-ended question that gives the member complete freedom of response. For instance, rather than asking John whether he has had any professors that were particularly good lecturers, you could ask "John, what are some of the characteristics that made your favorite lecturers particularly effective?" or "Mary, from your experience in listening to speakers, what would you select as most important elements of speaker effectiveness?"

When to ask questions is particularly important. Although we could list fifteen to twenty circumstances, let's focus on four purposes of questioning.

1. *To focus the discussion.* Individual statements usually have a point; the statements themselves relate to a larger point being made; and the general discussion relates to an issue or to an agenda item. You can use questions to determine a speaker's point or to determine the relationship of the point to the issue or agenda item:

"Are you saying that the instances of marijuana leading to hard-drug use don't indicate a direct causal relationship?"

To what has just been said: "How does that information relate to the point that Cindy just made?"

To an issue or to an agenda item: "In what way does this information relate to whether or not marijuana is a problem?"

2. *To probe for information.* Many statements need to be developed, supported, or in some way dealt with. Yet often members of a group apparently ignore or accept a point without probing it. When the point seems important, the leader should do something with it.

On a question of source: "Where did you get that information, Jack?"

To develop a point: "That seems pretty important, what do we have that corroborates the point?"

To test the strength of a point: "Does that statement represent the thinking of the group?"

To generate discussion: "That point sounds rather controversial—why should we accept it as stated?"

3. *To initiate discussion.* During a discussion, there are times when lines of development are apparently ignored, when the group seems ready to agree before sufficient testing has taken place. At these times, it is up to the leader to suggest as starting point for further discussion:

"OK, we seem to have a pretty good grasp of the nature of the problem, but we haven't looked at any cause yet—what are some of the causes?"

4. *To deal with interpersonal problems that develop.* Sometimes, there is a need to ventilate very personal feelings: "Ted, I've heard you make some strong statements on this point—would you care to share them with us?" At times, the group begins to attack a person instead of the information that is being presented: "I know Charley presented the point, but let's look at the merits of the information presented. Do we have any information that goes counter to this point?"

Questions by themselves are not going to make a discussion. In fact, some questions can hurt the discussion that is taking place. The effective leader uses questions sparingly but decisively.

Brainstorm When Needed

Most of the time a discussion is a rather orderly flow of information; and one of the goals of the leader is to see to it that ideas relate to each other, that an important idea is probed, explored, developed before the group goes on, that the group does not go too long without having ideas relate to key issues in the discussion. There are times, however, when the leader needs to direct the group to a completely freewheeling sharing of ideas regardless of their organization, value, or any other consideration. At such times, the leader should direct his group to brainstorm. *Brainstorming* is the process of stating and recording of every idea that is mentioned with no attempt made to evaluate a particular idea when it is mentioned. The philosophy of brainstorming is that within the atmosphere of complete freedom the presentation of ideas may, through free association, release the creative processes and enable the group to get a list of subjects that later can be sorted, developed, and evaluated.

For instance, Mary is leading a group of three persons who have for their charge the presentation of five good ideas for a senior-class present to the university. In such situations, the committee often bogs down after one or two suggestions have been rejected out of hand and no one can offer any more ideas. To free up the creative process, Mary could begin the meeting by suggesting brainstorming: "I've asked Suzy to sit in for a few minutes for the express purpose of taking down ideas that we come up with. Now, here's what I want you to do. In the next ten minutes or so I want you to say anything that comes to mind, regardless of how wild it may sound to you. Our only purpose is to see whether we can come up with at least 100 ideas. OK, let's get started."

Although ideas may come slowly at first, within a minute or so, all members should be contributing. The reason for an outsider taking short-hand notes is that participants should not do anything to slow down the process, yet they will want everything on paper. After a session, Mary might then say, "We'll type up the list and get copies to you later this afternoon. If you have any afterthoughts, add them to your list, and we'll meet tomorrow to begin processing what we've got." From that point on, the discussion could return to an orderly procedure.

Although this example illustrates getting a meeting started, you can use brainstorming in a discussion whenever the group needs to come up with just the right idea, word, or name.

Summarize Frequently

Often a group talks for a considerable period, then takes a vote on how they feel about the subject. A good problem-solving discussion group should move in an orderly manner toward intermediate conclusions represented by summary statements seeking group consensus. For instance, on the topic question "What should be done to lower the crime rate in the United States?" the group would have to reach consensus on each of the following questions:

What is the problem?

What are the symptoms of the problem? (Draw intermediate conclusion; ask whether group agrees)

What are the causes? (Draw intermediate conclusion on each cause separately or after all causes have been considered; ask whether group agrees)

What criteria should be used to test the solutions?

What is one criterion? (Draw conclusions about each criterion)

What are some of the possible conclusions? (Determine whether all possible solutions have been brought up)

What is the best solution?

How does each of the solutions meet the criteria? (Discuss each and draw conclusions about each; ask whether group agrees)

Which solution best meets the criteria? (The conclusion to this final question concludes the discussion; ask whether all agree)

During the discussion the group might draw six, eight, ten, or even fifteen conclusions before it is able to arrive at the answer to the topic question. The point is that the group should not arrive at the final conclusion until each of the subordinate questions is answered to the satisfaction of the entire group.

It is up to the leader to point up these conclusions by summarizing what has been said and seeking consensus on a conclusion. Everyone in the group should realize when the group has really arrived at some decision. If left to its own devices, a group will discuss a point for a while, then move on to another before a conclusion is drawn. The leader must sense when enough has been said to reach a consensus. Then he must phrase the conclusion, subject it to testing, and move on to another area. You should become familiar with phrases that can be used during the discussion:

"I think most of us are stating the same points. Are we really in agreement that . . ." (State conclusion)

"We've been discussing this for a while and I think I sense an agreement. Let me state it, and then we'll see whether it does summarize group feeling." (State conclusion)

"Now we're getting on to another area. Let's make sure that we are really agreed on the point we've just finished." (State conclusion)

"Are we ready to summarize our feelings on this point?" (State conclusion)

Maintain Necessary Control

Regardless of personal style, a leader must maintain control. Remember, absence of leadership leads to chaos. Group members need to feel that someone is in charge. If the group has a set of formal rules, be sure that the rules are followed (at times bending is necessary—but total breaking does not help the group). As leader, remember that some members will be playing negative roles in the discussion; don't let them spoil the outcome. You are in charge—you are responsible—you have authority. You will need to exercise it on occasion for the benefit of the group. If Johnny is about to talk for the fortieth time, it is up to you to harness him; if Jack and Mary are constantly sparring with each other, it is up to you to harmonize their differences; if something internal or external threatens the work of the group, it is up to you to deal with it.

Close the Discussion Effectively

It is up to the leader to determine when the group has finished. A one-meeting group cannot finish until it has completed its task. But as soon as it is finished you should bring the meeting to a close. Ongoing groups

A LEADER MUST MAINTAIN CONTROL.

need to adjourn when useful discussion seems to have ended for that day, when the day's task is over, when fatigue is too great, or when the task is complete. Unfortunately, some groups meet by time instead of by task. Just because you are scheduled to meet from 1:00 to 2:00 P.M. does not mean that you cannot stop at 1:30 if you have done the job.

EVALUATING LEADERSHIP

Although some group discussions are leaderless, no discussion should be leadershipless. An important element of the evaluation process is to consider the nature of the leadership. If there is an appointed leader, and most groups have one, you can focus on that individual. If the group is truly leaderless, then you must consider all attempts at leadership by the various members.

The checklist in Appendix B-7, Leadership Analysis, provides an easy-to-use instrument for evaluating group leadership.

EXERCISE ———————————————————————

Each classroom is given or selects a task (a discussion question) that requires some research. Each group should be given approximately 30 to 40 minutes for discussion. While group A is discussing, members of group B should observe and after the discussion give feedback during the remainder of the class period. For practice in using the various instruments, one observer could be asked to do a decision analysis (Appendix B-4), one could be asked to do a group communication analysis (Appendix B-5), one could be asked to do a group process analysis (Appendix B-6), and one could be asked to do a leadership analysis (Appendix B-7). During the next class period, group B would discuss and group A would observe and critique. Example questions:

What should be done to improve *parking* or *advising* or *registration* on campus?

What should be done to increase the participation of women in college or university *athletic programs* or *governance* or *teaching*?

SUMMARY

Leadership is exerting influence to accomplish a goal. Although leaders may show greater degrees of ability, sociability, and motivation than others in the group, the presence of traits is not the answer to whether you will lead effectively.

Do you want to lead? If so, you will want to understand the group expectations, study the subject area, be prepared to work hard to get the job done, be willing to be decisive, be committed to the goals of the group, interact freely with members, and develop task and maintenance skills.

Still, how well you lead may depend upon your style and how you put it into operation. Some "leaders" adopt the laissez-faire style of no leadership; some leaders try to dictate what will be done, when, and how; but most effective leaders try to adopt the democratic style of giving the group direction, while letting them participate in decision making.

Once you hold a position of leadership you must establish a good working climate, plan an agenda, be able to direct the flow of discussion, summarize when necessary, and maintain the necessary control to keep the discussion from getting out of hand.

SUGGESTED READINGS

Dorwin Cartwright and Alvin Zander (Eds.). *Group Dynamics: Research and Theory,* 3rd ed. New York: Harper & Row, 1968. This book is basic to any library of group research and contains excellent material on leadership.

A. Paul Hare. *Handbook of Small Group Research,* 2nd ed. New York: The Free Press, 1976. This may be the single most complete survey of small group research available.

Marvin E. Shaw. *Group Dynamics: The Psychology of Small Group Behavior,* 2nd ed. New York: McGraw-Hill, 1976. Shorter and more readable. A superior source.

PART 4

PUBLIC SPEAKING

*Winston Churchill,
Franklin Roosevelt, and Martin
Luther King, Jr., are but
three speakers whose words
made history.
Whether our words will make
history or not, we will
often be called upon
by choice or by necessity to speak
our ideas in public. This unit then
considers the variables that
affect public speaking.*

PUBLIC SPEAKING: SELF-ANALYSIS

When you go from the safety of personal and group communication to expressing your ideas in front of considerably larger audiences, a great deal of pressure is placed on your communication ability. In public speaking your message must be prepared in its entirety (or at least well thought out) before you begin; you must speak without the verbal feedback that helps to sharpen message understanding; and you must do it alone.

Yet, of all the communication settings, public speaking effectiveness may be the most important. As a member of a community action group, a college governance group, a social group, or any of the many types of groups with whom you may meet, you have the power and the opportunity to make a difference. But, if you cannot or will not speak out on issues either because of fear or lack of speech experience, you, your group, and perhaps society may suffer for your failure. Your ideas count—you need to make the most of them!

For each of the paired statements of the following public speaking analysis, encircle the number that best indicates how you see your behavior. The numbers 1, 2, and 3 represent the negative end of the continuum—they suggest a need for work on the item; the numbers 5, 6, and 7 represent the positive end—they suggest a perceived competence with the behavior. The number 4 is the midpoint that represents a position between the extremes. It may also say you are not sure of your behavior.

I have considerable fear about speaking in public	1 2 3 4 5 6 7	I have confidence in my ability to speak in public
In my preparation I seldom consider whether I have developed ideas fully	1 2 3 4 5 6 7	In my preparation I am careful to be sure that I have developed ideas fully
When preparing to speak I seldom consider audience knowledge, needs, or interest	1 2 3 4 5 6 7	When preparing to speak I choose information to present on the basis of audience knowledge, needs, or interest

In my preparation I seldom consider the order of my ideas	1 2 3 4 5 6 7	In my preparation I work to organize material to follow some consistent pattern
When I speak, audiences show signs of restlessness and inattention	1 2 3 4 5 6 7	When I speak audiences are alert and listen attentively
When I speak, the "right words" never seem to come to me	1 2 3 4 5 6 7	When I speak I sense that my audience perceives my language as clear and vivid
I tend to avoid looking directly at members of my audience when I speak	1 2 3 4 5 6 7	I look directly at members of my audience when I speak
My public speaking voice tends to remain on the same levels of pitch, speed, and loudness	1 2 3 4 5 6 7	My public speaking voice shows variations in pitch, speed, and loudness
When I speak I never know what to do with my hands; I feel and look awkward	1 2 3 4 5 6 7	When I speak, my bodily actions help to supplement or reinforce my ideas; I feel and look involved
When I have finished, I seldom feel that I have made an impact on my audience	1 2 3 4 5 6 7	When I have finished, I usually feel I have achieved my speech objective

(1) Consider your analysis. Is the number you encircled indicative of where you would like to be in that category? If not, in different colored ink or pencil, encircle the number that represents your goal for this term. (2) If you would like verification of your self-analysis, have a close friend, one parent, and a working acquaintance complete a personal analysis as outlined on page 345 of Appendix B-1.(3) Select one of the areas in which your goals are farthest from your current behavior. Write a communication improvement contract similar to the sample contract on page 362 of Appendix C.

CHAPTER 11

SPEECH PREPARATION

She was conscious that she was in a vast room filled with people. "Where am I?" she thought. "I wish I had some clue—I never dreamed that I wouldn't know."

From somewhere in the room she heard a deep resonant voice: "Welcome, Phyllis."

She looked around to determine the source of the voice. Not knowing where she was distressed her. "I thought I'd have some clue—angels or fire or something. All these people here—they're smiling. Do they smile in Hell?" she wondered.

"Phyllis," the voice intoned, "we've been waiting for you."

"They know me, but that's no clue. I've got to find out."

"Phyllis, come forward," the voice echoed, and a man and a woman rose to escort her down a long center aisle to the front of the room. As if by magic a podium bathed in light suddenly appeared. "Are you ready, Phyllis?" the voice asked.

Phyllis was panic-stricken. "Ready, uh, for what?" she managed to stammer.

"To give your speech, Phyllis."
Phyllis now knew—
She was in Hell.

Most of us are just naturally gregarious—we like to talk. We think nothing of spending hours chatting with a next-door neighbor over a cup of coffee, talking with our office mate about last night's game, or thrashing out the latest about guys, girls, cars, new clothes, or any topic imaginable over a beer at the local bar. Likewise, we do not seem particularly concerned when we have been asked to work with some problem-solving group—especially if we have the time, if we see the value of the task, or if we are rather ego-involved in the solving of the particular problem. Yet, ask the average person to give a "speech" and you turn him into a bundle of nerves. As Phyllis's fantasy illustrates, for many people the thought of giving a speech is hell.

Think I exaggerate? According to their study, R. H. Bruskin Associates found that 40.6 percent of the population are frightened by speaking in public.[1] In this study people were asked to pick items from a list of things that frightened them. Results showed such predictable feared things as heights, 32 percent; insects, 22 percent; financial problems, 22 percent; deep water, 21 percent; sickness, 18 percent; death, 18 percent; flying, 18 percent; loneliness, 13 percent; dogs, 11 percent; darkness, 8 percent—but speaking in public, *40.6 percent!*

Whatever the cause of the fear, for a great many people the presence of fear is real—and it needs to be considered. People exhibit various behaviors in responding to their fear: some people tremble, perspire, and experience shortness of breath and increased heartbeat. As they go through their speech, they worry about themselves and lose all contact with the audience, they jump back and forth from point to point, and on occasion they forget what they had planned to say. Their anxiety is so great that some people cannot eat or sleep before a speech; and some people avoid speaking at any cost. With such uncomfortable or frightening prospects before you, why even try? Foremost, *because speaking is important.* It is through speaking that we show others what we are thinking. Each of us has vital information to share: we may have the data needed to solve a problem; we may have a procedure to follow that will save countless dollars; we may have insights that go beyond those of others involved. Think of the potentially tremendous loss to business, governmental, educational, professional, and fraternal groups, because fear prevents people from being heard!

Let's start with the assumption that you are indeed nervous—in fact, you may be scared to death. Now what? Experience has proven that people (and this includes you) can learn to cope with these fears. Consider the following points:

[1]"Fears," *Spectra,* Vol. 9 (December 1973), p. 4.

1. *Almost all people experience nervousness when they speak in public.* The difference in nervousness among people is a matter of degree. I can hear you now: "Don't give me that line—you can't tell me that [and you fill in the blank with some person you know] is nervous when he [or she] speaks in public!" You doubt me? Ask the person. He or she will tell you. This may surprise you: I would be disappointed if you were not nervous. Why? Because you must be a little nervous to do your best. Of course I do not mean that you should be blind with fear, but it requires a bit of nervousness to get the adrenaline flowing—to bring you to speaking readiness.

2. *Almost all people discover that despite nervousness, they can make it through a speech.* Very few people are so bothered that they are literally unable to function. You may not enjoy the experience—but you *can* do it.

3. *The more experience you get in speaking, the more able you become at coping with nervousness.* You learn to think about the audience and the speech and not about yourself. Moreover, you come to realize that audiences are not nearly so frightening to deal with as you assume they will be. You will come to find that having a group of people listening to you and you alone is a pretty satisfying experience.

Now let's get down to two specific recommendations:

1. *Think positive!* You can do it! Once you realize that you can succeed (and you can), you will be less likely to be concerned about nervousness. Each successful experience will make the next effort just a little bit easier. Now do not interpret this to mean that sometime soon you will not be nervous. No, it means only that you can learn to cope with the nervousness. Just before it is your turn to speak, give yourself a little pep talk. Psych yourself up a bit—it will help.

2. *Be prepared.* Of all the things you can think or do nothing is more important than being prepared. Much of the fear of speaking is a reaction to perceived inadequacy: the belief that you do not know enough to be talking. If our nation's love affair with big-time athletics has taught us anything, it is that careful preparation enables us to meet and to overcome adversity. Among relatively equal opponents, the team that wins is the team that is mentally and physically prepared for the contest. When a player says, "I'm going into this contest as well prepared as I can possibly be," he usually does his best. In this regard, speechmaking is not different from athletics. If you will assure yourself that you have carefully prepared and practiced your speech, you will do the kind of job that will make you proud.

The rest of this chapter is directed toward helping you get ready to speak. If you are willing to work and check what you are doing against a few easily understood principles, you can do a better job than most speakers you hear giving speeches—in classrooms, at church, or in the political arena.

In this chapter we look at four steps that take you through the complete speech preparation process: (1) determine the material you will present, (2) organize the material to develop the speech objective and to relate to the audience, (3) adapt your language directly to your audience, and (4) practice the delivery.

DETERMINING YOUR CONTENT

Benjamin Franklin once said "an empty bag cannot stand upright." The content of the speech is of utmost importance. Without something of value to say, there is no reason for speaking. Every effort should be made to come forward with the best material possible. You will find that determining content will involve four issues: selecting a topic, analyzing the background and interests of your audience, phrasing a specific speech objective, and discovering the material you can use to develop your objective. Although I will discuss them separately, they overlap and are often accomplished in a different order.

Selecting a Topic

If someone selects a topic area for you, this step is omitted; usually, however, and especially in the classroom, topic selection is up to you. This initial problem of topic selection may be the most terrifying part of the process (I have often heard "Oh, I can give a good speech—if only I could find a topic!"). Let me offer a suggestion: Talk about the topics you know about and topics that interest you. You need to work out a procedure for revealing what you know something about and what you are interested in. You will discover that your knowledge and interests probably lie in three areas: in your major (or prospective profession), in your hobby (or spare-time activity), or in current events or social issues you are concerned about.

In order to create specific topics from these general categories, I suggest a form of *brainstorming*. As we discussed in the group communication section, brainstorming is an uncritical, nonevaluative attempt at verbalizing responses to given stimuli, much like the old word-association process: When you think the word *music* associatively you may think of "rock," "dance," "electronic," and "amplifiers." Likewise, when you start with a word or idea related to your major areas of expertise or interest, you can often associate twenty, thirty, or even fifty other related ideas and concepts.

How do you start? One way is to take a sheet of paper and divide it into three columns. Label column 1 "Major" or "Vocation"; label column 2 "Hobby" or "Activity"; and label column 3 "Current Events" or "Social Issues." Work on one column at a time. If you begin with column 2, "Hobby," you might write "pool." Then you would jot down everything that comes to mind, such as "cue," "English," "games," "tables," "equipment." Work for at least five minutes on a column. Then begin with a second column. Although you may not finish in one sitting, do not begin an evaluation until you have noted at least twenty items in each column.

When you think you have exhausted your personal resources, look over your list and check the three or four items that "ring a bell," that best capture your concerns and interests. The point of this exercise is to enable you to take advantage of a basic psychological principle—it is easier to answer a multiple-choice question than it is to answer the same question without the choices. So instead of asking yourself: "What should I talk about?" you are asking yourself: "What are the one, two, or three best topics that I have listed under each heading?" You may find, however, that the words or phrases you select are still too general to give you direction. If so, start a new list with one of the general topics. If you make a selection of this kind from each of the three columns, you may realize that you have three good topics to choose from for your speech.

EXERCISE

1. Divide a sheet of paper into three columns labeled "Vocation" or "Major," "Hobby" or "Activity," and "Current Event" or "Social Issue"; complete a list of twenty to forty items in each column.

2. In order of preference, indicate the three topics that are most interesting or most important to you in each list.

Phrasing a Speech Objective

Your topic states the subject area. The topic selection process is continued by deciding what you plan to do with that topic in your speech. Although you may want to delay your decision until you have analyzed your audience or until you have explored available material, or *both*, let us consider the issue of speech goal now.

Some difference of opinion exists about whether the topic statement is best expressed as "a specific purpose" or as "a speech objective." The difference between the two is orientation: specific purpose is speaker-oriented and speech objective is audience-oriented. The *specific purpose* is a single statement that summarizes exactly what you want to do with the speech. For instance, the statement "to explain the four steps of a four-stroke engine" is a specific purpose. It contains your intention (to explain) and the limits of the topic (the four steps of a four-stroke engine). A *speech objective* is a single statement that summarizes exactly what behavior or response you want from the audience as a result of your speech. The statement "to understand the four steps of a four-stroke engine" is a speech objective. The limits of the subject are stated identically. The difference is in the infinitive (the *to* form of the verb). Rather than being stated from the speaker perspective ("to explain"), it is stated from the audience response goal ("to understand"). Since a speech is given for an audience, it seems to me that the best phrasing is the one that accounts for audience response. For the remainder of this text, then, I will use the term "speech objective" as the term that explains the topic statement. If you or your instructor prefers "specific purpose" to "speech objective," the change can be accomplished by merely changing the infinitive.

In the following statements, the behavior is underlined once and the substance of the speech follows. For you to get a more complete idea of the limiting process, the examples move from subject area to topic to speech objective (expected audience response):

Subject Area: Swimming

Topic: The butterfly stroke

Speech Objective (expected audience response): <u>To understand</u> the elements of the butterfly stroke

Subject Area: Home decoration

Topic: Macramé hangers

Speech Objective (expected audience response): <u>To understand</u> how macramé hangers may be used to enhance the beauty of your plants, to help conserve space in a small room, and to decorate a home

Subject Area: Energy crisis

Topic: Development of electric cars

Speech Objective (expected audience response): <u>To petition</u> automotive companies to produce electric cars

Subject Area: Theatre

Topic: The play *Godspell*

Speech Objective (expected audience response): <u>To attend</u> *Godspell* this weekend at Shuler Auditorium

With any topic, a number of speech objectives are possible. Choose the statement that best indicates what you want your audience to understand, to do, or to believe.

Since writing a good speech objective is so important, let us take a step-by-step look at the procedure:

1. *Write out several potential wordings of the objective.* You probably will not be satisfied with your first attempt. In fact you may find it difficult to compose a statement that clearly states your point.

2. *Make sure that the speech objective is written as a complete thought.* Do not stop with one word, several words, or a vague statement. For instance, suppose you want to talk about "capital punishment." You have an idea, but it is just the start of a complete thought. "Methods of capital punishment" indicates the aspect of the topic you want to consider. "Three methods of capital punishment" limits what you will say to a specific number. "To understand three methods of capital punishment practiced in the United States" is a complete, clear statement of speech objective.

3. *Write the objective so that it contains only one idea.* "To understand the three methods of capital punishment practiced in the United States and to see that all three are inhumane" includes two distinct ideas, either of which can be used—but not both. Make a decision. Do you want to talk about methods? Then the objective "To understand the three methods of capital punishment practiced in the United States" is the better statement. Do you want to talk about morality? Then the objective "To believe that the methods of capital punishment practiced in the United States are inhumane" is the better statement.

4. *Write the speech objective in declarative form.* "Is capital punishment inhumane?" is a good question for discussion, but it is not a good speech objective because it does not show direction. Likewise, "Capital punishment—man's inhumanity to man!" may be a clever title, but it, too, fails as a speech objective for much the same reason: It does not give clear enough direction. "To believe that capital punishment is inhumane" is a clear declarative statement.

5. *Precede the statement of thesis with an infinitive or infinitive phrase that shows the audience reaction desired.* If you regard your idea as noncontroversial, universally accepted, or an expression of observation, then your intent is basically informative and will be shown with such wordings as "to understand." If, however, your idea is controversial, a statement of belief, or a call to action, then your intent is persuasive and that intent will be shown with such statements as "to believe" or "to petition" or some infinitive incorporating a specific action.

After you have written a number of topic statements, you will note that almost all of them can be loosely classified either as speeches that are concerned with understanding information or as speeches that involve belief or action. Since one common way of assigning classroom speeches is by the nature of the response desired, assignments discussed later in the textbook are grouped under the headings of "Information Exchange," "Persuasion," and, in order to cover speeches meeting several ceremonial occasions, "Speeches for Special Occasions."

Why is it so important to have a clear topic statement early in speech preparation? First, the topic statement helps to limit your research. If you know you want to bring about "an understanding of the location of the world's greatest diamond mines," you can limit your reading to "locations" at a saving of many hours of preparation time. Second, a good topic statement will assist you in organizing your ideas logically—the main points of a speech grow directly from the topic statement. Third, with a clear statement, you have your topic in a form that will enable you to answer these four important questions:

1. Is your topic really clear?

2. Does it meet audience expectations? (In a classroom setting, the expectations are those outlined by the professor for the assignment.)

3. Can I cover it in the time allotted? (We sometimes get a bit ambitious about what we can accomplish in four to six minutes.)

4. Does it offer the possibility of providing new information, new insights, or reasons for change of opinion for my audience? (No audience is going to be much interested in a rehash of what they already know or a restatement of what they already believe.)

EXERCISE

1. For each of the topic statements below, underline the behavior desired once and the substance of the topic statement twice. The first one has been done for you.

   To understand the three major criteria for evaluating the quality of a diamond.

   To believe that football should be de-emphasized at most colleges.
   To understand the steps involved in customizing a car.
   To go to the Coq D'Or for dinner.
   To evaluate the prospects of the Cincinnati Reds this year.

2. For one of the topics you indicated a preference for on page 224, write three well-worded speech objectives. Then, test each by asking the questions that precede this exercise.

Analyzing Your Audience

Since you are planning to give your speech to a specific audience, before you go very far in speech preparation you need to analyze your audience very carefully. Audience analysis is a method of examining audience knowledge, interests, and attitudes to determine a set of criteria by which you can test the appropriateness of the selected topic and the speech objective. You will also use the results of this analysis to guide you in your selection of supporting material, organization, language, and delivery. The following three groups of questions provide a working framework for such analysis. As you gain experience, you may modify the phrasing of questions and add other appropriate questions.

DO LISTENERS HAVE AN
INTEREST IN YOUR TOPIC?

1. *What are the nature and extent of my listeners' knowledge of this topic?*

Is my listeners' knowledge of the subject area sufficient to allow them to understand my speech? For some subjects, special knowledge is necessary; for some others, a certain level of information may be necessary before what you plan to say will make sense (an explanation of calculus requires understanding of certain mathematical information).

Will developmental material provide new information to most of my listeners? A speech that does not provide either new information or new insights will need to be reconsidered.

What kinds of development and language will be most suitable in meeting their level of knowledge? Each audience will be receptive to certain kinds of material that best fit into the general frame of reference of its members.

2. *What are the nature and extent of my listeners' interest in this topic?*

Do my listeners already have an immediate interest? If not, can I relate my topic to their interest? It is the rare topic that will create an automatic interest, and some topics will require a special creative approach to make them interesting.

What kinds of material are most likely to arouse or to maintain their interest? Each audience will be receptive to certain ways of creating interest.

3. *What are the nature and the intensity of my listeners' attitude toward this topic?*

Will my listeners be sympathetic? Apathetic? Hostile? Knowing or at least attempting to determine audience disposition beforehand should help you determine procedure.

Can I expect them to have any preconceived biases that will affect their listening, understanding, or emotional reactions?

If sympathetic, how can I present my material so that it will take advantage of their favorable attitude?

If hostile, how can I present my material in a way that will lessen or at least not arouse their hostility?

Of course, to answer these questions completely, you have to know something about your audience. Since you are not likely to have the members available beforehand to give them a comprehensive examination, an aptitude test, or an opinion poll, you must get the information in some other way. How can you gather data on an audience beforehand?

If you know the audience, if you have spoken to the group before, you can gather data by direct observation and experience. Any familiar group, such as your family, your social organization, your political group, or your speech class, can be analyzed in this way.

If you are not familiar with the group, you can ask the chairperson or group contact to provide information for you. Perhaps immediately before you speak you will have a chance to observe the audience and talk with a few of its members. If you just cannot get information, you will have to guess. Such things as the kind of people most likely to attend a speech, the location of the meeting place, and the sponsor of the speech may be useful.

What are the clues you are looking for in an audience analysis? Judgments (guesses) about audience knowledge, interests, and attitudes can be made by gathering the following data:

Age:
What is the average age? What is the age range?

Sex:
Is the audience all or predominantly male? Female? Or is the sex of the group reasonably evenly balanced?

Occupation:
Is everyone of one occupation such as nurses? Bankers? Drill press operators? Is everyone of a related occupation such as professional men? Educators? Skilled laborers?

Income:
Is average income high? Low? Average? Is range of income narrow? Large?

Race, religion, nationality:
Is the audience primarily of one race, religion, or nationality? Or is the audience mixed?

Geographic uniqueness:
Are all the people from one state? City? Region?

Group affiliation:

Is the audience made up of members of one group such as a gardening club? Professional organization? Political group?

What you are really looking for in these data is how the members of the audience are alike and how they differ. The ways that they are alike will give you a key as to whether you have shaped your material so that it will adapt to them. For instance, a Chamber of Commerce group would be composed of men and women who (1) have a common interest in the community, (2) are concerned with attracting business and industry, and (3) have or can get information touting advantages of the location, services, and the like. These three similarities alone provide an excellent base for determining whether you have really adapted to them. Awareness of their differences—possible age spread, occupations, income, race, and religion—may help you eliminate examples that really do not relate to experiences of all members.

EXERCISE

1. Write an analysis of your class based upon age, sex, occupation, income, race, religion, nationality, and geographic uniqueness.
2. Take one of your topic statements from page 227 and answer the questions posed on pp. 228–229.

Developing Ideas

Once you know what behavior you want from your audience and once you know the nature of that audience, you can look for the materials that will develop your topic most creatively. As suggested on pages 169–170, communication material will come from your personal knowledge and observation, interviewing, and reading. To make sure you have uncovered the best published sources, go through the card catalog that lists all your library's holdings by author, title, and subject. Since much of your material may come from magazines, familiarize yourself with *Readers' Guide to Periodical Literature,* which is an index of such popular American magazines and journals as *Ebony, Time, Newsweek, Reader's Digest,* and *Vital Speeches.* Beyond these sources, your reference librarian may suggest various biographical sources, statistical sources, newspapers, government documents, and other materials the library holds that may provide material for your topic. Don't hesitate to ask the library staff for help; helping library patrons is a major professional responsibility and with very few exceptions librarians are delighted to help.

To develop your topic creatively, you should look for material that supports your points and material that is interesting. The following kinds of materials can be used as found, can be modified, or can be completely reworked to provide the most creative development of your speeches.

Examples and Illustrations   *Examples* are single instances that show or prove a point; *illustrations* are more detailed examples. Most examples you find will be real: "Advertisers must give the source of the tests of their products" is a real example supporting the statement "Television commercials are required to be true." Yet, examples may be fictitious or hypothetical. The turtle beating the hare is a fictitious example to support a statement that slow and steady wins the race. The statement "If you put a sheet of glass in a pool and removed it one hour later, a fish probably wouldn't attempt to go beyond the line where the glass was" would be a hypothetical example to prove the point that fish are easily conditioned. Fictitious and hypothetical examples may be very interesting but are probably less weighty than real examples.

Anecdotes and Narratives   *Anecdotes* are brief, often amusing stories; *narratives* are tales, accounts, or lengthier stories. Remember the last time one of your professors said, "That reminds me of a story"? Probably more people listened to the story than to any other part of the lecture. Inclusion of anecdotes and narratives will pay dividends in audience attention as well as in audience understanding. For instance, if you were making a point about the influence of television on behavior, you might relate the following story:

> When we went next door to hear our neighbor's new stereo set, he put on a record, sat down squarely in front of the machine and stared at it intently. Finally, I asked him what in the world he was looking at. Grinning sheepishly, he tried to settle back in his armchair. "I'm so doggone used to looking at television," he explained, "I just can't listen any other way!"

Comparisons and Contrasts   Probably the very best ways of giving meaning to new ideas are through comparison and contrast. *Comparisons*, of course, are forms of material that show similarities; *contrasts* show differences. Literal comparisons show similarities of real things: "It costs about as much as a luxury automobile," "It's about the size of a chestnut." Figurative comparisons express one thing in terms normally denoting another: "He's as fast as greased lightning"; "She's skinny as a pencil." Metaphors, figures of speech in which a word or phrase literally denotes one kind of object or idea used in place of another ("Advertising is the sparkplug that makes our system work"), and similes, figures of speech in which a thing or idea is likened to another ("He walks like an elephant"), are both forms of comparisons. "Unlike last year when our entire attack was on the ground, this year we've really been passing" illustrates the contrast. Because comparisons and contrasts talk about unknowns in terms of the familiar, they are excellent forms of explanation.

Statistics   Numerical facts, or *statistics,* such as "seven out of every ten voted in the last election" or "the cost of living rose 13.5 percent in 1979," enable you to pack a great deal of information into a small package. When statistics are well used they can be most impressive; when they are poorly used, they may be boring and, in some instances, downright deceiving. How can you use statistics effectively?

1. *Make sure you know when your statistics were true.* In 1971 only 12 out of 435 or 2.7 percent of Congress were women. If you wanted to make a point about the number of women in Congress today, you would want the most recent figures.

2. *Use statistics comparatively whenever possible.* For instance, to say that this year industry offered the nation's supermarkets about 5,200 new products does not take on meaning until you say that 5,200 products equals the total number presently on their shelves. In your comparisons, be careful not to present a misleading picture. For instance, if we say that during the last six months Company A doubled its sales while its nearest competitor, Company B, improved by only 40 percent, the implication would be misleading if we did not indicate the size of the base; Company B could have more sales, even though its improvement was only 40 percent.

3. Although statistics may be an excellent way of presenting a great deal of material quickly, *be careful not to overdo them.* A few well-used numbers are far more effective than a battery of statistics.

Quotable Explanations and Opinions   When you find an explanation or an opinion that seems to be just what you are looking for, you may quote it directly in your speech. Because we want to see *your* creative processes at work we do not want to hear long quotations strung together representing your speech. Nevertheless a well-selected quotation might be the perfect thing in one or two key places. If you keep quotations relatively short and few in number, they can and should serve you well. One last point—if you use a direct quotation, you should give credit to the source. Use of any quotation or close paraphrase that is not documented is plagiarism.

Visual Aids   The *visual aid* is a form of speech development that allows the audience to see as well as to hear about the material. A speaker will rarely try to explain complicated material without the use of visual aids, such as charts, drawings, or models. In information exchange, visual aids are especially important in showing how things work, are made, are done, or are used. Some common visual aids and their use are considered in Chapter 13.

Description   *Description* is the act of picturing verbally or giving an account in words. We think of description relating to concrete, specific materials. Thus, we try to describe a room, a city, a park, a dog, or any other object, place, person, or thing with the goal of enabling the audience to hold a mental picture that corresponds to the actual thing. The elements of description are discussed in Chapter 13.

Definition   A *definition* is a statement of what a thing is. Our entire language is built on the assumption that we, as a culture, share common meanings of words. Of course most of us can define only a fraction of the words in the English language. For instance, a standard collegiate dictionary may have more than 100,000 entries, whereas first-year students may have vocabularies ranging from 10,000 to 30,000 words. Since many of the words we want to use may not be totally understood by our audience, we need to offer definitions when they are appropriate. And, of course, the nature of the definition will determine whether the audience really understands. The types of definitions, their uses and functions, are discussed in detail in Chapter 13.

Any kind of material you plan to keep on file should be recorded on note cards. Try to keep each item on a separate 3×5 or 4×6 card. Although it may seem easier to record materials from one source on a single sheet of paper or on a large card, sorting and arranging material is much easier when each item is recorded separately. On each card, indicate the name of the source, the name of the author if one is given, and the page number from which it was taken. You will not necessarily need this material, but should you decide to quote directly or to reexamine a point, you will know where it came from. Figure 11-1 illustrates a useful note card form.

EXERCISE _____

1. Develop one of the following three examples with any *three* of the following types of development: an example; an illustration; an anecdote, or a narrative; a comparison; statistics; or a quotable explanation or opinion.

    Woman are careful (careless) drivers
    _____ has a very good _____ team this year
    _____ should win an academy award.

2. Complete two note cards for one of the speech objectives from page 227.

```
Topic:  Emphysema--scope of disease

"When combined with bronchitis, emphysema
kills an estimated 35,000 people in the United
States each year and contributes to the deaths
of 30,000 more."

                    "Clues to the Cause of Emphysema"
                    Newsweek, April 14, 1980, p. 111
```

Figure 11-1

ORGANIZING YOUR MATERIAL

Once you have the material that will provide the substance for your speech, you must organize it. There has been a lot of research related to organization, but nothing beats the standard advice: "Tell them what you're going to tell them; tell them; and then tell them what you've told them." We call these three parts of the speech the introduction, the body, and the conclusion. Let's look at these parts in the most effective order of preparation.

The Body

The body of a speech is the development of the speech objective. The major elements of the body are the main points that are suggested by the speech objective itself and the developmental material that explains or elaborates those main points. The main points provide the groupings or categories for all your information. If your objective is well worded, determining the main points will not be much of a job at all. For instance, if your speech objective is "to understand three steps of putting power into your tennis serve," each of the main points will be one of the steps. Likewise, if the response you seek is for the listeners "to support United Appeal," the statements that tell the listeners *why* will be the main points (reasons as main points for persuasive speeches will be discussed in more detail in Chapter 14).

How you then order the points depends upon the nature of the material. Still, most speeches follow a time order, a space order, or a topic order.

Time order follows a chronological sequence of ideas or events. It tells the audience that there is a particular importance to the sequence as well as to the content of those main points. This kind of order often evolves when you are explaining how to do something, how to make something, how something works, or how something happened. For instance, the objective "To understand the four simple steps involved in antiquing a table" would be developed in a time order as follows:

I. Clean the table thoroughly.

II. Paint on the base coat right over the old surface.

III. Apply the antique finish with a stiff brush, sponge, or piece of textured material.

IV. Apply two coats of shellac to harden the finish.

Space order follows a spatial relationship of main points. If a speaker's intent is to explain a scene, place, object, or person in terms of its parts, a space order will allow him or her to put emphasis on the description, function, or arrangement of those parts. Because we remember best when we see a logical pattern to the development, the speaker should proceed from top to bottom, left to right, inside to outside or any constant direction that the audience can follow visually. For instance, for a speech that is explaining the arrangement of the Student Union, the main points might be:

I. The basement contains the game room.

II. The first floor contains the various dining rooms.

III. The second, third, and fourth floors contain various meeting rooms and offices.

Topic order is an arbitrary order of topics that grow from the speech objective. Points may go from general to specific, least important to most important, or some other logical order that is at the discretion of the speaker. If all the topics are of equal weight, their order is unimportant—if topics vary in weight and audience importance, how you order them may well influence whether your audience understands or accepts them. Main points offered in support of the objective "support United Appeal" might be listed:

I. The United Appeal combines a wide variety of charities.

II. You can determine who gets all or most of your money.

III. The administration costs are very low, so that most money goes to the charities themselves.

As we will see in the chapter on persuasion, there are many variations of the topic order method.

Most of your speech material will relate to the labeled main points. Although some may provide a nice introduction to the speech or may supplement the conclusion you have planned, a good rule of thumb is that any material that does not further one of the points should be omitted— likewise, if any point is not developed fully enough you will need to get more information.

Let's summarize the guidelines for stating main points that have just been discussed:

1. State each main point as a complete sentence.

2. State each main point in a way that develops the key words in the speech objective. If the objective speaks of "several insights," then each main point should be an insight; if the objective speaks of the "steps" involved, then each main point should be a step.

3. State each main point as specifically and as concisely as possible. For example, saying "The clothes in our society indicate the emphasis most of us are likely to place on trying to look as youthful as we can" is less specific and less concise than saying "Our clothes indicate our emphasis on youthfulness."

4. State main points in parallel language whenever possible. If the first main point is begun with the words "Our clothes indicate . . . ," then each of the other main points should begin "Our clothes indicate. . . ."

5. Limit the number of main points to a maximum of five.

6. Organize the main points so that they follow a time order, a space order, or a topic order.

Taken collectively, your main points outline the structure of your speech. Whether your audience understands, believes, or appreciates what you have to say will usually depend upon the nature of your development of those main points. Earlier in the chapter you learned that examples, illustrations, statistics, comparisons, and quotations were the materials to look for. Now you must select the most relevant of those materials and decide how you will use them to develop each of the main points.

First, write down each main point and under it state the information that you believe develops that main point. For example, for the first main point of a speech with the objective "To understand the criteria for evaluating diamonds":

I. Carat is the weight of a diamond.
Recently standardized.
Used to be weighed against the seed of the cabob.
Now the weight is a standard 200 milligrams.
Weight is also shown in points.
How much a diamond costs depends on how big.
But the price doesn't go up in even increments—it multiplies: a ½-carat costs $600; a 1-carat, $3000.
The reason involves the amount of rock that has to be mined.

Once you have put down the items of information that make the point, you work to subordinate material so that the relationships between and among ideas are shown. You accomplish this organization by using a consistent set of symbols and by indenting some ideas more than others. For instance, organization of the statements about diamonds might evolve into the following outline form:

I. Carat is the weight of the diamond.

   A. Diamond weight has only recently been standardized.

      1. Originally, merchants measured weight of diamonds against the seed of the cabob.

      2. Now the carat has been standardized as 200 milligrams.

   B. As diamond weights increase, the costs multiply.

      1. A ½-carat stone will cost about $600.

      2. A 1-carat stone will cost about $3000.

For each of the subpoints you should have various examples, illustrations, anecdotes, and other material to use in the speech itself. Put down enough material on paper so that you can test both the quality and the quantity of your material. After we look at preparing the introduction and the conclusion of the speech, we will look at the total outlining process.

The Introduction

At this stage of preparation the substance of the speech, the body, is ready for practice. Now you must concern yourself with the strategy of getting your listeners ready for what you have to say. Although your audience is captive (few of them will get up and leave), having an audience present physically does not mean having an active, alert, listening audience. It is a good introduction that brings the audience to this state.

Any introduction has at least three potential purposes: (1) to get initial attention, (2) to create a bond of good will between speaker and audience, and (3) to lead into the content of the speech. These three are not necessarily synonymous. A speaker may get attention by pounding on the stand, by shouting "Listen!" or by telling a joke. The question is whether any of these approaches will prepare the audience for the body of the speech. If the attention does not relate to the speech topic, it is usually short-lived. You must consider a way that will get undivided attention on the speech topic.

A survey of suggested introductions would produce as many as twenty different ways of beginning a speech, most of them directed to getting attention. Let me here suggest some representative approaches that will work for short and long speeches; but keep in mind that how you begin is largely up to your imagination. The only way to be sure that you have come across a winner of a speech introduction is to try out three to five different ones in practice and pick the one that seems best.

How long should the introduction be? Introductions may range from less than 7 percent to nearly 50 percent of the speech. How long should yours be? Long enough to put the audience in the frame of mind that will encourage them to hear you out—and of course, the shorter the speech the shorter the introduction.

Startling Statement   Especially in a short speech, the kind you will be giving in your first few assignments, you must obtain your listeners' attention and focus on the topic quickly. One excellent way to do this is to make a startling statement that will penetrate various competing thoughts and get directly to the listener's mind. The following opening illustrates the attention-getting effect.

> If I came before you with a pistol pointed at you, you would be justifiably scared. But at least you would know the danger to your life. Yet every day we let people fire away at us with messages that are dangerous to our pocketbooks, our minds, and we seldom say a word. I'm talking about the television advertiser.

Question   The direct question is another way to get your listeners thinking about ideas you want them to think about. Like the startling statement, this opening is also adaptable to the short speech. The question has to have enough importance to be meaningful to the audience.

> Do you know how many triples Pete Rose got in 1979? Do you know how many double faults Billie Jean King committed in her last tournament? Don't

worry too much, the information's of little importance to anyone—including Pete Rose and Billie Jean King. Do you know the seven danger signals of cancer? You'd better—not knowing the answer to this question could kill you.

Anecdotes, Narratives, or Illustrations Nearly everyone enjoys a good story. When a speaker starts with a good story, she is sure to get audience attention or interest. However, remember that a good opening must lead into the speech as well as get attention. If your story does both, you probably have an unbeatable opening. If it is not related to the subject— save it for another occasion. Since most good stories take time to tell, they are usually more appropriate for longer speeches. Still, you can occasionally come across a short one that is just right for your speech. How do you like this one for the opening to a speech on "Making money from antiques"?

> At a recent auction, bidding was particularly brisk on an old hand-blown whiskey bottle, and finally a collector on my left was the successful taker at $50. When the purchase was handed over to him, an aged but sharp-eyed farmer standing nearby leaned over and took a good look at the bottle. "My God," he gasped to his friend, "it's empty!" To that farmer an empty bottle wasn't worth much. But in today's world anything that's empty might be worth a fortune—if it's old enough. Today I want to talk with you about what might be lying around your basement or attic that's worth real money; a branch of antiquing called "Collectables."

Personal Reference Since your audience is the object of your communication, a direct personal reference may be a particularly good way of opening. Of course, any good opening has an element of audience adaptation to it—the personal reference is directed solely to that end. A personal reference opening like this one on exercising may be suitable for any length of speech.

> Say, were you panting when you got to the top of those four flights of stairs this morning? I'll bet there were a few of you who vowed you're never going to take a class on the top floor of this building again. But did you ever stop to think that maybe the problem isn't that this class is on the top floor of the building? You know it just might be that you are not getting enough exercise.

Quotation A particularly vivid or thought-provoking quotation makes an excellent introduction for any length speech. Still, you need to use your imagination to develop the quotation so that it yields maximum benefits.

> Shakespeare wrote: "If music be the food of love, play on." A modern-day poet might write: "If music be the food of love as well as making you

a lot of money, write on." And that's exactly what a lot of people are doing. Pop music is big business—one of the biggest. And those people who write those cute words are budding millionaires.

Suspense   An extremely effective way of gaining attention is through suspense. If you can start your speech in a way that gets the audience to ask, "What is he leading up to?" you may well get it hooked for the entire speech. The suspense opening is especially valuable when the topic is one that the audience might not ordinarily be willing to listen to if started in a less dramatic way.

Consider the attention-getting value of the following:

> It costs the United States $20 billion in *one* year. It has caused the loss of more jobs than a recession. It caused the death of more than 35,000 Americans. No, I'm not talking about a war; but it is a problem just as deadly. The problem is alcoholism.

Although each has been discussed individually, the various types of introductions may be used alone or in combination, depending upon the time you have available and the interest of your audience. The introduction is not going to make your speech an instant success, but an effective introduction will get an audience to look at you and listen to you. That is about as much as you have a right to ask of an audience during the first minute of your speech.

The Conclusion

So now you have a body of the speech and you have a way to start it. But before you think you have licked this organization problem, you had better think a little bit about how you are going to end it. Too many speakers either end their speeches so abruptly that the audience is startled or ramble on aimlessly until they exhaust both the topic and the audience. A poor conclusion (or no conclusion at all) can destroy much of the impact of an otherwise very effective speech. Even the best conclusion cannot do much for a poor speech; but it can help to heighten the effect of a good speech and, equally important, it can tie the speech together into a compact, concise package for the audience. Look at it this way: You may have talked for five minutes or fifty-five minutes, but when you get near the end you have only one last chance to put the focus where you want it. So, even though the conclusion will be a relatively short part of the speech, seldom more than 5 percent, it is worth the time to make it good.

The Summary   By far the easiest way to end a speech is by summarizing the main points. Thus, the shortest appropriate ending for a

A POOR CONCLUSION CAN DESTROY
AN EFFECTIVE SPEECH.

speech on the warning signals of cancer would be, "So remember, if you experience a sudden weight loss, lack of energy, blood in your urine or bowels, then you should see a doctor immediately." The virtue of such an ending is that it restates the main points, the ideas that are after all the key ideas of the speech.

Because the conclusion may be important for heightening the emotional impact of the speech, even when you are using a summary you may want to supplement it in some way so that your message is impressed upon the audience. Speakers have found numerous ways to supplement and occasionally supplant the summary. Let us look at a few.

The Appeal The appeal is a frequently used conclusion for a persuasive speech. It is as though you tell your listeners that now they have heard all the arguments you will describe the behavior you would like them to follow. An example would be:

> So, we've seen that Janet Hartnet is dedicated, experienced and a creative problem solver—that she would make a superior Student Body President. I hope that next Tuesday you will exercise your right to vote. But most important, I hope you will vote for the best candidate—Janet Hartnet.

An even better conclusion is one that drives home the most important point(s) with real emotional impact. Consider the powerful way General Douglas MacArthur finished his speech when he ended his military career:

But I still remember the refrain of one of the most popular barrack ballads of that day which proclaimed most proudly that—

"Old soldiers never die; they just fade away."

And like the old soldier of that ballad, I now close my military career and just fade away—an old soldier who tried to do his duty as God gave him the light to see that duty.

Goodby.

EXERCISE

Each person should work out a tentative opening for the topics listed on page 227. One person will give his introduction. The rest of the class will then try to improve upon the introduction given until five or six have had a chance. After you have worked on three or four separate speech introductions, follow the same procedure for working on speech conclusions.

Outlining the Speech

Perhaps after you have thought about the body and worked on the introduction and conclusion for a while, you may figure that you are pretty well organized. Yet, before you actually get into practicing the speech, I suggest that you write an outline. In fact, of all the skills related to speech organization, outlining may be the most important.

A speech outline is a short, complete-sentence representation of the speech that is used to test the logic, organization, development, and overall strength of the structure before any practice takes place.

Does a speaker really need an outline? Most of us do. Of course, there are some speakers who do not prepare outlines, who have learned, through trial and error, alternate means of planning speeches and testing structure that work for them. Some accomplish the entire process in their heads and never put a word on paper—but they are few indeed. As a beginner, you can save yourself a lot of trouble if you learn to outline ideas as suggested. Then you will *know* the speech has a solid, logical structure and that the speech really fulfills the intended purpose.

What rules should you use to guide your writing of the development of the speech? The following five rules will help you test your thinking and produce a better speech. In my years of working with beginning speakers, I have observed ample proof of the generalization that there is a direct relationship between outlining and the quality of speech content.

1. *Use a standard set of symbols.* Main points are usually indicated by Roman numerals, major subdivisions by capital letters, minor subheadings by Arabic numerals, and further subdivisions by small letters. Although greater breakdown can be shown, an outline will rarely be subdivided further. Thus an outline for a speech with two main points might look like this:

I.
  A.
     1.
     2.
  B.
II.
  A.
  B.
     1.
        a.
        b.
     2.

2. *Use complete sentences for major headings and major subdivisions.* By using complete sentences you are able to see (1) whether each main point really develops the thesis of your speech objective and (2) whether the wording really makes the point you want to make. Although a phrase or key-word outline is best when the outline is to be used as a speaker's notes, for the planning stage—the blueprint of the speech—complete sentences are best. Unless you write key ideas out in full, you will have difficulty guaranteeing accomplishment of the next two rules.

3. *Each main point and major subdivision should contain a single idea.* By following this rule you will assure yourself that development will be relevant to the point. Let us examine a correct and an incorrect example of this rule:

Incorrect	*Correct*
I. The park is beautiful and easy to get to.	I. The park is beautiful. II. The park is easy to get to.

Development of the incorrect example will lead to confusion, for the development cannot relate to both the ideas at once. If your outline follows the correct procedure, you will be able to line up your supporting material confident that the audience will see and understand the relationship.

4. *Minor points should relate to or support major points.* This principle is called *subordination.* Consider the following example:

  I. Proper equipment is necessary for successful play.
    A. Good gym shoes are needed for maneuverability.
    B. Padded gloves will help protect your hands.
    C. A lively ball provides sufficient bounce.
    D. And a good attitude doesn't hurt.

Notice that the main point deals with equipment. A, B, and C (shoes, gloves, and ball) relate to the main point. But D, attitude, is not equipment, and should appear somewhere else, if at all.

5. *Main points should be limited to a maximum of five.* A speech will usually contain from two to five main points. Regardless of the length of time available, audiences will have difficulty really assimilating a speech with more than five points. When a speech has more than five points, you usually can group points under headings in such a way that they will appear as fewer. It is a simple psychological fact that audiences will better remember two main points with four divisions each than eight main points.

6. *The total words in the outline should equal no more than one third to one half of the total number anticipated in the speech.* An outline is a skeleton of the speech and should be a representation of a speech—not a manuscript with letters and numbers. One way of testing the length of an outline is by computing the total number of words that you could speak during the time limit and then limiting your outline to one-third of that total. Since approximate figures are all that are needed, you can assume that your speaking rate is about average—160 words per minute. Thus, for a two- to three-minute speech, which would include roughly 320 to 480 words, the outline should be limited to 110 to 160 words. The outline for an eight- to ten-minute speech, which will contain roughly 1200 to 1500 words, should be limited to 400 to 500 words.

Now let us look at an example. The outline shown in Figure 11-2 illustrates the principles in practice. In the analysis I have tried to emphasize each of the rules, as well as to make suggestions about some other facets of outlining procedure.

ADAPTING TO THE AUDIENCE

The third step in the speech preparation process is to adapt your language to the audience. Unlike written communication where wording evolves through editing and finally appears on the printed page, wording in speech communication develops through oral practice. Unless the speech is to be delivered from a manuscript, it never really becomes final until it is presented to the audience.

Think of the process of wording this way. Through careful outlining of your speech you have produced a skeleton that includes anywhere from 20 percent to 50 percent of the words that could be used in the speech. During the first practice you fill out the outline to speech length. Then through several practice periods you sample various wordings: your mind retains wordings that seem especially effective and seeks to modify awkward, hesitant, or otherwise ineffective phrasings. You continue until you are confident that the speech itself will do what you intended.

Outline	Analysis
Speech Objective: to understand the meaning of and the effects of hypochondria.	Written at the top of the page, the speech objective is used to remind the speaker of his objective and to test the relevance of the outline's points.

Introduction

I. Do you feel sick when you have to give a speech or cut the grass?

II. You just may be a hypochondriac.

The word "introduction" sets this section apart as a separate unit. The introduction gets attention and, often by stating the behavioral objective of the speech, leads into the body.

Body

I. Hypochondria, a psychological problem, is an abnormal anxiety over one's health.

    A. Encyclopaedia Britannica calls it "a morbid mental preoccupation . . . with a tendency to find evidence of disease from insignificant signs."

    B. Early classics referred to the disease as melancholia or the vapors.

    C. Today, hypochondriacs account for up to 20 percent of our national health budget.

The word "body" sets this section apart as a separate unit. Main point I reflects a topical relationship of main ideas. It is stated as a complete, substantive sentence.

The main point could be developed in many ways. These subdivisions further elaborate on the definition and quantify its extent.

II. The psychological state of hypochondria may lead to actual physical discomfort or disease.

    A. At times a hypochondriac convinces himself so well that he actually suffers pains and symptoms.

        1. Fear causes panic and damaging overload of adrenaline discharges.

        2. Fear causes psychosomatic symptoms.

    B. Hypochondria often leads to "Secondary Gain": psychic effects from unpleasant situations.

        1. A friend's girl friend faked pregnancy to gain attention.

        2. Athletes exploit minor injuries.

    C. Hypochondria in its worst state results in Munchausen's syndrome.

        1. A man faked pulmonary embolism to the degree of injuring himself.

        2. Many people spend their healthy lives in hospitals.

Main point II continues the topical relationship. Notice that each main point considers one major idea.

Ordinarily, subordination is shown by the following set of symbols: major points—I, II, III, etc.; subdivisions—A, B, C, etc.; subdivisions of subdivisions—1, 2, 3, etc. Words and phrases are often substituted for complete sentences after the first two stages of subordination.

The substance of the outline should be tested by asking:

1. Is the speech objective a clear, concise statement?
2. Are the main points stated as clear, substantive sentences?
3. Do the main points develop the speech objective directly?
4. Does each main point consider only one idea?
5. Do the various subpoints really support or develop the division they are subordinate to?

Conclusion

I. Hypochondria is something we kid about, but convincing yourself that you are sick when you are not may have serious results.

II. Oh, I feel a pain in my chest—I'd better sit down.

The word "conclusion" sets this apart as a separate unit.

The content of the conclusion may take any form that ties the speech together and leaves a lasting impression.

Figure 11-2

The steps of speech practice—including a discussion of how this practice is handled *without resulting in memorization*—will be discussed later in this chapter in the section on practicing the delivery. Here we will consider what criteria we can use to measure whether or not the words we are using in practice will result in an effective oral style. To put it another way, what wording can we use that is instantly intelligible as heard by our *specific* audience? To help achieve an oral style adapted to the specific audience, we need to test our language for clarity, vividness, emphasis, and appropriateness.

Clarity

Clarity contributes to achieving instant intelligibility by eliminating ambiguity and confusion. Suppose a teacher commenting on a student said, "He does pretty well on tests, he gets his other stuff done in pretty good order, and he talks in class—no complaints." Would you know much about that student's work? Suppose instead the teacher said, "He gets B grades or better on tests, completes all his homework and turns it in on time, and his class discussion shows his understanding of basic theory—he's a pleasure to have in class." With the second phrasing, you would have a clear picture of exactly what kind of student he was.

Clear language is accurate, specific, and concrete. Are these words familiar? We dealt with them in Chapter 3 in the discussion of sending messages accurately. To refresh your memory on the effects of accurate, concrete, specific language, consider the differences in meaning of the sentence, " 'Bring me the paper,' John *said*," when we substitute "growled," "snarled," "pleaded," "purred," "shouted," and "whispered" for "said."

Vividness

Beyond the clarity that helps the audience see meaning, effective public speaking language should be vivid. Vivid language paints meaning in living color. *Vividness* means full of life, vigorous, bright, and intense. If your language is vivid, your audience will picture your meanings in striking detail. "Jackson made a great catch" is an evaluative statement that states the speaker's opinion but creates no images. "Jackson made a great one-hand catch against the wall" is more vivid. "Jackson, racing with his back to the infield, leaped and made a one-hand stab just as he crashed into the center field wall" is even more vivid, because it paints a verbal picture of the action.

Vivid speech begins with vivid thought. You must have a striking mental picture before you can communicate one to your audience. If you cannot feel the bite of the wind and the sting of the nearly freezing rain, if you cannot hear the thick, juicy sirloin strip steaks sizzling on the grill, if you cannot feel that empty yet exhilarating feeling as the jet climbs from takeoff, you will not be able to describe these sensations vividly. The more imaginatively you can think about your ideas, the more likely you can state them vividly.

Emphasis

A third important element of style is *emphasis.* In a 500-word speech, all 500 words are not of equal importance. We neither expect nor necessarily want an audience to retain the memory of every word uttered. Still, if you leave it up to listeners to decide which words are most important, they may select the wrong ones. You are the speaker; you know what you want to stand out. How can you do it? Emphasis may be made through organization by idea subordination, through delivery by voice and bodily action, and through language itself, by means of proportion, repetition, and emphasis.

Proportion means spending more time on one point than on another. If an employer in interviewing people for the job of secretary tells them that typing and answering the telephone are the two principal duties, talks for fifteen minutes about the typing and only one minute about the telephone, applicants would assume that typing is the more important duty—since the interviewer spent more time talking about it. Even though this is a good way, it is still a little subtle for some audiences.

Another way to emphasize an idea is by *repetition.* If I say, "There are 500 steps—that's 500," a listener will probably perceive the repetition as an indication that the point must have greater importance and should, therefore, be remembered.

A third kind of emphasis is the carefully phrased *transition.* Transitions are the words, phrases, and sentences that show idea relationships. Transitions summarize, clarify, forecast, and, in almost every instance, emphasize.

Our language contains a number of words that show idea relationships. Words like "also," "likewise," and "moreover" forecast additional material; words like "therefore," "all in all," and "in short" bring ideas together to show results; words like "but," "however," "on the other hand" indicate changes in direction; and words like "in other words," "for example," and "that is to say" explain or exemplify.

Moreover, we can make statements that call special attention to words and ideas. One special attention statement is the kind that acts like a tour guide through the speech. At the start of the body of the speech a speaker might say, "This speech will have three major parts." After a main heading in a process speech, a speaker might say, "Now that we see what the ingredients are, let's move on to the second step, stripping the surface."

In addition to acting like a tour guide, special-attention transitions can announce the importance of a particular word or idea. For instance, speakers might say such things as "Now I come to the most important idea in the speech," or "If you haven't remembered anything so far, make sure you remember this," or finally, "But maybe I should say this again, because it is so important." These examples represent only a few of the possible expressions that interrupt the flow of ideas and interject the speaker's subjective keys, clues, and directions to stimulate audience memory or understanding.

Appropriateness

The final way of achieving instant intelligibility is through *appropriateness*. Appropriateness means using language that adapts to the needs, interests, knowledge, and attitudes of the audience. Appropriate language cements the bond of trust between the speaker and his audience. In most situations, the more personal you can make your language the more appropriate it will be.

Using Personal Pronouns Often by merely speaking in terms of "you," "us," "we," and "our," you will give the audience a verbal clue to your interest in them. Suppose you were talking about some of the intricacies of football. Instead of saying, "When *an individual* goes to a football game, *he* often wonders why players make certain maneuvers," why not try, "When *you* go to a football game *you* may often wonder why players make certain maneuvers." Although this may seem to be a very small point, it may make the difference between audience attention and audience indifference.

Using Audience Questions Although public speaking is not direct conversation with your audience, you can create the impression of direct conversation by generating a sense of personal involvement through *audience questions*. For instance, if we take the same example we used above, we can make one more change in phrasing that would heighten the audience adaptation. Now instead of leaving the statement as "When you go

to a football game, you may often wonder why players make certain maneuvers," why not try "When you go to a football game, have you ever
asked, 'I wonder why Kessel moved to the other side of the line before the
snap' or 'I wonder why Jones started to rush the passer and then all of a
sudden stepped back'?"

Audience questions generate audience participation; and of course,
once an audience is participating, they will see the content as more meaningful to them. One caution: Because direct audience questions—trying to
get the audience to answer aloud—may disrupt your flow of thought (and
sometimes yield unexpected answers), the rhetorical question—a question
requiring only a mental response—is usually safer. The speaker's rhetorical
questions encourage the same degree of involvement and they are easier
to handle. Moreover, questions are good means of adaptation because they
are appropriate at any place in the speech.

Alluding to Common Experience   If you think your audience has
had common experiences, then you should try to allude to them in the
speech. Your disclosure of your understanding of these experiences will
allow your audience to identify more with you. For instance, if you were
talking to a group of Boy Scouts, in order to drive home the point that
sometimes important tasks can only be accomplished through hours of
hard work, you might say, "Remember the hours you put in working on
your first merit badge? Remember wondering whether you'd ever get the
darned thing finished? Also, do you remember how good it felt to know
that the hours you put in paid off on something you could really be proud
of?" (Notice how this example incorporates all three of the special devices
we have mentioned.) When an audience identifies with you as a speaker,
the members will become more receptive to what you have to say.

Building Hypothetical Situations   Although you cannot involve the
audience directly with every topic, you can often simulate involvement by
placing the audience into a hypothetical situation. Suppose you were talking to a garden club about chartering an airplane for a group vacation. You
might develop the speech along these lines:

> Let's say that for your project this month you wanted to go to the Tulip
> Festival in Holland, Michigan. Now you could drive, but 500 miles is rather
> a long trip, and let's say that several of you wanted to go. You could fly, but
> individual passage from here to Holland, Michigan, would be _____ plus
> it would require two intermediate stops. Now, if you chartered an airplane
> you could make the flight directly from here to Holland for only _____
> per person.

EXERCISE

1. For each of the following ideas, try two or three different ways of making them clearer and more vivid:

   The game was fun

   The dinner was tasty

   He talks mean

   The class is yucky

2. Divide into groups of three (this may be combined with the previous exercise). A talks with B, and C acts as observer. During the discussion, C should try to keep track of words—analyze them as vivid versus trite, common; clear versus unclear. After five minutes of discussion, observer feeds back word usage. Then switch speakers and observer.

3. Each person makes up a short three- or four-word sentence, such as "Sidney flunked the course" or "Milo bought the shovel." When it is his turn, he or she says the sentence trying to emphasize one of the words. The group considers which word, if any, seemed to stand out significantly. If the group is wrong or is not sure, the person tries again.

4. Divide into groups of three. Each person prepares a one-minute statement containing at least *five* facts on a topic, such as "this year's team record," "crime in the city," or "a discussion of a good movie, play, or television show." In presentation of the statement, the speaker should use various language devices to indicate which of the five is most important, which are of lesser importance, and which are least important. After the presentation, the two listeners indicate the order of importance of the facts as they perceived them. Each person should be given one or two opportunities to speak.

5. What lines of development could you use to relate the following ideas to your class?

   People are afraid to report venereal disease to the authorities.

   Horseshoes (or any other participation sport for two to four people) is fun.

   Bolivia's copper prices are rising.

   The average American watches a lot of television.

PRACTICING THE DELIVERY

There is an old saying: "It's not what you say, but how you say it that counts." Like so many popular sayings there is at least a grain of truth to it. Although you cannot communicate much if you do not have anything to say, not many will listen to you at all if your delivery of the speech is dull. So the final skill we will consider in the preparation process is practicing delivery until the speech comes alive. *Delivery* is the use of voice and body to help convey the message of the speech. Although the best delivery will not save the poorly prepared speech, particularly poor delivery may well harm your speech so much that even exceptional content and organization are negated. Speech delivery may be the deciding factor in the audience's estimation of your effectiveness.

Voice, Articulation, and Bodily Action

Your voice, articulation, and bodily action are the basic elements of your speech delivery. What are you attempting to achieve through their use? Most good speakers will achieve the following three results:

   1. *Show enthusiasm for what you have to say.* We call this quality the desire to communicate. If you care—I mean really care—about your material, your listeners will care. If you do not care—and your listeners will be able to tell if you do not—they certainly are not going to get excited. Enthusiasm is infectious.

   2. *Look at the audience while you talk.* You know what you think of your professors who bury their noses in their notes while they lecture—they put you to sleep. You gain attention, sustain interest, and build trust in your ideas by looking directly at the audience. How do you accomplish good eye contact? It is, of course, physically impossible to look at your whole audience at once. What you can do is talk to individuals and small groups of people in all parts of the audience throughout your speech. Do not spend all of your time looking front and center. The people at the ends of rows and those in the back of the room are every bit as important as those right in front of you.

   3. *Be spontaneous.* You must give the impression that the ideas you present are being formed at the time they are spoken. When words are memorized, they usually sound that way. Furthermore, audiences do not get turned on by listening to people read manuscripts. However, if you can speak spontaneously, you can get an audience excited. We will discuss spontaneity in more detail as we get into the mechanics of speech practice.

Now that we have looked at the basic criteria, let's consider the mechanics of voice, articulation, and bodily action that go together to produce what most speech teachers call a conversational quality.

   Voice   Your voice is a combination of pitch, volume, rate, and quality. *Pitch* refers to the highness or lowness of your voice. Your voice is produced in the larynx by the vibration of your vocal folds. In order to feel this vibration, put your hand on your throat at the top of the Adam's apple and say "ah." Now, just as the change in pitch of a violin string is brought about by making it tighter or looser, so the pitch of your voice is changed by the tightening and loosening of the vocal folds. Fortunately, most people use a pitch that is about right for them. A few persons do have problems related to pitch. If you have questions about your pitch level, ask your professor about it. If you are one of the very few persons with a pitch problem, she can refer you to a speech therapist for corrective work.

Volume is the loudness of the tone we make. When we exhale normally, the diaphragm relaxes, and air is expelled through the trachea. When we speak, we supplement the force of the expelled air on the vibrating vocal folds by contracting our abdominal muscles. This greater force behind the air we expel increases the volume of our tone. To feel how these muscles work, place your hands on your sides with your fingers extended over the stomach. Say "ah" in a normal voice. Now say "ah" as loud as you can. If you are making proper use of your muscles, you should feel the stomach contraction increase as you increase volume. If you feel little or no muscle contraction, you are probably trying to gain volume from the wrong source, and such a practice will often result in tiredness, stridency, and lack of sufficient volume to be heard in a large room. Each of us, regardless of size, is capable of a great deal of vocal volume. If you have trouble getting sufficient volume, work on exerting greater pressure from the abdominal area.

Rate is the speed at which we talk. Although most of us talk between 140 and 180 words per minute, the best rate is a highly individual matter. The test of rate is whether an audience can understand what you are saying. Usually even the fastest rate is acceptable if words are well articulated and if there is sufficient vocal variety and emphasis.

Quality is the tone, timbre, or sound of your voice. Voices are described as being clear, nasal, breathy, harsh, hoarse, strident, and other such adjectives. If your voice seems to have too great a degree of some undesirable quality, consult your professor. Although you can make some improvement on your own, improvement requires a great deal of work and rather extensive knowledge of vocal anatomy and physiology. Severe problems of vocal quality should be referred to a speech therapist.

Vocal variety and expressiveness involve our use of the voice to stimulate meaning. The *variations* of pitch, volume, rate, and quality give voice the dimension that aids or limits audience attention and understanding. Take the simple sentence "I am not going to the movie." The entire meaning of the sentence depends upon which word you say with more volume or in a higher pitch. If you emphasize "not," the sentence means you are answering the question of *whether* you are going; if you emphasize "movie," the sentence means you are answering the question of *where* you are going. If you were to speak the sentence in a monotone with all words at the same pitch and the same volume, the listener could not be sure what question you were answering. The more variety and emphasis, the more meaning is communicated.

If you want to check your variety and emphasis, get someone to listen as you read short passages aloud. Ask the person to tell you which words were higher in pitch, or louder, or slower. When you find that you can give a speech in such a way that the person recognizes which words you were trying to emphasize, you will be showing improvement in using vocal variety to clarify meaning.

Articulation This aspect of speech is concerned with the shaping of speech sounds into recognizable oral symbols that go together to make up a word. Articulation is often confused with pronunciation, the form and accent of various syllables of a word. In the word "folklore," articulation refers to the shaping of the six sounds (f, o, k, l, o, r); pronunciation refers to the grouping and accenting of the sounds (fok' lor).

Although true articulatory problems (distortion, omission, substitution, or addition of sounds) need to be corrected by a speech therapist, the kinds of articulatory problems exhibited by most students can be improved individually during a single term. The two most common faults for most of us are slurring sounds (running sounds and words together) and leaving off word endings. "Who ya goin' ta see" for "Who are you going to see" illustrates both these errors. If you have a mild case of "sluritis," caused by not taking the time to form sounds clearly, you can make considerable improvement by taking ten to fifteen minutes a day to read passages aloud, trying to overaccentuate each of the sounds. Some teachers advocate "chewing" your words; that is, making sure that you move your lips, jaw, and tongue very carefully for each sound you make. As with most other problems of delivery, you must work conscientiously every day for weeks or months to bring about significant improvement.

Bodily Action Your nonverbal communication, or bodily action, says the same kinds of things in a speech as it does in normal interpersonal or group communication. It is true that when we get in front of an audience we may have a tendency to freeze up—that is, to limit our normal nonverbal action—and occasionally the speaking situation may bring out nervous mannerisms that are not so noticeable in our daily speaking. My personal belief is that if you are thinking actively about what you are saying your bodily action will probably be appropriate. If you exhibit either too much or too little bodily action, your instructor can give you some pointers for tempering or actuating your nonverbal behavior. Although you may find minor errors, you should not be concerned unless your bodily action calls attention to itself—then you should determine ways of controlling or changing the behavior.

During practice sessions you may try various methods to monitor or alter your bodily action. If you have access to video tape, you will have an excellent means of monitoring your bodily action. You may want to practice in front of a mirror to see how you look to others when you speak. (Although some speakers swear by this method, others find it a traumatic experience.) Perhaps the best is to get a willing listener to critique your bodily action and help you improve. Once you have identified the behavior you want to change, you can tell your helper what he should look for. For instance, you might say, "Raise your hand every time I begin to rock back and forth." By getting specific feedback when the behavior occurs, you can make immediate adjustment.

EXERCISE

1. Divide into groups of three to six. Have each person give a personal experience—something that happened to him or her that can be told to the rest of the group. Each person should have at least two minutes to relate the experience. The other members of the group should observe for any problems in vocal variety and emphasis, articulation, and body action.
2. After each person has had a chance to speak, the group should discuss how emphasis was achieved and what kinds of articulation problems were most noticeable.

Guidelines for Practice

Most speeches you will be giving, in class and out, will follow the extemporaneous mode. An extemporaneous speech is prepared and practiced, but the exact wording is determined at the time of utterance. Now let's consider how a speech can be carefully prepared without being memorized.

Novice speakers often believe that preparation is complete once the outline has been finished. Nothing could be further from the truth. If you are scheduled to speak at 9 A.M. Monday and you have not finished the outline for the speech until 8:45 A.M. Monday, the speech is not likely to be as good as it could have been had you allowed yourself sufficient practice time. Try to complete your outline early enough to make best use of the practice period. Practice gives you a chance to revise, evaluate, mull over, and consider all aspects of the speech.

One good way to practice is to make the practice period as similar to the speech situation as possible:

1. Stand up and face your imaginary audience.
2. Read through your outline once or twice before you begin.
3. Put your outline out of sight.

4. Look at your watch to see what time you begin.

5. Begin the speech. Keep going until you have finished the ideas.

6. Note the time you finish.

7. Look at your outline again to see what you omitted, what you discussed too briefly, and what you spent too much time on, if anything.

8. Go through the entire process again. If you can get a friend or relative to listen to later practices, so much the better.

After you have completed two sessions of practices and criticism, put the speech away for a while. Although you may need to practice three, four, or even ten times, there is no value in going through all the sessions consecutively. You may well find that a practice session right before you go to bed will be beneficial; while you are sleeping, your subconscious will continue to work on the speech. As a result, you will often note a tremendous improvement at the first practice session the next day.

Should you use notes in practice or during the speech itself? The answer depends upon what you mean by notes and how you plan to use them. My advice would be to avoid using notes at all for the first short speech assignments. Then, when assignments get longer, you will be more likely to use notes properly and not as a crutch. Of course, there is no harm in experimenting with notes to see what effect they will have on your delivery.

Appropriate notes are composed of key words or phrases that help trigger your memory. Notes will be most useful to you when they consist of the fewest words possible written in lettering large enough to be seen instantly at a distance. Many speakers condense their written preparatory outline into a brief word or phrase outline. A typical set of notes made from the preparatory outline illustrated on page 245 would look like this:

Nature of hypochondria
   Abnormal anxiety
      Morbid mental preoccupation
      Melancholy or vapors
      Accounts for 20% of health budget
   Effects
      Actual suffering
      Secondary gain
      Munchausen's syndrome

During practice sessions you should use notes the way that you plan to use them in the speech. Either set them on the speaker's stand or hold them in one hand and refer to them only when you have to. Speakers often find that the act of making a note card is so effective in helping cement ideas in the mind that during practice or later during the speech itself they do not need to use the notes at all.

In any event, you should practice the speech until you gain a complete understanding of meaning and order of ideas—do not try to memorize the words. When a person memorizes he repeats the speech until he has mastered the wording—when a person stresses the learning of ideas, he practices his speech differently each time. For instance: Practice 1: "A handball court is a large rectangular box 20 feet wide, 40 feet long and 20 feet high." Practice 2: "A handball court is 20 by 40 by 20—a lot like a large rectangular box." In both practices, the ideas are the same but the wording is different. When you are not tied to a particular phrasing, you can adapt to reaction of the audience at time of delivery; moreover, because each experience builds on the last, the speech itself is often better than any wording used during practice.

EXERCISE

Make a diary of your program of practice for your first speech. How many times did you practice? At what point did you feel you had a mastery of substance? How long was each of your practice periods?

PUBLIC SPEAKING EVALUATION

Perhaps more than any other form of communication, the speech is subject to almost instant evaluation by nearly everyone who hears it. Public speeches are fair game. However, if the evaluation is to benefit the speaker, those who did not hear the speech, and, for that matter, the critic, some system of analysis is necessary. In this section, we want to develop a public speaking analysis that considers the key elements that may or should be considered. Our goal is not only to put a label of "good" or "bad" on the speech, but to determine what made the speech more or less effective in achieving its behavioral goal.

When is a speaker successful? On the surface, a speaker is successful when he or she is able (1) to achieve the behavioral objective sought or (2) to bring the audience significantly closer to that objective. If as a result of what a speaker says you go to see the suggested movie or you are convinced that Congress should enact laws to control possession of handguns or you understand how the pyramids were built, then the speech has been successful. Yet sometimes the speaker is successful even when the desired behavior is not achieved. If none of the members of the audience were planning to go see the suggested movie, but after hearing what the speaker had to say some were willing to consider going; if most members of the audience were hostile to any form of gun control legislation, but now they are willing to weigh the arguments; or if the majority of the audience had no idea how the pyramids were built, but now they have some comprehension, then the speaker has achieved a measure of success.

Is a successful speaker a good speaker? Success is the goal of any speaker. But success alone does not make a good speaker. Hitler was successful; Senator Joseph McCarthy was successful; nearly every demagogue of history can thank speaking skill for at least part of his success. A speaker can always increase his chances of success by lying to his listeners, by distorting, by relying on emotion to inflame the passions, or by other unethical means. But an unethical speaker cannot be called a good speaker. A speaker in the public forum has a great responsibility; the speaker who cannot or will not bear that responsibility achieves his success only through trickery.

What are the elements of speechmaking that a critic evaluates? First, the setting can help or it can hurt the speaker's cause. If a speaker faces 5,000 people in the University Field House but the public address system is bad and the seating arrangements unfavorable, the speaker will have little chance of success even though the majority of the audience are advocates of her ideas.

Second, the nature of the audience is also important in determining and in predicting speaker success. The age, sex, occupation, religion, socioeconomic level, attitudes, interests, and knowledge of the audience all affect how that audience will view the speaker's ideas. For instance, although an audience of auto dealers is not likely to be receptive to Ralph Nader's ideas on methods of controlling air pollution, it is likely to be receptive to those of Henry Ford II.

In addition to the setting and the audience, the reputation, appearance, and demeanor of the speaker himself will affect his relative success. Speaker credibility is the keystone of motivation; if the speaker is not trusted by the audience, this lack of trust will affect the prospects of success.

Yet, in the final analysis the burden of evaluation will be on the speech itself—specifically, the content, the organization, and the presentation of that speech. Since we have covered each of these elements of the speech in detail earlier, let's move right to the evaluation instrument (Appendix B-8).

EXERCISE

Use the material presented in Appendix B-8 to evaluate a speech.

SUMMARY

Fear of speaking may be eased, if not entirely overcome, through careful speech preparation. Effective preparation follows four broad steps. The first is to determine your content. Select a topic that you are interested in and that you know something about, phrase a clear speech objective, analyze your audience to discover how you will want to shape and direct your content, and find material that will develop your ideas and adapt them to audience knowledge and interests.

The second step is to organize the material. First work on the body of the speech, the main points and development that accomplish the speech objective. After you have the material organized into main points you can work on an introduction that gains attention and leads into the body of the speech and a conclusion that ties the speech together and leaves it on a high note. The logic and development of the speech are tested through analysis of the speech outline.

The third step is to adapt your language to the audience. Speech language must be clear, vivid, emphatic, and appropriate to the audience.

The final step is to practice the delivery. Good delivery requires enthusiasm, good eye contact, and spontaneity. You achieve good delivery through voice, articulation and bodily action. Between the time the outline has been completed and the time the speech is to be given, you will want to practice the speech several times—weighing what you did and how you did it after each practice.

SUGGESTED READINGS

Karlyn Kohrs Campbell. *Critiques of Contemporary Rhetoric.* Belmont, Calif.: Wadsworth, 1972 (paperback). Three good background chapters on rhetorical criticism, followed by several examples of contemporary rhetoric and critiques.

Anthony Hillbruner. *Critical Dimensions: The Art of Public Address Criticism.* New York: Random House, 1966 (paperback). This short paperback gives a good overall view of the subject of speech criticism.

Edwin Newman. *Strictly Speaking: Will America Be the Death of English?* New York: Warner Books, 1975 (paperback). A highly readable and popular look at contemporary problems of English usage. A best seller.

CHAPTER 12

PRINCIPLES OF INFORMATION EXCHANGE

As Claude got into the car he casually asked Phyllis, "How'd things go today?"

"Oh," Phyllis said as she shrugged her shoulders, "Mindy lost her ball."

"She's always doing things like that," Claude chuckled, "Did . . ."

"But Ken found it."

"Ken found it?" Claude responded with a note of disbelief in his voice. "Ken isn't known for helping Mindy under any circumstances. Just the other day . . ."

"Well, I guess saying Ken found it isn't quite accurate," Phyllis interrupted. "Actually saying his foot found it would be a little more accurate."

"His foot what?" Claude asked totally confused.

"His foot stepped on it. Luckily the fall didn't hurt him too badly."

"He stepped on the ball and fell? What do you mean not too badly?"

"Well, Dr. Scott says he'll only be on the crutches a few weeks. In fact, he said a break like that is often less troublesome than a sprain."

"Ken broke a bone—and you say not hurt too badly?" Claude replied incredulously.

"In comparison to the picture window," Phyllis said indignantly.

"The picture window? How did the picture window get into this?" Claude asked nervously.

"Well, the lamp went right through it, of course," Phyllis replied matter of factly.

"Wait a minute, I thought we were talking about Ken falling and breaking a bone."

"We were," Phyllis said impatiently. *"But you were making such a fuss about a broken bone, and I just wanted to show you that the bone he broke was nothing compared to the window."*

"OK, what happened to the window?" Claude sighed.

"When Ken fell he landed on Rover who was sleeping. Rover leaped out of that sound sleep and bumped into the lamp which . . ."

"Fell through the picture window," Claude finished. *"Phyllis, is that all?"* Claude asked hesitantly.

"Isn't that enough?"

"Phyllis, that's more than enough, but the way you're talking I started to think there might be even more . . ."

"No, that's it—unless Mrs. Parker decides to sue."

"Our babysitter? Sue about what? Phyllis!" Claude shouted.

"Calm down, Claude. Oh I just knew you'd get all excited about this. Listen, when the lamp went crashing through the window, Mrs. Parker jumped up to see whether something had happened to Mindy and reinjured her sacroiliac. But I doubt she'll sue—after all, I offered to pay for the operation. But enough about this, Claude. How'd your day go?"

Information—it's difficult to do anything without adequate accurate information; and, as the opening story indicates, inadequately or poorly presented information can lead to frustration.

In spite of our most advanced technology for information retrieval and dissemination, we still get an amazing amount of the information we need or want through the spoken word. You listen to your radio or your television for the news of the day. You attend classroom lectures to learn psychology, economics, history, and the like. You may go to church to hear the minister's interpretation of the Bible. You listen to your friends, neighbors, and co-workers to find out how to get from here to there, how to bake a carrot cake, how the new computer works, and literally thousands of other topics.

Unfortunately our own abilities to process and disseminate information have not improved as fast as our technological means. As much as we talk, most of us are not nearly so good at information exchange as we could be. Yet learning to share information clearly and interestingly is not all that difficult. It does, however, require an understanding and application of basic principles. In this chapter, we will discuss those principles, most of which apply to any communication setting; in the next chapter, we will consider information skills in the context of speech assignments.

GOALS

In a speech communication course you are likely to be asked to give one or more "informative" speeches. On the surface, your goal appears to be simple enough: give information. But to what end? Of what value is the oral presentation of information? Giving an informative speech can be justified only so far as it facilitates the learning process. No one can "teach" another person anything—but one person can *help* another person in his or her learning of that material. How? (1) By opening the person to the information—helping him or her become receptive; (2) by helping the person to *understand* the material through vivid explanation and application; and (3) by devising means of helping a person *retain* the material he or she has received. An informative speech can focus on any one or more of these three goals.

EXERCISE

Consider the circumstances under which you are or have been active in facilitating the learning process. Were your efforts directed toward reception, understanding, or retention?

MEANS OF FACILITATING LEARNING

Now let us consider in some detail several basic principles of information exchange that will get audience attention, add to audience understanding, and increase the chances of audience retention of information. These principles are valid whether the format is public speaking, small-group interaction, or personal communication.

  1. *Information is more likely to get audience attention when it is perceived to be relevant.* Rather than acting like a sponge to absorb every bit of information that comes our way, most of us act more like filters—we pay attention only to that information we perceive as relevant.

  The ultimate in relevance is information perceived as vital, that is, information that is truly a matter of life and death. Just as police cadets are likely to pay attention when the subject is what to do when attacked, so will members of your audience pay attention when they think what you have to tell them is critical to them. Although very little of what you tell an audience will literally help them stay alive, you can focus on points that will improve the quality of that life. Students pay attention when the professor is telling them what's going to be on the midterm; men and women pay attention when someone talks about what can be done to insure fidelity of their boy-friend, girlfriend, or spouse; college seniors applying for graduate school pay attention to suggestions for increasing scores on graduate entrance exams.

  If your speech material can promise vital information you can and should take advantage of it. But even when what you have to say seems somewhat remote from audience experience you can usually build some relevance if you will think creatively and take the time to work at it. A speech on Japan can focus on the importance of Japanese manufacturing to our economy; a speech on the Egyptian pyramids can be related to our interest in building techniques. There is literally no subject for which some audience relevance cannot be shown. It is up to you to find that relevance and make a point of it in the speech.

A very good way of achieving relevance is to consider information as an answer to stated or implied questions that grow from perceived audience needs. Consider your need to know as related to today's weather. If you are planning to stay in your room all day to study, you probably have little need to know about outside temperatures and weather conditions; if, however, you are planning to go to a football game, a picnic, or take a hike, weather information will meet a felt need, and you will seek out and listen closely to weather forecasts. What do the people you are planning to talk with need to know? How does your information meet their needs?

2. *Information is more likely to get audience attention when it is perceived as new.* When people think they know something already, they are less likely to pay attention. It is up to you as speaker not only to find information that will be new to your audience but also to concentrate on the newness.

Even when you are talking about a topic that most of the people in your audience are familiar with, you can uncover new angles, new applications, new perspectives on the material. Just listen to people who are advertising such products as cellophane wrap, kitchen towels, and cheese. Nearly every commercial points to a new and different use for the various products. When it comes to speech material, the tests of "newness" are whether the information adds to audience knowledge or gives new insights to information members of the audience already possess.

3. *Information is more likely to be remembered when it is repeated.* The potential of repetition is unquestioned by those who study the memory process. For instance, when you meet someone for the first time, you will be more likely to remember the person's name if you repeat it a few times immediately after being introduced; when you are trying to learn a new definition, a formula for a compound, or a few lines of poetry, you will master them only after you have repeated them often enough to remember.

Putting repetition into speeches is perhaps one of the easiest devices. If you want the audience to remember exactly what you have said, then you can repeat it once or twice: "The number is 572638, that's 5,7,2,6,3,8"; or, "A ring-shaped coral island almost or completely surrounding a lagoon is called an atoll—the word is *atoll*."

There are times in a speech you will want the audience to remember an idea but not necessarily the specific language. Under these circumstances you will probably restate it rather than repeat it. Whereas repetition is the exact use of the same words, restatement is saying the idea again but in different words. For instance, "The population is 975,439—that's roughly one million people"; or "The test will be comprised of about four essay questions—all the questions on the test, about four, will be essay."

4. *Information is more likely to be understood and remembered when it is well organized.* Good organization does not necessarily influence the total amount of information remembered. If an audience listens to two thirty-minute

INFORMATION IS MORE LIKELY TO BE
REMEMBERED WHEN IT IS REPEATED.

speeches, one well organized and one disorganized, the audience is likely
to remember about the same amount of information. The difference is that
with the well organized speech, the speaker can predict better what the
audience will remember. So, the point of good organization is that it puts
the speaker in control.

Not only must information be well organized in your mind or on paper,
but also your listeners must be consciously aware of the presence of that
good organization. In the last chapter when we talked about speech organization we included the kinds of devices that a speaker must use to help
the audience *perceive* organization. A speaker who says, "In my speech I will
cover three goals, the first is . . . the second is . . . and the third is . . ." will
often have more success getting an audience to remember than one who does
not. Likewise, such reminder statements as "Now we come to the second
key point" or "Here's where we move from the third stage and go to the
fourth" have proven effective in directing audience thinking.

5. *Information is more likely to be retained when it has emotional impact.* Think
back over your life and recall what stands out most vividly about the past.
What you recall most readily are probably happenings, events, experiences,
or incidents that had highly emotional impact. Was it the day you got to drive
the family car for the first time? Or the time you fell off the ladder reaching
a little too far when you were painting? Or your first kiss? The artful speaker
can simulate this emotional impact through vivid anecdotes, illustrations,
and examples. The more vivid you can make your development, the more
powerful the emotional impact will be. Repetition can become boring when
used to excess, but audiences seldom tire of amplification that has sensory
impact.

Information is likely to have emotional impact when it is startling. Seeing your professor in a new sport coat may get your attention; seeing your professor come to class in a toga, a bearskin, or a loin cloth would be startling. Since the startling will have only momentary impact, its best use is as an attention-getter—either to get attention initially or to rekindle attention at flagging moments. The startling is often accomplished through action. Blowing up a balloon and letting it sail around the room to illustrate propulsion is startling.

6. *Information is more readily received and retained when it is presented humorously.* You do not have to be riotously funny or sprinkle your speech with jokes—in fact, both are likely to be more detrimental to your information than useful. To be most effective, the humor should be related to the topic. If you discover an amusing way of developing some point in your speech, your audience will listen. For instance, here is how one speaker heightened audience interest in his speech on hotel management:

Frankly, I think the hotel business has been one of the most backward in the world. There's been very little change in the attitude of room clerks in the 2000 years since Joseph arrived in Bethlehem and was told they'd lost his reservation.[1]

If trying to be funny makes you feel self-conscious, then do not force humor

DO NOT FORCE HUMOR INTO A SPEECH.

[1]James Lavenson, "Think Strawberries," *Vital Speeches,* March 15, 1974, p. 346.

into your speech. But if you think humor is one of your strengths, then make the most of it.

7. *Information is more likely to be understood and retained if it is associated.* When you walk into a room of people, you seek out the familiar faces. Likewise, when you are confronted with information that you do not readily understand, your ear listens for certain familiar notes that will put the new information into perspective. A speaker can associate through vivid comparisons and take advantage of this tendency on the part of the audience by associating new, difficult information with the familiar.

Association is defined as the tendency of a thought to recall others similar to it. That means when one word, idea, or event reminds you of another, you are associating. A speaker can associate through vivid comparisons and contrasts. For instance, if you were trying to show your audience how a television picture tube works, you could build an association between the unknown of the television tube and audience knowledge. The metaphor "a television picture tube is a gun shooting beams of light" would be an excellent association between the known and the unknown. The image of a gun shooting is a familiar one. A gun shooting beams of light is easy to visualize. If you made the association striking enough, every time your audience thought of a television picture tube, they would associate it with guns shooting beams of light. If you can establish one or more associations during your speech, you are helping to insure audience retention of key ideas.

8. *Information is more likely to be understood and retained when it is related visually.* You are more likely to make your point if you can show it as well as talk about it. Visual aids are effective in simplifying and emphasizing information as well as in holding interest. Their impact is a result of appealing to two senses at the same time: we listen to the explanation and we see the substance of the explanation. This double sensory impact helps cement the ideas in our mind. Visual aids will be discussed in some detail in the next chapter.

EXERCISE

Working with a set of facts like those included in exercise 2, pp. 285–286, practice ways of presenting these facts to facilitate reception, understanding, and retention. Work with at least three of the principles just discussed.

SUMMARY

Communication of information involves principles of reception, understanding, and retention. Basically information is more readily received and understood when it is relevant to receiver experience and is perceived as new information or at least as providing new insight. Information is more likely to be understood when it is well organized, when it is associated to previous knowledge or experience, and when it is related visually. Information is more likely to be retained when it is repeated and when it has some emotional impact.

SUGGESTED READINGS

John P. Houston. *Fundamentals of Learning.* New York: Academic Press, 1976. A good analysis of the total process of learning.

David Krech, Richard Crutchfield, and Norman Livson. *Elements of Psychology,* 3rd ed. New York: Knopf, 1974. See especially pages 359–446 for information about learning and memory.

Charles Petrie. "Informative Speaking: A Summary and Bibliography of Related Research." *Speech Monographs,* Vol. 30 (June 1963), pages 79–91.

CHAPTER 13

PRACTICE IN INFORMATION EXCHANGE

It was Phyllis's first day on the new job. For a week she had been putting in hours of time at home to learn all there was to know about the new Magic Power Super Electric Sweeper and Home Cleaning Outfit. And today was the first day she would have the chance to put her knowledge to use. She could scarcely wait for the first customer. Her mastery of the machine was complete—she had practiced the demonstration until she could do it smoothly without a flaw. Now all she needed was a customer.

"Miss," a voice said, shaking Phyllis from her dreams of hundreds of people gathered in admiration of her superb handling of the product. "Ah, my first chance," Phyllis said to herself.

"No doubt you are interested in how this magnificent piece of machinery works?"

"Er, could you . . ."

"Explain how you can save both time and money through this superbly engineered model? Why, it's no mystery. Let me show you how it works . . ." and Phyllis launched into her demonstration.

"Uh, no, Miss, I'm sure it works fine, but I . . ."

"Ah, you're interested in price—well, let me assure you that you can never guess how reasonable this revolutionary model is . . ."

"Uh, well, I'm sure it's a good price, but . . ."

"But you're wondering what you can do with your old, out-of-date machine? Well, let me tell you that for a limited time only, we will give you not a good, but the best trade-in you could imagine. We are . . ."

"Miss? Miss! Can you tell me where the men's room is?"

We can't blame Phyllis for being a bit overzealous in her desire to show her skill in demonstration. I hope you will be as well prepared and as enthusiastic as Phyllis, but I also hope you are more successful. To help you in your preparation, let us consider four specific skills that are most often included in information exchange: explaining processes, describing, defining, and using resource material. Although these skills may be used alone or in concert for any informational presentation, for purposes of speech practice, we will develop each in terms of a speech assignment that will incorporate and focus upon expertise with the skill.

EXPLAINING PROCESSES

When we give instructions to a friend on how to hit an overhead smash in tennis; when we share ideas with our neighbor on how to make tasty meals with ground meat; and when we talk with an employee of the telephone company on how a switchboard works, we are explaining processes: telling how to do something, how to make something, or how something works. In this unit we are working on the skills of clear, accurate process explanation.

Speech Topics

Since one way of working on the skills of explaining processes is to prepare a speech, you will need to discover a topic that is suitable for this assignment. As you analyze the brainstorming lists you made earlier (p. 224), you should find some that are best discussed as processes. These are possible examples:

Spare bowling	Getting elected	Using a slide rule
The American twist serve	Making fish flies	Mixing drinks
Sewing buttonholes	Designing a dress	Buying a car
Making glass	Grading beef	How a slot machine works

Skill with the Process

Of course, before you can ever attempt to successfully explain or demonstrate a process you must have the necessary knowledge and experience behind you. In many speech situations, you can find out what you need to know by reading about the topic. Successful process explanations go beyond cognitive understanding—they depend upon the presence of skill with the process. Thus if you are not a bowler, you may have difficulty in giving depth to an explanation of spot spare bowling; if you are not a seamstress, you may have difficulty in giving the ins and outs of hemming a dress. In both of these instances—and these are relatively simple examples—success of explanation requires more than a list of steps. Only from your knowledge and experience can you tell how much you will have to compensate if bowling alleys are fast or slow—or whether a certain stitch will work well with a certain material. Moreover, knowledge and experience build "speaker credibility." When you are explaining a process, you are projecting yourself as an authority on that particular subject. How well the audience listens will depend a great deal upon the credibility you can establish on this topic. We are inclined to listen when Julia Child tells us how to make chicken cacciatore or when Rod Carew tells us how to hit a curve or when Neal Armstrong tells us how a moon rover works. Your audience will listen to you if you make them confident in your knowledge and experience of the process you are explaining.

Organization of a Process

All but the simplest processes require many steps in the explanation. A process may have nine, eleven, or even fifteen steps. And of course, you cannot omit any of them. Since audiences find it much more comfortable to retain three to five steps, you should develop the skill of learning to group steps under common headings. A principle of learning states that it is easier to remember and comprehend information in units than as a series of independent items. Of course, you do not want to sacrifice accuracy just to limit your process to five steps—still, if it's at all possible, use some way to reduce this total. Notice how this was accomplished in a speech on woodwork.

A
1. Gather the materials
2. Draw the pattern
3. Trace the pattern on the wood
4. Cut out the pattern so that tracing line can still be seen
5. File to the pattern line
6. Sandpaper edge and surfaces
7. Paint the object
8. Sand lightly

B
1. Plan the job
   A. Gather materials
   B. Draw a pattern
   C. Trace the pattern on wood
2. Cut out the pattern
   A. Saw so the tracing line can be seen
   B. File to the pattern line
   C. Sandpaper edge and surface

9. Apply a second coat of paint
10. Varnish

3. Finish the object
   A. Paint
   B. Sand lightly
   C. Apply a second coat of paint
   D. Varnish

Although both sets of directions are essentially the same, the inclusion of the arbitrary headings in B enables us to visualize the process as having three steps instead of ten. As a result, most people would tend to remember the second set of directions more easily than the first.

Visualization

Although your audience can visualize a process through vivid word pictures—in fact, in your impromptu explanations in ordinary conversation it is the only way you can proceed—when you have the time to prepare, you will probably want to make full use of visual aids. With processes perhaps more than with any other kind of information exchange, carefully prepared visual material may be essential to receiver understanding.

Anything that is used to appeal to the visual sense is a visual aid. Let's look at the ones we are most likely to see used in speeches.

The Speaker   Sometimes through his use of gestures, movement, and personal attire the speaker himself can become his best visual aid. Through descriptive gestures he can show the size of a soccer ball, the height of a tennis net, and the shape of a lake; through his posture and movement, he can show the correct stance for skiing, a butterfly swimming stroke, and methods of artificial respiration; and through his own attire, he can illustrate the native dress of a foreign country; the proper outfit for a mountain climber, a cave explorer, or a scuba diver; or the uniform of a fireman, a policeman, or a soldier.

Objects   The objects you are talking about make good visual aids if they are large enough to be seen and small enough to carry around with you. A vase, a basketball, a braided rug, or a sword is the kind of object that can be seen by the audience and manipulated by the speaker.

Models   When an object is too large to bring to the speech or too small to be seen, a model will usually prove a worthwhile substitute. If you were to talk about a turbine engine, a suspension bridge, an Egyptian pyramid, or the structure of the atom, a model might well be the best visual aid. Working models are especially eye-catching.

Chalkboard   Because every classroom has a chalkboard, our first reaction is to make use of it in our speeches. As a means of visually portraying simple information, the chalkboard is unbeatable. Unfortunately, the chalkboard is easy to misuse and to overuse. The principal misuse students and teachers make of it is to write a volume of material while they are talking. More often than not what we write while we talk is either illegible or at least partly obscured by our body while we are writing. Furthermore, the tendency is to spend too much time talking to the board instead of to the audience.

The chalkboard is overused because it is so readily available. Most people use it in an impromptu fashion, whereas good visual aids require considerable preplanning to achieve their greatest value. By and large, anything that can be done with a chalkboard can be done better with a pre-prepared chart, which can be introduced when needed.

If you believe you must use the chalkboard, think about putting the material on the board before you begin, or use the board for only a few seconds at a time. If you plan to draw your visual aid on the board before you begin, get to class a little early so that you can complete your drawing before the period. It is not fair to your classmates to use several minutes of class time completing your visual aid. Moreover, it is usually a good idea to cover what you have done in some way. If you do plan to draw or to write while you are talking, practice doing that as carefully as you practice the rest of the speech. If you are righthanded, stand to the right of what you are drawing. Try to face at least part of the audience while you work. Although it seems awkward at first, your effort will allow your audience to see what you are doing while you are doing it.

Pictures, Drawings, and Sketches   These three elements probably account for most visual aids used in speeches in or out of the classroom. Pictures, of course, are readily available; however, you must make sure that they are large enough to be seen. The all-too-common disclaimer, "I know you can't see this picture but . . ." is of little help to the audience.

You may want to draw your own visual aid. If you can use a compass, a straightedge, and a measure, you can draw or sketch well enough for speech purposes. A drawing need only be a representation of the key ideas. Stick men may not be as aesthetically pleasing as professional drawings, but they work every bit as well. The important thing about this kind of visual aid is to make your lettering large enough to be seen easily by the person sitting farthest away.

Charts   A chart is a graphic representation of material that compresses a great deal of information into a usable, easily interpreted form.

Word charts, maps, line graphs, bar graphs, and pie graphs are all possible. To get the most out of them, however, you should be prepared to make intelligent interpretations. Since charts do not speak for themselves, you should know how to read, test, and interpret them before you try to use them in speeches.

Films, Slides, and Projections   In a classroom presentation, you will seldom have the opportunity to use films, slides, and projections. The scheduling of projectors, the need for darkened classrooms, and the tendency for these visual aids to dominate the speaker all combine to outweigh possible advantages of their use. Nevertheless, slides, opaque projections, and overhead projections can make even a classroom speech more exciting. If possible, use a partner to run the machinery for you while you are speaking. Make sure that each picture really relates to, supplements, or reinforces what you are saying.

Using Visual Aids

As with any other speech skill, you must practice using visual aids to get the most from them. The following are some useful guidelines for you to consider in your practice.

1. *Show visual aids only when you are talking about them.* You are competing with visual aids for attention. When you are using a visual aid to make a point you expect audience attention to be directed to it. But if your visual aids are still in view when you are talking about something else, the audience will still be inclined to give attention to the visual aid. So, when the visual aid does not contribute to the point you are making, keep it out of sight.

2. *Talk about the visual aid while you are showing it.* Although a picture may be worth a thousand words, you know what you want your audience to see in the picture. You should tell your audience what to look for; you should explain the various parts; and you should interpret figures, symbols, and percentages.

3. *Show visual aids so that everyone in the audience can see them.* If you hold the visual aid, hold it out away from your body and point it to the various parts of the audience. If you place your visual aid on the chalkboard or easel or mount it in some way, stand to one side and point with the arm nearest the visual aid. If it is necessary to roll or fold your visual aid, bring some transparent tape to mount it to the chalkboard or wall so that it does not roll or wrinkle.

4. *Talk to your audience and not to your visual aid.* You may need to look at the visual aid occasionally, but you want to maintain eye contact with your audience as much as possible to see how they are reacting to your visual

DON'T OVERDO THE USE OF VISUAL AIDS.

material. When a person is too engrossed in his visual aid, he tends to lose audience contact entirely.

5. *Don't overdo the use of visual aids.* You can reach a point of diminishing returns with them. If one is good, two may be better; if two are good, three may be better. But somewhere along the line, you will reach a point where one more visual aid is too many. Visual aids are a form of emphasis; but attempts to emphasize too many things result in no emphasis at all. Decide where visual aids would be of most value. A visual aid is an *aid* and not a substitute for good speech making.

6. *Pass objects around the class at your risk only.* People look at, read, handle, and think about something they hold in their hands; and while they are so occupied, they may not be listening to you. Moreover, when something is being passed around, the people who are not in possession often spend their time looking for the objects, wondering why people are taking so long, and fearing that perhaps they will be forgotten. If you are going to pass things out, have enough for everyone. Then keep control of audience attention by telling them what they should be looking at and when they should be listening to you. Anytime you actually put something in your listeners' hands, you are taking a gamble—make a conscious decision whether it is worth the risk.

7. *Demonstrate your process if possible.* When the task is relatively simple, you may want to try a complete demonstration. If so, practice until you can do it smoothly and easily under the pressure of facing an actual audience. Remember that in the actual speech the demonstration may take longer than in practice.

For a relatively complicated process, you may want to consider the modified demonstration. For a modified demonstration, you complete the demonstration in various stages at home and do only part of the actual work in front of the audience. For instance, if you were going to demonstrate construction of a floral display you would have a complete set of materials to begin the demonstration, a mock-up of the basic floral triangle, and a completed floral display. During the speech you would first talk about all the materials you need and then you would begin the demonstration of making the basic floral triangle. Rather than trying to get everything together perfectly in a few seconds, you could draw from a bag or some concealed place the partially completed arrangement that illustrates the floral triangle. This you would use in your demonstration, adding flowers as if you were planning to complete it. Then from another bag you could draw the completed arrangement that illustrates one of the possible effects you were discussing. Although this demonstration is modified, it is probably better than trying to complete an entire demonstration within a short time limit.

Throughout your demonstration, speak slowly and repeat key ideas often. Moreover, if you can work in audience participation—we learn best by doing—you may be even more successful. For instance, in a speech on origami, Japanese paper folding, you may want to give your audience paper so that each person can go through a simple process with you. You could explain the principles; then you could pass out paper and have the audience participate in making a figure; finally, through other visual aids you could show how these principles are used in more elaborate projects. Actual participation will increase interest and insure recall.

EXERCISE _____

1. Work in groups of three or five or individually to develop visual aids that would show the following:

   Comparative temperatures or rainfall in major U.S. cities
   The field, court, or layout for a sport
   How to play a musical instrument

   Show and explain the completed visual aids to the entire class.

2. Prepare a speech of three to six minutes in which you show how something is made, how something is done, or how something works. An outline is required. Criteria for evaluation will include quality of topic, use of visual aids, and skill in organization and presentation.

DESCRIBING

Next to showing a visual aid (a procedure which may or may not be "worth a thousand words") the next most effective method of portraying pictorial information is through vivid description. Because the act of "seeing" information is so important, learning to describe effectively is fundamental to good information exchange. A descriptive speech assignment gives you a chance to focus on and to sharpen your skills of describing.

Topics

As you analyze your original brainstorming lists, you should look for those topics that are best communicated by means of physical description of their properties, such as objects, structures, or places. The following examples suggest the kinds of topics that will help you focus on description:

Crossbow	Tent trailer	Disneyland
Eiffel Tower	Geyser	Pikes Peak
St. Louis Golden Arch	The ocean floor	Space capsule

Essentials of Description

Description is achieved through clear and vivid word pictures. To enable your receivers to get a mental image that corresponds with your perception, you need skill in describing size, shape, weight, color, composition, age and condition, and location of subordinate items. Description may of course be made considerably easier with visual aids. Since the purpose of this assignment is the development of verbal skills, you should accomplish the description without use of visual aids.

Size We describe size subjectively by "large" or "small" and objectively by dimensions. Often a good description of size will contain some comparison. Statements like "It's a small car" or "It's 12 feet long" are not very descriptive. On the other hand, "The car is only 12 feet long; that's a foot shorter than a Volkswagen Rabbit" would be descriptive.

Shape We describe shape in terms of common geometric forms. "Round," "triangular," "oblong," "spherical," "conical," "cylindrical," and "rectangular" are all descriptive. A complex object is often best described as a series of simple geometric shapes. Even though most objects do not conform to perfect shapes, you can usually get by with approximations and with comparisons to familiar objects: "The lake is oval," "The lot is pie shaped," or "The car looks like a rectangular box," all give reasonably accurate impressions. Shape is further clarified by such adjectives as "jagged," "smooth," or "indented."

Weight   We describe weight subjectively as "heavy" or "light" and objectively by pounds and ounces. Thus, "The object is really rather light, only about an ounce—approximately the same weight as your standard lead pencil" would be descriptive.

Color   This basic element of any vivid description is difficult to describe accurately. Although most people can visualize black and white, the primary colors (red, yellow, and blue), and their complements (green, purple, and orange), very few objects are quite these colors. Perhaps the best way to make description of color vivid and accurate is to couple it with a common referent. For instance, "lime green," "brick red," and "sky blue" are helpful in giving accurate approximations.

Composition   Knowing the composition and texture of an object helps us to visualize it. A ball of aluminum does not look the same as a ball of yarn. A brick building looks different from steel, wood, or glass buildings. Sometimes you will refer to what the object seems like rather than what it is. An object can appear metallic even if it is not made of metal. Spun glass can have a woolly texture. Nylon can be soft and smooth as in stockings or hard and sharp as in toothbrush bristles.

Age and Condition   Whether an object is new or old, in good or poor condition, can make a difference in its appearance. Since age by itself may not be descriptive, it is usually best to couple it with condition. Books become ragged and tattered, cars become rusty and dull, clothes become worn, dull, and threadbare with age.

Location of Subordinate Items   If your object is complex, the parts must be put into their proper relationship before a mental picture emerges. Remember the story of the three blind men who described an elephant in terms of what each felt? The one who felt the trunk said the elephant was like a snake; the one who felt a leg said the elephant was like a tree; and the one who felt the body said the elephant was like a wall. Unless we show how the parts fit together no accurate picture can emerge.

One helpful suggestion is to arrange your discussion according to a space order—top to bottom, left to right, upper right corner to lower left corner, clockwise around an object, or the like. For practice, look around your study room. Select three or four objects and describe them as clearly and as vividly as you can. For instance:

> A lead pencil. The pencil is about six inches long. The shaft, a hexagonal shape, dark yellow in color, is imprinted with black lettering. At one end the pencil looks like a cone coming to a blunt point; at the other end a ¾-inch

metal band attaches a red eraser to the shaft. The band is a dull gold color with two blue bands about $\frac{1}{16}$-inch wide and $\frac{1}{16}$-inch apart near the center of the band. The eraser is worn down to about two thirds of its original size.

EXERCISE

1. Study the description just given of the lead pencil. How many elements of description were used? Which were most descriptive? Which were least?

2. Write out descriptions of each of the following relatively simple objects:

   Your speech book
   Your room key
   A lamp in your room
   Your chair
   Your home
   Your car

3. Working in groups of three to five, discuss your descriptions. Whose was clearest? Most vivid? Who did the best job of using comparisons to sharpen the description?

4. Prepare a two- to four-minute speech describing an object, a building, or a place. An outline is required. Criteria for evaluation will include clarity and vividness of the description.

DEFINING

Each of us has a working vocabulary of many thousand words. Yet when we are asked for a complete, clear definition of even relatively simple words we see how fuzzy our understanding of words really is. Since we cannot solve problems, learn, or even think without meaningful definitions, the ability to define clearly and vividly is essential for the effective communicator. Since Plato first attacked the Sophists for their failure to define and to classify, students of public speaking have seen definition as a primary tool of effective speaking. In fact, Richard Weaver, representing the view of many modern scholars, has labeled definition as the most valuable of all lines of development.[1]

Topics

As you examine your original brainstorming list you may be surprised at the number of topics that depend upon definition if they are to be under-

[1]Richard Weaver, "Language Is Sermonic," *in* Richard L. Johannesen (Ed.), *Contemporary Theories of Rhetoric: Selected Readings* (New York: Harper & Row, 1971), pp. 170–171.

stood. The most informative speeches are often those that develop definitions for the audience. The following are some terms that are well worth defining:

Impressionism (art, theatre)	Nongraded elementary
Jury rigging	High fidelity
Jazz	Apartheid
Octane rating	Archeology
Vitamins	Sextant

Methods

The following are the four most common methods of defining. In your communication, they can be used separately or in combination.

Classification and Differentiation   When you define by *classification*, you give the boundaries of the particular word and focus on the single feature that gives the word a different meaning from similar words. Most dictionary definitions are of the classification-differentiation variety. For instance, a dog may be defined as a carnivorous, domesticated mammal of the family Canidae. "Carnivorous," "mammal," and "family Canidae" limit the boundaries to dogs, jackals, foxes, and wolves. "Domesticated" differentiates dogs from the other three.

Synonym and Antonym   Synonym and antonym may be the most popular means of defining. Both enable the speaker to indicate approximate if not exact meaning in a single sentence; moreover, because they are analogous to comparison and contrast they are often vivid as well as clear. *Synonyms* are words that have the same or nearly the same meanings; *antonyms* are words that have opposite meanings. Defining by synonym is defining by comparison. For instance, synonyms for "arduous" would be "hard," "laborious," and "difficult." Antonyms define by contrast. Antonyms for "arduous" would be "easy" and "simple." Synonyms are not duplicates for the word being defined, but they do give a good idea of what the word means. Of course, the synonym or antonym used must be familiar to the audience or its use defeats its purpose.

Use and Function   Another effective way to define is to explain the *use or function* of the object a particular word represents. Thus when you say "A plane is a hand-powered tool that is used to smooth the edges of boards," or "A scythe is a piece of steel shaped in a half circle with a handle attached that is used to cut weeds or high grass," you are defining tools by indicating their use. Since the use or function of an object may be more important than its classification, this is often an excellent method of definition.

Etymology and Historical Example   *Etymology* is the derivation or an account of the history of a particular word. Since words change over time, origin may reveal very little about modern meaning. In some instances, however, the history of a word reveals additional insight that will help the audience remember the meaning a little better. For instance, a censor originally was one of two Roman magistrates appointed to take the census and, later, to supervise public morals.

Definition Development

A word can be defined by synonym with one other word or by use in a single sentence. To practice the skill of definition, you should work on extended definitions that explore the various aspects of the word involved. In essence, you have two choices for your development. One is to develop the speech topically with coordinate headings each of which stands as a part of the definition. The other method is to develop the speech topically with subordinate headings in which the first point defines the word in general and subsequent points define the word in specific.

In coordinate development, the major aspects of the definition become the main points of the speech. For instance, expressionism in drama is characterized by the nonobjective use of symbols, stereotyped characters, and stylization. Like most dictionary definitions, this further requires an understanding of the elements used in the definition. A speech of definition then would concentrate on these elements. For instance, your structural outline would look like this:

> *Speech Objective:* To understand the three major elements of expressionism in drama.
>
>   **I.** Expressionism is characterized by nonobjective use of symbols.
>   **II.** Expressionism is characterized by stereotyped characters.
> **III.** Expressionism is characterized by stylization.

If you sought to develop your own definition instead of adopting a dictionary definition, the principle involved would be much the same. For example, if you wanted to define "academic responsibility," you would think of the criteria that a professor must meet. If you determined that these criteria were teaching, public relations, publication, and university service, then your structural outline would look like this:

Speech Objective: To understand the elements of academic responsibility.

   I. Academic responsibility is characterized by good teaching.

   II. Academic responsibility is characterized by dedicated research and publication.

   III. Academic responsibility is characterized by university service.

   IV. Academic responsibility is characterized by public relations.

Subordinate development proceeds somewhat differently. Sometimes you will discover that the word you wish to define is most clearly defined through various examples and illustrations that *limit* the boundaries of the definition. Under these circumstances, rather than developing the speech topically, with each main point standing as a part of the definition, you may elect to develop the speech subordinately. In subordinate development, your first major point presents the total definition *in general*. Then your remaining points present degrees, limits, or other specific aspects of the definition. In a speech on social customs, a speaker might define the word *norm*. The definition itself is rather simple—norms are rules that define accepted behavior in society. Much of the real understanding of the word, then, must come through various examples that consider the degrees of norms. In brief, the skeleton of the outline might look like this:

Speech Objective: To understand the two different degrees of norms.

   I. Norms are rules that define what is required in certain situations in society.

   II. One degree of norms is illustrated by folkways.

   III. Another degree of norms is illustrated by mores.

The strength of this kind of development is that in moving from general to specific, you give your audience a clear and vivid understanding of the word being defined.

In developing an extended definition, you are not restricted to any particular procedure. Your goal is to give the clearest, most meaningful definition possible, utilizing any or all of the preceding methods of definition.

EXERCISE

1. For practice, working in groups of three to five or alone for presentation to a small group or the class itself, develop short but accurate definitions of some of the following terms. Try to define by at least two different methods for each.

a pencil	a rocket	a fondue pot
a chair	beef stroganoff	a dog
a pizza	a tape recorder	a guitar
a griddle	a telescope	a houseboat

2. Prepare a two- to four-minute speech of definition. An outline is required. Select a word or concept that is not readily definable by most members of the class. Criteria for evaluation will include clarity of the definition and quality of the development of the various aspects.

USING RESOURCE MATERIAL

With processes, description and definition, we were working with skills related to shaping and amplifying information. Information exchange, however, often requires use of source material beyond the experience of the speaker. In this section, the information-exchange skill we are developing is how to incorporate research information in communication.

Topics

Research speeches are most often found under the categories of political, economic, and social issues; historical events and forces; and theories, principles, or concepts. The following topics may give you some ideas of what to look for in your brainstorming sheets.

Political, Economic, and Social Issues:

Methods of solving air pollution	Effects of drug abuse
Modernization of police forces	Goals of women's liberation
Pesticides and wildlife	Effects of TV violence on children

Historical Events and Forces:

Greek drama	Oriental use of gunpowder
Roman roads	Napoleonic wars
Chivalry	Witchcraft

Theory, Principle, or Law:

Harmonics	Law of diminishing returns
X-rays	Law of supply and demand
Magnetism	Relativity

Research Evaluation

One of the criteria you should apply to your research is whether it is comprehensive. Comprehensive means researching until you have discovered all the relevant information. Although comprehensive research on any subject could take a team of researchers weeks or more—for a class assignment, we expect the speech to be comprehensive "within reason." This might be defined as utilizing at least four different authoritative sources of information. My advice would be to look into eight or ten different sources and then focus your efforts on the best three or four.

If you research properly, you will have on hand more material than you can read completely. In order to locate and record the best material, you should develop a system of evaluation that will enable you to review the greatest amount of information in the shortest period of time. A skill that facilitates this process is *skimming*. Let's define skimming by showing how it works. If you are appraising a magazine article, spend a minute or two finding out what it covers. Does it really present information on the phase of the topic you are exploring? Does it contain any documented statistics, examples, or quotable opinions? Is the author qualified to draw meaningful conclusions? If you are appraising a book, read the table of contents carefully, look at the index, and skip-read pertinent chapters asking the same questions you would for a magazine article. During this skimming period, you will decide which sources should be read in full, which should be read in part, and which should be abandoned. Minutes spent in evaluation will save you from hours of useless reading.

A second criterion you should apply to your research is whether the material you plan to use is accurate and objective. Determining accuracy can be a long and tedious job. In most instances, accuracy can be reasonably assured by checking the fact against the original source if one is given or against another article or book on the same subject. Although checking accuracy may seem a waste of time, you will be surprised at the difference in "facts" reported in two or more sources. If at least two sources say about the same thing, you can be a little more confident. Objectivity is tested much the same way. If two or more sources give different "slants" on the material, then you will know that what is being discussed is a matter of opinion. Only after you have examined many sources are you in a position to make the kind of value judgment that a thinking speaker needs to make.

Citation of Source Material

A special problem of a research speech is how to cite source material in the speech. In speeches, as in any communication in which you are using ideas that are not your own, you should attempt to work the source of your material into the context of the speech. Such efforts to include sources not only will help the audience in their evaluation of the content but also will add to your credibility as a speaker. In a written report ideas taken from other sources are designated by footnotes; in a speech these notations must be included within the context of your statement of the material. In addition since an expository speech is supposed to reflect a depth of research, citing the various sources of information will give concrete evidence of your research. Your citation need not be a complete representation of all the bibliographical information. Here are some examples.

> According to an article about Margaret Thatcher in last week's *Time* magazine . . .

> In the latest Gallup poll cited in last week's issue of *Newsweek* . . .

> But in order to get a complete picture we have to look at the statistics. According to the *Statistical Abstract,* the level of production for the Common Market rose from . . .

> In a speech before the National Association of Manufacturers given just last spring, Philip Dumbar, an authority on advertising, said . . .

Creativity

Perhaps one of the most important skills of presenting resource material is creativity. A creative speech is new; it is not copied, imitated, or reproduced. This means that your speech must be a product of, but entirely different from, the sources you used. You find material, you put it in a usable form, then you inject your own insights—your own personality into the speech.

Some people believe that creativity is possible only for a "gifted personality." Actually, we all have the potential for thinking creatively—some of us just have not given ourselves a chance to try. First, and perhaps most important, you need to give yourself enough time for the creative process to work. Once you think you are prepared (say, when you have completed your outline), you need time, perhaps two or three days, for your mind to reflect upon the material. You may find that the morning after a few uninspiring practices you suddenly have two or three fresh ideas for lines of development. While you were sleeping, your mind was still going over the material. When you awoke, the product of unconscious or subconscious thought reached the level of consciousness. Had there been no intervening time between those unrewarding practice sessions and actual speech delivery, your mind would not have had the time to work through the material. So, sometimes we are not creative simply because we have not given our minds time to process the material we have.

WHILE YOU ARE SLEEPING,
YOUR MIND IS STILL GOING
OVER THE MATERIAL.

But time alone is not enough. You must be receptive to new ideas, and you must develop the capacity to evaluate comparable ideas. Too often we are content with the first thought that comes to mind. Suppose for your speech on plastics, you thought you would begin the speech with "Today, more and more items are made out of plastic. But what are we going to do to meet our needs for plastic in light of the energy crisis?" Now, there is probably nothing wrong with that opening, but is it the best you could do? There is no way for you to know until you have tried other ways. Brainstorm a little. Try to start your speech in two, three, or even five different ways. Although several attempts will be similar, the effort to try new ways will stretch your mind, and chances are good that one or two of the ways will be far superior and much more imaginative than any of the others.

Being receptive also means noticing ideas that come to you when you are doing other things. Have you ever noticed how ideas come to you while you are washing dishes or shining your shoes or watching television or waiting at a stop light? Also, have you noticed that when you try to recall those ideas later many have slipped away? Many speakers, writers, and composers carry a pencil and paper with them at all times; and when an idea comes, they make note of it. Not all of these inspirations are the flashes of creative genius—but some of them are good, or at least worth exploring. If you do not make note of them, you will never know whether they were good or not.

Creativity is also the product of hard work. By being familiar with possible lines of development and by trying to take an idea along each of the possible lines, you can work out alternative methods of presenting factual material. In the section on speech preparation, we discussed examples, illustrations, stories, comparisons, and contrast as developmental material. With any given set of facts you may be able to create one of these lines of development. For instance, let's say that you are to give a speech about England. You learn that London is a city of seven million people, it rests roughly at the fifty-first parallel, its average temperature in the summer is mid-sixties and winter is mid-forties, and it is the leading city in a nation of some 50,000 square miles. With only these four facts about London, you could do a great deal. You could develop a comparative line by showing each of these in comparison with a familiar spot in the United States. You could develop a generalization example line by making a statement using each of the facts as an example. Or, you could develop an illustration or story line by taking one of the facts and developing a hypothetical situation. The potential is limited only by your willingness to work with the materials that you have available.

So, if you will give yourself time, if you will be receptive to ideas, and if you are willing to work with your materials, you can create.

EXERCISE

1. Citing material: Indicate various ways that you could cite the sources you used to make the evidence cards on page 283.

2. Creativity: From the following data about the book and television program *Roots,* write two separate paragraphs. In the first, make a statement about *Roots* and develop it by example and illustration; in the second, make a statement about *Roots* and develop it by comparison and contrast.

> *Roots* is both a book and a television program.
> By mid-1977, more than a million hard-cover copies had been sold.
> At least some 130 million Americans watched at least some parts of the television dramatization.
> 80 million tuned in for the final installment.
> First television showing of *Gone With the Wind*—only weeks before the dramatization of *Roots*—broke all previous ratings records. It was surpassed by *Roots.*
> *Roots* was the first television series to be shown for eight consecutive nights.

Roots won awards on every awards show of the year for which it qualified. Alex Haley is the author of the book and served as an advisor on the television dramatization.

3. Prepare a four- to seven-minute speech. An outline and a bibliography are required (at least four sources). Criteria for evaluation will include the quality of the content, the use of source material in the speech, and the creativity shown in developing ideas. The speech should be informative and interesting. A question period of one to three minutes will follow (optional).

SUMMARY

Effective information exchange involves not only the steps of speech preparation and a knowledge of principles of information exchange but also ability in explaining processes, describing, defining, and using resource material.

We are often called upon to show how to do something, how to make something, or how something works. The effectiveness of our explanations is facilitated by learning to use such visual aids as the speaker, objects, models, chalkboard, pictures, drawings, sketches, charts, films, slides, and projections.

Information clarity and vividness is likely to be a function of the quality of your description. Describing requires skills in recognizing and portraying size, shape, weight, color, composition, age and condition, and location of subordinate items.

Since effective communication is dependent upon sharing meaning, clarity of definition is often prerequisite to information exchange. Effective definition involves the understanding of methods of definition: classification and differentiation, synonym and antonym, uses and function, and etymology and historical example.

One of the most important information skills is using resource material. By knowing how to evaluate your research, how to cite sources in the speech, and how to develop resource material creatively you can give a speech that is both informative and interesting.

SUGGESTED READINGS

Rudolph Verderber. *The Challenge of Effective Speaking,* 4th ed. Belmont, Calif.: Wadsworth, 1979.

CHAPTER 14

PRINCIPLES OF PERSUASION

The convention was at a standstill. For hours the two sides had battled back and forth on the key plank of the platform. Three times votes were taken and three times no majority could be obtained to resolve the issue. Tempers were flaring and chaos threatened to break loose, when from the back of the room Claude made his way forward to the speaker's stand. As he mounted the stand and faced his party a hush fell over the crowd. Claude began. For an hour he coolly assessed the issue. Every facet was carefully examined. How one man could have at his fingertips such a volume of information! How one man could sort out the wheat from the chaff with such unerring accuracy after so many of the best minds of the party had snarled and snagged the issues was the wonder of all who listened in amazement. As Claude finished, the entire membership rose as a body and cheered. Immediately cries of take a vote were heard throughout the auditorium. "All those in favor say aye," the chairman shouted, and as one, everyone roared "aye" as a testament to Claude's lucid and persuasive argument.

The chairman proclaimed, "The aye's have it—unanimously." As the tumult echoed, he turned to the party leaders and said, "Thank God for Claude—what we'd do without his keen, cool mind, I'll never know."

As Claude walked to his seat people reached out to pat him on the back and those who could not touch him chanted "Claude . . . Claude . . . Claude . . ."

"Claude! Claude! Wake up, Claude!" Phyllis shouted as she shook Claude's shoulder. "Claude—wake up—you're supposed to be working on your speech."

Like Claude, I think each of us has dreamed of holding an audience in the palm of his hand. Although we may never give the speech that turns the party convention around, each of us is likely to have that chance to make a statement that will change an audience's attitude or move an audience to action. Basically, that is what persuasion is all about—changing attitudes and moving people to action. Still, rather than seeing persuasion as a different category of speaking, you should look at it as an extension of the information-exchange process. As Plato asserted more than two thousand years ago, persuasion without an informative base is "empty rhetoric"—it does not contribute to the best interests of society. So in this chapter we are concerned not only with success in achieving objectives but also with achieving those objectives ethically.

Persuasive speaking is without a doubt the most demanding of speech challenges. Moreover, there is no formula for success—no set of rules to guarantee effectiveness. The highest paid advertising firms do not guarantee success—they suggest they will prepare advertising campaigns with high probability of success. So if you are seeking a sure-fire measure of success perhaps you should look elsewhere. Still, in the centuries that scholars have been studying the process, they have learned to identify many variables of persuasion. In this chapter we will explore the principles of persuasive speaking that if properly considered should enable you to increase the *probability* of achieving your objective. A speech is more likely to be persuasive (1) if the speech objective is a clearly written statement calling for a change in belief or action; (2) if the speech is organized to adapt to audience attitudes; (3) if the speech uses materials that are logical, emotional, credible, and ethical; and (4) if the speech is delivered with conviction.

DETERMINING A PERSUASIVE SPEECH OBJECTIVE

Although any random statement may influence another person's actions (merely saying "I see the new Penney's store opened in Western Woods" may "persuade" another person to go to Penney's for some clothing need), the successful persuader does not leave the effect of the message to chance. How then should you begin your preparation? The same as with any type of speech—by determining a clearly worded speech objective. The persuasive speech objective, often called a proposition, indicates specifically what you want your audience to do or to believe. Although persuasive messages may be phrased to strengthen a currently held belief, the two most common types of statements are those that (1) seek to change a belief held by an audience or those that (2) seek to move an audience to action. "The Bluebirds are the best team on the circuit," "State lotteries should be outlawed," and "Social Security taxes should be lowered" illustrate statements seeking to create or to change beliefs. Many theorists consider the creation or the change of belief as an intermediate step in getting an audience to act. Once a belief is established, the believer may (or may not) be open to further persuasion to take action on his belief. "Buy a box of wheat puffs the next time you go shopping" and "Write to your congressman" illustrate statements seeking to move to action. Although a persuader can sometimes see the effect of her message (if her listeners are moved to immediate direct action), much of the persuasion that takes place is on the attitudinal or belief level.

So any clearly worded statement calling for a belief or action will qualify as a starting point in the planning stage; but before you go much further, you must consider the potential for success of your efforts. Your goal must give you some chance for success or else you are wasting your time. A speech to the Soviet Presidium calling for them to change to free enterprise capitalism would be foolhardy, if not outright dangerous. What tests can you apply to an examination of your speech objective? Before you make a final decision on wording of your speech goal, you should consider the following principles:

1. *The farther from the focus of audience belief, the less likely the chances for achieving your objectives.* Attitudes can be changed and behavior can be modified, but to expect 180-degree shifts in attitude or behavior as a result of a single speech is unrealistic and probably fruitless. William Brigance, one of the great speech teachers of this century, used to speak of "planting the seeds of persuasion." If we present a modest proposal seeking a slight change in attitude, we may be able to get an audience to think about what we are saying. Then later when the idea begins to grow, we can ask for greater change. For instance, if your audience believes that taxes are too high, you are unlikely to make them believe that they are not. However, you may be able to influence them to see that taxes are not really as high as they originally thought or not as high as other goods and services.

The further your goal is from the focus of audience belief, the more time it will take you to achieve that goal. Major attitude change is more likely to be achieved over a period of time rather than in a one-shot effort. One author encourages "seeing persuasion as a campaign—a structured sequence of efforts to achieve adoption, continuance, deterrence, or discontinuance."[1] Attitude change is most effective over a long-range, carefully considered program in which each part in the campaign is instrumental in bringing about

---

[1] Wallace Fotheringham, *Perspectives on Persuasion* (Boston: Allyn & Bacon, 1966), p. 34.

later effects. Still, much of your speaking allows for only one effort—and you want to make the most of it. So, we have to look for principles to guide us when we have just one opportunity.

2. *The more you call for your audience to do or the more difficulty required in doing what you call for, the less likely the chances for achieving your objective.* When we call for members of an audience to act, we are usually asking them to modify their behavior in some way. This action or behavior modification is always done at some cost (in time, money, or energy) to the audience. When the cost is negligible or token, an audience may well go along with you. For instance, if you ask your listeners to write a note to their congressman, the time and expense involved in the writing and mailing may be more than they care to handle at that time. However, if you *give* them pre-addressed post-cards, they are likely to take a minute right then to dash off a few lines. Or if you ask them to give five dollars to a particular charity, they may see that as more than they can spare or they will not have the cash on them or they say they will do it "sometime." The result is, no money gets contributed. If, on the other hand, you ask them to reach into their pocket and pull out the change they are carrying and drop it in the hat as it is being passed, they are more likely to follow through.

The greater the demand you place on the audience, the more prepared you must be to meet resistance and the more prepared you must be to get less than maximum involvement. Even when you are asking for minimal expense of time, energy, or money, you must continue to show the audience how easy it is to follow up on your proposition.

3. *The more ego-involved the members of the audience are, the less likely you are to achieve your objective with them.* Ego-involvement is related to face-saving. There are times when we realize that we are wrong but feel that to change should somehow make us look bad. It is difficult, for example, for one who has worked hard for years to get authorization and funding for a hydroelectric dam to admit that the building of such a dam would be a bad idea—it is difficult for a devoted fan of a particular team to admit that his team lost because the players just were not good enough.

4. *The more basic the change, the less likely you are to achieve your objective.* Consider the subject of diet. You may be able to get a person to change from one brand of ham to another rather easily—you're still talking about ham. Considering comparative prices, you may be able to get a person to eat more chicken and turkey and less beef—you're still talking about meat. However, it would be far more difficult to convince a beef eater to become a strict vegetarian. For most Americans eating meat is part of basic behavior patterns, whereas the choice of type of meat or brand of meat product is less basic.

EXERCISE

Write a speech objective that you would consider for your persuasive speech. What is the probability of your success with this objective?

USING MATERIALS OF PERSUASION

Persuasion is more likely to occur when the speaker makes good use of the various materials of persuasion. These materials are the same as those you have used in your informative speeches: examples; illustrations; statistics; quotations; along with facts and opinions that you get from experience, observation, reading, and interviewing. The difference between the materials in informative and in persuasive speeches is in their use. In contrast to the informative speech when you use materials to explain, clarify, and promote understanding, in the persuasive speech you use materials to prove and to motivate, to change beliefs, and to bring others to action. These goals are accomplished through materials that provide logical proof, that arouse the emotions, that are perceived as being delivered by a credible source, and that are used ethically. Let us consider each of these in turn.

Reasoning

Persuasion is more likely to be achieved when you can show the audience logical reasons for supporting the proposition. As human beings we take pride in considering ourselves "rational." We seldom do anything without some real or imagined reason. Sometimes these reasons are not clearly stated; sometimes the reasons we state for our behavior are neither the real ones nor very good ones. And sometimes the reasons come after we do something rather than before. Nevertheless, whether the reasons are good or bad or whether they come before or after the fact we seek reasons for our actions and beliefs. If you wish to affect an audience, you have to provide reasons.

Reasons are statements that answer the question Why? For instance, today I am thinking about how I can convince my colleagues to support a return from the quarter to the semester calendar. Why should they? Semesters give more time for the student, cut down the number of registrations and grading periods, give a student fewer courses to worry about for one calendar year, and they are a change. Each of these statements is a reason.

Think over some one of your actions during the past couple of days. You probably can identify a reason or set of reasons that affected your action or later explained it. Did you watch television last night? Why? Because you needed a little relaxation? Because the program you watched is almost always "good"? Because a friend wanted to watch? Because you were bored and had nothing else to do? Each of these is a reason.

If you want to influence other persons' beliefs or actions, you must present reasons why those persons should modify their beliefs or actions. You must determine a number of possible reasons and choose the ones that seem best for persuasion.

How do you compile a list of reasons? Sometimes the reasons will become apparent if you just think about the issue. What are some reasons for favoring a semester calendar? Let us summarize the ones mentioned earlier:

Proposition: You should support a return to a semester calendar. Why?

    I. Semesters give more time for the student to master the material.

    II. Semesters cut down the number of registrations and grading periods.

    III. Semesters give a student fewer courses to take in one calendar year.

    IV. Semesters provide a change.

For most topics you must do more than just think about the issue. Although creative thinking will supply some reasons, others will be suggested by observing, interviewing, and reading. If you wished to give a speech in support of the proposition that the United States should overhaul the welfare system, you might, through thinking and research, arrive at the following list of possible reasons:

    I. The welfare system costs too much.

    II. The welfare system is inequitable.

    III. The welfare system does not help those who need help most.

    IV. The welfare system has been grossly abused.

    V. The welfare system does not encourage people to seek work.

    VI. The welfare system does not provide means for persons to better themselves.

In a speech you cannot use (nor would you want to use) all the reasons you can think of or find. Remember that any speech should have only two to five main points, and for a persuasive speech you want to focus on two to five reasons. How do you decide which reasons to use? Make your decision primarily on the following three criteria:

1. *The reason must really support the proposition.* Sometimes statements look like reasons but really don't supply much support. The statement "Semesters will provide a change" is certainly true and is a reason, but it doesn't give much in the way of real support to the proposition; that is, because it provides a change does not show that the calendar will be any better.

2. *The reason must itself be supportable.* Some reasons are quite good in themselves, but if they cannot be supported with facts, then they should be abandoned. For instance, the reasons "The welfare system has been grossly abused" is a good reason in support of a proposition calling for "An overhaul of the welfare system"—if you can find the facts to support it. If in your reading you cannot find supporting material, then you should not use that reason.

You cannot be sure that a reason is supportable until you have done some research. If you think you have a good reason, you'll need to do the research necessary to uncover supportive facts. Nevertheless, if after a given amount of time invested, you find a lack of solid support drop it from consideration.

3. *The reason must have an impact upon the intended audience.* Suppose you are trying to convince your audience to "Eat at the Sternwheeler" the next time they elect to eat at a restaurant. Suppose that one of the reasons that you had listed is "The seafood is excellent." In support of this reason suppose that you had plenty of good factual material. Even though excellent seafood is a good reason which can be supported, it would be a poor reason to use in a speech if you knew that the majority of the audience *did not like seafood!*

A reason will have impact on an audience if that audience is likely to accept it. Sometimes you cannot be sure about the potential impact of a reason; if, however, you know your audience, you can make a reasonably good estimate of possible impact. We have already considered the issue of audience analysis. On the basis of your audience analysis you can make a choice. For instance, on the topic of eating out, a college audience is very likely to consider price as a major criterion for selecting a restaurant. If one of your reasons is that comparable dishes cost less than at other similar restaurants, you can be reasonably sure that you should include that reason in the speech.

Motivation

Persuasion is more likely to be achieved when the language of the speaker motivates the audience. Through reasoning we may be convinced of the soundness of an idea. Yet intellectual agreement may not be enough to affect behavior. I may believe that giving to the United Appeal is a good idea, but I may not have given. I may believe that the handicapped should be helped by the government, but I may not have voted for legislation directed toward helping the handicapped. What makes the difference between believing in something and acting in its behalf? Often it is the degree of motivation inherent in the case for the action. Motivation is the driving force behind our actions. It is the prod that pokes or nudges us from passive to active. Unless properly motivated we may sit idly by and *do* nothing.

EMOTIONAL APPEAL IS A
SUPPLEMENT TO REASONING.

Various researchers[2] have attempted to determine the effect of the use of emotional appeals in persuasive communication. So far, the results of such research have been inconclusive and at times contradictory. The effectiveness of emotional appeals seems to depend a great deal on other related factors, such as mood of the audience, attitude of the audience, and construction of the appeals. My experience has been that the value of emotional appeal is as a supplement to reasoning. Good speech development then is logical-emotional development. I like to look at logic (the reasons) and emotion as inseparable elements within a speech. Thus you should not look for some additional material that will arouse an emotion; you should look for a good, logical supportable set of reasons that if properly phrased and developed will arouse emotions.

Suppose that in a speech in which you call for a more humane treatment of the elderly in our society you want to make the point that present options for dealing with the elderly alienate them from the society they worked so many years to support. In reference to this statement you have facts and figures to show the effects of present options. Then you ask the question, "How can I phrase the information in a way that will incline my

[2]*See* Ronald L. Applbaum and Karl W. Anatol, *Strategies for Persuasive Communication* (Columbus, Ohio: Charles E. Merrill, 1974), pp. 102–103, for a summary of conflicting research studies.

listeners to feel guilty about treatment of the elderly, to feel a responsibility for care of them, and to feel sadness about the results of our current behavior?" Contrast the following two statements:

> Currently the elderly are alienated from the society that for so many years they supported. A high percentage of elderly live in nursing homes, live on relatively small fixed incomes, and are by and large outside of the mainstream of society.

> Currently the elderly are alienated from the society that for so many years they supported. What happens to the elderly in America? They become the forgotten segment of society. They are often relegated to "old people's homes" so that they can live out their lives and die without being "a bother" to their sons and daughters. Because they must exist on relatively small fixed incomes they are confined to a life that for many means separation from the very society that they helped to create.

What do you do to create a mental state for yourself in which you can phrase statements that will have emotional impact—that will motivate?

1. *Get in touch with your own feelings about the topic.* If you think enough of a topic to give a persuasive speech, then it is likely that you have some strong feelings about the people, conditions, or situations that relate to that topic. What are they? Are your feelings ones of sadness? Happiness? Guilt? Anger? Caring? Grief?

2. *Construct mental pictures that portray your feelings.* On the topic of the elderly if you feel sadness, anger, and grief you may well see pictures of nursing homes, elderly huddled together in wheelchairs in front of televisions with blank looks on their faces, and so forth.

3. *Practice describing your feelings and your mental pictures so that the audience can empathize with those feelings and pictures.* Your first practices are likely to be clumsy—maybe even laughable. As you work with your descriptions, you will find yourself speaking more and more vividly and with more feeling.

The speaker's major means of motivating is through language that is adapted to the needs of the specific audience and language that touches the emotions and drives us to respond. In any speech, but especially in a speech where your goal is audience action, you must ask, "How can I make my points so that they will have the greatest emotional effect on this audience?"

Credibility

Persuasion is more likely to be achieved when the audience likes, trusts, and has confidence in the speaker. The Greeks had a word for this concept—they called it *ethos*. But whether we call it ethos, image, charismatic effect, or the word I prefer—*credibility*—the effect is the same: almost all studies confirm that speaker credibility has a major effect on audience belief and attitude.[3]

Why are people willing to take the word of someone else on various issues? Since it is impossible for us to know all there is to know about everything (and even if it were *possible,* few of us would be willing to spend the time and effort), we seek shortcuts in our decision making. We rely on the judgment of others. Our thinking often goes something like this: Why take the time to learn about the new highway when someone we trust tells us it is in our best interest? Why take the time to try every restaurant in town when someone we are willing to rely on tells us that Barney's is the best? Why take time to study the candidates when our best friend tells us to vote for Smith for councilman? Each of us places such trust in some people in order to take shortcuts in our decision making.

How do we determine whom we will rely on? Is it blind faith? No, the presence (or our *perception* of the presence) of certain qualities will make the possessor a *high credibility* source. Although the specific number of distinguishing characteristics of credibility differs somewhat in various analyses of that quality, most analyses include the characteristics of competence, intention, character, and personality.

Competence is that quality of being properly or well qualified, of being capable. It may well be that your attraction toward your favorite professor is based upon competence. Although all professors are supposed to know what they are talking about, some are better able to project this quality in their speaking. As a rule of thumb, we believe that people are competent when we believe they know far more than what they are telling us now. For instance, when a student interrupts with a question, the competent professor has no difficulty in discussing the particular point in more detail—perhaps by giving another example, perhaps by telling a story, perhaps by referring the student to additional reading on the subject. Often our judgment of competence is based upon a past record. If we discover that what a person has told us in the past has proven to be true, we will tend to believe what that person tells us now.

A second important characteristic of credibility is *intention*. A person's intentions or motives are particularly important in determining whether another person will like him, trust him, have respect for him, or believe him. For instance, you know that clothing salespersons are trying to sell

[3]Kenneth E. Andersen and Theodore Clevenger, Jr., "A Summary of Experimental Research in Ethos," *Speech Monographs,* Vol. 30 (1963), pp. 59–78.

you the garments they help you try on, so when they say to you, "This is perfect for you," you may well question their intentions. On the other hand, if a bystander looks over at you and exclaims, "Wow, you really look good in that!" you are likely to accept the statement at face value because the bystander has no reason to say anything—his or her intentions are likely to be good. The more positively you view the intentions of the person, the more credible his or her words will seem to you.

Character is a third component of credibility. By character, we mean what a person is made of. We trust and believe in a person who has a record of honesty, industry, trustworthiness, dependability, inner strength, fortitude, and ability to hold up under pressure. We will often overlook what are otherwise regarded as shortcomings if the person shows character.

Personality, the fourth component, is the personal impression a person creates. Sometimes we have a strong "gut reaction" about a person based solely on a first impression. Some people strike us as being friendly, warm, nice to be around. They are enthusiastic, positive in approach, go-getters. Because they have a ready smile and really seem to care, we just cannot help liking them.

Most of these qualities are known to members of the audience (or at least exist) before the speech begins. Still, some of these can be demonstrated during the speech itself. When it comes to the quality of competence, you can let the audience know that you have experienced what you are talking about or that you have made an exhaustive study. For instance, if you are giving a speech on police public relations, you might say, "I had read about police public relations, but I wanted to see for myself, so I spent several days talking with police, watching how they worked, riding around in squad cars . . ." Intention can be shown by placing emphasis on how members of the audience can and will benefit from what you say and how their needs have affected your plans. Although personality and character are more projections of what you are, in a speech you can attempt to show that you are friendly, that you care, that you are sincere, honest, and trustworthy.

Credibility is not something that you can gain overnight or turn off or on at your whim. Nevertheless, you can avoid damaging your credibility and perhaps even strengthen it somewhat during a speech or a series of speeches. You will probably see the cumulative effect of credibility during this term. As your class proceeds from speech to speech, some individuals will grow in stature and some will diminish. Being ready to speak on time, approaching the assignment with a positive attitude, showing complete preparation for each speech, giving thoughtful evaluation of others' speeches, and demonstrating sound thinking—all these will contribute to your credibility.

Ethics

Persuasion is more likely to have a lasting effect if it is ethical. So far we have looked at the persuasive effect of reasoning, motivation, and credibility, but overriding all of these is the principle of ethics. Especially when we believe strongly in the righteousness of our cause, we are faced with the temptation of bowing to the belief that the end justifies the means—or, to put it into blunt English, that we can do *anything* to achieve our goals. As we observe the world around us, we are all too well aware of the many people who have ridden roughshod over any moral or ethical principles operating within the society. Yet, just when we appear to be ready to give up on mankind something happens that proves that a society does have its ethical limits.

What are *ethics*? Ethics are the standards of moral conduct that determine our behavior. Ethics include both how we ourselves act and how we expect others to act. Whether or how we punish those who fail to meet our standards says a great deal about the importance we ascribe to our ethics. Although ethical codes are personal, society has a code of ethics that operates on at least the verbal level within that society.

What is your code of ethics? The following four points reflect the standards of hundreds of students that I have seen in my classes during the last few years. I believe that these four make an excellent starting point for consideration in determining your standards. These are not rules someone made up. They are statements of attitudes held by large numbers of individuals within the society.

1. *Lying is unethical.* Of all the attitudes about ethics, this is the one most universally held. When people *know* they are being lied to, they will usually reject the ideas of the speaker; if they find out later, they often look for ways to punish the speaker who lied to them.

2. *Name-calling is unethical.* Again, there seems to be an almost universal agreement on this attitude. Even though many people name-call in their interpersonal communication, they say they regard the practice by public speakers as unethical.

3. *Grossly exaggerating or distorting facts is unethical.* Although some people seem willing to accept "a little exaggeration" as a normal product of human nature, when the exaggeration is defined as "gross" or "distorted," most people consider the exaggeration the same as lying. Because the line between "some" exaggeration and "gross" exaggeration or "distortion" is often so difficult to distinguish, many people see *any* exaggeration as unethical.

4. *Condemning people or ideas without divulging the source of the material is unethical.* Where ideas originate is often as important as the ideas themselves. Although a statement may be true regardless of whether a source is given,

people want more than the speaker's word when a statement is damning. If you are going to discuss the wrongdoing of a person or the stupidity of an idea by relying on the words or ideas of others, you must be prepared to share the sources of those words or ideas.

Remember, these are but starting points in your consideration of ethical standards. Effective speaking should be ethical speaking.

EXERCISE

In terms of the objective you wrote for the exercise on page 290, what means of persuasion are you likely to stress in the development of the speech? How? Why?

ADAPTING TO AUDIENCE IN ORGANIZATION

Persuasion is more likely to occur when the speaker organizes material according to expected audience reaction.

Although most persuasive speeches follow a topical organization, many different topic frameworks are available for meeting expected audience reaction. The major determinant for the kind of organization you use will depend upon whether the members of the audience favor your proposition and to what degree. Except for polling the audience, there is no way of being sure. By examining the data in the way described in Chapter 11, you will be able to make reasonably accurate estimates of whether your audience has no opinion, is in favor, or is opposed.

If your listeners have no opinion, they are either uninformed or apathetic. If they are uninformed, you should use an organization that will give the necessary information first—then you can work on persuading them. If they are apathetic, all of your effort can be directed to breaking them out of their apathy.

If your audience is in favor, you can devote most of your time to bringing them to a specific action. Many times people are in favor of doing *something*, but they are not in agreement on *what* to do. Your job is to provide a specific course of action they can rally around. When you believe your audience is on your side, do not just echo their beliefs. Try to crystallize their attitudes, recommit them to a particular direction, or suggest a specific course of action that will serve as a rallying point.

If your audience is opposed, their attitudes will range from slightly negative to thoroughly hostile. If an audience is slightly negative you can approach them rather directly with your plan, hoping that the weight of argument will swing them to your side. If they are hostile, you will usually have to approach the topic indirectly—work hard to develop common ground—and perhaps you must be content with planting the seeds of persuasion and not expecting much at the moment.

The following organizational methods may prove useful to adopt as stated or they may suggest an organization that you believe will work for your audience given the material you have to work with.

Statement-of-Reasons Method

For purposes of illustrating this and other methods, I will use the same proposition and the same (or similar) arguments. The point to be made is that each of these represents a different form. It is true that with some topics and some material only one or two of the forms will work for you; with some propositions (and some material) you will have complete freedom of choice. Try to make your decision on which line of development makes best use of your material and stands the best chance of success with your audience. Let me emphasize that by making this decision you are not changing the facts, you are only choosing the best way of packaging them for the particular audience.

When you believe your listeners have no opinion on the subject, are apathetic, or are perhaps only mildly in favor or opposed, the straight-

CHOOSE THE BEST WAY TO PACKAGE
FACTS FOR A PARTICULAR AUDIENCE.

forward topical statement of reasons may be your best organization. In brief, in the statement-of-reasons method, each reason presented is a complete statement of justification for the proposition. Thus, in outline form, the statement-of-reasons method will look like this:

Speech objective: To have the audience vote in favor of the school tax levy on the November ballot.

I. Income will enable the schools to restore vital school programs.

II. Income will enable the schools to give teachers the raises they need to keep up with the cost of living.

III. The actual cost to each member of the community will be very small.

Problem-Solution Method

If you are attempting to prove to the audience that a new kind of procedure is needed to remedy some major problem, the problem-solution method will provide you with the framework for clarifying the nature of the problem, and for illustrating why the new proposal is the best measure for accomplishing the purpose. There are usually three main points of a problem-solution speech: (1) there is a problem that requires a change in attitude or action; (2) the proposal you have to offer will solve the problem; and (3) your proposal is the best solution to the problem. This organization may be best for an audience that has no opinion or is mildly pro or con. Now let's see how a problem-solution organization would look for the school tax levy proposition:

Speech objective: To have the audience vote in favor of the school tax levy on the November ballot.

I. The shortage of money is resulting in serious problems for public education.

II. The proposed increase is large enough to solve those problems.

III. For now, a tax levy is the best method of solving the schools' problems.

Comparative-Advantages Method

In your proposed speech, you may not be trying to solve a grave problem as much as you are suggesting a superior alternative course of action. You want to show that your plan is better than either what is being done or what the audience is considering doing. This organization is suggested for any audience attitude except frank hostility. A comparative-advantages approach to our school tax levy proposition would look like this:

Speech objective: To have the audience vote in favor of the school tax levy on the November ballot.

I. Income from a tax levy will enable schools to raise the standards of their programs.

II. Income from a tax levy will enable schools to hire better teachers.

III. Income from a tax levy will enable schools to better the educational environment.

Criteria-Satisfaction Method

When you are dealing with audiences that are opposed to your ideas, you need procedures that will help you cope with the hostility. The criteria-satisfaction method, which is one of two organizations that are particularly effective in these circumstances, involves developing a "yes" response before you introduce the proposition and reasons. A criteria-satisfaction organization for our school tax levy proposition would look like this:

Speech objective: To have the audience vote in favor of the school tax levy on the November ballot.

I. We all want good schools.
  A. Good schools have programs that prepare our youth to function in society.
  B. Good schools are those with the best teachers available.

II. Passage of the school tax levy will guarantee good schools.
  A. Passage will enable us to increase the quality of vital programs.
  B. Passage will enable us to hire and to keep the best teachers.

Negative Method

The other method that is particularly effective for hostile audiences is the negative method. In this you show that something must be done but that the possible alternatives just will not work. To persuade a hostile audience to vote for a tax levy, you might use this organization:

Speech objective: To have the audience vote in favor of the school tax levy on the November ballot.

I. Saving money by reducing services and programs will not help the schools.

II. The federal government will not increase its help to the schools.

III. The state government will not increase its help to the schools.

IV. All we have left is to pass the tax levy.

Knowing what you are trying to do, looking for a variety of means of accomplishing your goal, and organizing the material to adapt to audience needs will get you ready to speak. From here on the success of your speech will rest on how it is delivered.

EXERCISE _____

For the speech objective you wrote for the exercise on page 290, write two potential organizations of material. Which is best for your audience? Why?

SPEAKING CONVINCINGLY

Persuasion is more likely to occur when the speaker shows conviction in his or her ideas.

Effective delivery for persuasion is no different from effective speaking for any speech. Still, because delivery is so important it is worth a moment to focus on one key aspect of delivery that is especially relevant to persuasion: The effective persuader shows conviction about his subject. With some people conviction is shown through considerable animation. With others it is shown through a quiet intensity. However it is shown, it must be perceived by the audience. If the audience does not perceive some visual or auditory sign of conviction, what you say is likely to be suspect. And if you really do have a strong conviction, there is a good chance that your voice and your bodily action will reflect it.

SUMMARY

At the beginning of this chapter we said that no formula for success could be given, but we did promise a set of principles that can serve as guidelines for your procedure.

First, determine a speech objective that takes into account existing audience attitudes. Not only must you be specific in determining your objective, but also you must phrase it in a way that gives you at least a chance to succeed.

Second, use several means of persuasion. By combining good reasons and emotional development and by utilizing your own credibility with the particular subject you give yourself the best chance to affect the audience.

Third, organize your speech following some pattern that adapts to the prevailing audience attitude. How you proceed depends to a large extent on whether you perceive your audience as in favor, apathetic, un-informed, slightly opposed, or hostile.

And last, deliver your speech with conviction.

SUGGESTED READINGS

Winston L. Brembeck and William S. Howell. *Persuasion: A Means of Social Influence,* 2nd ed. Englewood Cliffs, N.J.: Prentice-Hall, 1976.

Charles U. Larson. *Persuasion: Reception and Responsibility,* 2nd ed. Belmont, Calif.: Wadsworth, 1979.

Vance O. Packard. *The Hidden Persuaders.* New York: Pocket Books, 1975 (paperback). This popular book, first published in the 1950s, still makes for excellent reading about the problems and excesses of persuasion.

CHAPTER 15

PRACTICE IN PERSUASION

Chet rapped on the door and a grandmotherly woman answered.

"Uh, you wouldn't want to buy any greeting cards, would you?"

"Young man, you're not going to sell any cards that way!"

"Huh?"

"Do you remember what you asked me?"

"I said, you wouldn't want . . ."

"Stop right there. You have to be positive. Don't start with 'you wouldn't.' Let's see, what's your name?"

"Chet."

"Last name?"

"Abbott."

"Who are you selling these for?"

"The Little Bats baseball team."

"OK—Start 'Hello. My name is Chet Ab-bott. I'm a member of the Little Bats baseball team. We're selling greeting cards this year . . .' Why are you selling them?"

"To buy uniforms."

" 'To make money to buy uniforms. We've got an excellent selection at only . . .' how much do they cost?"

"A dollar fifty a box."

" 'At a dollar fifty a box. Let me show you . . .' Hm, these are nice looking cards. Say, I'll take one box of these . . . and one of these . . . and two of those. See? You've even sold me. Here's your six dollars."

"Thank you ma'am." Slowly Chet walked to the next house and rapped on the door. A young woman answered.

"Huh, you wouldn't want to buy any greeting cards, would you?"

You can read about persuasion and you can listen to people tell you about persuasion, but as Chet's experience shows, the principles of persuasion will do you little good unless you can put them into practice. In this chapter, we offer suggestions for applying persuasion in speeches of convincing, actuating, and refuting.

CONVINCING

You can put what you have learned about reasoning into practice by preparing and presenting a speech of conviction. A speech of conviction or a speech of reasons, as it is sometimes called, is an attempt to develop the propositions with clear reasons and sound support for the reasons. Your goal in accomplishing this assignment is to gain conviction through sound arguments. Let's first take a brief look at "reasoning" and then let's consider preparing a speech to convince.

Reasoning

Reasoning is the process of drawing inferences from facts or proving inferences with facts. Although the study of logical reasoning is worthy of an entire course, in this short section we can only sketch the basics. For instance, in the morning you are confronted with the question, "What kind of a coat (if any) should I wear today?" You look out the window and say to yourself, "It's raining now and it looks like it's going to rain all day. To be safe, I'd better wear my raincoat." On the basis of the fact (it's raining now) and the opinion (it looks like it's going to rain all day) you *reason* that you should wear a raincoat.

In persuasive speaking instead of drawing inferences from facts, reasoning is more likely to be the process of proving inferences with facts. You get into a conversation with a friend about the home team's chances in tonight's game. Your friend is unsure of the outcome. To convince him that everything will come out all right you *reason* with him. You say, "You seem worried, but *the Tigers are going to win tonight* (the conclusion you've drawn and that you wish to prove to your friend). Our overall record is better. We've played two common teams—we beat them both and they lost both—and most of all, we're playing at home." You reasoned by presenting facts in support of a proposition.

How do we know whether our reasoning is sound? First, we can apply various tests to the reasoning process. (We will look at several common tests in the next section on refutation.) Second, we can decide whether the reasons are good ones. In the last chapter we said that good reasons are ones that can be supported and ones that relate directly to the proposition. In short, they are the reasons that an audience will accept as proving the proposition.

Preparing a Speech to Convince

Preparing a speech to convince is not without real-life application. When you consider your persuasive strategy, you may decide that as a result of the audience position on a proposition or as a result of the nature of the audience itself, presenting the merits of the proposition is your best procedure. Under these circumstances the speech-of-conviction model will be the one you will follow. This does not mean your speech will be devoid of motivation or that you as a speaker can ignore the value of your credibility. It does mean that the final evaluation of your effort will be on the soundness of your case.

The objective of a speech of conviction is usually a proposition phrased to change a belief held by an audience—for example, "All states should adopt a no-fault automobile insurance program" or "Jones is the best man for president." In both cases the assumption would be that the propositions are in opposition to the attitude or belief of the audience to which the speeches will be given.

In order to determine what should be the main points of a speech of conviction, you look for statements that answer *why* a proposition is justified. Sometimes the sources you read suggest reasons; sometimes you have to develop your own statement of reasons.

Let's examine a series of propositions (a *proposition* is a persuasive speech objective) and see the reasons that we could suggest in their support:

> To go see the theatrical production of *Chorus Line*. Why? (The question "why?" leads you to the reasons and helps you test both the quality and the persuasiveness of the particular reason.)
>
> **I.** The story is moving.
>
> **II.** The acting is excellent.
>
> **III.** The music is contemporary.
>
> **IV.** The production is a sell-out wherever it plays.
>
> **V.** The cost is nominal.
>
> To vote for Colletta. Why?
>
> **I.** She will provide council with needed female representation.

    II. She has served successfully in two previous posts.

    III. She works for the people.

    IV. She is extremely intelligent.

    V. She has worked at HEW where she gained an understanding of qualifying for federal support.

To believe that we need to provide more money for space exploration. Why?

    I. Findings from space exploration yield new data about our universe.

    II. Costs are low in comparison with information received.

    III. Space technology has application to business, industry, and defense.

As you determine a list of reasons, you must decide the value and persuasiveness of each to a particular person or audience. If a person is made to see the soundness of a reason and sees how it relates to him, he is likely to be persuaded.

The next related skill that is required is discovering the best evidence (material) to support the reasons and to show their relevance to the audience. Reasons are only generalizations. Although some are self-explanatory and occasionally even persuasive without further support, most do require development before people will either accept or act upon them. For instance, saying that the reason for going to the Park Restaurant is because food is priced lower than in comparable restaurants for comparable dishes is a generalization. If you support the generalization with the statement that the Park charges $5.95 for a six-ounce club steak dinner including potato and salad where others charge a minimum of $6.25, that is evidence. Further examples and illustrations would make the generalization even more solid and perhaps more persuasive.

The two major kinds of evidence are fact and opinion. *Facts,* the best support for any reason, are statements that are verifiable. That metal is heavier than air, that World War II ended in 1945, and that Oakland won the World Series in 1972 and 1973 are all facts. If you say "It's really hot today—it's up in the nineties" and the thermometer registers 94°, your support (temperature up in the nineties) is factual.

Although factual support is best, there are times when the facts are not available or when facts are inconclusive. In these situations, you will have to support your conclusions further with opinion. The quality of *opinion* as evidence is dependent upon whether the source, the person giving the opinion, is expert or inexpert. If your gasoline attendant says it is likely that there is life on other planets, the opinion is not expert—his expertise lies in other areas; if on the other hand, an esteemed space biologist says there is a likelihood of life on other planets, her opinion is

THE QUALITY OF OPINION
DEPENDS UPON THE SOURCE.

expert. Both statements are only opinion, but some opinions carry more weight than others. Of course, opinions are most trustworthy when they are accompanied by factual data. If it is an automotive engineer's opinion that a low-cost electric car is feasible, his opinion is valuable, since automotive engineering is his area of expertise. If accompanying his opinion, he shows us the advances in technology that are leading to a low-cost battery of medium size that can run for more than 200 hours without being recharged, his opinion is worth even more.

Let's illustrate by developing a proposition by fact and opinion.

Shop at Schappenhouper's food stores. Why?

I. Prices are lower for comparable food items.

    A. Evidence by fact:

        If we look at prices for five basic foods: eggs, chopped meat, lettuce, potatoes, and milk at four major markets we find the following: eggs: Schappenhouper's 87¢; A, 91¢; B, 96¢; C, 89¢.
        sirloin steak per lb.: . . . , and so on.

    B. Evidence by opinion:

        Mrs. Goody, fraternity cook who comparison shops every week, says, "I shop at Schappenhouper's because prices are lower for comparable foods."

EXERCISE

1. For each of the following propositions, write at least three reasons:

   Go to see——————movie Watch——————on television Vote for——————for——————
   Why?

1.	1.	1.
2.	2.	2.
3.	3.	3.

2. Divide into groups of three to five and consider (1) the phrasing and quality of reasons and (2) the kinds of evidence that could be used to develop each reason.

3. Prepare a three- to six-minute speech of conviction. An outline is required. The speech should have a short introduction that leads into the proposition. By the end of the speech (probably by the end of the introduction), the audience should be aware of the specific behavioral objective—the proposition. The major portion of the speech should be on the statement and development of two to five *good* reasons. Development should both prove the truth of the reasons (through facts or opinions—or, preferably, both) and indicate the relevance of the reasons to the audience. A brief conclusion will summarize the reasons or in some way re-emphasize the importance of the proposition.

ACTUATING

Reasoning provides a solid logical base for your persuasion and a sound rationale for change of audience attitude. But what if sound reasoning is not enough to bring action? What can you do to complement or supplement reasoning? What can you do when your listeners recognize the relative merits of your proposition—but they are not acting? The catalyst for firing the imagination, causing commitment, and bringing to action is the psychological aspect of persuasion called *motivation*. In this section we will consider how to motivate by applying the theories of motivation and the language of motivation. For practice in focusing attention on the development of motivation in speeches, we will consider a specific speech assignment, the speech to actuate.

Applying Theories

Through the years many individuals have set forth rhetorical and psychological theories of persuasion. To help you with your strategy for motivation, I will explain the basic theory and material in support of three such strategies. These are not the only ones available—nor are they necessarily the only ones that work.

What is likely to bring an audience to action? We can summarize the strategies involved as follows:

1. People are more likely to act when they see the suggested proposition as presenting a favorable cost-reward ratio.
2. People are more likely to act when the suggested proposition creates dissonance.
3. People are more likely to act when the proposition satisfies a strong unmet need.

Cost-Reward   If you'll recall, we looked at John Thibaut and Harold Kelley's explanation of social interactions in terms of rewards received and costs incurred when we were discussing theories explaining relationships. The theory can also be applied to persuasion. Let's consider an example. Suppose you are asking your audience to give money to a charity. The money you are asking them to give is a negative outcome—a cost; however, giving money may be shown to be rewarding. That is, members of the audience may feel civic minded, responsible, or helpful as a result of the giving. If in the speech you can show that those rewards outweigh the cost, then you can increase the likelihood of the audience giving.

Strategies growing from this theory are easy for most people to understand because the theory is so easily supported by our own "common sense" observations. What makes this theory work for you is your ability to understand the cost-reward ratios in relation to the particular topic operating within your particular audience. Suppose that you are, in fact, trying to motivate the audience to give money to a charity. Assuming that this audience has nothing against this particular charity and assuming they agree that giving to this charity has merit, how do you proceed? You could ask each person to give ten cents. Since the cost is very low, you are unlikely to meet much resistance and you will probably get a high percentage of donations; but you will not be making much money for that charity. What if you decide to ask for a donation of $10 from each person? Since $10 is likely to represent a lot of money to members of a college audience, they must be shown that $10 really is not that much money (a difficult point to make for any audience) or they must be shown that the reward for giving $10 is worth that $10 gift. For most of your audience, talking about how good giving makes a person feel will not be enough. You will have to show them some very tangible rewards.

In general then, the higher the cost to the individual, the greater the reward must be. Thus, the higher the perceived cost, the harder you will have to work to achieve your goal. In summary, (1) people will look at calls for action on the basis of a cost-reward ratio; (2) either you must show that the time, energy, or money investment is small; or (3) you must show that the benefits in good feelings, prestige, economic gain, or other possible rewards are high.

Cognitive Dissonance   A second theory from which your persuasive strategies may be drawn is the theory of cognitive dissonance. *Cognitive dissonance* is an inconsistency that occurs between two or more cognitive elements. A *cognition* is a thought or a knowledge about some situation, person, or behavior. For example, if you worked hard to save $35 for a gift for your friend, the amount you had saved would be one cognitive element. If you proceed to spend $75 for the gift, the amount you have actually spent would be a second cognitive element. The inconsistency between money available and money spent would create a discomfort. This discomfort is what Leon Festinger, the originator of this theory, calls cognitive dissonance.[1]

Festinger holds that whenever you get yourself in one of these states of discomfort (and some of us may find ourselves in this state quite often), you have a great desire to *reduce the discomfort*. The greater the degree of discomfort experienced, the greater the desire to reduce it.

The degree of discomfort will depend on the complexity of the situation and its importance to you. The more complicated the dissonance, the greater the discomfort. So, you may experience some dissonance with a high paying job that carries low prestige (two elements in competition); you will have a great deal more dissonance with a higher paying job and a better location in competition with low prestige, little chance for advancement, and less desirable duties. The second factor is the importance to you. You'll experience less discomfort over a decision about buying a pair of shoes than you will over a decision about buying a house.

Relief from dissonance comes from changing your attitude about a decision, changing your behavior, or finding other compensating factors. So, what does this have to do with helping you make a speech more motivating?

As a speaker, you have opportunities to create dissonance in the mind of each person in the audience and then to provide the means of relieving the dissonance you have created. If you can show an audience that they have been buying a product primarily on the basis of unethical advertising, you may be able to create a dissonance within that audience for buying that product. Then you can give a plan for relieving the dissonance. You

---

[1]Leon Festinger, *A Theory of Cognitive Dissonance* (Evanston, Illinois: Row, Peterson, 1957), p. 13.

may ask them to write letters of protest to the company, or you may ask them to stop buying the product.

In general then, the greater the degree of dissonance you can create, the more likely the audience will look for a way of relieving that dissonance, and the more likely the audience will accept your proposal. We can summarize as follows: (1) people will look for ways to relieve dissonance when confronted with conflicting cognitions; (2) you can create dissonance through presentation of conflicting cognitions; and (3) the proposition of your speech can be perceived as a way of relieving the dissonance you have created.

Basic Needs   A third theory from which persuasive strategies may be developed is based upon Abraham Maslow's theory of the hierarchy of needs. Persuasion is more likely to occur when the proposition meets a specific need of members of the audience. If people have a need for food, they will be more likely to listen to a message about where to eat, where to shop, or what to buy than if they do not have that immediate need. Thus, if you are able to identify audience needs, you have a good start for planning your persuasive strategy. Abraham Maslow[2] classifies basic human needs in five categories:

1. Physiological needs
2. Safety needs
3. Belongingness and love needs
4. Esteem needs
5. Self-actualization needs

Notice that he places these needs in a hierarchy: one set of needs must be met or satisfied before the next set of needs emerge. Your physiological needs for food, drink, life-sustaining temperature are the most basic; they must be satisfied before the body is able to consider any of its other needs. The next level consists of safety needs—security, simple self-preservation, and the like; they emerge after basic needs have been met, and they hold a paramount place until they, too, have been met. The third level includes your belongingness or love needs; these involve the groups that you identify with: your friends, loved ones, and family. In a world of increasing mobility and breakdown of the traditional family, it is becoming more and more difficult for individuals to satisfy this need. Nonetheless,

[2]Abraham H. Maslow, *Motivation and Personality* (New York: Harper & Row, 1954), pp. 80–92.

once your belongingness needs are met, your esteem needs predominate; these involve your quest for material goods, recognition, and power or influence. The final level is called, by Maslow, the self-actualizing need; this involves developing one's self to meet its potential. When all other needs are met, this need is the one that drives people to their creative heights, that urges them to do "what they need to do to fulfill themselves as human beings."

What is the value of this analysis to you as a speaker? First, it provides a framework for and suggests the kinds of needs you may appeal to in your speeches. Second, it allows you to understand why a line of development will work on one audience and fall flat with another. For instance, if your audience has great physiological needs—if they are hungry—an appeal to the satisfaction of good workmanship, no matter how well done, is unlikely to impress them. Third, and perhaps most crucial, when your proposition is going to come in conflict with an operating need, you will have to be prepared with a strong alternative in the same category or in a higher-level category. For instance, if your proposition is going to cost money—if it is going to take money in the form of taxes—you will have to show how the proposal satisfies some other comparable need.

Let's look at just three of the traditional motives for action. This brief analysis is meant to be suggestive of the kind of thinking you should be doing.

Wealth   The desire for *wealth*, the acquisition of money and material goods, is a motive that grows out of an esteem need. Does your proposition affect wealth or material goods in any way? If it does in a positive way, you may want to stress it. If your plan calls for giving up money, you will need to be prepared to cope with your listeners' natural desire to resist giving up money—you will have to involve another motive from the same category (esteem) or from a higher category to override the loss of money or the money they have to give up.

Power   Another esteem need is *power*. For many people, personal worth is dependent upon their power over their own destiny, the exercising of power over others, and the recognition and prestige that comes from such recognition or power. If your proposition allows a person, group, or community to exercise power, it may be worth emphasizing. On the other hand, if your speech takes power away from part or all of the audience, you will need to provide strong compensation to be able to motivate them.

Pleasure   When you are given a choice of actions, you often pick the one that gives you the greatest pleasure, enjoyment, or happiness. On at least one level, *pleasure* is a self-actualizing need; however, it also operates as an esteem need. If your speech relates to something that is novel, promises excitement, is fun to do, or offers a challenge, you can probably motivate your audience on that basis.

These are only three possible motives for action growing out of basic audience needs. Conformity, sex appeal, responsibility, justice, and many others operate within each of us. If you discover that you are not relating your material to basic audience needs, you probably need to revise your procedure.

Practicing Language Patterns

In addition to applying theories of persuasion, you must also practice the use of language patterns that motivate. Three frequently used language patterns for motivation are yes-response, common ground, and suggestion. Please be aware that these language patterns are two-edged swords. When used ethically, they can work on your behalf; but unethical use will work against you even if you appear to achieve short-term gains. Learn to use these language patterns ethically and learn to recognize their unethical use by others.

"Yes" Response   Psychologists have found that when a person gets in the habit of saying "yes," he is likely to continue to say "yes." If you can phrase questions that establish areas of agreement early in your speech, the audience will be more likely to listen to you and perhaps to agree with your proposition. For instance, if you asked, "Do you like to have a good time? To get your money's worth? To put your money into a worthy cause? To support your community if you will profit from the support?" and then asked, "You'll support Playhouse-in-the-Park?" you would be using the "yes" response method.

Common Ground   This motivational device is based on an establishment of the same type of response pattern as the "yes" response, but the initiation of the response pattern follows a somewhat different route. Essentially, the overall response sought is: "We agree, or have so much in common, on so many various points that we can reach agreement on a single point of difference." In trying to get support for his latest program a politician will often try to show the audience that he has the same background, the same set of values, beliefs, and attitudes, the same overall way of looking at things so that a point of difference does not represent a difference in philosophy.

Suggestion   Suggestion involves planting an idea in the mind of the listener without developing it. It is an idea stated in such a way that its acceptance is sought without analysis or consideration.

Suggestion may be direct, as in bumper stickers that say SEE MAMMOTH CAVE or VOTE FOR SMEDLEY. Suggestion may also be indirect. The speaker who says, "Let's see, we could act now—a stitch in time often saves nine" has found an indirect way of saying, "If I were you, I'd act now before the problem gets any worse, causing us to take even more drastic action later." Suggestion may be positive ("Play soccer") or negative ("Don't walk on the grass"). Positive suggestion is usually more effective. Negative suggestion often leads to the very behavior it decries. Who can avoid putting a finger on the wall when the sign says DO NOT TOUCH—WET PAINT? Suggestion may be in the form of countersuggestion. *Countersuggestion* is a manipulative form that can and often does backfire. You use countersuggestion when you want to go swimming, and you say to a bullheaded friend, "Let's go fishing"—and she replies, as you hoped, with "Naw, let's go swimming." Of course, if she had said "yes" to fishing, your countersuggestion would have backfired.

One writer, Robert Oliver, says that suggestion works best when "(1) the audience is inclined to be favorable to the proposition; (2) the

COUNTERSUGGESTIONS
CAN OFTEN BACKFIRE.

audience is in a generally agreeable state; and (3) the audience is polarized to such a degree that judgment is inhibited."[3]

As an ethical speaker, however, you will find your use of suggestion limited. One prevalent use of suggestion in speechmaking is the use of directive. Such expressions as "I think we will all agree," "As we all know," and "Now we come to a most important consideration" are forms of suggestion that will help you to direct audience thinking. Another use of suggestion is to associate the name of a prominent individual to add prestige to a proposal. Of course, ethical use of this method is limited to those individuals who have given their backing to that particular proposal. In contrast to saying that a proposal is favored by notable people, you can say that Senator X, who received an award for his work on air-pollution control, favors the proposal to curb air pollution. This kind of use helps the audience to make the association between the proposal and responsible public officials. A third way to use suggestion is by phrasing ideas in specific, vivid language. Audiences are drawn to favor proposals that are phrased in memorable language. In 1946 Winston Churchill, who is regarded by many as the most effective speaker of the twentieth century, introduced the use of the term "Iron Curtain" in a speech at Fulton, Missouri. This term suggested an attitude about Russian ideology that has permeated Western thinking for more than thirty years. Because the subtle, less obvious statement of an idea may be more easily accepted by an audience, suggestion is an aid to persuasive speaking.

Preparing a Speech to Actuate

Practice with motivation may be best accomplished with a speech of actuation assignment, a speech calling for the speaker to bring her audience to action.

Propositions for speeches to actuate are often phrased as directives, such as "Eat at Barney's," "Give to the United Appeal," "Go to the antique automobile show." Although you may call for any action, you will be wiser to select propositions that your listeners already favor in principle or ones toward which they are apathetic, ignorant, or only mildly opposed. Although you can try to get a group of hard-core Republicans to vote for a Democrat or get a group of conservatives to support a social welfare pro-

---

[3]Robert T. Oliver, *The Psychology of Persuasive Speech* (New York: David McKay, 1957), pp. 151–152.

gram, you are probably doomed to failure before you begin. It takes a highly skilled speaker and particularly favorable circumstances to bring an audience from hostility or strong opposition to willingness to take direct action in one speech.

Any persuasive speech is built upon sound reasons. Regardless of how you decide to proceed in the speech, you must have a logical framework to support your proposition. Although your speech may not be a "one, two, three" statement and development of reasons, it should be logically conceived and logically based.

As we said in Chapter 14, there are many organizations of reasons to choose from. Under some circumstances the statement-of-reasons method may prove best; under others a more indirect approach such as criteria-satisfaction method may be better.

The success of your speech will depend on how you appeal to audience needs and emotions. Here are a few suggestions:

1. Keep the language audience-oriented. In this speech it is especially important to use personal pronouns, to build common ground, and to involve the audience emotionally.

2. Either avoid pedantic and dry statements of points or supplement such statements with emotional language. For instance, you may decide to use the statement "one out of every eight children suffers some birth defect." As impressive as that statement appears to be, you will develop far more emotional involvement by supplementing the statement with a short case history or one specific example. People do not see or feel statistics.

3. In writing the outline, make sure that every main point and major subdivision is stated with emotional appeal in mind. "The atmosphere is good" is not nearly as impressive as "The atmosphere of palatial elegance adds to your dining pleasure."

4. Put a special emphasis on your introductions and your conclusions. You cannot persuade an audience that is not listening. If only ten members of a class of twenty-five are listening to you, your potential is severely limited. Likewise, you must leave your audience excited about the action you call for. Think creatively to determine the very best way of closing your speech.

If there is any speech where delivery effectiveness is crucial, this is it. You must practice this speech until you are in total command. The more careful you are in practice of wording and delivery, the better you will be in the actual speech.

EXERCISE

Prepare a four- to seven-minute persuasive speech on a topic designed to bring your audience to action. An outline is required. In addition to clarity of purpose and soundness of rationale, criteria for evaluation will include your credibility on the topic, your ability to satisfy audience needs, and your ability to phrase your ideas in a way that will motivate.

REFUTING

When you are attending some decision-making group meeting, how do you proceed when someone says something that you think is wrong? Do you rise to reply? Or do you just sit there waiting for someone else to say something? In order to make the best use of your potential in social, legislative, vocational, and other decision-making bodies, you must develop some confidence in your abilities to reply.

By definition, refutation is the process of proving that a statement is false or erroneous—or at least doubtful. Someone says, "Billie Jean King will win the match," and you say, "No, she isn't even entering the tournament." Someone says, "We need more governmental control of basic industry," and you say, "No, according to Milton Friedman, that's about the *last* thing we need." What you say in reply is refutation. The following discussion is concerned with what can be refuted and how refutation is prepared and presented.

What Can Be Refuted

Refutation begins with anticipation of what the opposition will say. For any controversial issue you should know the material on both sides—if you have an idea how an opponent will proceed, you will be in a much better position to reply. If the opponent talks for very long, you should probably take at least some notes; you do not want to run the risk of being accused of distorting what your opponent really said. What do you consider in your opponent's statement? You can base your refutation on quantity of evidence, quality of evidence, or reasoning from the evidence.

Quantity of Evidence If someone has asserted that something is true without giving any evidence to support the assertion or if he has presented very limited evidence, you can refute the argument on that basis alone. Reliance on this as a form of refutation has a shortcoming: If the opponent brings up evidence, you must take another attack. You will find some occasions when this is the only way to proceed.

Quality of Evidence A better method of refutation is to attack the quality of the evidence. If sheer amount of evidence were the most important consideration in proving a point, the person with the most would always be most persuasive. However, there often is no direct relationship between total amount of evidence and quality of proof. A statement by a judge who has studied the rights of individual citizens to privacy would be worth far more than several opinions on the rights of privacy from athletes, musicians, or politicians who have not studied the subject. For every bit of evidence that is presented you should ask: (1) *Is the evidence fact or opinion?* As we said earlier, fact is usually worth more than opinion and expert opinion is worth more than inexpert opinion. (2) *Where does the evidence come from?* This question involves both the persons who offered the opinions or compiled the facts and the book, journal, or source where they were reported. Just as some persons' opinions are more reliable than others, likewise some printed sources are more reliable than others. Just because something appeared in print does not make it true. If data come from a poor source, an unreliable source, or a biased source, no reliable conclusion can be drawn from them, and you should refute the argument on the basis of dubious quality. (3) *Is the evidence recent?* Products, ideas, and statistics often are obsolete as soon as they are produced. You must ask when the particular evidence was true. Five-year-old evidence may not be true today. Furthermore, an article in last week's news magazine may be using five-year-old evidence in the story. (4) *Is the evidence relevant?* You may find that the evidence has little to do with the point being presented. This question of relevancy may well lead you into the reasoning process itself.

Reasoning from the Evidence   Although attacks on evidence are sometimes effective means of refutation, the form of refutation that is most telling and most difficult to reply to is the attack upon the reasoning from the evidence. Each argument presented in a persuasive speech is composed of at least three elements: (1) evidence or data from which a conclusion is drawn, (2) the conclusion itself, and (3) a stated or implied link that takes the speaker from her evidence to the conclusion she has drawn. Analysis of reasoning focuses on that stated or implied link. Because the link is more often implied than stated, you must learn to phrase it before you can proceed to attack the argument. For instance, if your opponent says:

> Our point is that once a government agency begins uncontrolled gathering of information, abuses—serious invasions of privacy—are inevitable. According to X the Army's efforts at gathering information have led to the following abuses: . . . . According to Y the FBI's efforts at gathering information have led to the following abuses: . . . . According to Z the Census Bureau's efforts at gathering information have led to these abuses: . . . .

Since in this argument the conclusion is clearly stated as a reason and the evidence is documented and appears above reproach, you would have to determine the reasoning link so you could determine whether or not the conclusion really followed from the evidence. In the preceding example the speaker is reasoning that if abuses resulted from information-gathering efforts in each of three government agencies analyzed, then it is reasonable to conclude that similar abuses would follow from information-gathering efforts of any or all government agencies.

Once you have the reasoning link stated rather than implied, you can begin to apply the proper tests to the reasoning. Perhaps the best way to approach the problem of phrasing the reasoning link is to ask: "How could the relationship between evidence and conclusion be stated so that the conclusion does follow from the evidence?" Then, to begin your testing of the soundness of the link, you can ask: "What circumstances would need to be present to prevent the conclusion from coming about even if the evidence is true?"

Our goal here is not to explain, exemplify, and provide tests for every kind of reasoning link that can be established. What we want to consider are the major forms that will work for you in the great majority of circumstances.

1. *Reasoning by generalization.* You are reasoning by generalization when your conclusion states that what is true in some instances is true in all instances. Generalization links are the basis for polls and predictions. Take, for example, the evidence, "Tom, Jack, and Bill studied and got As" and the conclusion based on it: "Anyone who studies will get an A." The reasoning link can be stated: "What is true in these representative instances will be true in all instances." To test this kind of argument you should ask: "Were enough instances cited? Were the instances typical? Were the instances representative?" If the answer to any of these questions is "no," you have the basis for refutation of the reasoning.

2. *Reasoning by causation.* You are reasoning by causation when your conclusion is a result of a single circumstance or set of circumstances. Causation links are one of the most prevalent types of arguments you will discover. An example would be: *Evidence:* "We've had a very dry spring"; *conclusion:* "The wheat crop will be lower than usual." The reasoning link can be stated: "The lack of sufficient rain *causes* a poor crop to result." To test this kind of argument you should ask: "Are the data (is the evidence) alone important enough to bring about the particular conclusion? If we eliminate the data, would we eliminate the effect?" If the answer to one of these questions is "no," then you have the basis for refutation of the reasoning by causation. "Do some other data that accompany the cited data cause the effect?" If so, you have the basis for refutation.

3. *Reasoning by analogy.* You are reasoning by analogy when your conclusion is the result of a comparison with a similar set of circumstances. Although reasoning by analogy is very popular, it is regarded as the weakest form of reasoning. The analogy link is often stated: "What is true or will work in one set of circumstances is true or will work in another comparable set of

circumstances." An example would be: *Evidence:* "A state lottery has proved very effective in New Jersey"; *conclusion:* "A state lottery will prove effective in Ohio." The reasoning link can be stated, "If something works in New Jersey it will work in Ohio, because Ohio and New Jersey are so similar." To test this kind of argument you should ask: "Are the subjects really capable of being compared? Are the subjects being compared really similar in all important ways?" If the answer to these questions is "no," you have the basis for refutation of the reasoning. "Are any of the ways that the subjects are dissimilar important to the conclusion?" If so, then the reasoning is not sound.

4. *Reasoning by definition.* You are reasoning by definition when your conclusion is a definition or a descriptive generalization that follows from agreed-upon criteria. Again, this is a very popular form of reasoning. An example would be: *Evidence:* "She takes charge; she uses good judgment; her goals are in the best interests of the group"; *conclusion:* "She is a good leader." The reasoning link could be stated: "Taking charge, showing good judgment, and considering the best interests of the group are the characteristics most often associated with good leadership." To this kind of argument you should ask: "Are the characteristics mentioned the most important ones in determining the definition? Are those characteristics best labeled with the stated term?" If the answer to these is "no," you have the basis for refutation of the reasoning. "Is an important aspect of the definition omitted in the statement of the characteristics?" If so, then the reasoning is not sound.

5. *Reasoning by sign.* You are reasoning by sign when your conclusion is based upon the presence of observable data that usually or always accompanies other unobservable data. If, for example, Martha breaks out in hives, the presence of that data (breaking out in hives) is usually or always associated with another variable (an allergy reaction) and we can predict the existence of the other unobserved variable. Signs are often confused with causes, but signs are indications, not causes. Hives are a sign of an allergy reaction. Hives occur when a person is having such a reaction, but the hives do not *cause* the reaction. To test this kind of argument, you would ask: "Do the data cited always or usually indicate the conclusion drawn? Are sufficient signs present?" If not, you have the basis for refutation of the reasoning.

How to Refute

Although you do not have as long to consider exactly what you are going to say, your refutation must be organized nearly as well as your planned speeches. If you will think of refutation as units of argument each of which is organized by following four definite steps, you will learn to prepare and to present refutation effectively:

1. State the argument you are going to refute clearly and concisely. (Or as an advocate replying to refutation, state the argument you are going to rebuild.)

2. State what you will prove; you must tell the audience how you plan to proceed so that they will be able to follow your thinking.

3. Present the proof completely with documentation.

4. Draw a conclusion; do not rely upon the audience to draw the proper conclusion for you. Never go on to another argument before you have drawn your conclusion.

In the following abbreviated statement, notice how the four steps of refutation (stating the argument, stating what you will prove, presenting proof, and drawing a conclusion) are incorporated. For purposes of analysis, each of the four steps is enumerated:

(1) Miss Horan has said that buying insurance provides a systematic, compulsory savings. (2) Her assumption is that "systematic, compulsory savings" is a benefit of buying insurance while you are young. But I believe that just the opposite is true—I believe that there are at least two serious disadvantages resulting from this. (3) First, the system is so compulsory that if you miss a payment you stand to lose your entire savings and all benefits. Most insurance contracts include a clause giving you a thirty-day grace period, after which the policy is cancelled . . . (evidence). Second, if you need money desperately, you have to take a loan on your policy. The end result of such a loan is that you have to pay interest in order to borrow your own money . . . (evidence). (4) From this analysis, I think you can see that the "systematic, compulsory saving" is more a disadvantage than an advantage for people who are trying to save money.

EXERCISE

Working with a classmate, select a debatable proposition and clear the wording with your professor. Phrase the proposition so that the first speaker is in favor of the proposal. Advocate's first speech—four minutes; opponent's speech—five minutes; advocate's second speech—two minutes.

The advocate's four-minute speech should be prepared as a speech of reasons. The opponent has two choices for the presentation of his speech: (1) He may spend his entire time in direct refutation of the reasons presented; or (2) he may wish to spend a couple of minutes stating and proving his own negative reasons and then spend the rest of his time in direct refutation. The advocate's second speech will be direct refutation for the purpose of analyzing the flaws in his opponent's reasons (if any were given) or to rebuild his original set of reasons. Criteria for evaluation will include soundness of argument and skill in refutation.

SUMMARY

Persuasive speakers increase their effectiveness as they learn to sharpen their skills for gaining conviction, bringing to action, and refuting.

Conviction is basically a product of selecting and supporting solid logical reasons. Although reasoning should not be isolated from the other means of persuasion, giving a speech to convince helps the speaker focus on the logical aspects of persuasion.

Actuating involves motivating an audience to respond. To bring an audience to action, a speaker needs to understand his audience's needs and must develop emotional appeals that will arouse.

At times a speaker comes into direct confrontation with another speaker. In these situations, the speaker must know how to refute the arguments of others and defend his own against attack. To do this effectively, speakers know what to refute, how to test reasoning, and how to proceed with refutation.

SUGGESTED READINGS

Howard Kahane. *Logic and Contemporary Rhetoric,* 3rd ed. Belmont, Calif.: Wadsworth, 1980 (paperback). This excellent source gives you some outstanding pointers on the use and development of logical argument and a considerable emphasis on identifying and eliminating the fallacies of reasoning.

Russel R. Windes and Arthur Hastings. *Argument and Advocacy.* New York: Random House, 1965 (paperback). This is a short book on debate, reasoning, and refutation.

CHAPTER 16

SPEECHES FOR SPECIAL OCCASIONS

"It is with great honor that I present to you today a man who . . . No, I don't like that," Phyllis said with disgust at her inability to come up with the perfect wording for her speech.

"Seldom in the course of human events . . . No, that won't do."

"Two score and three years ago . . . No, too cutesy."

"I am indeed proud to come before you on this important occasion to introduce . . . Yuck!"

"These are the times that try men's souls, but . . . No, that won't work."

"I am pleased, excited, indeed proud to come before you to introduce a man who . . . Now I'm back to this 'man who.' "

"Mom?"

"Don't bother me, Dottie, I'm going crazy trying to get this introduction done."

"Mom, I know—why don't you just say, 'Girls, Claude wants to talk with you.' "

"Not bad, honey—I like the sound of it."

Although most of your speeches will involve information exchange or persuasion, there are times when you will be called upon to speak under circumstances that are best described as ceremonial. In these speeches you will not only give information or persuade, but also you must meet the conventions of the particular occasion. This chapter is short, but the skills discussed will serve you well when you speak on such special occasions.

Even though no speech can be given by formula, certain occasions require at least the knowledge of conventions that have been observed by various speakers and that may be expected by audiences. Of course, as Phyllis's experience shows, these conventions can be a problem. Because a speaker should always use her own imagination to determine how to develop the theme, she should never adhere slavishly to those conventions. Still, you must know the conventions before you can decide whether to deviate from them or ignore them entirely.

INTRODUCTIONS

This occasion calls for a *short* but very important speech. The purpose of this speech is to pave the way for the main speaker. An audience wants to know who the speaker is, what the person is going to talk about, and why they should listen. If you make the introduction in such a way that the audience is psychologically ready to listen to the speech, then you have accomplished your purpose. Sometime before the speech you should consult with the speaker to ask what he would like to have told. Ordinarily you want the necessary biographical information that will show who the speaker is and why he is qualified to talk on the subject. The better known the person is the less you need to say about him or her. For instance, the introduction of the president is simply, "Ladies and gentlemen, the president of the United States." Ordinarily, you will want enough information to allow you to talk for at least two or three minutes. Only on rare occasions should a speech of introduction go more than three or four minutes; the audience assembled to hear the speaker, not the introducer. During the first sentence or two, then, you will establish the nature of the occasion. In the body of the speech, you will establish the speaker's credibility. The conclusion will usually include the name of the speaker and the title of the talk.

There are some special cautions concerning the speech of introduction: First, do not overpraise the speaker. If expectations are too high, the speaker will never be able to live up to them. For instance, overzealous introducers may be inclined to say: "I've heard this man speak before. He is undoubtedly one of the greatest speakers around today. See whether you don't agree with me that this will be one of the best speeches you've ever heard." Although this may appear to be paying a compliment, it is doing the speaker a disservice by emphasizing comparison rather than speech content. A second caution is to be familiar with what you have to say. Audiences question sincerity when an introducer has to read his praise. Many of us have been present when an introducer said, "And now it is my great pleasure to present that noted authority . . ." and then had to look down at some notes to recall the name. Finally, get your facts straight. The speaker should not have to spend time correcting your mistakes.

EXERCISE

Assume that you are introducing the featured speaker for some specific occasion. Limit your speech to no more than four minutes.

PRESENTATIONS

The purpose of a speech of presentation is to present an award, a prize, or a gift to an individual or group. In some circumstances a presentation accompanies some long tribute to an individual. In most cases the speech of presentation is a reasonably short, formal recognition of some accomplishment. Your speech usually has two goals: (1) to discuss the nature of the award, including history, donor or source, and conditions under which it is made; and (2) to discuss the accomplishments of the recipient. If a competition was held, you will describe what the person did in the competition. Under other circumstances, you will discuss how the person has met the criteria for the award.

Obviously, you must learn all you can about the award and about the conditions under which such awards are made. Although the award may be a certificate, plaque, or trophy that symbolizes some achievement, the contest may have a long history and tradition that must be mentioned. Since the audience wants to know what the recipient has done, you must know the criteria that were met. For a competition, you must know the number of contestants and the way the contest was judged. If the person earned the award through years of achievement, you need to know the particulars of that achievement.

Ordinarily, the speech is organized to show what the award is for, to give the criteria for winning or achieving the award, and to state how the person won or achieved the award. If the announcement of the name of

AVOID THOSE EMBARRASSING MOMENTS WHEN THE RECIPIENT DOESN'T KNOW WHAT TO DO.

the recipient is meant to be a surprise, all that is said should build up to the climax, the naming of the winner.

For the speech of presentation there are only two special considerations. (1) During the speech avoid overpraising. Do not explain everything in such superlatives that the presentation lacks sincerity and honesty. (2) If you are going to hand the award to the recipient, you should be careful to hold the award in your left hand and present it to the left hand of the recipient. At the same time, you want to shake the right hand in congratulations. If you practice, you will find that you can present the award and shake the person's hand smoothly and avoid those embarrassing moments when the recipient does not know quite what he is supposed to do.

EXERCISE

Prepare a speech of one to two minutes in which you present a gift, plaque, or award to a member of the class.

WELCOMINGS

The purpose of a speech of welcome is to express pleasure in the presence of a person or organization. In a way the speech of welcome is a double speech of introduction. You introduce the newcomer to the organization or city, and you introduce the organization to the newcomer.

You must be familiar with both the person or organization you are welcoming and with the situation you are welcoming the person to. It is surprising how little many members of organizations, citizens of a community, and students at a college or university really know about their organization or community. Although you may not have the knowledge on the tip of your tongue, it is inexcusable not to find the material you need to give an appropriate speech. Likewise, you want accurate information about the person or organization you are introducing. Although the speech will be brief, you need accurate and complete information to draw from.

After expressing pleasure in welcoming the person or organization, you will tell a little about your guests and give them the information about the place or the organization to which they are being welcomed. Usually the conclusion is a brief statement of your hope for a pleasant and profitable visit.

Again, the special caution is to make sure the speech is brief and honest. Welcoming guests does not require you to gush about them or their accomplishments. The speech of welcome should be an informative speech of praise.

EXERCISE

Prepare a speech welcoming a specific person to your city, university, or social organization.

TRIBUTES

The purpose of a speech of tribute is to praise some individual's accomplishments. The occasion may be, for example, her birthday or the announcing of her taking office, her retirement, or her death. A formal speech of tribute given in memory of a deceased person is called a eulogy. The key of an effective tribute is sincerity. Although you want the praise to be apparent, you do not want to overdo it.

You must know the biographical information about your subject in depth. Since audiences are primarily interested in new information and specifics that characterize your assertions, you must have a mastery of much detail. You should focus on the person's laudable characteristics and accomplishments. It is especially noteworthy if you find that the person had to overcome some special hardship or meet some particularly trying condition. All in all, you must be prepared to make a sound positive appraisal.

One way of organizing a speech of tribute is to focus on the subject's accomplishments. How detailed you will make the speech will depend upon whether the person is well known or not. If the person is well known, you will be more general in your analysis. If the person is little known, you will have to provide many more details so that the audience can see the reasons for the praise. In the case of very prominent individuals you will be able to show their effects on history.

Remember, however, no one is perfect. Although you need not stress a person's less glowing characteristics or failures that might have been experienced, some allusion to this kind of information may make the positive features even more meaningful. Probably the most important guide is for you to keep your objectivity. Overpraise is far worse than understatement. Try to give the person his or her due, honestly and sincerely.

EXERCISE

Prepare a speech paying tribute to some person living or dead.

MANUSCRIPTS

During the public speaking portion of this text, we have been emphasizing the extemporaneous speaking method. I believe that no speaker should face an audience without thorough preparation; yet, I believe that neither the manuscript speech nor the memorized speech provides the speaker with the opportunity to adapt directly to his audience the way the extemporaneous method does. Nevertheless, you may be called upon to speak on occasions when the wording of the speech is far more important than the spontaneity or potential for audience adaptation.

The final draft of your manuscript should be extremely well worded. You will want to show all that you have learned about making ideas clear, vivid, and appropriate. In your preparation you should proceed as if you were giving an extemporaneous speech. Then record what you would ordinarily consider your final speech practice. Type up the manuscript from your recorded practice, and then work on polishing the language. This procedure will ensure your working from an oral style rather than from a written essay style.

After the manuscript is fully prepared, you should practice using it effectively. You should be sufficiently familiar with the material that you do not have to focus your full attention on the manuscript as you read. I would suggest going over the manuscript at least three times in these final stages of practice. You will discover that even when you are reading you can have some eye contact with your audience. By watching audience reaction, you will know when and if to deviate from the manuscript.

So that the manuscript will be of maximum value to you I would suggest the following tips for preparing it:

1. The manuscript should be typed, preferably on a typewriter that is pica sized or larger. Some radio, television, or student newspaper rooms are equipped with typewriters that have extra large type. You may be able to gain access to such a machine. Whatever size type you use, it is wise to double or even triple space the manuscript.

2. For words that you have difficulty pronouncing you should use phonetic spelling, accent marks, or diacritical marks to help you in your pronunciation.

3. Make markings that will help you determine pauses, places of special emphasis, or where to slow down or speed up. Also make sure that the last sentence on each page is completed on that page to assure no unintended pauses.

4. Number pages boldly so that pages are kept in their proper order. You may also find it valuable to bend the corner of each page slightly for assisting you in turning pages easily.

5. Make sure to doublecheck that there will in fact be a lectern or speaker's stand upon which the manuscript can be placed.

EXERCISE

Prepare a four- to six-minute manuscript speech. Criteria for evaluation will include clarity, vividness, emphasis, and appropriateness of language and the quality of delivery.

IMPROMPTUS

There is no question that by far the greatest number of "speeches" you give are impromptu. When you answer a question posed by a professor in class, when you rise to speak on a motion made at a club meeting, when you talk about the events of your vacation at a party, you are giving an impromptu speech. But just because a speech is impromptu (given on the spur of the moment) does not mean that it need not be prepared. It is just that the preparation time is reduced to a matter of seconds or at most a matter of minutes.

Yet, if all the time we spent on information exchange and persuasion is going to be worthwhile, there must be some carryover into these im-

JUST BECAUSE A SPEECH
IS IMPROMPTU DOES NOT MEAN
THAT IT NEED NOT BE PREPARED.

promptu settings. Even in a few seconds you can form a topic statement—or at least a line of development; you can determine two or three points you will pursue in the development, and if time permits, you may even be able to think of a good one-line opening. Just as extemporaneous speaking improves with practice, so does impromptu speaking. The following assignment can be used to help test your preparation and delivery facility even when preparation time is minimal.

EXERCISE

Your instructor will have words and phrases on 3 × 5 cards, such as "Today's television," "Women's Liberation," "Astroturf," "Does the end justify the means?" "The ideal male (or female)," "Sex in the movies." At the beginning of the round, a student (usually a volunteer) draws three topics. Each student is given two to three minutes, or in the case of subsequent speakers, as long as the previous speaker has talked, to prepare a speech on one of the topics selected. Speeches should not exceed four minutes in length.

SYMPOSIUMS

A symposium is a special occasion for which each speaker is prepared to talk on one portion of a larger topic. For instance, in a one-hour symposium on drugs, one speaker might talk for ten minutes on types of drugs, one might talk on drug abuses, one might talk on means of deterring use of drugs, and one might talk on rehabilitation centers and drug clinics. At the end of the forty-minute speaking time, the participants usually answer questions from the audience and interact with each other.

The value of a symposium is that it gives a unity to the program. It also provides an opportunity for relatively comprehensive and orderly coverage of a topic.

EXERCISE

Divide the class into groups of four to six people. Each group selects a topic upon which all speeches will be prepared. Each speech should be five to seven minutes long. Criteria for evaluation include all criteria given in Appendix B-8, Speech Evaluation.

SUMMARY

At times you may be called upon to make a short but important speech for a special occasion. In this chapter we have looked at directions for giving introductions, presentations, welcomes, and tributes. Further, we have considered elements of manuscripts, impromptus, and symposiums.

SUGGESTED READINGS

Robert G. King. *Forms of Public Address.* New York: Bobbs-Merrill, 1969 (paperback). This short paperback is quite inexpensive. See particularly pp. 58–113.

Edward Rogge and James C. Ching. *Advanced Public Speaking.* New York: Holt, Rinehart & Winston, 1966. This comprehensive book on public speaking formats has a good section on speeches for special occasions.

APPENDIXES

APPENDIX A
SAMPLES AND ANALYSES

1. Interpersonal Conversation and Analysis
2. Informative Speech and Analysis
3. Persuasive Speech and Analysis

APPENDIX B
ANALYSIS CHECKLISTS

1. Feedback Analysis
2. Personal Communication Analysis—Form A
3. Personal Communication Analysis—Form B
4. Group Communication Analysis—Form A, Decision
5. Group Communication Analysis—Form B, Individual
6. Group Process Analysis
7. Leadership Analysis
8. Speech Evaluation

APPENDIX C
SPECIAL MATERIALS

1. Communication Contract
2. Employment Interview

APPENDIX A:

SAMPLES AND ANALYSES

Samples can be a useful means for studying the principles of any speech communication format. Each of the following is a sample that was presented by students much like yourself to meet a communication assignment. The first is an interpersonal conversation; the second is an informative speech; the third is a persuasive speech. Each contains enough examples of successful applications of principles to make them worth analysis. Your goal is not to copy what others have done but to read and analyze in order to better test the value of what you are planning to do.

In each case my suggestion is to read the sample and make your own judgments about which parts are good, bad, or indifferent. After you have made your analysis, read the critique and compare it with your own.

INTERPERSONAL CONVERSATION AND ANALYSIS

Dating

Sheila and Susan talk about the advantages and disadvantages of dating exclusively within one's own religion. Read the conversation aloud in its entirety. After you have considered its merits, read it again, this time noting the analysis in the left-hand column.

ANALYSIS	CONVERSATION
Susan introduces the subject with a question.	**Susan:** How are you and Bill getting along these days?
Sheila's answer is neither as specific nor as concrete as it could have been.	**Sheila:** Not too well. I think you could say our relationship is coming to an end. The feelings just aren't there, and so many problems have been building up.
Susan responds with a *perception check* wording when a *feelings paraphrase* wording would be better. She's	**Susan:** I get the impression from the expression on your face that you're having problems. Is there one specific problem?

Conversation presented in Interpersonal Communication class, University of Cincinnati. Reprinted by permission of Sheila Slone and Susan Lautman.

ANALYSIS

responding both to Sheila's spoken words and to what she is implying. Better: "From the way you're talking, I get the impression that you're very sad about the outcome of the relationship."

Sheila says, "It really does make a difference," but she doesn't go on to say what the difference is. We would expect Susan to ask about the difference.

Susan assumes she understands. She needs a question or a content paraphrase here. Instead, she changes the emphasis to her own experience. Now apparently the conversation will focus on Susan and an implied contrast in upbringing.

Although Sheila's paraphase is satisfactory, the wording could be even more specific. "It seems like you were a little upset at first, but now that you're older you have a better understanding of your parents' position."

Susan's response has a slightly superior ring to it. Note the implications of the word *predicament*. Susan needs to empathize with Sheila more directly.

Sheila's reaction is to defend her parents' policy. Then she makes a statement about the value of independence. Notice that even though the statements are at odds, Sheila and Susan seem to be maintaining a good climate.

Sheila says "feel," but she's not really describing feelings

Susan begins a response to the subject of the last sentence: choices. But then she returns to her parents' policy.
Good, clear statement of position.

Sheila's acknowledgment of Susan's feelings is in the right direction, but her

CONVERSATION

Sheila: Well, there are a lot, but one that I didn't think would make such a difference at the beginning of the relationship that's made a difference now is the fact that we're from different religions. I'm Jewish and he isn't, and at first I never thought it would affect me, but it does make a difference.

Susan: I think I was kind of lucky, well, lucky in the long run. When I was in high school, my parents wouldn't allow me to go out with anybody who wasn't Jewish. I really resented that at first, but now I'm kind of glad since I'm thinking about the future now. And as my parents said, you don't know what could come out of a high-school relationship.

Sheila: It seems like you were a little upset at first, but now you're pretty happy with the whole situation.

Susan: Yes, now that I look around, I'm not in the predicament that you are of having to get out of a relationship for something that's not what you want.

Sheila: I can see what you mean, but I'm also happy that my parents didn't restrict me because I think I would have felt a lot of pressure just to always . . . I wouldn't have had a choice of whom to go out with, and I wouldn't have felt very independent. But I feel I have to make my own choices. As long as I know what I want, I feel it's all right.

Susan: That was my problem—having to pick and choose. My parents would say, "Oh, is he Jewish?" "I don't know, should I ask him?" They wanted me to say, "Are you Jewish? Oh, you're not? Well, you can't go out with me, then."

Sheila: I can see how you feel—that's a tough situation, but I see now that I feel pretty frustrated because I want to date

ANALYSIS

wording appears a bit half-hearted. She needs a good paraphrase of feelings. In the midst of her response, she switches to a description of her feelings. The rest of the sentence is well-worded. She needs a clearer division between her response to Susan and her description of feelings.

This is probably one of the best responses in the dialogue. Although it is cast in question form, it is still a good attempt at seeking clarification of Sheila's feelings.

Notice the use of the word *feel* when *believe* or *think* would be more appropriate.

A nicely phrased personal feedback statement—a nice compliment.

Sheila again describes her feelings quite well.

Here's one of the few times when Susan focuses her attention on Sheila. Good question.

Sheila states her plans and continues to describe her feelings.

Susan gives advice that is meant to be supportive of Sheila's predicament.

In trying to help Sheila deal with her problem, Susan probably spent too much time talking about her own background

CONVERSATION

people who are Jewish, but I'm not going to go around picking on them saying this one is and this one isn't. It's too hard to do that. You can't turn your feelings on and off. You have to be interested in someone. So I get pretty frustrated a lot of times.

Susan: Are you saying that you are kind of glad that your parents didn't restrict you in that manner, or are you saying that you're glad they didn't but wish they had?

Sheila: I guess I'm glad they didn't, but maybe it would have been better if they had. I would have been more conscious about it.

Susan: In the long run, I feel it's best to start early to get an idea in your mind of what you really want to do. I never thought a relationship in high school would go anywhere, but the man I'm dating, it's been four years already. That's a long time.

Sheila: You seem happy together. I saw you the other day and that's really nice. I wish I could find somebody that . . .

Susan: I saw you start shrugging Bill off and just ignoring him.

Sheila: Yes, that's a hard situation. I get pretty depressed about it, too. I just never thought religion could make such a big difference. But it means a lot to me, and that's why it makes such a difference.

Susan: What are you planning on telling him?

Sheila: Well, I guess I'll just say that it won't work out. It depresses me to think about that, too.

Susan: You should really try to go easy—don't let it upset you too much. It's what you want, right?

Sheila: I guess so. I'll have to try to do the best I can.

ANALYSIS

and situation. Although some of her remarks show that she heard what Sheila was saying, some of her comments did not deal directly with Sheila's problem. Since the dialogue began as a response to Sheila's problem, Sheila's attempts at directing conversation to her problem are in order.

Both speakers made satisfactory attempts at paraphrasing and describing feelings; however, there were no good examples of perception checking. Still, the conversation was friendly (nonverbal responses were very supportive, but you can't see that on paper), and no major barriers developed.

CONVERSATION

INFORMATIVE SPEECH AND ANALYSIS

In Search of Noah's Ark

ANALYSIS

The speech opens with a good historical narrative designed to get the attention of the class.

Notice the use of rhetorical questions to lead into the speech objective.

In this case the speech objective is stated at the end of the speech introduction and leads into the body of the speech. If you are going to state or paraphrase your speech objective, this is the place to do it.

Here the body of the speech begins. The first main point—that historical writings suggest the presence of a real Ark—is implied rather than stated directly. Although you should probably state each main point clearly, in this speech the method fits well with the historical

SPEECH

In 1916 during the first World War, in the Russian-occupied sector of eastern Turkey, a Russian airman, W. Roskavitsky, swore that while flying over one of the slopes of Mount Ararat he saw a large vessel. This amazing report was taken all the way to the Czar, who himself organized an expedition to climb Mount Ararat, and this expedition brought back the description of just such a large vessel half-submerged in the glacial lake. The Czar's commission believed that they had found Noah's Ark. Could this be? Is it possible that Noah's Ark is real? In this speech, I'd like to examine with you some of the historical documentation supporting the statement that an ark, vessel, or boat is on top of Mount Ararat—and that the vessel is in fact Noah's Ark.

First, and probably most familiar to us, of this historical evidence is the Biblical account of Noah's Ark and the Flood. In Genesis 8:4 it says that the Ark came to rest upon Mount Ararat. Second, Flavius Josephus, the Jewish historian, wrote in his history, *Jewish Antiquities*, in 37 A.D., that it had been reported that the Ark had been found on top of Mount Ararat. Finally, more than one thousand years

Speech given in Fundamentals of Speech class, Miami University. Printed by permission of Thomas Grossmann.

ANALYSIS

narrative approach—an approach that is designed to draw you into the resolution of the mystery.

Here the speaker confuses the date of Josephus' birth, A.D. 37, with the date of the writing of *The Antiquities of the Jews*, which was A.D. 93 or 94.

Here again a main point is stated differently from what we usually expect. In outline form, the main point would be stated: Actual sightings of the Ark have been reported.

Here and throughout the speech the content is excellent. You should keep one criticism in mind, however. Since the source of this material is important and perhaps necessary for building and maintaining speaker credibility, the speaker should have introduced the sources of the various facts with a statement such as "As Jones pointed out in his book on ———." The speaker presented a good bibliography on his outline of the speech, but he did not introduce enough of the sources directly in the speech.

Still, the examples are good, and the use of the examples helps to gain and hold attention.

Here we get into the third main point that recently actual material has been brought back from the source.

The speech continues with specific details.

I particularly like the way this speech fits together. The audience feels in on the

SPEECH

later, in 1300 A.D., Marco Polo wrote in his book called *Travels* that on his way through Turkey to China, he had heard that the Ark was on top of Mount Ararat. For a long time historians had held this information suspect. First, it was difficult to believe that a boat was on top of a mountain; second, all the documentation was hearsay. Proof in the way of verifiable sightings was needed.

But these actual sightings did come. On two separate occasions, expeditions on Mount Ararat have seen the prow or side of a large wooden vessel sticking out of the glacial ice pack. First, a Turkish expedition in 1840 sent to Mount Ararat to build barricades against avalanches came back and reported that a large prow or side of a vessel was sticking out of the glacial ice pack. In 1952, more than 100 years later, an almost identical sighting was made by an American oil pipeline mining expedition. This expedition, headed by George Jefferson Green, also found the large prow or side of a vessel sticking out of the glacial ice pack.

Even though these sightings were documented no one had actually been able to bring a piece of this supposed Ark back for study. And often in history supposed firsthand observations had proved to be wrong. With this goal of getting tangible evidence, Ferdinand Navara, a French explorer, climbed Mount Ararat in 1955, and at an elevation of 14,000 feet, he dug down into the glacial ice pack and found an estimated 50 tons of wood. He was able to bring back some of this wood to France where it was analyzed by the Pre-history Institute of the University of Bordeaux on April 15, 1956. The conclusion of this report said that it was definitely wood, it was white oak, it was more than 5,000 years old, it was covered with pitch, and the wood was hand hewn. The wood was also studied by the Forestry Institute of Research and Experimentation in Madrid, Spain, and they reached the same conclusions. This finding of wood may not appear to offer support for the presence of an Ark until another aspect is considered—this wood was found on Mount Ararat at a height some 300 feet higher

ANALYSIS

drawing together of the various materials.

This is an excellent summary. It states the three main points of the speech—points that were only alluded to in the speech itself. Moreover, the rhetorical question and the last statement leave the speech on a high note—a note of mystery and speculation.

Although there are a few problems with this speech (and as you'll discover there are some problems with almost any speech), it is a good one.

SPEECH

than the highest tree in the entire world! Moreover, Mount Ararat itself is 300 miles away from the closest living tree.

So let's see what we've discovered. Historical documentation dating back as far as 1000 B.C. has said that an Ark or boat rests upon Mount Ararat. Three separate expeditions—one Turkish, one Russian, and one American—have all found something that looks like a boat on top of Mount Ararat. A Frenchman by the name of Ferdinand Navara has actually found more than 50 tons of wood on top of Mount Ararat 300 feet above the highest tree line and 300 miles from the nearest tree. What does this mean? In eastern Turkey, in the area of cold Armenia, on top of a volcanic mountain named Mount Ararat, there rests a very large boat-like object—an object that many believe to be Noah's Ark.

PERSUASIVE SPEECH AND ANALYSIS

Open Your Eyes

ANALYSIS

Much of the strength of this speech is a result of the speaker's ability to involve members of the audience personally and get them to feel what she is saying. This opening is a striking example of audience involvement. She does not just tell the audience what it would be like—she has them experience the feeling. The speaker very successfully lays the emotional groundwork for total audience reception of her words.

Here the speaker begins the body of her speech by telling us about the role of the cornea. Notice throughout the speech the excellent word choice, such as "The bright world we awake to each morning is brought to us by. . . ."

SPEECH

Would all of you close your eyes for just a minute. Close them very tightly so that all the light is blocked out. Imagine what it would be like to always live in a world of total darkness such as you are experiencing right now, though only for a moment. Never to see the flaming colors of the sunset, or the crisp green of the world after the rain—never to see the faces of those you love. Now open your eyes, look all around you, look at all of the things that you couldn't have seen if you couldn't have opened your eyes.

The bright world we awake to each morning is brought to us by two dime-sized pieces of tough, transparent, semielastic tissue; these are the cornea, and it is their function to allow light to enter the lens and the retina. Normally, they are so clear that we don't even know they are there; however, when they are scratched or scarred either by accident or by disease, they tend to blur or blot

Speech given in Fundamentals of Speech class, University of Cincinnati. Printed by permission of Kathleen Sheldon.

ANALYSIS

Here again she does not just tell us what it is like but asks us to imagine for ourselves what it would be like if. The "rain-slashed window pane" is an especially vivid image.

The speaker continues in a very informative way. After asserting that corneal transplants work, she focuses on the two key points that she wants the audience to work with—the operation works, but it must be done within seventy-two hours.

Notice that there is still no apparent direct persuasion. Her method is one of making information available in a way that will lead the audience itself to thinking about what effects the information might have on them personally.

In this segment of the speech, she launches into emotional high gear. Still, her approach remains somewhat indirect. Although we stress the importance of directness in language in this speech, the use of "no one" repeatedly through the examples is done by design. Although a more direct method might be effective, in this case the indirectness works quite well.

The real effectiveness of the section is a result of the parallel structure and repetition of key phrases: "no one who has seen . . . human tragedy . . . great joy . . . can doubt the need or the urgency." As this portion of the speech was delivered, the listeners were deeply touched by both the examples themselves and their own thoughts about the examples.

Also note how the examples themselves are ordered. The first two represent a personal effect; the final one a universal effect.

SPEECH

out the light. Imagine peering through a rain-slashed window pane or trying to see while swimming under water. This is the way victims of corneal damage often describe their vision.

"To see the world through another man's eyes." These words are Shakespeare's, yet today it can literally be true. Thanks to the research by medical workers throughout the world, the operation known as a corneal transplant or a corneal graft has become a reality, giving thousands of people the opportunity to see. No other generation has held such a profound legacy in its possession. Yet, the universal ignorance of this subject of cornea donation is appalling. The operation itself is really quite simple; it involves the corneas of the donor being transplanted into the eyes of a recipient. And if this operation takes place within seventy-two hours after the death of the donor, it can be 100 percent effective.

No one who has seen the human tragedy caused solely by corneal disease can doubt the need or the urgency. Take the case of a young woman living in New Jersey who lost her sight to corneal disease. She gave birth to a baby and two years ago, thanks to a corneal transplant, she saw her three-year-old baby girl for the first time. And no one who had seen this woman's human tragedy caused solely by corneal disease nor her great joy at the restoration of her sight can doubt the need or the urgency. Or take the case of the five-year-old boy in California who was playing by a bonfire when a bottle in the fire exploded, flinging bits of glass, which lacerated his corneas. His damaged corneas were replaced with healthy ones in an emergency operation, and no one who has seen this little boy's human tragedy caused solely by corneal laceration nor the great joy to his young life of receiving his sight back again can doubt the need or the urgency. Or take the case of Dr. Beldon H. Scribbner of the University of Washington School of Medicine. Dr. Scribbner's eyesight was damaged by a corneal disease that twisted the normally spear-shaped cornea into cones. A corneal transplant gave Dr. Scribbner a twenty-twenty corrective vision and allowed him to continue work on his invention—the artificial kidney machine. And no one who has seen this man's human tragedy caused solely by corneal disease, nor the great joy brought not only to Dr. Scribbner but to the thousands of people his machine has helped save, can doubt the need or the urgency.

ANALYSIS

At this point in the speech the audience should be sympathetic with the problem and encouraged by the hope of corneal transplants. Now the speaker must deal with the listener's reactions of "That may be a good idea for someone else, but why me?" It is in this section that she offers reasons for our acting. If the speech has a weakness, it may be here. I'd like to have heard a little further development of the reasons or perhaps the statement of an additional reason.

Here she brings the audience from "Good idea—I'll do something someday" to "I'd better act now."

She reminds them of the critical time period. And tells them how they can proceed to make the donation. In this section it might be worth a sentence to stress that the donation costs nothing but a little time.

Here the speaker brings the audience full circle. Although she could have used different images, the repetition of those that began the speech takes the emphasis off the images themselves and places it in what the audience can do about those who are in these circumstances.

The last line of the speech is simple, but in the context of the entire speech it is direct and quite moving.

SPEECH

There are many philosophies behind such a gift. One of them was summed up by a minister and his wife who lost their daughter in infancy. They said "We feel that a part of her goes on living." Or take the case of the young woman who was dying of cancer. She donated her eyes and did so with this explanation: "I want to be useful; being useful brings purpose and meaning into my life." Surely if being useful is important there are few better ways than to donate your eyes to someone who lives after you. But no matter which philosophy you do adopt, I hope each of you will consider donating your eyes to another who will live after you and who otherwise would have to survive in the abyss of darkness. It will do you no good to leave your eyes in your regular will if you have one; for as I mentioned earlier, there is a seventy-two-hour critical period. If you wish to donate your eyes, I would suggest you contact Cincinnati Eye Bank for Sight Restoration at 861-3716. They will send you the appropriate donor forms to fill out, which should be witnessed by two of your closest friends or by your next of kin so that they will know your wishes. Then, when you die and no longer have need for your sight someone who desperately wants the chance to see will be able to.

Will all of you close your eyes again for just a moment? Close them very tightly, so that all the light is blocked out. And once more imagine what it would be like to live always in a world of total darkness such as you are experiencing right now, never to see the flaming colors of a sunset, or the crisp green of the world after a rain—never seeing the faces of those you love. Now open your eyes . . . Won't you give someone else the chance to open theirs?

APPENDIX B-1:

FEEDBACK ANALYSIS

To indicate your rating of _____ on Personal Communication, Group Communication, and Public Communication, encircle the number for each statement below that best corresponds with your evaluation of the particular behavior. The numbers 1, 2, and 3 represent the negative end of the continuum—they suggest a need for work on the item. The numbers 5, 6, and 7 represent the positive end of the continuum—they suggest a perceived competence in terms of the behavior. The number 4 represents a midpoint between the extremes.

PERSONAL COMMUNICATION

When he or she has something to say, he or she doesn't worry about how it comes out or how another person might take it	1 2 3 4 5 6 7	When he or she has something to say, he or she tries hard to word thoughts and feelings carefully taking into account the feelings of others
Has trouble phrasing ideas precisely	1 2 3 4 5 6 7	Speaks clearly in specific and concrete language
Conversation is cluttered with meaningless expressions like "uh," "well uh," and "you know," or stumbles and gropes for words	1 2 3 4 5 6 7	Conversation is fluent without meaningless expressions like "uh," "well uh," and "you know," or without stumbling around for the right word
Either withholds negative feelings about others' behavior toward him or her	1 2 3 4 5 6 7	Describes objectively to others negative feelings about their behavior to-

or blows up at what they've said or done

Does not pay full attention when listening so misses words and ideas 1 2 3 4 5 6 7 Listens carefully and attentively

When he or she doesn't understand something, acts as if he or she does 1 2 3 4 5 6 7 When not sure whether he or she understands, seeks clarification

Method of responding to others makes them react defensively—they feel as if they're being attacked 1 2 3 4 5 6 7 Method of responding to others seems to encourage them to talk openly and honestly

Has little interest in hearing about what others may think of him or her 1 2 3 4 5 6 7 Is willing to listen to what others think of his or her behavior—in fact, often asks for reactions from others

Is completely oblivious to the nonverbal cues that others give 1 2 3 4 5 6 7 Looks for and tries to understand what other peoples' nonverbal behavior is saying

Is easily intimidated and will seldom give an opinion when he or she feels likelihood of conflict 1 2 3 4 5 6 7 Is willing to state what he or she thinks and feels regardless of the other person's status

GROUP COMMUNICATION

Gives impression that working in groups is a waste of time 1 2 3 4 5 6 7 Appears to enjoy working in groups

Seldom appears to do advance preparation for group discussions 1 2 3 4 5 6 7 Appears to prepare carefully for group discussions

Contributes to the group only when called upon 1 2 3 4 5 6 7 Contributes freely and openly in groups

Seldom provides valuable material or insights to the group 1 2 3 4 5 6 7 Contributions are very helpful to the group in accomplishing its task

ward him or her without withholding or blowing up

Seldom says things that help a group work better together	1 2 3 4 5 6 7	Often is the one to say something that helps the group get along better
Appears to avoid making decisions	1 2 3 4 5 6 7	Appears to enjoy making decisions
Looks for others to lead the group	1 2 3 4 5 6 7	Tries to provide group leadership
When called upon to lead seldom provides much direction	1 2 3 4 5 6 7	When called upon to lead provides the group with a well thought out suggested procedure
Not likely to support group decision	1 2 3 4 5 6 7	Abides by group decision even when appears to be opposed

PUBLIC SPEAKING

Has considerable fear of speaking in public	1 2 3 4 5 6 7	Appears to have confidence in ability to speak in public
Speeches do not seem to consider audience knowledge, needs, or interests	1 2 3 4 5 6 7	Speeches seem to consider audience knowledge, needs, or interests
Speeches are not fully developed	1 2 3 4 5 6 7	Speeches are fully developed
Speeches seem disorganized	1 2 3 4 5 6 7	Speeches follow some consistent pattern in organization
Audiences are restless or inattentive	1 2 3 4 5 6 7	Audiences are alert and listen attentively
Appears to have trouble selecting "the right word"	1 2 3 4 5 6 7	Audiences perceive language as clear and vivid
Avoids looking directly at members of audience when speaking	1 2 3 4 5 6 7	Looks directly at members of audience when speaking
Speaking voice tends to remain on the same level of pitch, speed, and loudness	1 2 3 4 5 6 7	Public speaking voice shows variations in pitch, speed, and loudness

Does not appear to know what to do with hands; appears awkward	1	2	3	4	5	6	7	Bodily actions appear to help supplement or reinforce ideas; appears to be involved
Seldom makes an impact on the audience	1	2	3	4	5	6	7	Usually achieves his or her speech objective

APPENDIX B-2:

PERSONAL COMMUNICATION ANALYSIS—FORM A

Participants:

Apparent purpose of the encounter:

Outcome—what was the result?

Describe the entire encounter. Use dialogue wherever possible.

On the back of this sheet, list the reasons for success or failure of the communication. Discuss those reasons in terms of presence or absence of various skills and barriers.

APPENDIX B-3:

PERSONAL COMMUNICATION ANALYSIS—FORM B

Participants:

Apparent purpose of the encounter:

Outcome—what was the result?

Play back the dialogue as you remember it. On the back of this sheet, describe the entire encounter. Use specific dialogue wherever possible. Indicate whether or not various skills were used in the dialogue. Describe their use and consider their relative effectiveness. Check those below that you will be discussing in your analysis.

Message Formation and Response Skills:

☐	Asserting	☐	Paraphrasing
☐	Dating	☐	Supporting
☐	Indexing	☐	Questioning
☐	Describing feelings	☐	Interpreting
☐	Listening	☐	Descriptive feedback

Nonverbal Considerations:

☐	Environment	☐	Paralanguage

- ☐ Personal style
- ☐ Body motions

- ☐ Perception checking

Barriers Encountered:

- ☐ Transfer stations
- ☐ Information overload
- ☐ Noise
- ☐ Hidden agendas

- ☐ Defensiveness
- ☐ Inappropriate responses
- ☐ Conflict

APPENDIX B-4:

GROUP COMMUNICATION ANALYSIS—FORM A, DECISION

Analysis of group characteristics: Indicate which if any of the following characteristics affected group performance. Discuss how the group was affected.

- ☐ Size
- ☐ Cohesiveness
- ☐ Commitment to task
- ☐ Norms

_____

Did the group arrive at a decision? Explain.

_____

What action was taken as a result of that discussion? Explain.

_____

Was the group decision a good one? Explain.

_____

Was quality information presented?

_____

Were the data fully discussed?

_____

Did interim conclusions reflect group discussion?

_____

Were conclusions measured against some set criteria?

_____

Did the group agree to support the decision?

APPENDIX B-5:

GROUP COMMUNICATION ANALYSIS—FORM B, INDIVIDUAL

For each of the following questions, rate the participant on a 1 to 5 basis: 1, high; 2, good; 3, average; 4, fair; 5, poor.

	1	2	3	4	5
Preparation:					
Seems to be well prepared?	☐	☐	☐	☐	☐
Analyzes the problem?	☐	☐	☐	☐	☐
Suggests possible solutions?	☐	☐	☐	☐	☐
Tests each solution?	☐	☐	☐	☐	☐
Organization:					
Is aware of the problem?	☐	☐	☐	☐	☐
Analyzes the problem?	☐	☐	☐	☐	☐
Suggests possible solutions?	☐	☐	☐	☐	☐
Tests each solution?	☐	☐	☐	☐	☐
Talking Productively:					
Interacts?	☐	☐	☐	☐	☐
Maintains objectivity?	☐	☐	☐	☐	☐
Deals with conflict?	☐	☐	☐	☐	☐
Shows leadership?	☐	☐	☐	☐	☐

	1 2 3 4 5

Carrying Out Roles:

	1	2	3	4	5
As information or opinion giver?	□	□	□	□	□
As information or opinion seeker?	□	□	□	□	□
As expediter?	□	□	□	□	□
As idea person?	□	□	□	□	□
As analyzer?	□	□	□	□	□
As game leader?	□	□	□	□	□
As harmonizer?	□	□	□	□	□
As gatekeeper?	□	□	□	□	□
As compromiser?	□	□	□	□	□
As active listener?	□	□	□	□	□

Carrying Out Negative Roles: (For this category a 1, high, would show that the person was not playing that negative role)

	1	2	3	4	5
As aggressor?	□	□	□	□	□
As blocker?	□	□	□	□	□
As competer?	□	□	□	□	□
As special pleader?	□	□	□	□	□
As joker?	□	□	□	□	□
As withdrawer?	□	□	□	□	□
As monopolizer?	□	□	□	□	□

Write an analysis of the person's group participation (two to five paragraphs) based upon this checklist.

APPENDIX B-6:

GROUP PROCESS ANALYSIS

Place a tally-mark in the category that best represents each statement or nonverbal action in the discussion as it is made.

	1 (Name)	2 (Name)	3 (Name)	4 (Name)	5 (Name)
Task Functions:					
Gives information (example, illustration, statistics, quotation, and all explanation)	☐	☐	☐	☐	☐
Gives personal opinion	☐	☐	☐	☐	☐
Asks for information	☐	☐	☐	☐	☐
Asks for personal opinion	☐	☐	☐	☐	☐
Expedites	☐	☐	☐	☐	☐
Analyzes	☐	☐	☐	☐	☐
Originates an idea	☐	☐	☐	☐	☐
Positive Maintenance Functions:					
Game Leads	☐	☐	☐	☐	☐
Harmonizes	☐	☐	☐	☐	☐
Gatekeeps	☐	☐	☐	☐	☐
Compromises	☐	☐	☐	☐	☐
Contributes to well-being (agreeing, being friendly)	☐	☐	☐	☐	☐
Negative Maintenance Functions:					
Is aggressive	☐	☐	☐	☐	☐
Blocks	☐	☐	☐	☐	☐
Competes	☐	☐	☐	☐	☐

	1	2	3	4	5
Special pleads	☐	☐	☐	☐	☐
Withdraws (only the act of withdrawing)	☐	☐	☐	☐	☐
Monopolizes (only acts that show desire to monopolize)	☐	☐	☐	☐	☐
Detracts from well-being (tension, hostility, or unfriendliness)	☐	☐	☐	☐	☐

APPENDIX B-7:

LEADERSHIP ANALYSIS

For each of the following questions, rate the leadership on a 1 to 5 basis: 1, high; 2, good; 3, average; 4, fair; 5, poor.

	1	2	3	4	5

Leadership Traits:

	1	2	3	4	5
Seems intelligent and alert?	☐	☐	☐	☐	☐
Has sufficient knowledge?	☐	☐	☐	☐	☐
Stimulates the group?	☐	☐	☐	☐	☐
Has a sense of humor?	☐	☐	☐	☐	☐

Meeting Task Functions:

	1	2	3	4	5
Has an agenda?	☐	☐	☐	☐	☐
Promotes systematic problem solving?	☐	☐	☐	☐	☐
Clarifies and crystallizes ideas?	☐	☐	☐	☐	☐
Summarizes and expresses group ideas?	☐	☐	☐	☐	☐
Arrives at decisions by means of consensus or voting?	☐	☐	☐	☐	☐

Meeting Maintenance Functions:

	1	2	3	4	5
Opens the discussion effectively?	☐	☐	☐	☐	☐
Creates and maintains a suitable atmosphere?	☐	☐	☐	☐	☐
Shows respect for and interest in group members?	☐	☐	☐	☐	☐
Demonstrates sensitivity to attitudes and reactions?	☐	☐	☐	☐	☐
Maintains impartiality and avoids antagonism?	☐	☐	☐	☐	☐
Encourages balanced participation?	☐	☐	☐	☐	☐
Refrains from dominating the group?	☐	☐	☐	☐	☐
Prevents arguments from developing?	☐	☐	☐	☐	☐

	1	2	3	4	5
Deals with conflict?	☐	☐	☐	☐	☐
Brings discussion to a satisfactory close?	☐	☐	☐	☐	☐

Write an analysis (two to five paragraphs) based upon this checklist.

APPENDIX B-8:

SPEECH EVALUATION

Speaker:

Location:

Speech Objective:

Check your opinion of how well speaker met major criteria:

	Yes	Partially	No

Content:

	Yes	Partially	No
Was the speaker prepared?	☐	☐	☐
Did the speaker have specifics to support or to explain major statements?	☐	☐	☐
Was the support well related to points made?	☐	☐	☐
Did material and development meet your ethical standards?	☐	☐	☐

Organization:

	Yes	Partially	No
Did the introduction gain attention and lead into the speech?	☐	☐	☐
Were the main points clearly stated?	☐	☐	☐
Did they follow some identifiable pattern?	☐	☐	☐
Did the conclusion end the speech appropriately?	☐	☐	☐

	Yes	Partially	No

Style:

Were ideas presented concretely and
specifically? ☐ ☐ ☐
Was the language vivid? ☐ ☐ ☐
Were transitions used effectively? ☐ ☐ ☐
Was the language related to audience needs
and interests? ☐ ☐ ☐

Delivery:

Was the speaker enthusiastic about the
material? ☐ ☐ ☐
Did the speaker look at the audience
throughout the speech? ☐ ☐ ☐
Was the delivery spontaneous? ☐ ☐ ☐
Did the speaker use sufficient vocal variety
and emphasis? ☐ ☐ ☐
Was the speaker poised? ☐ ☐ ☐

Analysis:

Encircle your opinion of the speech:

Excellent   Good   Average   Fair   Poor

Using the data from the checklist write on an attached sheet of paper two to five paragraphs of analysis of the speech supporting your encircled evaluation. Also include any aspects of speech setting (size of room, lighting, heating, and the like) or speech audience (size, age, sex, race, attitudes, interests, and the like) that may have affected the speech effectiveness.

APPENDIX C:

SPECIAL MATERIALS

THE COMMUNICATION CONTRACT

Before reading each of the major parts of this textbook (personal, group, and public communication), you were encouraged to complete a self-analysis to identify areas of weakness and to write a communication contract. A communication contract should include (1) a statement of your goal, (2) a description of the present problem, (3) a step-by-step action plan to reach the goal, and (4) a method of determining when the goal has been reached.

1. *Statement of goal.* After considering the rating scales in the self-analysis section preceding each unit, you will probably realize that one or more of your communication behaviors listed in the analysis could profitably be changed over the period of this term. When you have selected a specific change you feel a need to make, write your goal specifically. *Example 1:* "Goal: To increase my listening efficiency with my close friends." *Example 2:* "Goal: To look at people more directly when I'm giving a speech."

2. *Description of the problem.* Here you describe to the best of your ability the specific nature of that communication problem. *Example 1:* "Problem: Currently when my roommate tries to say something to me, I find myself daydreaming or rehearsing my replies. Consequently, I sometimes miss important points or misinterpret what is being said." *Example 2:* "Problem: Usually when I get up to speak in class or in the Student Senate I find myself burying my head in notes or looking at the ceiling or walls."

3. *A step-by-step action plan.* Read the procedures for implementing a skill or coping with a problem in the sections of the text where the skills or problems are discussed. From these discussions you can decide on the procedures you wish to include in your plan. When you have a plan in mind, write it out in enough detail that any reader could understand your plan. *Example 1:* "Step-by-step Action Plan: (1) I will consciously attempt to 'clear my mind' when my roommate is speaking. (2) I will learn to employ the skill of paraphrasing in order to check the accuracy of my perception of what I have heard." *Example 2:* "Step-by-step Action Plan: I will take time to practice oral presentations aloud. (1) I will stand up just as I do in class or at Student Senate. (2) I will pretend various objects in the room are people, and I will consciously attempt to look at those objects as I am talking. (3) In the actual

Communication Contract

1. Goal:

To look at people more directly when I'm giving a speech.

2. Statement of the problem:

Currently when I get up to speak in class or in Student Senate I find myself burying my head in notes or looking at the ceiling or walls.

3. Step-by-step action plan:

I will take time to practice oral presentations aloud. (1) I will stand up just as I do in class or at Student Senate. (2) I will pretend various objects in the room are people, and I will consciously attempt to look at those objects as I am talking. (3) In the actual speech setting, I will try to be aware of when I am looking at my audience and when I am not.

4. Method of determining when the goal has been reached:

This goal will be considered achieved (1) when I am conscious of when I am looking at my audience and (2) when I am maintaining eye contact most of the time.

Signed: _Sarah Gordon_

Date: _September 26_

Witnessed by: _Phil Backlin_

speech setting, I will try to be aware of when I am looking at my audience and when I am not."

4. *A method of determining when the goal has been reached.* Here you will write the minimum requirements for having achieved your goal. *Example 1:* "Test of Achieving Goal: This goal will be considered achieved (1) when I have completed two weeks of listening during which my roommate never has to repeat something for me to get it and (2) when I have internalized para-phrasing to the extent that I remember to do it and do it well." *Example 2:* "Test of Achieving Goal: This goal will be considered achieved (1) when I am conscious of when I am looking at my audience and (2) when I am maintaining eye contact most of the time."

After completing the contract you should sign it. We would further suggest that you have another person in class witness the contract. (Perhaps you can witness his or her contract in return.) At the end of the term (or at the end of each unit), you can meet with the witness to determine whether or not your contracts have been fulfilled.

EMPLOYMENT INTERVIEW

Although there is some question about the interview as a really valid tool for personnel selection, nearly every major position in nearly any field requires that the applicant go through at least one interview. At its worst, an interview can be a waste of time for all parties involved; at its best, an interview can be an integral part of the process of selection and placement. Since you will undoubtedly go through at least one (and probably more than one) interview before you get a job, let us consider some of the procedures and methods that are most likely to be beneficial to you.

Responsibilities

You will want to approach the interview seriously and systematically. Re-member that all you have to sell is yourself and your qualifications. You want to show yourself in the very best light. Therefore, you should be concerned about your appearance; if you really want a particular job, you will dress in a way that will be acceptable to the person or organization that may hire you. Moreover, you should be fully prepared for the inter-view. Two important responsibilities that you must meet before the inter-view itself are the résumé and the cover letter.

Before most employers will even talk with you, they will want to see your résumé with a cover letter. A survey of the recruitment and employment policies and practices of the 500 largest U.S. corporations revealed the following information:[1]

1. Most want the letter and résumé typewritten.

2. A high percentage (more than 75 percent) want the following information included:

   Personal information—date of birth, phone, address, marital status, number of dependents

   Listing of special interests such as accounting, statistics, sales, finance, ·economics

   Specific educational qualifications—major, minors, and the like

   Willingness to relocate

   List of scholarships, awards, and honors

   Previous work experience—jobs, dates of employment

   Statement of physical or health status

   Social organizations and offices held

3. More than a third expect to find the following information included:

   Salary requirements

   Source of applicant's college financing

   Name of high school, class rank, and date of graduation

   Grades in major and minor subjects

   Special skills such as typing, fluency in foreign language, operating computers

   A list of references

4. Most prefer one- to two-page résumés; 30 percent prefer only one page.

5. The cover letter should be short, contain specific areas of interest and availability; it should explain or amplify elements of the résumé; it should be creative; and it should be clear, neat, and well typed.

The Interview

Before the interview itself, it is a good idea to give yourself a practice session. Try to anticipate some of the questions you will be asked and think carefully about the answers. You need not write out and practice answers; but, before the actual interview, you should have anticipated key questions, and you should have thought about such subjects as salary expectations, possible contribution to the company, special skills, and so forth.

---

[1]"As You Were Saying—The Cover Letter and Résumé," *Personnel Journal*, Vol.48 (September 1969), pp. 732–733. This article is a summary of information provided by Harold D. Janes, Professor of Management, University of Alabama.

In the interview itself you should consciously avoid the common complaints that interviewers have about applicants. Although the following list was compiled more than twenty years ago, it still contains cautions that any applicant for employment will find valuable to consider:[2]

The undesirable applicant:

1. Is caught lying

2. Shows lack of interest

3. Is belligerent, rude, or impolite

4. Lacks sincerity

5. Is evasive

6. Is concerned only about salary

7. Is unable to concentrate

8. Is indecisive

9. Is late

10. Is unable to express himself clearly

11. Wants to start in an executive position

12. Oversells case

If these are what you should not do, then what should you attempt to do? Let us consider some positive approaches that will help you give the best possible impression.

1. *Do your homework.* Know about the company's services, products, ownership, and financial health. Knowing about a company shows your interest in that company and will usually impress the interviewer.

2. *Be prompt.* The interview is the company's only clue to your work behavior. If you are late for such an important event, the interviewer may well conclude that you are likely to be late for work. Give yourself plenty of time in travel to cover any possible traffic problems, and so forth.

3. *Be alert and look at the interviewer.* Remember that your nonverbal communication tells a lot about you. Company representatives are likely to consider eye contact and posture as clues to your self-confidence.

4. *Give yourself time to think.* If the interviewer asks you a question that you had not anticipated, give yourself time to think before you answer. It is better to pause and think than to give a hasty answer that may cost you the

---

[2]Selected from Charles S. Goetzinger, "An Analysis of Irritating Factors in Initial Employment Interviews of Male College Graduates," unpublished Ph.D. dissertation, Purdue University, 1954. Reported in Charles J. Stewart and William B. Cash, *Interviewing: Principles and Practices* (Dubuque, Iowa: Wm. C. Brown, 1974), pp. 162–163.

job. If you do not understand the question, paraphrase it before you attempt to answer.

5. *Ask questions about the type of work you will be doing.* The interview is your chance to find out if you would enjoy working for this company. You might ask the interviewer to describe a typical work day for the person who will get the job. If the interview is conducted at the company offices, you might ask to see where you would be working.

6. *Don't engage in long discussions on salary.* On your résumé you have probably indicated a range of salary expectations. If the company representative tries to pin you down, ask, "What do you normally pay someone with my experience and education for this level position?" Such a question allows you to get an idea of what the salary will be without committing yourself to a figure first.

7. *Don't harp on benefits.* Detailed questions about benefits are more appropriate after the company has made you an offer.

INDEX